CECIL KUHNE

NEAR DEATH
ON THE
HIGH SEAS

Cecil Kuhne is the editor of two previous anthologies on adventure travel, *On the Edge* and *The Armchair Paddler*. A former whitewater rafting guide, he has also written nine books about rafting, kayaking, and canoeing. He lives in Dallas.

ALSO EDITED BY CECIL KUHNE

On the Edge

The Armchair Paddler

NEAR DEATH

ON THE

HIGH SEAS

NEAR DEATH
ON THE
HIGH SEAS

TRUE STORIES OF
DISASTER AND SURVIVAL

EDITED BY
CECIL KUHNE

VINTAGE DEPARTURES
Vintage Books
A Division of Random House, Inc.
New York

A VINTAGE DEPARTURES ORIGINAL, MARCH 2008

Library of Congress Cataloging-in-Publication Data
Near death on the high seas : true stories of disaster and survival /
edited by Cecil Kuhne.
p. cm.–(Vintage departures)
ISBN 978-0-307-27934-7
1. Shipwrecks.   2. Adventure and adventurers.
I. Kuhne, Cecil, 1952–
G525.N34 2008
910.4'52–dc22
2007043573

Book design by Rebecca Aidlin

www.vintagebooks.com

Printed in the United States of America
10 9 8 7 6 5 4 3 2 1

CONTENTS

PREFACE

Slamming into the teeth of an ocean swell has a way of instantly transforming even the largest and most stable sailboat into a very small one. Which may explain why maritime literature seems to produce more than its fair share of robust adventure tales. In the end, the sea is a great leveler, and stories about its encounters reach the depth of human emotion precisely because they rouse that most basic of fears—death by drowning.

Launching a boat into the open sea has sometimes been compared to being propelled into the vastness of space. The water is very dark out there, and unfortunately, there are no handholds. The howling wind first begins, causing the sails to flap and the mast to creak a little. Then the roiling gale grows louder and louder, and soon your boat becomes a wild pendulum out of control. Before you know it, you are left with only viciously cold waves and strange creatures lurking below the churning surface. What started off as a grand adventure in a beautiful craft on a sheet of glass with spectacular sunsets has become a fight for survival. And unless you are fortunate indeed, there is rarely anyone around to help you.

The modern essays collected in this anthology were chosen because they were the finest writing I could find, and because they cover such a wide span of ocean experiences. Some of those who write here were heading out for a short pleasure cruise when things went horribly wrong. Others were engaged in dramatic round-the-world races that lasted months. The crafts in which these various mishaps occurred ran the gamut from the most sophisticated vessel imaginable to a simple balsa wood raft with a sail on top.

Some of the sailors were forced to abandon their sinking craft in order to take refuge in small inflatable life rafts. They often faced that most helpless of situations: they spotted large ships—which could have rescued them but didn't see them—slide slowly out of view and disappear forever. Those who stayed with their boats held on for dear life as they were buffeted by high winds and crashing walls of water. Many survived, but others died tragically. And often they perished in horrifying numbers when a storm hit as their flotilla raced toward the finishing line.

The authors assembled in these pages are gifted individuals, being as talented with pens as they are with mainsails. And they all possess two other characteristics in common—a great love of and deep respect for the power of the sea. It is important to note that those who survive the ordeal almost always return, proving true Richard Henry Dana's words almost three hundred years ago that "there is a witchery in the sea, its songs and stories, and in the mere sight of a ship."

Cecil Kuhne
Dallas, Texas

FOREWORD

William F. Buckley Jr.

The best explanation I ever heard for man's compulsive race to get to the moon was offered by a shrewd and attractive lady, wife of a law school don at the University of Indiana. "Don't you understand?" she asked after the company had worn each other down with elaborate scientific explanations. They wheeled toward her. "Boys will be boys."

The rhetoric, of course, can be escalated without difficulty, making the statement read: "Men will be men." That takes the hint of mischief out of it all, but it is much better with the mischief left in. Because there is a bit of mischief in adventure, and men who go off grandiloquently to meet their destiny often feel a trace of the excitement a boy feels when he goes out for the first time on an overnight hike. There is, of course, no fun at all in the pursuit of adventure if, as so often is the case, you die en route. No fun at all, when you feel fear and loneliness and helplessness. It is man's capacity to expose himself to the certainty that he will be lonely and afraid that makes possible great adventures of the human spirit.

And it takes a boyish zest for adventure for staid and middle-aged men to engage in such a dazzling adventure as Robert Manry's aboard *Tinkerbelle*, the 13½-foot converted dinghy in which he crossed the Atlantic Ocean, covering

3,200 miles in eighty days. The chances of surviving such a voyage were less than the chance our astronauts will survive their orbits around the planet, covering, in one-tenth the time, a distance 1,000 times as long. The astronauts convince us that heavenly rendezvous are possible between assorted flying objects and that man's body can endure eight days of weightlessness and immobility. Mr. Manry proved that a few planks of wood, none of them more than 13½ feet long, and strips of cloth, put together by a single carpenter of moderate skill, can, using only nature's power, transport a man across the most treacherous ocean in the world.

One feels nothing but admiration for the astronauts. Theirs is, above all, a mission to press their fragile bodies against the unknown and in an experiment so mechanized that they are left with little to do except to obey the signals they hear. It must put a special tax on the spirit to be left with so little latitude. Mr. Manry, by contrast, had great latitude. He could point the nose of his boat in any direction he chose, except in the direction the wind was coming from, and he could leave both sails up, or take down one of them, or take down both of them, or trim one or both, or drag his sea anchor. An almost infinite number of possibilities. And if he made a serious mistake, he would drown. And he might have drowned anyway, because a truly determined sea will not respect the right of so frail a challenger to claim safe passage across the haunted area.

Mr. Manry, who was almost fifty and made his living as a copy reader in Cleveland, knew enough of the literature of the sea to know that for every sailor the sea is the enemy, that it must be treated as the enemy, and that the enemy is formidable enough to have wrecked whole navies in her time. And the astronauts know that nothing in the world is more mysterious than science, that the most fastidious preparations, projections, and calculations are sometimes confounded by utterly inexplicable scientific back talk or because someone didn't turn the screwdriver hard enough.

Even so, boys will be boys, and some boys have the makings of heroes: Astronaut Gordon Cooper has reported that "once, in the middle of the night, at an altitude of over 150 miles, over the middle of the Indian Ocean," he prayed. Mr. Manry may have had room in his cluttered dinghy for the Thirty-third Psalm: By the word of the Lord, the heavens were established, and all the powers of them by the spirit of His mouth. Gathering together the waters of the sea, as in a vessel, laying up the depths in storehouses.

NEAR DEATH
ON THE
HIGH SEAS

Sailing single-handedly in a regatta from Spain to Antigua, Steve Callahan was just west of the Canary Islands when he realized that he had a serious problem—his boat was sinking. Fortunately, he did have on board a five-foot life raft and a survival manual. The fight for his life had begun.

ADRIFT

Seventy-six Days Lost at Sea

STEVEN CALLAHAN

Log of *Napoleon Solo*

It is late at night. The fog has been dense for days. *Napoleon Solo* continues to slice purposefully through the sea toward the coast of England. We should be getting very close to the Scilly Isles. We must be very careful. The tides are large, the currents strong, and these shipping lanes heavily traveled. Both Chris and I are keeping a sharp eye out. Suddenly the lighthouse looms on the rocky isles, its beam high off the water. Immediately we see breakers. We're too close. Chris pushes the helm down and I trim the sails so that *Solo* sails parallel to the rocks that we can see. We time the change in bearing of the lighthouse to calculate our distance away—less than a mile. The light is charted to have a thirty-mile range. We are fortunate because the fog is not as thick as it often is back in our home waters of Maine. No wonder that in the single month of November 1893 no fewer than 298 ships scattered their bones among these rocks.

The next morning, *Solo* eases herself out of the white fog and over the swells in a light breeze. She slowly slips into the bay in which Penzance is nestled. The sea pounds against the granite cliffs of Cornwall on the southwest coast of England, which has claimed its own vast share of ships and lives. The jaws of the bay hold many dangers, such as the pile of rocks known as the Lizard.

Today the sky is bright and sunny. The sea is gentle. Green fields cap the cliffs. After our two-week passage from the Azores with only the smell of salt water in our lungs, the scent of land is sweet. At the end of every passage, I feel as if I am living the last page of a fairy tale, but this time the feeling is especially strong. Chris, who is my only crew, wings out the jib. It gently floats out over the water and tugs us past the village of Mousehole, which is perched in a crevice in the cliffs. We soon glide up to the high stone breakwater at Penzance and secure *Napoleon Solo* to it. With the final neat turns of docking lines around the cleats, we conclude *Solo*'s Atlantic crossing and the last of the goals that I began setting for myself fifteen years ago. It was then that Robert Manry showed me not only how to dream, but also how to fulfill that dream. Manry had done it in a tiny boat called *Tinkerbelle*. I did it in *Solo*.

Chris and I climb up the stone quay to look for customs and the nearest pub. I look down on *Solo* and think of how she is a reflection of myself. I conceived her, created her, and sailed her. Everything I have is within her. Together we have ended this chapter of my life. It is time to dream new dreams.

Chris will soon depart and leave me to continue my journey with *Solo* alone. I've entered the Mini-Transat Race, which is a singlehanded affair. I don't need to think about that for a while. Now it is time for celebration. We head off to find a pint, the first we've had in weeks.

The Mini-Transat runs from Penzance to the Canaries and then on to Antigua. I want to go to the Caribbean anyway. Figure I'll find work there for the winter. *Solo* is a fast-cruising boat, and I'm interested to see how she fares against the spartan racers. I think I have a shot at finishing in the money since my boat is so well prepped. Some of my opponents are putting in bulkheads and drawing numbers on sails with Magic Markers in frantic pandemonium before the start. I indulge in local pasties and fish and chips. My last-minute jobs consist of licking stamps and sampling the local brew.

It is not all fun and games. It is the autumn equinox, when storms rage, and within a week two severe gales rip up the English Channel. Ships are cracked in half and many of the Transat competitors are delayed. One French boat capsizes and her crew can't right her. They take to their life raft and manage to land on a lonesome, tiny beach along a stretch of treacherous cliffs on the Brittany coast. Another Frenchman is not so lucky. His body and the transom of his boat are found crumpled on the Lizard. A black mood hangs over the fleet.

I make my way up to the local chandlery for final preparations. It is nestled in a mossy alleyway, and no sign marks its location. No one needs to post the way to old Willoughby's domain. I was warned that he talks a tough line, but in my few visits I have warmed up to his cynicism. Willoughby is squat, his legs bowed as if they have been steam-bent around a beer barrel, causing him to walk on the sides of his shoes. He slowly hobbles about the shop, weaving back and forth like an uncanvased ship in a swell. Beneath a gray tousle of hair, his eyes are squinted and sparkly. A pipe is clamped between his teeth.

Turning to one of his clerks, he motions toward the harbor. "All those little boats and crazy youngsters down there, nothin' but lots of work and headaches, I can tell you." Turning back to me he mutters, "Here to steal more bosunry from an old man and make him work like the devil to boot, I bet."

"That's right, no rest for the wicked," I tell him.

Willoughby raises a brow and twirks the faintest wrinkle of a grin, which he tries to hide behind his pipe. In no time he is spinning yarns big enough to knit the world a sweater. He ran away to sea at fifteen, served on square-riggers in the wool trade from Australia to England. He's been round Cape Horn so many times he's lost count.

"I heard about that Frenchman. Why you fellas go to sea for pleasure is beyond me. 'Course we had some fine times in my day, real fine times we had. But that was our stock in trade. A fella who'd go to sea for pleasure'd sure go to hell for a pastime."

I can tell the old man has a big space in his heart for all nautical lunatics, especially the young ones. "At least you'd have somebody to keep you company then, Mr. Willoughby."

"It's a bad business, I tell you, a bad business," he says more seriously. "Sorry thing, that Frenchman. What do you get if you win this here race? Big prize?"

"No, I don't know really. Maybe a plastic cup or something."

"Ha! A fine state of affairs! You go out, play tag with Neptune, have a good chance to end up in old Davy Jones' locker—and for a cup. It's a good joke." And it is, too. The Frenchman has really affected the old man. He cheerily insists on slipping a few goodies onto my pile, free of charge, but his tone is somber. "Now don't come back and bother me any more."

"Next time I'm in town you can bet on me like the plague, or the tax man. Cheers!"

A little bell jingles laughingly as I close the door. I can hear Willoughby inside pacing to and fro on the creaking wooden floor. "A bad business, I tell you. It's a bad business."

The morning of the race's start, I make my way past the milling crowds to the skippers' meeting. Whether the race will start on time or not has been a matter of speculation for days. The last couple of gales that swept through had edged up to hurricane force. "Expect heavy winds at the start," a meteorologist tells us. "By nightfall they'll be up to force eight or so."

The crowd murmurs. "Starting in a bloody gale . . . Quiet, he's not finished yet."

"If you can weather Finisterre, you'll be okay, but try to get plenty of sea room. Within thirty-six hours, all hell is going to break loose, with a good chance of force ten to twelve and forty-foot waves."

"Lovely," I say. "Anybody want to charter a small racing boat—cheap?" The crowd's talk grows loud. Heated debate breaks out between the racers and their supporters. Isn't it lunacy to start a transatlantic race in these conditions? The talk subsides as the race organizer breaks in.

"Please! Look, if we postpone, we might not get off at all. It's late in the year and we could get locked in for weeks. We all knew it would probably be tough going to the Canaries. If you can get past Finisterre, you'll be home free. So keep in touch, stay awake, and good sailing."

The quay around Penzance's inner harbor is packed with people gawking and snapping pictures, waving, weeping or laughing. They will soon return to the comfort of their warm little houses.

I yell "Cheerio!" as *Solo* is towed out between the massive steel gates, which are opened by the harbormaster and his men pacing round an antique capstan. *Solo* and I are as prepared as we can be. My apprehension gives way to high spirits and excitement. The seconds tick by. My fellow racers and I maneuver about the starting line, making practice runs at it, adjusting our sails, shaking our arms to get the butterflies out of our stomachs. Those prone to seasickness will have a hard time. Warning colors go up. Get ready. Waves sweep into the bay; the wind is already growing, a rancorous circus sky flies in from the west. I reign *Solo* in, tack her over. Smoke puffs from the starting gun; its blast is blown away in the wind before it reaches my ears. *Solo* cuts across the line leading the fleet into the race.

At night the wind is stiff and the fleet fights hard against rising seas. I can often see the lights of the other boats, but by morning I see none. The bad conditions have abated. *Solo* slices quickly over the large, smooth swell. I spot a white triangle ahead, rising up and then disappearing behind the waves. I shake the reef out of the jib and one of the reefs out of the mains'l. *Solo* races on to catch the other boat. In a few hours I can see the white hull. It is an aluminum boat that was rafted next to me in Penzance, sailed by one of the two Italians in the race. Like most of the competitors, he's a friendly guy. Something seems slightly wrong. The foot of his jib, which has been reefed, is flogging around and bangs on the deck. I yell across, but get no response. I film the boat as I pass, then go below and radio him several times. No answer. Perhaps he's asleep. As night falls, I hear one of the other racers talking to the organizer on the radio. The Italian has sunk. Luckily he has been picked up. When I rode by him, he was probably in trouble and trying to keep the leak contained.

On the third day, I see a freighter pass about a mile away. I radio to him and learn that he has seen twenty-two of the twenty-six boats in the fleet behind me. I'm greatly encouraged. The wind grows. *Solo* beats into stiff seas. I must make a choice, either to risk being pushed into the notorious Bay of Biscay and try to squeak past Finisterre, or to tack and head out to sea. I choose the bay, hoping for the front to pass and to give me a lift so I can clear the cape. But the wind continues to increase, and soon *Solo* is leaping over ten-foot waves, pausing in midair for a second, and then crashing down on the other side. I have to hold on to keep from being thrown off of my seat. Wind screams through the rigging. For hours *Solo* weaves and slips sideways, shaking at every punch. Inside, the noise of the sea pounding against the hull is deafening. Pots and cans clatter. An oil bottle shatters. After eight hours of it, I adjust. It is dark. There is nothing to do but push on. I crawl aft into my cabin, which is a little quieter than forward, wedge myself into my bunk, and go to sleep.

When I awake, my foul-weather gear is floating about in a pool of water. I leap through the pool and find a crack in the hull. With every passing wave, water shoots in and the crack grows longer. The destruction of *Solo* would follow like falling dominoes. As quick as a mongoose, I rip down the sails, cut lumber, and shore her up. For two days I guide her slowly to the coast of Spain.

Within twenty-four hours of my arrival in La Coruña, seven Mini-Transat boats arrive. Two have been hit by cargo ships, one has broken a rudder, others are fed up. It appears that *Solo* ran into some floating debris. Her hull is streaked with dents. Perhaps it was a log. I've seen plenty of them— even whole trees adrift. Over the years I've spoken with voyagers who have sighted everything from truck containers that fell off of ships to spiky steel balls that resembled World War II mines. One boat off the coast of the United States even found a rocket!

The race is finished for me. I speak no Spanish, so it is difficult to organize repairs. I can't find a Frenchman who will agree to drive over the rocky and pitted Spanish roads to retrieve *Solo*. I have little money. My boat is full of seawater, spilled cooking oil, and broken glass. My electronic self-steering is fried. Then I become ill, with a fever of 103°. I lie among the soggy mess, thoroughly depressed.

Still, I am more fortunate than others. Out of the twenty-five boats that started, no fewer than five have been totally lost, although luckily no one has drowned. Only half of the fleet will reach the finish in Antigua.

It is four weeks before I complete my repairs and put *Napoleon Solo* to sea again. I don't know if I have enough stores and money to reach the Caribbean, but I don't have enough to go home. Luckily the Club Nautico de La Coruña is kind. "No charge. We do what we can for the man alone." For four weeks gales daily ravage Finisterre. The harbor is full of crews waiting to escape to the south. We are all just a little late in the season. In the morning there is frost on the deck. Each day it remains longer before melting off. When *Solo* finally claws past Finisterre, I feel as though I've passed Cape Horn.

I've picked up one person to crew, a Frenchwoman named Catherine Pouzet. I needed someone to steer. Catherine's only previous ocean experience was on a boat that was dismasted in the Bay of Biscay. In a panic they had radioed for assistance, were picked up by a tanker, and had watched their boat—the dream they'd worked years for—drift away. They had operated under the delusion that the tanker would save their boat, too. Catherine was not easily put off. She "auto-stopped" her way to La Coruña and there tried yacht-stopping for a ride south.

Catherine loves my little boat, and she is lovely herself, but I feel no desire for romance. I want only for past pain to melt away in the sun of the south. With Catherine's help, I expect to reach the Canaries in fourteen days.

For four weeks we crawl south to Lisbon. Between zephyrs we flop about on a mirrored sea. In my reflection in the glassy water, I get a hint that I am going nowhere, but I begin to fall into the slow pace of the cruising life. My disappointment at not completing the Mini-Transat begins to fade.

On the coast of Spain, ancient river valleys cut deeply into the country. In these rugged *rías*, modern machinery consists of donkeys pulling oxcarts with wooden wheels and axles. Peasants collect animal bedding from the uncultured grasses of mountainside clearings. Women gather at community basins to beat clothes clean on rocks or concrete. In one port the officials pore over our entry forms, carrying them from office to office, like children trying to decipher hieroglyphics. We are the first yacht to anchor in their waters in over a year.

We proceed along the coast into Portugal, cutting through dense fog and dodging freighters, which on a clear night appear like strings of Christmas tree lights, sixteen or seventeen visible at any time. To one side of us is a coast of rocky teeth and seething seas, on the other the *drum, drum* of heavy engines. When the sails hang lifeless, we row. Often we make only ten miles a day.

It would have been simple to remain at anchor. Latin life and lazy weather are drugging. We begin to soak up tranquility like a sponge. Among the cruising community we make many friends traveling in the same general direction. Many are French. All planned to be into the Pacific by January, but their plans have been tempered. "Maybe we'll hole up in Gibraltar for the winter." But there is something inside of me itching to push on. It is more than the need to get to a place where I can refill my purse. Catherine sometimes pouts, wishing I would open up to her more. "You are a hard man," she tells me, but I do not respond by becoming softer. I only become more resolved to reach the Canaries and then push on alone.

We sail from Lisbon in decent wind and reach the peaks of Madeira, pause there, and then proceed south to Tenerife. Our two-week voyage has taken six. I say good-by to Catherine. My ship and I are at peace with one another once again.

Solo is well received wherever she goes. The local people, who would often steer clear of big, expensive yachts, flock to *Solo* like bears to honey. She is as small as their open coastal fishing boats. It is unbelievable to them that she has come all the way from America. In one small port, all of the fishermen and boatbuilders come down early each morning and perch along the quay, patiently waiting for me to wake up. They are eager for me to tell them more stories in my broken Spanish and convoluted sign language.

I come very close to mooring *Solo* for a winter. It has happened to many others, sailing in for a week's visit and staying for years. They make ends meet by making ships in bottles or collecting pinecones in the mountains. German tourists cover the beaches and buy anything with a For Sale sign. I might draw pictures, and I have some writing to do.

I need more than just looking on, playing tourist. I need to be productive, to create, and, of course, to earn money again since I have only a few dollars left and debts to repay.

I am caught in the sailor's inevitable dilemma. When you are at sea you know you must reach harbor, to restock and, you hope, rest in a warm caress. You need ports and often can't wait to get to the next. Then when you are in port, you can't wait to get back to sea again. After a few glasses of cold beer and a few nights in a dry bed, the ocean calls, and you follow her. You need mother earth, but you love the sea.

In most ports you can find a crew who wants to go in the same direction you do. But now most people who wanted to get to the Caribbean for the winter have left some time ago. I don't think that the trip will be difficult alone. One of my new-found friends on Tenerife has repaired my self-steering gear, and the pilot chart promises that there is only a 2 percent chance of encountering gales. The trade winds should be steady. It'll be a milk run.

I make my way to the sparsely populated island of Hierro. Steep cliffs rise from the Atlantic to the east, topped by lush hills and green valleys. The island slopes away to the west and ends with a moonscape of small volcanoes, rocky rubble, and hot red sand. I finish stocking in a tiny man-made port on the western end. On the final day my throat is dry and gravelly. I slap my last pesetas down on the bar. In fumbling Spanish I tell the familiar bartender that the coins will do me no good at sea. *"Cerveza, por favor!"* The beer is cold. The bartender sits down beside me.

"Where to?"

"Caribbean. Work. No more pesetas."

He nods, contemplating the length of the voyage. "Such a small boat. No problema?"

"Pequeño barco, pequeño problema. No big problem yet, any-way!" We laugh and talk while I finish my beer, bum a last cig-arette, sling my provisions over my shoulder, and head for the quay.

One of the old fishermen stops me. "You come from Amer-ica?" he asks as he slits open part of his catch, cleans it, and flops it onto a scale. A woman dressed in black pokes the fish, chattering away to herself.

"Yes, America." I wonder if her man was a fisherman lost at sea, like so many others.

"Ooh ho!" he says. "In such a small boat? *Tonto!*" Fool.

"It's not so small, it's my whole house."

The old man gestures toward his lower abdomen with

cupped hands as if holding gigantic organs. We laugh at his joke as I shake my head no, open my eyes wide, and shiver as if frightened. The woman grabs him by the arm, obviously telling him the fish is overpriced, and begins bargaining, an ageless custom as ritualized as the dominoes played by the men seated at a folding card table on the stony beach.

The night of January 29 is clear, the sky peppered with bright stars. Blocks squeak as I pull up the sails and glide out of the harbor. I thread my way through the offshore fishing fleet and point *Solo* toward the Caribbean. It feels good to be at sea again.

Nerves Exposed

I am experiencing a rare time for a sailor, a week of peace. With uncharacteristic gentleness, the sea and wind wrap my boat in a motherly caress that sends her skipping toward Antigua. I am comforted by the sea yet am continually awed by her. Like an old friend she is always familiar, yet she is always changing and full of surprises. I recline on the after-deck and feel the regular files of waves approach, lift my ship three or four feet as they roll under her, then ease her down gently as they rush on, slipping into the horizon ahead. The breeze rustles the pages of my novel while the sun browns my skin and bleaches my hair.

An age ago oceanic greyhounds—great clipper ships, whalers, and fast cutters full of slaves—plied this route from the Canaries to the Caribbean. Trade winds filled the cloud-like sails that hung from their towering spars: stuns'ls, tops'ls, royals, all set. The rattling of *Solo*'s spars and the hum of her auto pilot mix with the running wind and blow into my ears a fantasy of tapping feet in a hornpipe danced to the song of a concertina.

Solo smoothly cuts westward with twin jibs spread from her bow. Her bubbling trail curls across the waves astern. When not reading, I scratch out stories and letters, scribble pictures of sea serpents with bow ties, and waste inordinate amounts of film, shooting the sea, boat maneuvers, sunsets. I stuff myself with fried potatoes, onions, eggs, cheese, and grains— bulgur, rolled oats, millet. I exercise—pushups, pullups, and yoga—thrusting, twisting, and stretching in rhythm with the rolling boat. A spidery, animated maze of mast, boom, struts, and poles dips, rises, and spreads the sails to catch the wind. In short, I and my ship are in fine shape, and I am having a wonderful and leisurely sail. If good fortune continues, I will reach my destination before February 25.

On February 4 the wind rises and begins to whistle through the rigging. A gale begins to sweep in. A blanket of clouds races overhead. Seas build and begin to crash down all around us. I want to return to peaceful sailing. I speak to the sky. "Come on, hit me if you must, and then go quickly."

My little boat continues to slice across undulating foothills that are rapidly growing into small mountains. The water that was sparkling clear now reflects the dark, threatening sky. Waves froth and spit at us as we carve around them toward the sinking sun. *Solo* is kept more or less on course by the electric automatic pilot. Its motor hums a fatiguing song as it constantly works overtime. Despite the occasional waterfalls that cascade across the deck, I am not too uncomfortable. I joke in front of my movie camera, gnaw on a greasy sausage, and belch in a Long John Silver croak: "Aargh, matey, as you can see, we's havin' just fine weather. Course we could do with a bit o' wind." I crawl up on the foredeck and stuff one of the jibs into its sack. Cold water runs down my spine and up my arms.

The sky grows darker as dusk approaches. When *Solo*

slides into the wave troughs, the sun dips to the horizon. Dip, dip, and it finally drowns in the west. *Solo* slashes on into the night. The waves and wind seem to grow fiercer at night. I cannot see the waves far off—and then suddenly they are here, breaking and rushing down on us. Then they scurry away again into the shadow of the world almost before I am aware that they have struck.

For over ten thousand miles and one and a half Atlantic crossings, my ship and I have kept each other company. She has seen worse, much worse. If things significantly deteriorate, I can adopt storm tactics: reduce sail, and either heave to or run downwind. The pilot chart promises infrequent gales of minor intensity for this part of the south Atlantic and time of year. The wind can pipe up to force seven or so, enough to muss one's hair and guarantee a bathing on deck, but not enough to loosen one's dentures. In about two weeks I will be lying in the baking sun of the Caribbean with a cold rum punch in hand. *Solo* will be placidly anchored with sails furled beneath some palm-studded beach.

Fortunately I rarely have to be on deck, only to reef the sails or to change jibs. I have provided the boat with an inside steering and central control station. I sit beneath a Plexiglas hatch that looks like a boxy jet canopy. From here I can steer with an inside tiller, adjust the sails by reaching out through the open washboard to the cleats and winches beside the hatch, and keep watch, all at the same time. In addition, I can look at the chart on the table below me, chat on the radio beside me, or cook up a meal on the galley stove, all without leaving my seat. Despite the acrobatics of the sea, the cabin remains relatively comfortable. Save for an occasional drip of water feeling its way through the crevices of the hatch, my surroundings are dry. The air hangs heavy with the dampness of the coming storm, but the varnished wood of the cabin glows warmly in the soft light. The shapes contained in the wood grain become animals, people, companions. They calm me. The small amount of coffee that I manage to transfer from my lurching cup to my mouth warms me and props my eyes open. My stomach, made of some noncorroding, inexplodable, and otherwise nonimpressionable alloy, does not yearn for a dry biscuit diet; instead, I eat heartily and plan for my birthday dinner two days from now. I can't bake a cake, having no oven, but I will have a go at chocolate crêpes. I'll stir a tin of rabbit I've saved into a curry, ignoring the French superstition that even the slightest mention of *lapin* assures a crew the most wretched luck.

Though I feel secure in my floating nest, the storm reawakens my caution, which has slumbered for a week. Each ten-foot wave that sweeps by contains more tons of water than I care to imagine. The wind whistles across the deck and through the rigging wires. Occasionally *Solo*'s rear is kicked, and she brings her head to wind as if to see the striking bully. The jib luffs with a rustling rattle, then pulls taut as *Solo* turns off to continue on her way. Visions of a rogue wave snap into my mind. Caused by the coincidence of peaks traveling in different directions or at different speeds, a rogue can grow to four times the average wave height and could throw *Solo* about like a toy. Converging wave troughs can also form a canyon into which we could plunge. Often such anomalies flow from different directions, forming vertical cliffs from which seas tumble in liquid avalanches.

Six months ago *Solo* fell with a thunderous bang in just such a cascade off the Azores. The sky disappeared and nothing but green was visible across the deck hatch. The boat immediately righted and we sailed on, but it was a hard knock. My books and sextant leaped over the tall fiddle rails, smashing on the chart table and splintering its moldings. If they had not hit the table, they would have landed in my face. I was lucky that time; I must be more cautious.

Disaster at sea can happen in a moment, without warning, or it can come after long days of anticipation and fear. It does not always come when the sea is fiercest but may spring when waters lie as flat and imperturbable as a sheet of iron. Sailors may be struck down at any time, in calm or in storm, but the sea does not do it for hate or spite. She has no wrath to vent. Nor does she have a hand of kindness to extend. She is merely there, immense, powerful, and indifferent. I do not resent her indifference, or my comparative insignificance. Indeed, it is one of the main reasons I like to sail: the sea makes the insignificance of my own small self and of all humanity so poignant.

I watch *Solo*'s boiling, phosphorescent wake as it dissipates among the somersaulting waves. "Things could be worse," I muse. Then voices from the past speak to me. "Each time you have chanted that phrase, things have inevitably gotten worse." I think of the pilot chart figures, which are averages taken from ships' data. There might be some truth to the idea that charted estimates of gale strengths tend to be low. After all, if a captain hears of bad weather, he doesn't usually head his rust bucket for the center of it in order to get some fresh air. No doubt I will be a bit uncomfortable for a few days.

I check my gear over and make sure all is as secure and shipshape as a floating fool can make it. I inspect the hull, deck, bulkheads, cabinetry, and all of the joints that hold my wooden jewelry box secure. The kettle is filled for coffee or steaming lemonade. A lump of chocolate is at hand beside the radio. All essential preparations have been made.

It is about 22:30 Greenwich Mean Time. The moon hangs full, white, and motionless, undisturbed by the tempest and the tumultuous sea. If conditions continue to worsen, I will have to head more southerly. For the time being, I can do nothing more, so I lie down to rest. At 23:00 I get up and undress. I lie down again clothed only in a T-shirt. A watch circles my wrist, and around my neck is a slab of whale tooth on a string. It is the most I will wear the next two and a half months.

My boat slues around the rushing peaks, her keel clinging to the slopes like a mountain goat, her port side pressed down against the black, rolling ocean. I lie on my bunk, slung upon the lee canvas, hanging as if in a hammock.

BANG! A deafening explosion blankets the subtler sounds of torn wood fiber and rush of sea. I jump up. Water thunders over me as if I've suddenly been thrown into the path of a rampaging river. Forward, aft—where does it come from? Is half of the side gone? No time. I fumble with the knife I have sheathed by the chart table. Already the water is waist deep. The nose of the boat is dipping down. *Solo* comes to a halt as she begins a sickening dive. She's going down, down! My mind barks orders. Free the emergency package. My soul screams. You've lost her! I hold my breath, submerge, slash at the tie-downs that secure my emergency duffel. My heart is a pounding pile driver. The heavy work wrings the air from my lungs and my mind battles with my limbs for the opportunity to breathe. Terminal darkness and chaos surround me. Get out, get out, she's going down! In one rhythmic movement I rocket upward, thrust the hatch forward, and catapult my shaking body onto the deck, leaving my package of hope behind.

Less than thirty seconds have elapsed since impact. The bow points toward its grave at a hesitating low angle and the sea washes about my ankles. I cut the tie-downs that secure the raft canister. Thoughts flash about me like echoes in a cave. Perhaps I have waited too long. Perhaps it is time to

die. Going down . . . die . . . lost without trace. I recall the life
raft instructions: throw the bulky hundred pounds overboard
before inflation. Who can maneuver such weight in the
middle of a bucking circus ride? No time, quickly—she's going
down! I yank. The first pull, then the second—nothing, nothing! This is it, the end of my life. Soon, it will come soon. I
scream at the stubborn canister. "Come on, you bastard!"
The third pull comes up hard, and she blows with a bursting
static *shush*. A wave sweeps over the entire deck, and I simply
float the raft off. It thrashes about on the end of its painter.
Solo has been transformed from a proper little ship to a submerged wreck in about one minute. I dive into the raft with
the knife clenched in my teeth, buccaneer style, noticing that
the movie camera mounted on the aft pulpit has been turned
on. Its red eye winks at me. Who is directing this film?
He isn't much on lighting but his flair for the dramatic is
impressive.

Unmoving and unconcerned, the moon looks down upon
us. Its lunar face is eclipsed by wisps of clouds that waft
across it, dimming the shadow of *Solo*'s death. My instincts
and training have carried me through the motions of survival, but now, as I have a moment to reflect, the full impact
of the crash throbs in my head. Never have all of my senses
seemed so sharp. My emotions are an incomprehensible mix.
There is a wailing anguish that mourns the loss of my boat.
There is a deep disappointment in myself for my failures.
Overshadowing it all is the stark realization that what I
think and feel will not matter much longer. My body shakes
with cold. I am too far from civilization to have any hope
of rescue.

In the space of a moment, myriad conversations and
debates flash through my mind, as if a group of men are chattering within my skull. Some of them joke, finding comic relief

in the camera's busily taking pictures that no one will ever see. Others stoke a furnace of fear. Fear becomes sustenance. Its energy feeds action. I must be careful. I fight blind panic: I do not want the power from my pumping adrenaline to lead to confused and counterproductive activity. I fight the urge to fall into catatonic hysteria: I do not want to sit frozen in fear until the end comes. Focus, I tell myself. Focus and get moving.

I see my vessel, my companion, my child, swallowed up like a crumb too small for the deep Atlantic to taste. Waves bury her and pass. *Solo*'s white decks emerge. She's not going down, not yet. Wait until she goes before cutting the painter. Even though I have added canned water and other gear to the raft's supplies, I will not live long without additional equipment. Wait and salvage everything you can. My body shakes even more with fright and cold, and my eyes sting from the salt. I must get some clothes, some cover, anything. I begin hacking off a piece of the mains'l. Don't cut the raft, be careful, careful. Once cut, the sailcloth rips off easily. The raft flips about as I pull the horseshoe life preserver and man-overboard pole off of *Solo*'s stern. Foam and sea continue to sweep across her, but she rises each time. My mind coaxes her. Please don't go, not yet, please stay up. The watertight compartments that I designed and installed have combined with pockets of air trapped inside of her. She fights back. Her jib snaps with loud report. Her hatch and rudder bang as the ocean beats her. Perhaps she will not sink after all. Her head is under but her rear hesitates like a child at the shore, unable to make the final plunge.

I ache with cold; the stench of rubber, plastic, and talc fill my nostrils. *Solo* may sink any moment now, but I must get back inside. There isn't much time. I pull up to the side of the boat, climb aboard, and stand for a second, feeling the strange sensation of being in the sea and on deck at the same time. Waves rear up and bury the boat, but time after time *Solo* struggles to the surface. How much battering will she take before water feels its way into the few remaining air spaces? How many moments are left before she will disappear for the last time?

Between towering crests that wash over me, I lower myself into the hatch. The water below is peaceful compared to the surrounding tempest. I duck into the watery tomb, and the hatch slams shut behind me with a crack. I feel for the emergency bag and cut away the lines that secure it. Waves wander by, engulf us, and move on. I gasp for air. The bag is freed but seems to weigh as much as the collected sins of the world. While struggling in the companionway, pushing and tugging to get the gear on deck, I fight the hatch, which beats against my back. Heaving the bag into the raft requires all the strength I have.

As it tumbles into the raft, I turn to reenter the hatch. My hand turns aft and finds a piece of floating cushion wedged against the overhead. Jerking at it, I arise for a gulp of air. There is none. In that moment I feel as though the last breath in the galaxy has been breathed by someone else. The edge of the sea suddenly rips past. I see the surface shimmering like a thousand candles. Air splutters in, and I gasp as the clatter of *Solo* becomes muffled by the coming of the next wave.

I tie the cushion to the end of a halyard and let it float about while I submerge to retrieve my bed. Bundling up my wet sleeping bag is like capturing an armful of snakes. I slowly manage to shove, pull, and roll the bag into the raft. With the final piece of cushion, I fall in behind. I have successfully abandoned ship.

My God, *Solo* is still floating! I see her slowly rolling farther onto her side as I gather up items that float out of the cabin one by one: a cabbage, an empty Chock Full o' Nuts coffee can, and a box containing a few eggs. The eggs will probably not last long, but I take them anyway.

I am too exhausted to do any more. I will not part from *Solo*, but should she want to leave I must be able to let go. Seventy feet of ⅜-inch line, tied to the end of the mainsheet, allows me to drift well downwind. *Solo* disappears when we dip into the waves' troughs. Great foaming crests of water grind their way toward us. There is a churning up to windward like the surf on the shore. I hear it coming; I hear the clap and bang and snap that are *Solo*'s words to me, "I'm here." The raft rises to meet the head of the wave that rushes toward me. The froth and curl crash by just to port.

The entrance fly on the tent-type cover snaps with a ripping sound each time the Velcro seal is blown by the wind. I must turn the raft or a breaker may drive through the opening. While on a wave peak, I look aft at *Solo*'s deck mounting on the next swell. The sea rises smoothly from the dark, a giant sitting up after a sleep. There is a tight round opening in the opposite side of the tent. I stick myself through this observation port up to my waist. I must not let go of the rope to *Solo*, but I need to move it. I loop a rope through the mainsheet which trails from *Solo*'s deck and lead it back to the raft. One end of this I secure to the handline around the raft's perimeter. The other I wind around the handline and bring the tail through the observation port. If *Solo* sinks I can let go of this tail and we will slip apart. Wait—can't get back in . . . I'm stuck. I try to free myself from the canopy clutching my chest. The sea spits at me. Crests roar in the darkness. I twist and yank and fall back inside. The raft swings and presents the wall of the tent to the waves. Ha! A good joke, the wall of a tent against the sea, the sea that beats granite to sand.

With a slipknot I tie *Solo*'s line to the handhold webbing

that encircles the inside of the raft. While frantically tying all
of my equipment to the webbing, I hear rumbling well to
windward. It must be a big wave to be heard so far off. I listen
to its approach. A rush of water, then silence. I can feel it rising over me. There is a wrenching rubbery shriek from the
raft as the wave bursts upon us and my space collapses in half.
The windward side punches in and sends me flying across the
raft. The top collapses and water shoots in everywhere. The
impact is strengthened by the jerking painter, tied to my ship
full of water, upwind from where the sea sprang. I'm going to
die. Tonight. Here some 450 miles away from the nearest
land. The sea will crush me, capsize me, and rob my body of
heat and breath. I will be lost, and no one will even know until
I'm weeks overdue.

I crawl back to windward, keeping one hand on the cord to
Solo, the other hand clutching the handline. I huddle in my
sodden sleeping bag. Gallons of water slosh about in the bottom of the raft. I sit on the cushion, which insulates me from
the icy floor. I'm shivering but begin to warm up. It is a time
to wait, to listen, to think, to plan, and to fear.

As my raft and I rise to the crest of a wave, I can see *Solo*
wallowing in the following trough. Then she rises against the
face of the next wave as I plummet into the trough that had
cradled her a moment before. She has rolled well over now,
with her nose and starboard side under and her stern quarter
fairly high. If only you will stay afloat until morning. I must
see you again, must see the damage that I feel I have caused
you. Why didn't I wait in the Canaries? Why didn't I soften
up and relax? Why did I drive you to this so that I could
complete my stupid goal of a double crossing? I'm sorry, my
poor *Solo*.

I have swallowed a lot of salt and my throat is parched.
Perhaps in the morning I can retrieve more gear, jugs of water,

and some food. I plan every move and every priority. The
loss of body heat is the most immediate danger, but the sleeping bag may give me enough protection. Water is the first priority, then food. After that, whatever else I can grab. Ten
gallons of water rest in the galley locker just under the companionway—forty to eighty days' worth of survival rations
waiting for me just a hundred feet away. The raised stern
quarter will make it easier to get aft. There are two large duf-
fels in the aft cabin, hung on the topsides; one is full of food—
about a month's worth—and the other is full of clothes. If I can
dive down and swim forward, I may be able to pull my survival suit out of the forepeak. I dream of how its thick neo-
prene will warm me up.

Waves continue to pound the raft, beating the side in,
pouring in water. The tubes are as tight as teak logs, yet they
are bent like spaghetti. Bailing with the coffee can again and
again, I wonder how much one of these rafts can take and
watch for signs of splitting.

A small overhead lamp lights my tiny new world. The
memory of the crash, the rank odor of my surroundings, the
pounding of the sea, the moaning wind, and my plan to
reboard *Solo* in the morning roll over and over in my brain.
Surely it will end soon.

I am lost about halfway between western Oshkosh and
Nowhere City. I do not think the Atlantic has emptier waters.
I am about 450 miles north of the Cape Verde Islands,
but they stand across the wind. I can drift only in the direction she blows. Downwind, 450 miles separate me from the
nearest shipping lanes. Caribbean islands are the closest possible landfall, eighteen hundred nautical miles away. Do not
think of it. Plan for daylight, instead. I have hope if the raft
lasts. Will it last? The sea continues to attack. It does not
always give warning. Often the curl develops just before it

strikes. The roar accompanies the crash, beating the raft, ripping at it.

I hear a growl a long way off, toward the heart of the storm. It builds like a crescendo, growing louder and louder until it consumes all of the air around me. The fist of Neptune strikes, and with its blast the raft is shot to a staggering halt. It squawks and screams, and then there is peace, as though we have passed into the realm of the afterlife where we cannot be further tortured.

Quickly I yank open the observation port and stick my head out. *Solo*'s jib is still snapping and her rudder clapping, but I am drifting away. Her electrics have fused together and the strobe light on the top of her mast blinks good-by to me. I watch for a long time as the flashes of light become visible less often, knowing it is the last I will see of her, feeling as if I have lost a friend and a part of myself. An occasional flash appears, and then nothing. She is lost in the raging sea.

I pull up the line that had tied me to my friend, my hope for food and water and clothing. The rope is in one piece. Perhaps the loop I had tied in the mainsheet broke during the last shock. Or the knot; perhaps it was the knot. The vibration and surging might have shaken it loose. Or I may have made a mistake in tying it. I have tied thousands of bowlines; it is a process as familiar as turning a key. Still . . . No matter now. No regrets. I simply wonder if this has saved me. Did my tiny rubber home escape just before it was torn to pieces? Will being set adrift kill me in the end?

Somewhat relieved from the constant assault on the raft, I chide myself in a Humphrey Bogart fashion. Well, you're on your own now, kid. Mingled with the relief is fright, pain, remorse, apprehension, hope, and hopelessness. My feelings are bundled up in a massive ball of inseparable confusion, devouring me as a black hole gobbles up light. I still ache with cold, and now my body is shot through with pain from wounds that I've not noticed before. I feel so vulnerable. There are no backup systems remaining, no place to bail out to, no more second chances. Mentally and physically, I feel as if all of the protection has been peeled away from my nerves and they lie completely exposed.

Postscript: Steve Callahan eventually spent seventy-six days at sea. Emaciated from lack of food and scorched by the sun and salt water, he fought off sharks with a makeshift spear and watched nine ships pass by without noticing. His raft developed a hole after forty-three days, but amazingly, he was able to control the leak until his rescue twenty-three days later.

Gordon Chaplin and Susan Atkinson first met when she married his college roommate. Twelve years later, when both of
their marriages ended, the two became romantically involved
and decided to sail through the Marshall Islands in the
Pacific. A fearsome typhoon hit them one night, and some
critical mistakes were made. His story of their ordeal is a
frightening one indeed.

DARK WIND

A Survivor's Tale of Love and Loss

GORDON CHAPLIN

Paradise

On *November 9, just before*
sunset, we dropped anchor in the lee of one of the little islets
strung like pearls along the encircling barrier reef of Wotho
atoll, in the northwestern Marshalls. I could see the anchor
lying on white sand fifteen feet below the boat as if I were looking down through air. Terns and frigate birds were floating like
fish in a golden liquid element around the palms overhanging
the little beach, while surf from the open ocean where we'd been
an hour earlier broke blue and white on the reef outside.

Susan shut down the engine, walked up the deck, and

joined me on the bow. The boat was eerily steady and quiet. From what seemed a vast distance came the trafficky sough of the surf and the high, wild cries of the terns.

As the light deepened and the colors intensified, Susan whispered, "This is paradise. And you made it possible."

Any decent spiritual travelogue will tell you that you don't find paradise on purpose. If you're living right, it just happens. One day you look around, and you're there.

We'd made our first landfall in the Marshalls at Bikar, as planned, but the current in the narrow pass had been too strong to risk an entry. We'd heaved to for the night, waiting for slack water, and a trailing jib sheet had fouled the prop. It froze with a heart-stopping crash, yanking the shaft back several inches, loosening the stuffing box, and even bending the engine mounts.

We were taking water through the box, though the bilge pump could handle it, and after I cut the rope away (not easy in ten-foot seas), the prop was still functioning. We needed to get somewhere to make repairs, and since the current was still too strong through the Bikar pass, Wotho—about 270 miles southwest—was one of the closest along our route. From the chart and the pilot, entry looked easy enough, and there were some nice protected anchorages. In 1962, according to the pilot, the population of Wotho was 56. Our tourist guide reported that in the old days Marshallese royalty had favored it as a vacation spot.

Wotho Lagoon is a rough oval, about eight miles across at its longest point. We entered through the southern pass and anchored at the far end from Wotho Island, where the village is, because we wanted to indulge a feeling that this atoll, like Bikar, was uninhabited. The village was well out of sight. We were alone.

I hung the swimming ladder, stripped off my clothes, and

dove over the side. The water was cooler than the humid air, with a silkiness I hadn't felt before anywhere. About ten feet down I opened my eyes. The evening sun made the water peach-colored, like the sky.

Still underwater, I swam to the anchor chain and hung there, holding on. I felt no need to come up, as if I were absorbing oxygen directly from the water around me like a frog can. The silk played around every part of my body.

I let go finally and rose to the surface without swimming. Susan was at the rail, smiling down at me.

"You look like a fish. In your element."

"Jump in. There's something amazing about this water."

"What about sharks? Don't they come in at sunset?"

"Do you see them eating me? This is paradise, don't forget. You live forever."

"Do you just get older and older? That sounds awful."

"Of course not. You stay any age you want."

"Okay. I'll settle for twenty-eight."

"You've got to get in the water, though. It only works if you're in the water."

Almost shyly she stepped out of her shorts. Still in her T-shirt, she reached through the wheelhouse window for a barrette. When I begged her not to pin up her hair, she put the clip back and pulled the jersey over her head. Her breasts always surprised me. They looked like Marilyn Monroe's— cheerleader, Hollywood, 1950s breasts.

It was now the 1990s, and we were both middle-aged. But boat life is better than Elizabeth Arden. Joshua Slocum was fifty-four when he finished his epic single-handed round-the-world voyage in 1898 and wrote:

Was the crew well? Was I not? I had profited in many ways
  by the voyage. I had even gained flesh, and actually weighed

a pound more than when I sailed from Boston. As for aging, why, the dial of my life was turned back till my friends all said, "Slocum is young again." And so I was, at least ten years younger than the day I felled the first tree for the construction of the *Spray*.

I watched Susan carefully descend the swimming ladder. From the back, she was smaller and more rounded than Marilyn Monroe. More domestic. More vulnerable. More lovable.

She put a toe in the water, sighed, and committed herself, looking at me with a little wrinkle of worry on her forehead as if even now she wasn't sure she remembered how to swim. Her long hair spread out from her shoulders. "You're right," she said breathlessly. "This water is amazing."

"It feels different, doesn't it?"

"Yeah. It feels . . . safe." She looked surprised.

I exhaled a little and pushed myself underwater with a couple of upward hand strokes. Her body glowed in the slanting light beams, her breasts high and weightless, her belly a pale moon tapering to a dark triangle and dark tanned legs, her hair floating up.

"God," I said when I resurfaced, "you're a mermaid."

Jury-rigging the stuffing box to stop the leak turned out to be easier than we'd thought. A complete repair would mean remounting the engine, but that would have to wait. We could get by, at least until Ponape.

But once you find paradise, you don't want to leave. Who knows when or if you'll ever find it again? Under the boat, ample proof that God is an artist, were pastel reticulated brain corals, fire corals, plate corals, five-foot-wide anemones filled with giraffe-maculated brick-and-white clownfish, Kabuki-like but deadly poisonous lionfish. And farther out, nimble

inquisitive gray reef sharks, wary dolphins, blundering graceful sea turtles, hundred-pound blue-green Maori wrasses, and
giant tridacna clams with soft brown neon-spotted lips and
intricately chambered opalescent interiors. (Like all explorers,
we were prone to lists.)

Around noon on the second day, the village launch
showed up with the mayor, who asked us for our clearance
papers and cruising permit, which of course we didn't have.
We were the first yacht here he could remember. He looked
dubious when we explained that we were here for emergency
repairs and showed him the jury-rigged stuffing box.

The launch took us in tow to the village, where he radioed
Majuro for advice. Then, smiling beatifically, he told us we
could stay as long as we liked, go anywhere, do anything. He
handed Susan a cardboard box and opened the lid to reveal a
giant crab. "Him good eat. Welcome to Wotho."

The crab lived on coconuts, husked with its powerful
claws. It had a large soft body, almost like a hermit crab's
without the shell. That evening we poached it carefully, and
the meat had a tender coconut flavor. It was heavenly.

As soon as we went ashore a group of girls attached themselves to Susan. Holding her hand, they led her around to
places of interest, taking down her long hair to comb or braid
it, giving her coconut candy, ripe breadfruit, papayas, pan-
danus baskets, and coral trinkets and teaching her Marshallese words and songs in return for English ones. She
learned all their names, forgot them, and had to be told again.
They never got tired of her. "I can't believe how sweet they
are," Susan said. "They're angels."

We decided to write a piece on Wotho but to use a different
name and not reveal exactly where it was. To name it would
have been almost blasphemous. Wasn't it enough for people

to know a place like this was out there, and they could stumble on it by accident themselves?

I explored and catalogued the reefs, the lagoon, and the uninhabited islands while Susan learned the lore of the village. In a soft, effortless procession the days slipped by like tradewind clouds. We were sustained by what I could catch in the sea and what the villagers gave Susan: crab, clams (a smaller species, related to the tridacna, which tasted almost as fine as abalone when sautéed), conch, snapper, and more fruit. We never argued anymore; there was nothing to argue about. The issues between us resolved themselves or faded into insignificance.

Time was different here. We had a feeling it could go on forever.

Typhoon Gay

We were watching the sky, where the storm would come from.

In the morning, hazy cumulus clouds shot past, alternating with searing blasts of white sunlight. The air glowed with humidity, and quick, luminous terns rode the damp currents like trout. Our skins were shiny and sticky and we were always a little short of breath.

"I feel like a frog," Susan said. "I smell like a frog."

"How does a frog feel?"

"Permanently damp."

"How does one smell?"

"Aquatic. Fertile. Kind of like a pond in summer."

"We're in the same boat," I said, sniffing.

"Luckily," she said. "I better not kiss you, you might turn back into a prince."

By midafternoon the clouds had thickened and turned gray. The air currents had settled down and were moving with steady force across the surface of the lagoon. The formerly electric blue element now matched the air in color, except for small, luminous whitecaps that stood out as strongly as the terns had a few hours earlier.

The wind was pouring through the gray coconut palms of Wotho Island, making them writhe like water plants in a strong current. Kids played excitedly on the grayish-yellow beach. We saw the minister in his white long-sleeved shirt come out of his cinder-block house, look at the sky, look out across the three hundred feet of clear, warm, choppy water that separated him from our vessel, and wave. That morning, after we'd gone ashore and Susan was off with her girls, he'd said she'd be welcome to spend the night in the church—along with himself, his wife, and his congregation. He knew better than to invite the captain.

I told Susan about it as we were walking down to the dinghy. "Give it some thought," I'd joked, knowing that she wouldn't. "If anything ever happened to you, I wouldn't want to be the one to have to tell Ashley and Page."

The moment didn't seem important. The storm was going to miss us, we were sure it was. And there was a lot of work to do to get the boat ready. I needed her help.

It wasn't as if we were far from land. I could row her in later, after the work had been done.

If things looked bad.

If she wanted to go.

If I thought she should go.

We were stripping the *Lord Jim* of everything that might catch the wind: sails, sheets, awnings, dock lines, fenders, the boarding ladder. We stowed everything below but the life raft and four large plastic bags of trash and garbage up on the wheelhouse roof.

The bags had been accumulating since Hawaii and some of the garbage was pretty ripe, but Susan had refused to let me bury it under the palms of the deserted island where we'd been anchored. Our first argument since coming to paradise.

The bulky brown bundles were in a different place when I came up from the cabin after stowing a load of gear—aft of the cockpit, in a little eddy of wind that curled around the wheel-house and blew the smell back inside it. They rose high over the cockpit combing, hid the dock lines, and made it hard to get to the dinghy.

"I moved them down there so they wouldn't blow off," she said.

I opened my mouth, thought better of it, closed it—and opened it again. "They'll blow off anyway. Look at them."

She never turned. "Fine. If they blow off, they were meant to blow off. At least it won't be us doing it."

I threw up my hands and thought, *She has no idea how bad it could be.* But later, when I'd had a chance to think about it a lot more, I realized that she might have had a better idea than I. Worrying about the garbage was her way to cut the storm down to size.

It was nothing short of miraculous to everyone who knew us that we'd managed to survive so much time together alone on a small boat. We'd had our spats—that morning, when she'd been unable to remove the mizzen, I'd suggested that after three years of living aboard she might have learned how. "You never showed me how," she'd shot back. "You never show me anything because you want to keep me helpless."

Helpless! First I'd laughed in amazement, and then I'd apologized. Yes, she was small of stature (about five foot four), but she'd been fired from at least one job for feminist militancy, had kicked an armed mugger out of her car, had thrown her husband out of their house for philandering, and almost jumped ship in Costa Rica. I admit I pushed her out of a dinghy once, but that was nothing compared to the Silent Treatment, her favorite weapon.

Sooner or later, though, we'd rediscover how much we loved what we were doing and how much we needed each other to make it work. Our love for each other flourished on the boat as nowhere else. All the extraneous elements were gone. There was just us between the sky and the water, and our tasks were clearly delineated: to help each other survive and make it over a new horizon to the next port.

The rushing grayness all around us was deepening into dusk as I put on my mask, snorkel, and fins and jumped overboard to check the anchors. The wind now was well over 20 knots, but we still had a good lee from the nearby island and the water wasn't too rough. It was as warm as the air or warmer, comfortable and reassuring. Angelfish and wrasses were playing near the bottom, glowing like jewels in the dim light.

Both the 45-pound CQR plow on the three-eighths-inch chain rode and the 40-pound Danforth on the three-quarter-inch nylon were well buried in soft mud, a great holding bottom. If the wind shifted, and it probably would, the boat had room to swing 360 degrees without coming close to coral.

The water felt so luxurious I didn't want to come out into the wind. I floated on my back, kicking slowly, enjoying its movement past my skin. The *Lord Jim* lay nicely to the two rodes, and Susan watched me from the wheelhouse. I took a few deep breaths, jackknifed my body to raise my feet in the air, and slid down toward the bottom twenty feet away. I moved slowly, so the fish wouldn't be alarmed, and headed back to the boat underwater about a foot from the bottom.

The 6 P.M. weatherfax from Honolulu came over clearly. Typhoon Gay was about 120 miles east-northeast and moving west-northwest at 7 knots. Maximum winds were 80 knots. When we tuned in WWVH, the powerful radio station in Kauai, Hawaii, that broadcasts time signals twenty-four hours a day for navigational purposes and emergency weather reports every hour at exactly forty-eight minutes after the hour, their report coincided with the weatherfax. Things looked good.

Four days earlier, when we'd first thought about leaving Wotho for Ponape, 480 miles southeast in the Carolines, an ominous low-pressure area had been hanging over the open water we had to cross. We waited another day; the low-pressure area divided like an amoeba. One of the new nuclei began to drift up to the northeast, in our general direction. Toward the end of the day it had become a tropical depression, with winds around 30 knots.

The next day it had reached the islands a few hundred miles eastward and intensified to a tropical storm, with winds up to 60 knots. We assumed it would now follow the usual storm track northwest and decided to wait until it was safely out of the area. But instead of moving out, it zigzagged north and south and continued to intensify.

When it finally resumed the storm track sometime in the middle of the night, it had become Typhoon Gay. Waiting it out still seemed best; our anchorage was protected to the north and east by the island and the curve of the reef. The track would take it more than sixty miles to the north of us. Winds at Wotho shouldn't be much stronger than the last storm's, where our two-anchor system had been more than adequate. There were no other boats around to break loose and drift into us. If we sailed south away from the storm, the winds would be less strong but we'd be in open ocean—at night.

Stripping the boat had made a big change in the way she rode. "I bet the wind's over thirty knots now, and she's perky and buoyant as can be," I said. "Just like you."

Susan was wearing a dark green tank top, over a black bra, and the pink jogging shorts she'd bought in Hawaii for our daily run in the park near Keehi Marine. Her hair was loose and windblown.

We were alone in the still-grayish darkness, although on shore we could now see the flickering kerosene lamps of the village and the single battery-powered electric light at the community center. No matter what, the night was going to be long and dark, and without her, after all those other nights we'd been through together, I would have felt only half there.

"I'm glad you're not ashore." I put my arms around her. "Really glad." Her body was warm and soft and smelled of sun and suntan lotion; her hair tickled my cheek. When I looked down at her, her eyes were closed.

"I am too," she said, a bit absently. "Listen, I really should call Ashley and Page. Page has probably been tracking this thing. She tracks all of them."

I groaned. We were out of range of High Seas Radio in San Francisco and had to place our calls now through Sydney Radio in Australia. Even in the best of weather the routine was long, complicated, excruciating. "Couldn't we call them all after the storm?" I said. "Please?"

She finally agreed. We uncorked a bottle of cold California Gewürztraminer from the refrigerator, poured ourselves glasses, looked at each other, toasted, and drank. The rising wind in the shrouds made a little trilling sound every once in

a while, like a songbird, and the faint but somehow reassuring
smell of the garbage curled through the cabin.

"Well," I said, "I guess tomorrow we'll know what we
should have done, won't we?"

We heated up two cans of extra-hot Hormel chili while
the wind rose steadily and backed into the north, so we were
no longer protected by the island. By 9 P.M. the sustained
force seemed to be approaching 50 knots (not that easy to
judge in the dark with no anemometer) with gusts over 60—
stronger than anything we'd been through before. The 9:48
weather on WWVH hadn't been updated, so we assumed
there hadn't been any major changes in the storm's direction
or intensity.

We called the village radio and asked them what they'd
heard. They said the storm was due to pass at around midnight or a little later. We drew its projected course on our
chart and figured that the wind might get a little stronger, but
not much. I went up on the bow to check the anchor lines,
adjust the antichafe guard on the nylon one, and let a little out
so that as the boat swung farther into the north the strain on
both rodes would remain the same.

As soon as I got out there, it seemed, the wind picked up. It
whistled in my teeth and blew a tune through my nose. Looking directly into it was difficult. My shorts flapped painfully
against my legs. When I got back I checked with Susan to see
if I'd imagined the change, and she said I hadn't.

At about 10 P.M. we started the big Perkins diesel, which
hadn't failed us yet. The idea was to warm it up and get it
ready to use later, if necessary, to take strain off the anchor
rodes by motoring slowly ahead.

As usual, one touch of the starter was enough. The needles

jumped in the dials and gradually settled into their accustomed places: temperature 80 degrees centigrade, oil pressure 50 psi, RPM 900, transmission pressure 140 psi, starboard alternator charging at about 20 amps. Under the floorboards, the engine was warm and purring.

When I went down in the cabin to take a leak (the wind was too strong to do it over the side anymore), there was a faint smell of decay. I assumed it was from the garbage bags back on the stern but noticed that instead of getting weaker as I moved forward toward the head, it got stronger. I realized it was coming from two gleaming black-spotted tiger cowrie shells we had found a couple of days earlier, alive, in shallow water just short of the drop-off on the barrier reef. I'd found one and, later, Susan had found the other.

At the time, I hadn't realized that shells in some cultures are considered bad talismans. But when I found my shell, glowing eerily in the darkness of its crevice, I'd felt an odd current that was not the joy of discovery. Still, I hadn't resisted taking it back to the boat and showing it to Susan. As she took its smooth, dark heaviness into her hands she had that same wide-pupiled look she'd had when we made landfall in Hawaii and dropped anchor here.

We let the animal in my shell gradually die and deliquesce until it could be washed out in salt water. The smell was so horrendous that we tried a different approach when she found hers, boiling it briefly to kill and harden the animal and then picking it out with a fishhook. Her way was more humane and the smell wasn't as bad, but the boiling had caused slight chipping and discoloration.

The two shells were now side by side in a sea-railed pocket on the drop-leaf teak salon table. It was too late to throw them overboard; the animals had already died. They were just beautiful skeletons now, and Susan had always been on good terms with skeletons. She collected bones of all kinds, went out of her way to visit cemeteries, and had once put together a photographic essay on the death markers along the Transpeninsular Highway of Baja California. She'd want to keep hers, and it would be wrong to heave mine even though it was the smellier.

No, the two shells should stay together, in death as in life.

The boat was beginning to pitch uneasily in the short chop when I came back up to the wheelhouse. Susan, holding on to the grab rails with her small, strong hands, was looking out the window at the one light still visible on shore: the generator-powered electric light in the community center. All the kerosene lanterns were gone now, and the boat could have been floating in outer space. Susan's face was lit from below by the amber numerals on the depth finder, the pale green glow of the GPS, and the lamps in each of the engine dials. Neither of us spoke.

In that same illumination I could see the face of my watch, a little after 11 P.M. We'd been in darkness for five hours and had at least seven more to go before dawn.

Land people, most of them anyway, tend to sleep through the night. It's different on a boat at sea. The watches continue, no matter what time it is. You sleep a few hours at night and a few hours during the day.

In our usual voyaging schedule, the last watch of the night carried over into daylight and Susan took that, while both of mine were in darkness. On long passages I seemed to be awake at night more than during the day, becoming a creature of the night—a small, vulnerable one. I was well acquainted with the stars, the Southern Cross, the moon (in all its phases), the feel but not the look of big ocean swells. It was a fearsome beauty.

Squalls always seemed to come at night. Cold, sharp, horizontally moving raindrops would rattle against the black windows of the wheelhouse, and the sails would begin to boom like shotguns. I'd cut the automatic pilot, trim the sheets, and try to find the wind, which would be shifting wildly through all points of the compass. Confused, choppy seas would broadside the hull, break into the cockpit, and make me worry about the thin glass in the wheelhouse. The seas would be invisible as always, except for the white foam running down their fronts, but they'd sound like sliding rocks.

Ships always passed at night, too, moving at more than 20 knots, so fast they could be on us twenty-five minutes after their lights appeared on the horizon. And once again I'd marvel at how, in the middle of nowhere, two boats on two different courses originating on opposite sides of a vast ocean could pass so terrifyingly close.

I've read a lot of rhapsodies on the joys of night sailing in the trades. Personally, I was always very glad to see the sun come up, to have survived yet another twelve hours of uncertainty, punctuated by not a few of those waking nightmares, snatches of disembodied conversation, lights and huge waves that didn't exist. When dolphins streaked through that darkness like glowing comets, with unearthly breathing and startling churnings and splashes, I'd tell myself they were the spirits of my dead father enjoying themselves and wishing me well on this voyage. But I never believed it.

The sustained force of the wind now seemed over 60 knots, with occasional gusts that felt well over 80. But how could you judge? It was a dark wind, while the storm in Honduras—

our only standard of comparison—had been a daytime one. Does being able to see what you're faced with make it worse or better? You'd think better, except that sometimes at sea, when the sun comes up and illuminates the waves you've been taking for granted all night, they look terrifying. All I can say for sure is that this warm, damp, heavy entity sometimes felt a little stronger than anything we'd experienced before, and sometimes quite a bit stronger.

"*Lord Jim*, how are you doing?" asked Wotho Radio. Usually it was the mayor himself who talked to us, but the mayor was away at the President's Invitational Billfishing Tournament at Kwajalein atoll about fifty miles southeast. The speaker's English was better than the acting mayor's, whom we'd met earlier in the day, so we couldn't put a face to the voice. It would have been nice to have been able to. "We're doing okay so far," I said. "Have you heard anything new?"

Nothing new. The storm center was still due sometime after midnight, it was still headed west-northwest, and the present latitude was about 11 degrees. It still should pass well to the north.

"Are you sure you don't want to come ashore?" Wotho Radio asked.

It was the voice of experience talking, and we should have listened. Maybe Susan did listen and wanted to go, but she didn't tell me. I didn't ask her. I couldn't make out her expression in the dim light. I wanted her to stay. I was confident in our technology and even more confident that as long as we stayed together, everything would be all right.

We couldn't have rowed ashore, of course. The inflatable dinghy would have been blown downwind like a balloon. But swimming ashore in the warm, cozy water would have been easy. It was only three hundred feet to the protected beach. I could have swum in with Susan and then swum back. Or I could have stayed ashore with her and let the *Lord Jim* fend for herself.

"We'll hang on here," I said, trying to make out Susan's face. "But your light is very helpful. It lets us know where we are."

"Okay, roger, roger. Wotho Radio standing by."

The idea of abandoning ship—our home, our career, our life—was unthinkable to me, at least at that point. We weren't in trouble, not even close. There were many things we could do if it got worse, but how much worse could it get? I was prepared to take a chance, and I assumed Susan was, too.

I went forward to check the anchors again and, as before, the wind seemed to pick up immediately. I could feel the features on my face changing under it into a wind-tunnel grimace—my lips pulled back over my teeth, my eyes squeezed shut, my cheeks flapping.

I had let out all hundred feet of the nylon rode and needed more, so I tied one of the braided orlon dock lines to it with a double fisherman's bend and fitted another polyethylene chafe guard on the other side of the knot. The wind blew through my fingers and made them clumsy as I paid the line out through the bowsprit roller and snubbed it. On the other bowsprit roller the anchor chain, held with a chain hook attached to a fifteen-foot length of springy one-inch nylon rope to absorb the jerks, still had some belly left in it.

I was cold and breathless by the time I got back to the wheelhouse. Susan handed me a towel. "It doesn't seem to like me going out there, does it?" I joked. I was always complaining that she took things too personally, even the weather. "That last gust was a good eighty knots, didn't you think?"

She nodded without smiling back.

"Maybe we ought to try putting it in gear," I said. "Take the strain off the lines." My hand was shaking slightly as I pushed the Morse control lever forward and watched the RPMs climb to 1,000, the slowest possible motoring speed. "I'll have to go up again and see what's happening."

She put a warm hand on my arm. "Oh, wear your harness. Please!"

It was the first time she'd sounded fearful; maybe she was wishing she was safely onshore. It should have worried me. "We're at *anchor*, Susan." Grinning. "We're not out in the middle of the ocean. If I fall overboard, I can climb back on. Actually, it would be really nice to be in the water." I meant it. The air was filled with cold 80-mph raindrops that stung like buckshot. The water, as I imagined it, would be comforting, almost motherly.

This time there was no question: as soon as I left the wheelhouse the wind gusted to the highest velocity yet. I could tell by the weight of it on my body. I had to crouch and shield my eyes. Through the tears, I could see that the engine had caused us to run up dangerously on the anchor rodes and at the same time fall off to port.

I let the wind carry me back to the wheelhouse and took the engine out of gear. Towel again. "Hope we didn't piss off the storm god," I said, with the old casual reassuring grin. I leaned out the wheelhouse door and shouted, "Sorry! For Christ's sake, we're s . . . o . . . o . . . o . . . o . . . r . . . r . . . y!"

Maybe if I'd known then what I know now, I wouldn't have shouted so cockily. Maybe. Though the WWVH weather broadcasts told us otherwise, by dusk the storm had actually turned 20 degrees to the southwest and was now headed right at us, with an intensifying wind speed of between 85 and 105 knots.

We were targeted.

The storm god hates technology. For the first time in the four years we'd owned the boat, the depth finder began to malfunction. It would register the correct depth of eighteen feet for a little while, but then the number would be replaced by a line across the screen, meaning that its range had been exceeded or that it was actually sitting on the bottom. The line would be replaced by arbitrary numbers, and then—at increasing intervals—the real ones would come on again. This was unsettling, because a change in depth would be the best way to tell if we were dragging.

Another way would be by the light onshore. But what if the light onshore went out?

A third way could be by means of the GPS, which was accurate to a quarter mile. I programmed a way point that corresponded to the spot where we were anchored so that later, if we seemed to be dragging, we could check our actual position against it.

By this time, Susan had taken up a position on the floor of the wheelhouse near the closed door leading out to the cockpit, the most protected space on board. I was on the settee next to the radio and weatherfax. The boat rolled and pitched sharply, and the noises around us had deepened in tone from a screaming to a deep thrumming vibration. Talk was difficult; there didn't seem to be much to say anyway. The wind outside blew our thoughts away, even though inside the air was calm.

I wondered idly whether the large wheelhouse windows would blow in. The big diesel pulsed. We hung on and waited for the clock to move, and it had never moved more slowly.

Sometime after midnight, I saw that the light onshore was no longer there, although I thought I could still see the loom of the island. There was a chance we could be dragging.

"I better go check the anchors again," I said.

"Oh, God, don't go out there."

I grinned and said something flip, even though I understood very well what she was worried about. To go out would make the storm worse. At the time, I didn't wonder how bad things would have to get before the insouciance she hated so much gave way to tenderness and sympathy.

I tugged the wheelhouse door open. "Well, anyway, the garbage is still on board."

Susan didn't answer. I turned to see why not (in the darkness I couldn't make out her expression), almost went back; almost put my arms around her, but instead I went out and closed the door behind me.

Standing upright on deck now was impossible, so I hauled myself forward from handhold to handhold in the crouch of a man who has had too much to drink—the old Hurricane Walk.

The anchors were holding, but the nylon rode was tight as a piano string and the thick nylon spring line on the anchor chain was stretching more than a foot with every heave of the boat. As it stretched, it chafed against the sharp edge of the bulwark next to the bowsprit. The belly in the chain was gone.

I considered letting out more chain but that would have meant a complicated series of maneuvers. Susan would have to add power from the engine to take the strain off the rodes. When the strain was off, I'd have to reach down with my hand and release the steel bar that locked into the cogs of the windlass and held it immovable.

As Susan cut back the power and the chain paid out, I'd have to control it with the windlass brake while slacking the nylon rode with my other hand. When they were both out enough, I'd have to snub them (the chain with the windlass brake and the nylon with the cleat) and attach the chain hook again. If the brake slipped while I was releasing or engaging the locking bar and the strain of the boat suddenly came back on the chain, I could easily lose a finger or a hand.

I decided not to try, to wait it out and hope for the best. How much worse could it get? We had a third 45-pound CQR plow anchor to throw in an emergency. But for the first time, I began to feel a hint of passivity, a slight inclination to say to myself, "It's gone too far; it's out of my hands."

Back in the cockpit, I saw that our ten-foot inflatable dinghy, which had served us faithfully and well since we'd bought the boat, was floating upside down behind us. As I watched, the wind blew it right side up again; then for a while it left the water completely and streamed out behind us at the end of its painter like a kite. I grabbed the line and shortened it up until the dinghy was snubbed against the hull, but the chafing was worse that way. I tried to haul the whole thing into the cockpit but didn't have the strength.

Finally, I just let it go, feeling that curious passivity gain a little. And, thinking about it later, I realized that the garbage must have blown away by then or it would have been in my way.

For the first time, Susan and I didn't talk about whether the wind had picked up while I was outside. "I don't think the spring line is going to hold much longer," I said as she handed me the towel, pushing it into my hand as she'd been trained to pass a scalpel to a surgeon in an operating theater. When I tried to check our position against the way point I'd programmed into the GPS, I noticed some unfamiliar symbols next to the numerals. The numerals didn't change when I punched the keys, they didn't respond. There was some malfunction in it, too.

Normally, I would have opened the chart table, taken out the GPS manual, and painstakingly gone through it to find out what the numerals signified. But I didn't. I just didn't seem to have it in me. I sat down on the settee to rest for a minute, and the feeling of inertia gained another notch.

Susan was back in her protected position by the wheel-house door, staring at me. We were witnessing a performance. What next? Nothing we had been through before in our lives had prepared us for this, but we stayed calm because we had each other. Because everything was going to work out. And because at that moment there was nothing else to do.

Except jump overboard and swim for shore. It would have been easy. But even now, I was pretty sure that the wind wasn't going to get much stronger, that if the spring line broke the chain would hold, that if the chain broke, the emergency anchor on another two hundred-foot three-quarter-inch nylon rode could replace it. If it didn't we could beach the boat under power, make her fast to some palm trees, and repair the damage when the storm had passed. The big propeller gave so much thrust that I still didn't want to put it in gear and risk overriding the rodes.

"Jesus," Susan said as a banshee gust once again stretched the limits of what we could imagine. Her eyes looked black. There was a heavy, dense thud and the hull lurched backward off the wind for an instant and came up again. "There goes the spring line," I said, on my way out the door. Up on the bow, the anchor chain was rigid as a steel rod. The lunatic wind blew my brain clean. There was nothing to do but let the force carry me back to the cockpit.

My head stayed empty—*too empty to put the engine in gear*—as we sat in the wheelhouse and waited for the chain to break. Or not. The passive feeling gained a few more notches. Five or ten minutes later the chain did break, with the same dense thud. The hull lurched backward again but did not seem to bring up.

Blessed action. The tonic of movement, of carrying out a plan. Susan was at the wheel, applying enough power to move the boat up parallel to the anchor we were still attached to. I was out on the foredeck again, struggling with the emergency anchor. The plan was: when we got into position I'd drop it, and we'd fall back again on the two rodes. I waved my arm, motioning her forward, but the boat had turned far enough broadside to the wind for the high deckhouse to catch its full force. We were blown over at a 45-degree angle and held there, as if the 8,800 pounds of ballast in the keel didn't exist.

We had entered the realm of the storm god. The performance had turned into a demonstration. We were his, now. He set the rules. He made the plans. He wrote the script.

Up on the bow, though, I was so busy reacting that I didn't have time to think. Everything seemed as natural as anything else, as in a dream.

The heavy anchor, the coil of rode, and I slid down the steeply inclined deck to leeward and brought up against the bulwark. I worked slowly and methodically to get things cleared away; the hull now broke the wind so I felt comfortable, as if I could work there forever.

Reality now being beyond question, it didn't surprise me in the least that our little waterproof flashlight, which I'd used on all previous ventures forward, was dimming out. And neither did it come as a great shock, when I finally got the anchor over the side and began to pay out the rode, that there was no strain at the other end. It wasn't holding.

Neither was there much strain on the other rode, when I

tested it. Maybe we were still drifting down on it, after having powered upwind to drop the emergency.

Anyway, the job was done. When I stood up to work my way aft, the wind caught me and for a second I was flying. I landed on my knees on our newly nonskidded deck and skidded over the sharp little nubbles, pushed by solid air, wondering how much skin and flesh would be left but, clambering into the tilted cockpit, too busy to look.

"Head her up in the wind!" I yelled at Susan. She was clinging to the wheel to stop herself from slipping down the floor. I closed the wheelhouse door and latched it and suddenly the enveloping nightmare outside turned stagy and unreal, like a movie from the thirties. I felt her warm, dry body against me as I turned the wheel into the wind and applied power.

We couldn't hear the engine but the tachometer registered 2,200 RPM, full power. It made no difference at all. The boat stayed broadside to the wind, held by it at 45 degrees from the vertical and drifting to leeward, not moving forward or heading up. The depth finder continued to malfunction, but I knew there were coral heads near us and expected one or both of the anchors to snag and pull the bow around. We had shipped no water, and once the bow was back in the wind the boat could straighten up again.

It was as if the anchors didn't exist. We continued to drift to leeward, and now I noticed the engine temperature was into the danger zone, well over boiling. No surprise: it was all part of what was happening. I shut it down, rather than run the risk of ruining it forever; both the propeller and the cooling system intake must have been out of the water.

My watch read 1:10 A.M. I noticed the clasp had been damaged as I'd wrestled with the anchor, so I took it off and carefully put it next to my glasses on the ledge under the wheelhouse windows. It was an old Rolex Oyster diving

watch my father had given me when I was eighteen, and I
didn't want to lose it. "Well," I said to Susan, "you better call
Wotho on the radio and tell them we're drifting"—I checked
the compass—"south, out of control."

She called, but (no surprise) there was no answer. Then
she said, "Do you think we better get our life jackets on?"

I shrugged and grinned, a strange reflex, but there it was.
I'd done all I could. Life jackets were her area of responsibil-
ity, her decision. To me they'd always been a little like the
EPIRB: a harbinger, a Jonah. An admission of defeat.

"Well, do you?" She sounded angry.

"I guess we should," I said.

The life jackets were inflatable Mae West–type U-shaped
vests. You put your head through the upside-down U. The
two ends of it were attached to a web belt that you fastened
around your waist with a jam buckle. You inflated it by blowing into a tube past a one-way valve. We put them on and
stood there on the tilted wheelhouse floor, looking at each
other. If anything, seeing Susan in the jacket made things even
less real than before.

"I guess we shouldn't blow them up completely right now,"
I said. "We need to be able to maneuver."

She put her mouth to the tube and blew hers up about two-
thirds of the way. When I tried to blow mine up, nothing happened. "Do you have to twist it or something?" I asked. "No
air is going in."

"No you don't have to twist it," she said impatiently. "Just
blow."

I blew as hard as I could, felt the one-way valve give reluctantly and the vest inflate. I stopped when it was one-
third full.

We drifted downwind in silence for a while. Inside the
wheelhouse it was still warm and dry. Someone in Kwajalein

was speaking English on the radio, about supplies he'd be delivering somewhere the next day. His call sign was "Mr. Bill."

"Sooner or later we're going to hit the reef," I said. "Or an island. I don't know how much time we have, but we've got to think about what we're going to need." My mind felt sluggish. We both seemed slow, in movement and thought, as if we were in a dream.

Gradually we assembled the emergency items that Susan had prepared: a grab bag of flares, another flashlight, a pocket knife, a compass, a signal mirror, a large polyethylene waterproof container with a first-aid kit and drugs, emergency rations, fishing line and hooks, ship's and personal papers, my swim fins, the EPIRB.

"You better put your watch and glasses in the waterproof container," Susan said.

It was an impressive, foresighted idea, but I never got around to implementing it. I was trying to coax my sluggish mind to think of more immediate things we'd need. *Wet suits?* We each had a three-millimeter-thick full-body surfing wet suit that would help buoy us up, protect us from the coral, and keep us warm, but they were in the forepeak locker, and the forepeak was full of stuff from on deck. I started down to get them anyway but Susan begged me not to. She was worried about a propane gas explosion, and indeed the red light of the gas sensor had been on for some time. But more than anything, anything in the world at that moment, she didn't want me to leave her alone.

Looking around the wheelhouse and the cockpit for more accessible things, I noticed the pile of dock lines formerly hidden by the bags of garbage. I selected a fifteen-foot three-quarter-inch line and tied the ends around our waists, using bowlines, a knot that doesn't slip tighter or jam. "Now you don't have to worry," I said. "I'll never leave you." I do believe I was grinning when I said it. "Is it tight enough?"

She pulled at it. "I don't think so."

I undid it and tied it again. I didn't want it too tight in case it snagged on something and she needed to get out of it. "How's that?"

She raised her eyes, looked me full in the face for a full count of five (I remember every count), and nodded.

We finally grounded with the kind of jarring lurch that usually makes a sailor's heart dive overboard, but all I felt was a strange relief. "Well, there's the reef." I nodded wisely. At last something had happened the way we'd thought it would.

The wheelhouse was still warm and cozy. Electronic equipment glowed blue, green, amber, and red. The radio crackled with snatches of talk. And the quarter-inch safety-glass windows still safely sealed us in.

Our keel bounced at shorter and shorter intervals but never completely settled as the surf picked it up and dropped it over and over again on the coral. I turned on the roof-mounted searchlight and spun it around, looking for land. There was nothing in sight but howling, undifferentiated blackness. The light made it worse.

Eventually, we slid open the heavy teak wheelhouse door and worked our way out into the real world. We were still removed, not really with it, like newborn babies. The tilted hull rose over our heads and broke the unimaginable force of the wind. To leeward a strange white element that was a mixture of water, air, and rocks hissed and rushed. Invisible surf from the lagoon pounded the exposed bottom of the hull at our backs while unseen waves coming across the reef from the open ocean occasionally broke directly into the cockpit and

threw us around. There was one thing, though, that we knew
for sure. The water was warmer than the air.

Side by side, clutching the things we'd gathered together,
we sat on the uptilted cockpit thwart, our feet braced on the
downtilted one. All the literature said to stick with the boat
until the last minute. There was no question of inflating the
life raft—it would have vanished immediately. Our best
chance was that the hull might work its way higher and higher
onto the shallow reef until it was solid. Meanwhile, the searchlight continued to play on nothingness, unless you called that
white firehosing element rushing at the leeward edge of the
cockpit something.

The boat was already breaking up. When I went into the
wheelhouse to look for the diving knife (still connected by
our fifteen-foot rope), I saw the leeward windows, closest to the
elements, had shattered. The teakwood components of the
wheelhouse had started to split off jaggedly from the fiberglass of the hull. Down in the cabin, the red warning light of
the propane gas sensor pulsed. Water, mixed no doubt with
acid from our new Surrette Type D batteries, was over a corner of the floorboards and climbing up the settee toward our
new blue canvas seat covers.

The knife was nowhere to be found. I reeled myself back
along the rope to the small wet person alone in the cockpit, sat
down next to her again, and put my arm around her. Automatically she leaned forward to clear her hair. She always did
that, because she hated to have it pulled.

The last wave held us underwater for too long. It was time to
go, and quite easy. We let the soft, almost blood-temperature
element carry us clear of the foundering hull.

We were holding hands. The searchlight, now only a few
feet up, shone away from us into blackness. The wind was

easier, with only our heads in it. The noise was somewhere in the background. We were breathing the element, and it seemed breathable.

Drifting downwind from the hull, Susan's voice came more like a thought. "Where are we?"

I heard my matter-of-fact answer. "I don't know." The searchlight was extinguished, leaving us in darkness. The boat was gone. I blew on the tube to inflate my vest the rest of the way but no air would go in. A wave from the lagoon broke over us, tearing her hand out of mine, scraping my back against the reef. It was not sharp coral here, but weed-covered smooth rock. That was lucky.

Three-foot waves began breaking over us about every fifteen seconds. In the darkness we couldn't see them coming. They were big enough to roll us over and disorient us, to hold us underwater for a few seconds, to scrape us against the rocks but not to smash us. I held Susan around the waist with one arm and with the other held on to my partially inflated life vest.

Its belt had come undone and the U-shaped part had slipped off my head. In the darkness, I couldn't make out how to put it back on. The valve was still stuck. All the things we had brought with us had disappeared by this time, or I would have put on my fins. They would have made swimming twice as easy.

In some of the waves we couldn't hold on to each other. We'd catch our breath, get oriented, get a new grip. Another wave would come and go. We'd start the process over. Then I lost contact with Susan completely. I pulled on the rope. There was no resistance; finally I felt the knot at my fingertips, the empty loop. Nothing was visible.

The energy I used up in the next three or four strokes equaled all the previous energy combined. But she was there, not far away. Quite near. My arm was back around her soft waist and her voice was back inside my head, almost like a thought. "I've come out of my jacket."

She was holding on to it now, like I was holding on to mine. Her wet round head, mouth open and facing up, was in silhouette—against what? Against blackness, and yet I could see it clearly, the first thing I'd been able to see since we'd left the boat. Between waves, I tried to fit the loop back over her shoulders, under her arms. And failed.

We were in deeper water, no more rocks under our feet. Had we drifted out over the reef into the open ocean? Her voice again. *"Hold me up."* An arm around my neck, a hug, an embrace, like so many times before.

"Not the neck, pet. Not the neck." Obediently, she took her arm away. Her back was to me, my arm was around her waist. A few more waves rolled through and I yelled, "Hold on to your jacket. Hold on to the rope. Are you all right? You have to tell me if you're not all right."

She was making an oddly reassuring noise, *"Oh, oh, oh, oh."* I knew it well. It was the noise she made when she was scared—as we rowed our tiny inflatable dinghy closer and closer to a sleeping whale or when a car shot out in front of us on the highway without warning. When she made that noise, I knew, there wasn't any real danger. When the danger was real—when our car actually left the road on a rainy, foggy night in upstate New York and flew through the air into a ten-foot-deep culvert; when the seventy-foot shrimp boat broke loose in the last storm in Honduras and began to drift down on us; when the Cessna 172 I was trying to land began to porpoise down the runway—there had been no noise from her at all.

I knew how she hated and feared being rolled in the waves even on a good day, but as long as she made that noise there couldn't be any problem. Things would work out. We were together.

We were underwater again. I opened my eyes and saw her clearly, as if she were outlined in black fire. She was relaxed. There was a little smile on her lips and her eyes were half closed. Her long hair spread out in the water. The top of her head was about a foot under the surface, and when I put my hand under her chin and tried to push up, another wave was there.

She moved farther away from me below the surface and the black light around her was extinguished. I reached out and felt her hair—the soft, fine ends. The tips of my fingers could still feel it as the tickly bubbles and warm currents of the next wave curled around me, wrapped me up, and did what they wanted with me.

I can feel it now.

The Voice

The voice started talking in the womblike dark water sometime after I lost Susan. I was dog-paddling with one hand, holding the limp life vest with the other. I seemed to be in the open ocean now, with infinity in all directions, but whether or not I was on the surface was unclear. I could feel myself breathing something—air, water, or both. The storm seemed vague. *You blew it,* the voice said, and I felt myself crying, but it didn't seem to matter very much. *She's gone.* I would soon be gone myself. Maybe I already was gone. Is this what drowning feels like?

If it is, then drowning is mostly a process of waiting. Waiting for it all to be over with and wondering every once in a while how you'd know. No revelations, no home movies of your life, no regrets. No strong concerns, either about Susan or myself. A lonely way to die, but then what isn't? "What is the answer?" Gertrude Stein was asked as she slipped away, and she answered, "What is the question?" Neither the voice nor the womblike element that I floated in offered anything profound. I did have a feeling, though, that when I died I'd be able to see again.

Our story was almost complete. It was going to have an honorable end—and in a way, a happy one. We weren't going to die in each other's arms, but we were going to die in the same storm, in the same element, probably just about at the same time. Death was not going to put us asunder—the storm had done that—it was going to join us together again for good.

So the feel of sand under my slowly kicking feet was out of place, unbelievable. Sand instead of coral could mean a beach. A beach could mean an island. The story was being botched, I felt dimly, but there was nothing I could do about it; when I lost Susan I lost all control. My body wanted to survive, and each time my toes touched the sand I felt them dig in and push as hard as they could. They touched more and more often—they knew what they were doing.

I knew I was on land when I felt myself leave the water on hands and knees, felt the screaming air sandpaper my body raw, felt my arms and legs move me up, over a small ledge and partially out of the blast. The land was shaking. The air boomed. I pulled my knees up to my chin, wrapped my arms around my head, and lay there. _So you made it,_ the voice said. _Nice going._

Someone was laughing, a booming, roaring, awful laugh. I burrowed into the dense, thorny brush in front of me until I was too tired to move.

———

Some time in the darkness the eye of the storm passed through, and in the half hour or so of calm I stumbled along the invisible beach calling for her until the wind screamed me down. Coming in from the southeast instead of the northwest, it seemed if anything stronger than before. The island vibrated in a deep base register, and big heavy things seemed to be flying over my head and into the water.

At first light, I began searching the parts of the beach that were protected enough to stand on (the wind had dropped a little from its full force). Now I could see, though fuzzily without my glasses, where everything had happened. I had washed ashore at the northern end of a long, thin, low island, part of the uninhabited chain that encircled Wotho lagoon. A spit of sand led out into open water, a kind of channel in the reef with large, curling brown waves indicating a fair depth and current. Barely visible through the rain, blown sand, spume, and the blur of nearsightedness was a small rock ledge a few hundred yards away on the other side of the channel.

The *Lord Jim* must have hit near the rocky ledge. After we abandoned her, we'd been swept into the rough channel. There was no sign of the boat. Everything was brownish-whitish-gray, the color of the wind blowing the tops off the dirty waves and mixing them with air. The things that had been roaring through the air over my head were the tops of palm trees. They were in the surf, washing up and down the beach along with other detritus. *How do you like it now, gentlemen?* the voice asked.

Each time I searched the beach, a figure was there, cottony and vague, like everything else appeared without my glasses. The first few times I ran toward it, fearing I'd die before I got there. It would recede ahead of me, fade out, or turn into something else. But even when I couldn't see it, I felt it was there. I began to dread it, but desperately needed it at the same time.

I couldn't imagine Susan herself—where she might be if she

wasn't on that beach. What she was thinking? It came to me later, as if transmitted by some celestial EPIRB: *Where is he? God, where did he go?*

I lost count of how many times I walked the two miles of coastline, searched through the high mounds of debris and dense thickets all the way to the other side, but the last few times there was nothing new, nothing more to come ashore. The narrative of shipwreck was starkly told by what was there, almost everything from the boat that wasn't bolted on and some things that were.

Nothing of Susan's was on the beach but—as if she'd arranged it before departing—I quickly and easily found all the things I needed to survive. There was the waterproof emergency container, which would have had my glasses and watch in it if I'd listened to her, but which did have the other things she'd stocked it with: beef jerky for protein and gumballs for quick energy, various antibiotic and pain pills for the coral cuts on my feet and legs; the ship's papers and our passports, which the authorities would need when I reported what had happened. There was her precious Class 1 EPIRB, still blinking away and transmitting its special coded message via satellite to the nearest U.S. Coast Guard station—probably Honolulu, more than two thousand miles to the northeast. Scattered up and down were most of the foam rubber cushions in their new canvas covers. I could lie on the foam and zip myself up in a cover like a sleeping bag for protection from the rain. And completely buried in sand except for one arm was my black full-body wet suit.

I uncovered it gently, and as I did so suddenly I was back in the boat's wheelhouse, drifting downwind out of control, about to go down to the forepeak and get our wet suits and hearing her say, "*No. Please don't leave me.*"

But this time I did go down. I got the wet suits and we put

them on in the wheelhouse. Their buoyancy kept us afloat after we'd abandoned ship, and the three-millimeter foam protected us nicely from the coral and kept us warm both in the water and after we'd crawled out on the beach and under the bushes. They were what saved us.

The scene had the reality of a drug hallucination. It was to be the first of many replays, each with its own new twist and each having a happy ending. They're still happening.

Postscript: Searching for absolution from his mistakes, Gordon Chaplin obsessively rehearsed how he could have avoided this tragedy. He conceded that the vivid memories will haunt him for the rest of his life.

At the age of sixty-five, Francis Chichester decided that he would sail his ketch *Gipsy Moth IV* around the globe. He left Plymouth, England, on August 27, 1966, with the goal of being the first to circumnavigate the world solo from west to east via the great capes. He was also in a hurry, as he wanted to beat the times of the great clipper ships of the nineteenth century.

GIPSY MOTH CIRCLES THE WORLD

SIR FRANCIS CHICHESTER

The Roaring Forties

Working up my sights at noon on October 18 I found that I was well over half way to Australia—at noon that day I had sailed 7,300 miles, and had 6,570 miles to go to Sydney Heads. As if to celebrate this achievement the day changed like magic from grey with misty low clouds and overcast to a bright blue clear sky, with a darker, but still bright, blue sea. Sunshine, however, did not free me from work. I had trouble with the genoa hanks which were always coming unfastened, and the big sails had to come down so that I could refasten them. I had to leave this operation with the sail down, because just before the hanks unfastened themselves I had been making ready dough for baking, and I had to rush to get it into the baking oven before it fell flat. I left the bread safely baking and went back on deck. I changed the big genoa for the three-hundred-footer jib, and found that the yacht went better for the change. The wind was veering, and the mizzen staysail had to come down to sail nearer to the wind. Dropping that mizzen staysail I was nearly lifted off my feet—it is amazing how the strength of the wind can creep up without one's noticing.

There were thousands of prions flying about. These are lovely birds, silvery white seen from below, and a soft whitish grey seen from above. They swoop fast over the waves, resembling swallows. I never saw one pick up anything, but there must be something in the sea for them to eat. They did not seem interested in *Gipsy Moth*—probably they thought her an incredibly slow and clumsy bird. A school of porpoises played around the bows while I was struggling with the sail, but I made rather a noise with the mizzen staysail as it came down, and in a flash they disappeared.

When all the sails were trimmed *Gipsy Moth* was on a close reach, and went beautifully. It was pleasant sailing through that sunny afternoon and evening, because the sails and blocks were asleep, and for what seemed the first time for many days my ears were not assailed by the cacophony of barking blocks and cracking sails. The ship sailed as if she were satisfied—to me this is like being on a good horse, riding fast, but within her strength.

I put away my South Atlantic charts, and got out the charts for the Indian Ocean. There were not many straight charts, but U.S. Hydrographic Office pilot charts, British Met Office current charts, a gnomonic chart, and plotting chart sheets. It was quite a thrill to shift from one ocean to another. It is not often that a yachtsman changes oceans in one voyage!

I was rounding the Cape of Good Hope, though well to the south of it, and the weather grew more boisterous. The Forties really were beginning to roar, with strong winds increasing suddenly to gale force. I was bothered still with cramp in my leg, and began to suffer from lack of rest. On the night of October 19–20 at 2.30 A.M. I fell into a sound sleep for what seemed the first time for ages, but just after 4.30 A.M. I had a rude awakening. A dollop of water from a wave coming on board landed on the head of my bunk, and it was followed quickly by a second and a third. It was my own fault, for leaving out the top washboard of the companionway into the cabin, but this did not make it any more pleasant. I got up at once, dressed, dropped the spitfire jib, and turned dead downwind, because I thought *Gipsy Moth* would run dead before the wind under bare poles. Conditions were rugged on deck, with a lot of wind and water, both sea and heavy rain. I had to make sure of a good grip handy all the time, because of the rolling, and the seas pitching into the hull. After dropping the sail I felt seasick, and went below again to lie down, and try to get some more sleep. It was no good. No sooner had I undressed from my deck clothes than *Gipsy Moth* broached to, and I had to scramble into all my deck gear again and get back on deck as quickly as I could. *Gipsy Moth* had been slewed round broadside on to the waves, and she refused to answer the helm to take up any other heading. I noticed that the self-steering vane had apparently slipped, and was no longer trying to turn the rudder. I decided to stream a drogue from the stern, in the hope of bringing the stern to the wind. This I did, after collecting a shackle, a swivel, some rope from the afterpeak and the drogue from the forepeak. It didn't work; the yacht had not enough way on her to give the drogue the power to haul the stern round.

Gipsy Moth under bare poles in a gale would do nothing but lie ahull, broadside on to wind and waves. I was convinced by what had happened that she could not be made to run downwind under bare poles in a seaway. The rudder could not control her without a storm jib on the foremast stay. This was a serious setback; it meant that her slowest speed running downwind in a gale would be 8 knots. I had never even considered that such a thing could happen! *Gipsy Moth III* had steered easily downwind under bare poles, or even with the wind on the quarter, and the American-designed *Figaro* had steered lightly and easily when we brought her up the English Channel one night under bare poles in a strong gale.

It was damnably uncomfortable. The wind went up to 55 knots, and the yacht was thrown about in all directions. Water kept forcing its way under the cabin hatch whenever a wave hit the deck. My sextant, which I stowed for safety in a cabin berth—fortunately in its box—was thrown out on to the cabin floor. I had one wave come right over me when I was in the cockpit; the water felt oddly warm, and the wave did not seem to strike with much force, I suppose because we were not moving. The air was biting cold with hail.

The self-steering vane was damaged. It had sheared the bolt and pin holding it to its upright mast or shaft, and I thought it remarkable that it had not blown away altogether. I could make no attempt at repair then, because it was impossible to work on it in that high wind and very rough sea. All I could do was to lash it up temporarily.

The storm went on all day. From time to time the wind would seem to ease a little, and I would go on deck to see if I could do anything with the self-steering gear. In one such interval I managed to dismantle the self-steering oar and haul it inboard, because it was getting such a pounding from the waves. It seemed amazing that the vane had not taken off into the air. But always after these lulls the wind came back again, and I could make no start on repairs. The seabirds got very excited about the drogue churning up white water astern. Watching their flight against the strong wind took my mind off my own miseries. They seemed to creep up the sides of the waves uphill, very close to the water. At three o'clock in the afternoon the birds lost whatever entertainment they had had from my drogue, because the warp attached to it parted, and the drogue went.

A big breaking wave struck *Gipsy Moth* and turned her right round, so that she faced north-west. I could do nothing to get her back without setting a sail, and it was too rough for making sail. I felt that it did not matter much which way she was headed because although we were being flung about all over the place, it was hard to tell if *Gipsy Moth* was moving through the water at all.

By that time I had not had anything to eat for twenty-four hours, and still I did not feel hungry. I scribbled in my log: "It is the queasiness which kills appetite, I think. This is not my merriest day, but it might be worse. It is very cold out."

By nightfall I managed to get the yacht going again. At last the wind lulled for long enough to enable me to raise the little spitfire jib, and I gybed round. I contrived a very temporary repair of the self-steering with cordage, but it was not doing a job—the self-steering oar was still on deck. I set the tiller to take advantage of the fact that *Gipsy Moth* liked to lie beam on to the wind, and I left things at that until next morning. It was still appallingly uncomfortable, but we were sailing. The seas were impressive. If I looked up while working on deck I felt that I had to hang on for dear life. It seemed impossible for the monster rolling down on top of us not to submerge boat and all. But always *Gipsy Moth* rode up again. Some waves I called "strikers"—they would slam into the yacht viciously. I think these were waves which started to break about 25 yards from the boat. They looked about 100 feet high, some of them, so I dare say they were about 40 feet. They treated the boat like a cork, slewing it round and rolling it on its side. I would trim the self-steering gear and go below, only to find the heading 40° off what it should have been, so back I would have to go to retrim the self-steering gear. I decided that the big waves, slewing the boat through an angle of 45–60°, must make things impossible for the self-steering gear.

Gipsy Moth's third vice was taking effect; she could not keep to her heading at the top of a wave face, but whipped round and broached to, lying broadside on to the wind and the waves. Sometimes the self-steering gear could bring her back on to her right heading, but often when the wind vane was suddenly swung 60° across the gale force wind, the pressure on it was too great; if the safety clutch had not given way, the vane must have broken. Broaching-to was the danger that was most dreaded by the clippers. Slewing round, broadside on to a big Southern Ocean storm, they would roll their masts down, and, if the sails went into the water, they were likely to founder, as many did. Leaving the danger aside (which, any-way, I did not consider as great for *Gipsy Moth* as for the clip-pers because *Gipsy Moth* ought to survive a knockdown which would cause a clipper to founder), those broachings seriously threatened the self-steering gear. To cut down the broaching, I was forced to cut down the amount of sail that I would have carried in northern waters. This was a big setback to my plans, because I had reckoned on making long runs in the westerlies down south. I had hoped, before I started the voy-age, that a long light boat, which *Gipsy Moth* was designed to be, would knock off runs of 250 miles, day after day. I am not a designer myself, and my opinion as to the cause of this trick of *Gipsy Moth*'s may not be of value, but I did have a long experience of the boat and, in my opinion, her tendency to flip round as easily as a whip is cracked was due to her having too short a forefoot, and no grip on the water there, combined with an unbalance of the hull which required an excessive load on the tiller to activate the rudder.

There were leak drips everywhere, and I made a list of them:

Leaks
Doghouse post over sink
Doghouse post over Primus
Doghouse join about Primus v. bad
Post above head of quarter berth
Cabin hatch lets water in freely, both sides (according to heel)
All bolts holding companion hatch cover leak
Foot of quarter berth under outboard edge of the cockpit seat
From deck beside head of portside berth in cabin
Starboard forward locker—everything wet through
Seacock in cloakroom
Both ventilators when closed

I had to force myself to eat something to keep up my strength, so I had a chew at some mint-cake. It was not a very successful meal, for in biting on a piece of the mint-cake a tooth broke in half. Luckily my tongue recognised the bit of broken tooth as not mint-cake, and I did not swallow it, but recovered it in the hope of later repairs. Nigel Forbes, my dentist, had given me a dental repair kit, and now had come the time to use it. But I could not tackle dentistry then and there, because it was still too rough. I cleaned and scraped the broken bit as per instructions and wrapped it up safely to await a session in *Gipsy Moth*'s do-it-yourself dental chair. I made myself a cup of tea and turned in.

I was up two or three times during the night to tend the
tiller lines. I wanted to try to keep heading 90° off the wind,
but I did *not* want a gybe. There seemed to be a devil of a lot
of strong wind about, but I was able to snooze a bit, after a
fashion. Around six o'clock in the morning *Gipsy Moth* did
gybe, and began rolling madly. I found that she was headed
WNW. It looked cold and unfriendly outside, but I had to get
on with repairs to the self-steering—clearly I could not go on
like this. It took me an hour to dress, make tea, collect my
tools and generally screw myself up to make a start. The
rolling was frightful, and I felt as feeble as a half-dead mouse. I
turn to my log some two hours later:

> 0909. Well, there we are. The vane is repaired, the self-
> steering oar in the water and in charge of the ship, the mizzen
> and genoa staysail are set. Of course the wind has dropped
> now and more sail is needed to move, but I am on strike and
> intend to have some breakfast first. After a 40–50 knot gale
> the sea is monstrously lumpy, and it was no picnic repairing
> the vane sticking out beyond the end of the boat. But it might
> have been a lot worse. The coffee is made, here's to it.

That day I had a successful radio transmission with
Cape Town, and felt much the better for it. Throughout this
part of the voyage I was harassed by poor radio conditions,
and it was always an immense relief to get through a message to the newspapers that were helping to make my voyage
possible. When I failed to make R/T contact I would worry
about it, for I hated not being able to do what I had said I
would do. In poor conditions even a successful R/T transmission could be a strain. It might take an hour and twenty minutes to get off a 250-word cable. That used to take the stuffing
out of me.

With conditions a bit better I felt some return of appetite, and my log records a notable meal on Saturday, October 22:

Ai, but that was good, that breakfast! A mug of hot choco-late and sugar, dried bananas and wheat, onion pancake (aimed at omelette with dried eggs!) home-baked whole-wheat toast and lime marmalade, mug of coffee.

I got out my dentist's repair kit, and spent an hour having a go at my tooth. I succeeded in cementing the broken piece on again, but in doing so I cemented in a fragment of cotton wool from a cotton wool pad I had put in my mouth to keep my tongue away from my tooth while I was working on it. I left the bit of cotton wool in the repair—I felt I dared not pull it for fear of pulling off the piece of tooth I had managed to stick on.

I found a handsome six-inch squid on deck. It had attractive, variegated colouring rather like tortoiseshell, not at all like the pallid ones I had met before. It seemed just the thing for a good bouillabaisse, but I couldn't face eating it.

Birds continued to bring much interest to my life. The prions would cavort madly round the yacht. They seemed to like flying through the wind shadows of the sails—I suppose the turbulence must be unexpected and intriguing. I threw out some old wheat grains, but they did not appear interested. When emptying my gash-bucket of scraps I would bang it on the rail, and that would bring along the Cape Hens (white-chinned petrels). They would alight and pick over the scraps. I had a feeling of meanness every time this happened—compared with the waste from a liner, my vegetable scraps, perhaps no more than a dessertspoonful, because I harboured my stores carefully, must have disgusted them.

At this time, too, I began to meet *real* albatrosses; not that my earlier albatrosses, or the birds I called albatrosses, weren't real, but they seemed tiny compared with the big fellows I met now. One beautiful bird soared by with a wing-span that must have been at least eight feet across.

Alas, my tooth-repair did not hold. I tried it out at supper time, and it was no good—the broken bit simply came off again as soon as I tried to bite. Perhaps the best dentists do not mix cotton wool with their cement. I had another shot at cementing, this time without cotton wool fragments, but the repair was no more successful. In the end I got a file and filed down the jagged edges of the piece of tooth still in my jaw, and left it at that.

What had I expected from the Roaring Forties? They are not seas that many yachtsmen frequent; indeed, few ships of any sort go there now, because with steam and the Suez Canal the modern route to Australia is quite different. From my reading of the clipper logs I had an impression of a steady, surging wind, strong, driving ships day after day on towards the east. Of course, life is never quite like the tidy pattern that imagination makes of it. The clippers had great passages, and it is these that stay in the memory, but they had days (and weeks) of exasperating frustration too. Then one can gain a quite misleading impression of the seas from the logs of big ships—compared with *Gipsy Moth*, *Cutty Sark*, *Thermopylae* and their peers were all enormous. A gale that forced me, single-handed, to lie ahull, at the mercy of wind and sea, to them might have been a good sailing breeze. I knew enough of single-handed sailing in small boats to have assessed these things rationally, but rational assessment, and emotional preparation for the reality of something in life, are by no means the same. From my reading, and study of the clipper passages, I had expected the Forties above all else to be *steady*. That is just what they were not—it seemed luff and puff, luff and puff all

the time. But it was luff and puff with a difference, nothing
gentle about it; the difference, one might say, between the
playful games of a kitten and the gambolling of a tiger cub.
The squalls with which the weather, as it were, changed gear,
were not a nice gentle change from, say, 20 mph in a car to
25–30 mph. They were like a fierce racing changing from 20
to 90–110 mph. Another thing which I find hard to describe,
even to put into words at all, was the spiritual loneliness of
this empty quarter of the world. I had been used to the North
Atlantic, fierce and sometimes awesome, yes, but the North
Atlantic seems to have a spiritual atmosphere as if teeming
with the spirits of the men who sailed and died there. Down
here in the Southern Ocean it was a great void. I seemed plan-
etary distances away from the rest of mankind.

Just as I was getting ready for breakfast on Sunday, October 23, I had a bad shaking. In England before I left, Sheila
Scott had given me a toy Koala bear, and it lived on a perch
beside my Marconi set. It was always falling off its perch and
that morning, as so many times before, I went to pick it up. I
was holding the bear with one hand and making my way
across the cabin from handgrip to handgrip with the other,
when a violent lurch caught me between handgrips and threw
me hard against the table. When I picked myself up, a place in
my ribs under my right arm felt very sore. I thought some ribs
must be broken though I could find nothing wrong. The same
old lesson was driven home to me forcibly again—*never to move
about below without one handgrip, or at least an eye on the next one, so
that it can be grabbed instantly if the boat lurches.* Those lurches, as a
beam wave caught her, made *Gipsy Moth* move like a whip
cracking. I consoled myself for my sore rib with the reflection
that I might have been much more seriously hurt, and that the
accident would have done good if it made me remember the
lesson about holding on.

When I had recovered from my shaking and had some breakfast I went on deck to replace the trysail with the main. The wind seemed lessening, and I felt that *Gipsy Moth* needed the main. I did not like that main, it was my least-favourite sail. For one thing, it required too much brute force to handle, for it was always pressing against a shroud or binding on a sheet; for another, I had to trot to and fro from mast to cockpit about six times during the hoisting. First I had to slack away the vangs as the sail began to rise; then to alter the self-steering trim to head more into the wind so that the head of the sail would not foul the lower aft shroud; then several times to slack away the sheet as the sail went up. After that the lower shroud runner had to be released, and the shroud tied forward to another shroud. Why, then, did I use the mainsail? Well, it was double the area of the trysail and had much more drive, and when I did get it up and trimmed, it set better. Furthermore, it was my collecting-sail for rain, and I needed more rainwater in my tanks. But man is adaptable, and before the end of the voyage I had devised a method of raising the mainsail in a Force 6 when going downwind with no trouble at all!

That evening I was involved in a silly accident to the rigging. I had the starboard levered shroud, which was slacked off, tied forward to another shroud with the lever released, so that the wire should not chafe the mainsail. Gradually the tie worked its way up the two shrouds, until it nearly reached the lower crosstree. As a result, I could not tauten the shroud with the lever when I needed to. I tried for half an hour to get down the tie with a boathook, but I could not shift it. Then it got dark, and I decided to leave it until daylight, when I intended to go up the mast to free it. During the night I worried about the safety of the mast with an un-tautened shroud, and at 1.30 in the morning I got up and shone a torch on the mast. It looked quite unmoved, but I dared not come up closer to the wind, which I wanted to do. At 5.30 I went on deck to tackle the shroud and determined to have one more try at freeing it before climbing the mast. I got my long burgee stick (5 feet 6 inches) and taped a foot-long carving knife to it. The knife had a sharp, narrow blade—I had carried it on board various boats for at least ten years, and this was the first time I had ever used it. By standing on the main boom, I could make the knife just reach the nylon tie binding the two shrouds together. I sawed and stabbed at it with the knife, and after a somewhat lengthy process I contrived to cut it through.

While I worked at the shroud, *Gipsy Moth* galloped along on a grey-green sea. There was too much heel for comfort, but I left the mainsail up, because I expected the wind to veer and free the boat, and I went below to try for a little more sleep. Alas, I was wrong, for instead of veering the wind backed, and soon *Gipsy Moth* was hard on the wind coming from the south-east. I sweated up the main to get it setting better, and felt most unfairly treated, because according to the U.S. Pilot Charts a south-east wind should have been pretty rare in that area of sea. I wrote in the log: "What an indignity to have to cope with an east wind in the Roaring Forties."

For the next twenty-four hours the wind went on backing, with intervals of light, flucky airs, or all-but calm. I was up and down at the sails, constantly fiddling at the trim to get the best out of the yacht, and became drowsy and doped with fatigue. At last, during the morning of October 25, the wind began to return to the west, and as it did so, it increased in strength. Suddenly, there was a major crisis. I suppose I should not have let myself get caught, but due to fatigue I was not at my best for dealing with emergencies. As I was trying to eat some breakfast, a particularly fierce squall struck. I grabbed my padded coat and rushed into the cockpit—still in my "indoor" slip-on sheepskin boots—to turn downwind and run before it. With so much sail set I could not move the tiller, even with the help of cords after I had disengaged the wind vane. Later, I realised my mistake; I had released the self-steering vane, but I ought to have released the self-steering tiller lines to the rudder quadrant as well. I was pushing the tiller against the immense power of the self-steering oar locked to one side. I redoubled my efforts with the cords, and suddenly the tiller responded. Before I could check the turn, *Gipsy Moth* had gybed.

The boom came over with an almighty "wham," the vang tearing a stanchion out of the deck. As it came across, the mainsheet slide shot across the track rail, and tore out the permanent stop screwed to the end of the rail. The slide holding two parts of the mainsheet came off the rail of horse.

I gybed back again, because of the headsails being on the other gybe. I did not notice that when the boom crashed over to starboard the first time the topping lift from masthead to boom end had hooked up behind the upper crosstree. It was amazing, and a great tribute to the rigging and spars, that the crosstree did not carry away when I gybed back. All this time I was still in my "house" boots, bareheaded, and without a safety harness. Fortunately I had stowed away a spare harness in the cubby hole at the side of the cockpit. I struggled into this, took off my boots, and dropped them into the cabin, thinking that I might as well keep them dry. I could not leave the cockpit in those boots, because without non-slip soles they would have been dangerous.

As soon as I had the tiller lashed so that it should give me sufficient time before gybing or tacking, I went forward along the deck in bare feet. I dropped the mainsail, letting most of it (the bunt) fall into the water—the boom was way out abeam. Then I dropped the genoa staysail, and the jib, in each case securing the halliard after removing it from the head of the sail—I did not want halliards winding round the crosstrees! I let the sails lie, partly in the water. As I left the cockpit I had freed the mizzen halliard, hoping that the sail would drop of itself. This it did not do, and was damaged. I told myself: "Never mind. It might have been much worse."

When I turned to the main boom I noticed the topping lift hooked up to the weather crosstree. First I furled and tied the sail in three places to reduce windage—it was blowing a stiff 45 knots—and then I brought the boom inboard by hauling on the weather vang. As soon as I could reach the end of the boom I freed the topping lift from it, and dropped the boom on deck, lashing it there. After that I hoisted the spitfire jib, and engaged the self-steering as soon as *Gipsy Moth* started moving again. I hurried over this for fear that the self-steering gear would be damaged while *Gipsy Moth* lay ahull. Waves knocking the gear from side to side shook the whole boat with shuddering bangs.

One's thoughts at these moments of crisis are sometimes curiously detached. My chief personal worry during the gybe and the troubles that followed it was that, without a cap to protect them, my spectacles would blow away. I had intended to have a washing bout that morning, and I reflected that at least my feet were getting their wash in advance.

Overcoming Disaster

I began to understand why these lonely seas are called "The Roaring Forties." It is the noise of the wind in the rigging. I would not call it a roar exactly, but I know of no other way of describing it—a hard, compelling noise that seems unique to those latitudes. In the days of the clippers, with their forests of masts and rigging, the noise must have been awe-inspiring.

My sense of spiritual loneliness continued. This Southern Indian Ocean was like no sea I had met before. It is difficult to paint the picture with words of what it was like down in the Southern Ocean in those spring months. I have sailed across the North Atlantic six times, three times alone, and experienced winds up to 100 miles per hour (87 knots) there, but looking back it seemed so safe compared with this Southern Ocean stuff. This Southern Ocean was totally different; the seas were fierce, vicious and frightening. The boat was under big accelerations from the powerful, monumental waves. It was hard to say what the speed was. From the deck it seemed slow, but the foam on the water and the whole water surface were moving fast themselves, which made it difficult to judge.

The squally weather was beginning to form a pattern. Phrases such as this kept on recurring in the log:

A 45 knotter threatened to flatten *Gipsy Moth*. I did not know if it was the start of another gale or what.

There is a big sea running, and a big one coming under the boat slews her stern round now and then.

It was so still below after dropping the genoa that I went up into the cockpit to see if we had stopped. It was still blowing 30 knots of wind, and we were sliding along at about 6½ knots.

Rolling and strong sideways accelerations.

Pretty rough going with strong winds.

The moon shines bright between clouds as if to stress how ordinary all this is for her.

Banging and slamming and throwing about all over the place—probably due to two or three different seas overriding each other.

The incessant squalls had one unexpected quality—often the sun would continue to shine brightly while the wind whipped the sea to fury. Somehow this didn't seem right. An Atlantic squall usually comes from a grey sky over a grey sea. The bright sunshine was good, but it seemed odd, and out of place. Why should the sun be out there enjoying himself, when conditions were so rugged for the rest of us?

The near-calms were the most exhausting ordeals for me. Time after time the ship would go about, with all the sails aback. I would have to wear round, and retrim the mainsail and mizzen. These near-calms seemed to last seven or eight hours, and usually occurred at night. I would be up and down to the cockpit time after time for retrimming, and I would be lucky to get more than a couple of hours' sleep during the night. Each swell passing under the boat brought its own little wind during a near-calm. First, the swell pushed the ship so that the sails were all aback as the crest passed under, then it made a wind from the opposite direction after the crest or summit had passed.

Aback, aback, aback—this is the constantly recurring entry in the log. Each time involved wearing the ship round and retrimming at least the mainsail and the mizzen, then half an hour to an hour coaxing the self-steering gear to take charge again. I attributed this trouble to the unbalance of the sails or hull, or both. A slight change of wind force would completely alter the balance, the boat would head off in a new direction, and the rudder was so hard to move that the self-steering gear could not cope with it. On October 29 the log reads:

It is heartbreaking to have a lovely sailing breeze and fine sunny weather, to be sailing well off the wind and able only to do under 5 knots. The sea surface is pretty smooth really, yet *Gipsy Moth* splashes down, sending out great sheets of spray at the bows, and slows down for 3 rocks on 3 little waves. It is like a charging elephant being stopped by a fly whisk.

The seabirds continued to fascinate me. The albatrosses' legs and feet shook and shuddered each time they flew into the turbulent wind shadow downwind of the sails. In a storm, the birds seemed to climb very slowly up the face of a wave, as if walking up it. I wondered if they could get up *only* by using their feet or if they had to use their wings as well. Whenever I could, I tried to feed the albatrosses. I liked watching them alight. They would put down their feet to act first as an airbrake, and then to stop them on the water.

Twice I entered the Forties, and was driven out by a gale. A 50-knot squall going through was like the infernal regions, with great white monsters bearing down out of a black void, picking up the boat and dashing it about. I hated the feeling of being out of control. Once a wave broke in the cockpit, not seriously, but the immense power it showed was frightening. I wrote: "It requires a Dr. Johnson to describe this life. I should add that the cabin floor is all running wet, and my clothes are beginning to get pretty wet too. Vive le yachting!"

On November 2 I could not understand why *Gipsy Moth* nearly gybed time after time. Several times I reached the companion just in time to push the tiller over (leaning out from the cabin) at the gybing point. If she had gybed in that wind with the boom right out, there would have been chaos and damage. Then the boat would come up to wind until the wind was abeam. I began to fear that something had broken in the self-steering gear, so put on a coat and went to investigate. I found that the self-steering gear was not connected to the rudder at all; the link arm between the wind vane and the steering oar had pulled out of its socket after shaking out the safety pin somehow. I was thankful it was no worse. That day my speedometer packed up. At first I was surprised how much I missed it, but as things turned out it did not matter much, for I found that my dead reckoning was as accurate as it had been when the speedometer was working. As a matter of fact, it was more accurate, because the speedometer had been under-registering at low speeds. Perhaps this was because the little propeller of the speedometer's underwater unit was getting foul with marine growth. After I had got over the feeling of loss when the speedometer failed, it was quite a relief not to have it. There was certainly more peace in not eyeing the speed all the time, wondering if it could be improved.

On November 3 I had been three days without a sun sight, three days of "blind going" as the clipper navigators called it. This was just what I hoped would not occur when I was approaching Bass Strait, with no position fix since Madeira. With strong currents during the gales, no wonder so many clippers were wrecked there. In the afternoon of the 3rd I got a sun sight for longitude. This gave a day's run of 227 miles, but again this depended on the dead reckoning being correct for the two previous days when the runs had been 155 and 138.

I wondered how much more speed I should have made if I had not got the high-powered radio telephone on board, and had not had to use it. My log is full of entries such as this: "Long R/T contact with Cape Town. I feel absolutely flattened out." Apart from the effort of transmitting and writing out reports, there was the matter of the great weight which had to be carried to operate the telephone. There was the weight of the radio telephone itself, which was four feet or so above the waterline, and therefore badly placed for the stability of the boat. Then there were the heavy batteries, the alternator for charging the batteries at high amperage, fuel for the charging motor, earthing plates down to the keel of the boat, two backstays rigged with big insulators top and bottom for transmitting aerials. On top of all this was the negative effect of transmitting; time after time I would delay sail setting because a radio telephone schedule was coming up during the next hour. Altogether the effect on the performance of the boat was considerable.

November 3 brought the first real fog of the passage, with visibility down to about one hundred yards. I had both flames of my Aladdin stove lit and full on, trying to dry out the inside of the boat which was oozing water everywhere. My rain-collecting system went on sending down water collected from the fog—no smoke particles there! It rained a good deal when it wasn't foggy, and by November 4 I had collected 27 gallons of fresh water in my tank. That made me secure as far as water for drinking and cooking was concerned, but did not give me enough for washing clothes. I could sit for hours watching the rainwater trickling through the transparent pipe leading to the tank. It gave me great pleasure and satisfaction. I can't explain why; I think some primeval instinct must have been involved.

I was fagged out, and I grew worried by fits of intense depression. Often I could not stand up without hanging on to some support, and I wondered if I had something wrong with my balancing nerves. I felt weak, thin and somehow wasted, and I had a sense of immense space empty of any spiritual—what? I didn't know. I knew only that it made for intense loneliness, and a feeling of hopelessness, as if faced with imminent doom. On November 5 I held a serious conference with myself about my weakness. When I got up that morning I found that I could not stand on my legs without support, just as if I had emerged from hospital after three months in bed. I was exhausted after a long struggle with the radio on the previous evening, and a long-drawn battle with the mainsail during the night finished me off. Then I thought, "Husky young men on fully-crewed yachts during an ocean race of a few days have been known to collapse from sheer exhaustion. I have been doing this singlehanded for more than two months. Is it any wonder that I feel exhausted?" That cheered me up a bit, and I made two resolutions: firstly, to try to relax and take some time off during each day; secondly, to eat more nourishing food. Because I was so tired I was not eating enough. I logged: "I must go more for things like honey, nuts, dried fruits. I ought to bake some more wholemeal bread."

My oven was a camping one which fitted over the Primus, and it baked very well. But I had rather got out of the habit of baking, which was a mistake, because I enjoyed my bread, and always felt that it did me good. But conditions were usually so rough and I felt such lassitude that often I did not have the energy to prepare the dough and bake. After my resolution I did bake more regularly.

Breakfast was my best meal, partly, perhaps, because I felt more like eating after getting some sleep, but partly, too, because breakfast always seemed important as a ritual after coming through the night safely—candy for the kid. So deliberately I took more time over my breakfasts. I was often up at dawn, and at it all day until dark without a let-up, followed probably by three or four dressings-up in deck clothes during the night. So I sat for as long as I could over breakfast, and sometimes went back to my bunk for a snooze after it. My bunk was the most comfortable place on the yacht, but I had to give up the quarter berth which I liked best because of leaks. My sleeping bag and everything else got so sopping that I was driven out to another berth in the cabin.

Those first weeks of November were hard going. There was constant rough work on deck in huge seas, and I was constantly afraid of another accidental gybe, which might have brought grave damage. I was fortunate that my earlier gybe had not done more damage than it did—I felt I had been lucky. Apart from the deck-fittings, which I contrived to repair or replace from my bosun's stores, the only real damage had been to the mizzen staysail. That, too, was mendable, and although sewing was difficult in the rough conditions, I managed to restore the sail.

I think that the patent hanks on my headsails caused me more cursing than any other item of equipment on the boat. Almost every time a sail was hoisted, some of them came undone. On November 8 I logged that it was quite a job getting the big genoa down because the wind was piping up, and all the hanks except four were unfastened, so that the sail began flogging as soon as I started to lower it. There was one hank left at the head of the sail, but with the strain on it that tore free of the sail. I would have given a lot to have the good old-fashioned hanks on my sails.

On the evening of November 9 I was transmitting to Cape Town for *The Guardian* and got half my message through when the lead came off the aerial. I was still able to hear the operator and he could hear a few words from me, which I think was amazing with no aerial at all, and a 2,500-mile transmission! Part of the message which they got wrong was that I liked having birds around me, but that they made me realise how completely I was alone. The message went through, "*because* they make me realise how I am completely alone!"

In 10,000 miles of sailing I had not seen a single fish in the water, only flying fish in the air, and on the deck. A few squid landed on the deck at night. The prions were my favourite birds then—most beautiful dove-grey birds with pointed wings, flying like big crazy swallows. They would play above the top of the mizzen mast, flying up to it and hovering there in the updraught, before turning and streaking downwind. I think it must have been a prion that I saw one midnight, flying silently round the yacht like a white ghost. The Cape Hens were the quickest to settle on the water, to examine the scraps I threw to them.

Sheila, on her way to meet me in Sydney in the P and O *Oriana*, sailed from Aden on November 10, and I looked forward to being able to talk to her on the radio telephone. I tried two or three times to call up *Oriana* but without success. I was bothered about this, because I knew they were expecting me to call them and feared they would worry if they could not pick me up. But making unanswered radio calls was an exhausting strain, and *Oriana* became a sort of nightmare. I felt that I ought to tune in to try to contact her twice a day, but I also felt that it was nonsense to be trying to reach a ship still some 3,000 miles away. I decided to wait and not to try again until *Oriana* was nearing Fremantle in Australia. After my last futile call on the night of November 11 I wrote:

> No luck with *Oriana*. I don't think I shall try till they are near Fremantle. It wears one down with uncertainty. I'm sure Sheila would understand that. I think she is the most understanding, sensitive woman I know.

On November 11 I got all my dispatch for the *Sunday Times* through to Philip Stohr in Cape Town, but it took me 1 hour 20 minutes. This made an inroad into my charging fuel, which was already running short.

Next day I pumped the bilge and found that it took 257 pumps to clear the water. I had last pumped on November 9, when it needed only 57 pumps. I wondered where all the water came from—257 pumps represents a lot of water. It had been heavy weather all the time, and I decided that the total of all deck leaks could probably be enough to account for the water; a lot of water always seemed to get in through the doors of the dinghy well. Still, 257 pumps *was* a lot of water. I added to my tasks the job of keeping a more frequent eye on the bilge, in case there was a leak below the waterline. In spite of my resolution I had another go at trying to call *Oriana* but not a squeak could I hear.

It grew steadily colder. My fingers used to get frozen with any work on deck, and on November 14 a squall brought hail instead of rain. The hailstones rattled on the skylight like piles of white peas. I had a good contact, however, with Perth radio, and got through a 412-word telegram to *The Guardian* quite easily. I asked them to tell *Oriana* that I had tried to get her, and to say that I would call again on November 16 and 17 at 14.00 hours.

Thursday, November 15, brought disaster. I woke to a 40-knot wind—a heavy weight of wind, but no worse than the rough weather over most of the past weeks. The burgee halliard parted, but that was small beer. At 12.15 I went aft to make what I thought would be a minor repair to the self-steering gear, and found that the steel frame holding the top of the steering blade had broken in half. There were two steel plates, one on each side of the top of the blade, to hold the blade and to connect it to the wind vane. Both had fractured. The oar blade was attached to the ship only by a rod used to alter its rake. It was wobbling about in the wake like a dead fish held by a line. I expected it to break away at any moment, and rushed back to the cockpit. I let all the sails drop with a run as fast as I could let the halliards go, so as to stop the ship and take as much strain off the gear as possible. Then I unshipped the blade, and got it aboard as quickly as I could, before the fitting which held the rod broke off and I lost the oar. The sight of the self-steering gear broken beyond repair acted like a catalyst. At first I turned cold inside and my feel-

ings, my spirit, seemed to freeze and sink inside me. I had a
strange feeling that my personality was split and that I was
watching myself drop the sails efficiently and lift out the broken gear coolly. My project was killed. Not only was my plan
to race one hundred days to Sydney shattered, but to make a
non-stop passage there was impossible, too. Then I found out
that I was not really crestfallen; it was a relief. I realised that I
had been waiting for this to happen for a long time. I went
below and stood myself a brandy, hot. Now my thoughts
began whirling round in tight circles, as I thought about what
had happened, and searched for the best course of action. I
went back to the stern and studied the breakage. Two steel
plates, 27 inches long, 6 inches wide and ⅛ inch thick connected the wooden steering oar to the rest of the gear. These
had both broken clean across, where a strengthening girder
had been welded on to the plates. I considered all the pieces of
sheet metal on the boat that I could think of, wondering if I
could make a repair. The best bet seemed to be the swinging
frame of the Primus stove, but it was not nearly as strong as
the original metal that had broken and, besides that, I had no
suitable nuts and bolts for bolting it to the broken pieces. The
self-steering gear could not be repaired on board—I was well
and truly in trouble. If I had had a normal boat I could have
trimmed her up to sail herself, but experience so far had convinced me that *Gipsy Moth IV* could never be balanced to sail
herself for more than a few minutes. The bald fact was that
she could only be sailed from now on while I was at the helm,
otherwise she must be hove to while I slept, cooked, ate, navi-
gated or did any of the other many jobs about the ship. I
should do well if I could average 10 hours a day at the helm;
that would give me 60 miles a day at 6 knots. Taking calms
and headwinds into consideration, I should do well to make
good, on an average, 50 miles per day. I thought I was 2,758

miles from Sydney which was a long way, only 200 miles less, for example, than the Great Circle distance from Plymouth to New York. It would take an age to reach it, 55 days at 50 miles per day, perhaps 3 months. On top of the 80 days I had spent on the passage so far, it seemed out of the question. The only course open to me was to head for the nearest place where I could get a repair. The nearest suitable place was Fremantle. Even that was 1,160 miles away which would mean a very long time at the helm. I worked out a course for Fremantle.

I started work. I hoisted a small sail and after rigging a line from the tiller to the side of the cockpit I played with the adjustment of this until I got the boat reluctantly to keep roughly to a heading. It was not the best heading, but it could have been worse. I logged: "How I shall get her to steer on any heading that is not nearly abeam I can't think at present. I'll have some lunch and try again with more sail, etc. Of course this 37-knot wind is pretty strong." Later I wrote:

> Life is going to be pretty good hell I imagine for the next fortnight or so. I have been out to the tiller several times in the past two hours, once to prevent a gybe when the wind dropped, another time because the wind had increased, making the boat gripe up to windward. Tomorrow I must try to lead tiller lines into the cabin so that I can steer from there. Otherwise I shall go barmy if I have to dress up each time I have to adjust the tiller. At the moment the wind direction is the best possible, because beam to wind is the boat's natural lie. What I shall do to make her go downwind I can't think at present. I am going to turn in for a sleep while I can.

It was a stinking night, and I was called out several times to find the boat headed west instead of east, with all the sails aback. On one of these occasions I lay drowsy in my berth reluctant to get up again, and I noticed that although the sails were aback, the boat was forging ahead slowly and—a most important fact—*she kept a much steadier course than when she was sailing in the right direction with the sails all drawing.* At the time I took these facts in without really being aware of them. They imprinted themselves, as it were, on my subconscious self.

At 6 A.M. I started the job of trying to make the boat sail itself in some way or other, so that I should be able to eat and sleep without having her stop dead. It looked desperate by breakfast time, when I had been trying for an hour to balance the sail pressure, etc., against the pull on the tiller. However, I had a good breakfast, even though I absent-mindedly dipped into the coffee jar instead of the marmalade pot. Some time during breakfast I recalled that *Gipsy Moth* had held a steady heading when she had been turned round facing west with the sails aback. This was a strange fact; surely I might be able to make use of it? During breakfast, when I was trying hard to squeeze something out of my brain, I had an idea. I devised something and by 10.20 I had the boat sailing herself, on course, and downwind. She was not going very fast, but by then there was only an 8-knot wind (thank Heaven). An albatross gravely insulted my efforts by swimming or paddling along a few yards astern, to keep up with *Gipsy Moth*.

All that day I was experimenting. I unshackled both the storm sails and changed them over, so that the smaller sail was on the staysail stay; then I hove the clew of this small storm staysail to windward, so that the sail was as she would be if the ship had turned right round and the sail was aback; then I linked the clew of this sail to the tiller by means of blocks on each side. After a lot of trial and error, the result was as follows:

When the yacht was on course, the sail was aback, and wind pressing on it pulled the tiller sufficiently to windward to counteract the tendency of the boat to turn up into wind.

If the boat *did* begin turning off course into wind, the pressure on the sail increased, with the result that the pull on the tiller increased, making the boat turn off the wind again.

If, on the other hand, the boat started turning downwind, this steering sail would presently gybe, as it were, and the wind would press on it from the other side, thereby exerting a pull on the tiller in the other direction to leeward, with the result that the boat turned towards the wind again.

Luckily the wind had fallen light that morning, and all day I was working in a gentle breeze of between 7½ and 10 knots. By noon I had sailed 91 miles on course for Fremantle since the self-steering gear broke. At 17.30 I logged: "Nearly becalmed. At least *Gipsy Moth* has steered herself all day which I regard as an achievement starting from scratch, even if it isn't right for other conditions."

My chief anxiety now was not to embarrass Sheila. Her ship was due in at Fremantle next day, and I had to get a message to her before then, so that she would not continue on to Sydney while I put into Fremantle. That evening I had a bad contact with *Oriana*. Her operator seemed to hear me better than I could hear him. I kept on repeating: "I am on my way to Fremantle, I am putting into Fremantle." The contact was too bad to explain why. I logged: "Poor Sheila, she will wonder what is happening."

That night was dark and it was raining. I saw a strange thing, bright blobs of phosphorescence up in the air passing the boat. As my eyes got used to the dark I realised that these bright patches were actually *in* the water, and the high waves had made them appear to be up in the air!

By noon of the 17th I was another 81 miles on the way to

Fremantle. But I was getting increasing fits of depression and sense of failure; I had set out to sail non-stop to Sydney. The prospect of putting in at Fremantle stuck in my gullet, and finally I decided that I could not stomach it. At 3.45 that afternoon I altered course back for Sydney.

All day I worked on my self-steering system, watching the effect on my steering arrangement and the tiller of any change in the heading or in the wind strength or direction. By the end of the day the heading required was dead downwind to a 33-knot wind, but my system was coping with it, though with a loud clatter of ropes and sails flapping.

I was now anxious to get another message through to Sheila, so that she would not get off at Fremantle while I sailed on to Sydney. I tried calling up *Oriana* again that night, but had a rotten contact. Altogether I tried five times on the 16th and 17th to contact *Oriana*. I thought they were hearing me, even if I could not hear them, and I repeatedly said that I was headed for Sydney again, and was not going to Fremantle. I asked for Sheila to speak to me on Perth Radio when she landed there.

My system took a minor squall pretty well, and I was pleased with it. The day's run to the 18th was up to 111 miles. I felt happier than I had been at any time previously during the voyage. I had been waiting for the self-steering gear to fail, and apprehensive all the time that I should be helplessly stuck with a badly balanced boat. That I had been able to rig up gear to make her sail herself was deeply satisfying. I hate turning back; I hate giving up; and I hate being diverted from my course; it was a seaman's job to get over difficulties. I think this compensated for my chagrin at failure of the one-hundred-day project, which did seem impossible now for two reasons—firstly, because the steering sail was depriving me of one of my best driving sails when on the wind, and secondly, because part of the steering sail was actually acting *against* the forward movement of the boat, pulling against the other sails. I knew I had set a very high target with 100 days, but I believed that I stood a fair chance of achieving it if the self-steering gear had not bust. At the time that happened I had 2,758 miles to go and 20 days left of the 100. In the previous 20 days I had sailed 2,920 miles.

On the night of the 18th I had a long radio session with Perth, and explained the whole situation during eighty minutes. Just before midnight I was called out by a minor shemozzle, to find all the sails aback, including the mizzen staysail. "And that," I logged, "is something to have aback." I had set too high a standard for my steering system, asking it to control the boat with the mizzen staysail set in a light wind which was something the self-steering gear itself had often failed to accomplish.

The fourth day's run with my system produced 138 miles and I began to warm up my hopes: could I possibly do it in one hundred days after all? Of course there were a lot of miles lost in the first three days which I should have to make up, and that would be a big handicap. Again I kept at it all day, fiddling with the system and ironing out minor troubles.

The petrels and one or two albatrosses stayed with me, and they would come from quite far when I banged my scrap tin before emptying it—to call them to dinner. Then they kept on flying round close, for more scraps. I loved watching them. To make things better still, that evening I made contact on the radio with *Oriana*, and had a long talk with Sheila. It was a joy to hear her, and to be able to talk directly to her. This cheered me up immensely, and I wrote in the log:

I have been leaning over the garden gate, in this case the washboards of the companionway, looking out at the hazy moon and the water sliding by; I am more at peace than at any time before on this passage. I think that the damned self-steering gear was a constant worry to me, waiting for it to bust. Now we seem to be really sailing and I feel happy.

On the 20th I had got the day's run up to 168 miles. My system could keep the boat pretty steady on a heading downwind, or across wind, but for a wind half way between them the going was very tricky.

Next day I could only jog along in a 40-knot gale. There had been a quiet roar in the rigging all day and I had trouble getting the steering sail to control the boat when there was only one sail drawing. I logged: "My experience of these gales is that you can't set sail again seriously until the noise in the rigging, a mild roar, one might call it, eases." I was feeling very feeble physically again; it seemed as if the gale had taken the stuffing out of me. I meditated why, wondering whether my feebleness was due to the incessant effort of holding on and straining to keep a position without being thrown, or to damp, not enough food, or the nervous strain tensing up for the next time the hull was hit, thrown down or over. The day's run dropped to 82 miles.

I could not hoist the trysail right the way up, because the loose end of the broken burgee halliard was twisted round the trysail halliard and everything else aloft. I was afraid to use the winch, and there was too much wind to wiggle things free. I do not get on well with burgee halliards, and logged: "It could easily happen that that burgee halliard stops everything from moving up there! Curse it, this has always happened on every ocean crossing I have done. I should get rid of the damned thing before I start."

My great interest every day of the voyage was to get an accurate sun fix, so that I could know what the ship had sailed during the past day, and ponder on my tactics for the coming days. On November 22 I recorded:

> I got four shots at the sun with some difficulty, and then a surfing wave took charge of the boat. The crest coamed into the cockpit giving the sextant a real sea bath. However, I rinsed it in warm fresh water with some detergent in it. Just after I finished, a 45-knot squall hit the boat. I was sheltered in the cabin helping out the tiller in overpowering gusts. The hatch was only open an inch to allow passage of the cords to the tiller, but the rain was so heavy that it was driving 7 feet into the cabin through that small crack. I put on a raincoat and a hat standing in the cabin.

That afternoon I dropped the jib, and stopped the ship. All the battens had been torn out of the working jib, and the sails were taking a beating. It was hard to stand on the deck. Waves were coming into the cockpit, and hail sounded like rifle fire. It was also very cold, and my hands were half numb. The seas, squirting through the closed hatch, had swollen the woodwork in the galley so that I could not open two of the drawers there. That was irritating, because there were several things I wanted in those drawers.

In the evening I got *Gipsy Moth* sailing again, but I had to come to the rescue of the steering system several times next day, both to prevent a turn downwind from becoming a gybe, and a turn up into the wind from stopping the boat. Undoubtedly the system had its disadvantages. I could not use the mainsail, because the boom would have fouled the steering lines from the sail to the tiller. And the cockpit was so full of lines that it was dangerous to set the mizzen staysail. The boat was like a birdcage. It was difficult to make way along the deck, and when I came out of the cabin it was easier to crawl under the tiller than to move over it.

But I was improving all the time, and on November 24 I logged:

Still driving hard through grey-green seas, and grey sky of low overcast. The rig seems to be spoiling me, keeping course at 7 to 7½ knots all through the night, except for periodic roarings in the rigging and bashings of waves over the deck when a wave throws the boat's head off to the northeast or even further to the north; but each time so far, after rough going for a few minutes, the steering sail has brought her back on course. It is 9½ hours since I touched tiller or rope. Long may it continue; it smacks of the marvellous to me!

I got quite a thrill when I found suddenly that I was well past the western end of Australia, which I might not have noticed if I had not run off the end of the chart of the Indian Ocean. Perhaps I should add that I was then five hundred miles south of the land, so that there was no likelihood of charging into it because of not noticing that I was passing it. It was exciting to dig out the chart of Australia. I was now only about 1,200 miles from Bass Strait which was a daunting (if exhilarating) prospect after no sight of land since Madeira.

I still had no log or speedometer, but I found my dead reckoning much better than expected. One gets used to judging speed. For instance, the previous day's run was 158 miles by sun fixes, and my dead reckoning run, based on judging the speed at intervals, was only 3½ miles short of this.

An extraordinary thing happened after I had finished my radio telephone dispatch on November 25. As the light over my chart table had failed temporarily, I connected an inspection lamp at the end of a lead to give me light to work the telephone. I hung this lamp on the wire lead to the speedometer.

Suddenly the speedometer began to work again. I found that the wire leading to the speedometer had snapped (probably it had been damaged when the radio telephone was being fitted), and the weight of the inspection lamp somehow managed to connect the two ends again inside the insulating cover! I had tried that particular connection between the wire and the speedometer about eight times, but never thought of the wire itself being snapped. Now I had a speedometer again (though I didn't actually repair the lead until the next day). I was glad to have it, for I should need it among the islands of Bass Strait, but I reflected ruefully that my peace of mind would probably be less.

I fitted up a tackle with two blocks from the tiller to the windward side of the cockpit, and the running part of this tackle led into the cabin. On the lee side of the tiller I had at first a plain line leading from the tiller to the side of the cockpit, and from there into the cabin, but later I found that this was insufficient, and rigged a second tackle with two blocks on that side too. These two tackles were invaluable; they enabled me to control the tiller and help out the steering sail from the cabin, without having to dress up in deck clothes and go on deck. For example, on November 25 two smashing waves broke right on to the boat, picked it up and swung it round through a change of heading of no less than 140°. The steering sail might have brought the heading back again in time, but not without a lot of sail flogging. (It's a wonder any sail can survive flogging in a 45-knot gale!) By hauling on the weather tackle, I brought the heading back on course quickly without going up into the cockpit.

That evening a big swell began running in suddenly from the west; big, I would say fifty feet. There were a number of Mother Carey's Chickens about, which nearly always forecasts a storm, whatever meteorologists may say to the contrary. I could see them picking things out of the water while on the wing, but not what the things were. An hour before midnight a wave gybed *Gipsy Moth*, and put her aback, headed south. The steering sail could not move the tiller with the sails aback; nor could I with the tackle and the tiller line into the cabin. So I had to dress up in hard weather rig, and *still* I could not move the tiller by hand. I had to sit down on the lee side of the cockpit and, with my back to the side of the cockpit, and both feet on the tiller, I was able to move the rudder slowly and turn *Gipsy Moth* downwind, and gybe back on to course. It was really rather a splendid night. There was a bright moon, with some silvery clouds, and there were white manes to the waves. *Gipsy Moth* tore through the water at a good 7½ knots. Shortly after midnight I was woken up again with the ship aback, in a very unpleasant squall. I had to stick this one out in the cockpit, nursing the tiller to keep *Gipsy Moth* near downwind until the squall blew out. It was wild rocketing downwind, and I was very cold with only pyjamas under a quilted coat and trousers. As soon as I got a chance I put on a sweater and safety harness, and dropped the working jib. I hated losing the good speed, but a ship out of control is hell. At 5.30 in the morning I was woken again by the ship aback. I logged: "My steering sail, let's face it, will not control the boat in winds of Force 8 (35 knots) or more. It has not the power to work the tiller to bring the heading off the wind after a wave slew. That helm needs the strength of an elephant, anyway."

That was not my lucky day. Besides being turned out so often to rescue the helm, my drawer full of electrical spares, fuses, valves, etc., shot out, and on to the cabin floor. Next, all my rolls of chart fell from their nest close under the cabin ceiling on to the cabin floor; then I delved in the clothes locker under my cabin bunk, and found everything there running water, except what I had put in plastic bags. At noon I was in the middle of some sun shots when a big breaking sea surfed *Gipsy Moth* along with it until *Gipsy Moth* broached to on the starboard gybe, sails aback again. I felt that I needed a tent pitched in the cabin to keep things dry.

Two and a half hours later I logged: "Well! That was a near go." I was standing facing the companionway, and looking at the speedometer repeater dial above my quarter berth, to see if it was working properly. Suddenly the needle shot up hard against the stop at the limit, 10 knots, and stayed there. For a second or two I thought that the speedometer had bust again. Then the boat went over on to its side and, looking out, I saw that *Gipsy Moth* was on the crest of a big breaking wave. This breaker slewed the boat round broadside to it, knocking her down forwards, so that the masts were horizontal, pointing in the direction in which the wave was going. From where I stood on the side of the bunk I could see the mizzen mast lying flat along the surface of the boiling, seething surf. I would say that the boat was travelling sideways at a speed of 30 knots. There was nothing I could do. I was not frightened; I watched interested. Would the masts dip in? If they dipped a few more degrees below the horizontal they must dive into the water, and inevitably the boat must then roll over. They didn't; the surf passed leaving *Gipsy Moth* broached to. She righted herself, and presently the steering sail brought her back through 90° on to her previous heading.

On November 27 I was 710 miles from Cape Otway, and I decided that I must adjust the lead of the steering sail lines so that I could hoist the mainsail again. I had to have it, because I could not now pole out either of the big running sails. I had robbed the main boom of its topping lift tackle for one of my tiller lines, and had to rig up another. There was a pale greeny blue sky like I have known before a terrific wind in Europe.

There were also some strongly developed mares' tails in a straggly line across the sky. But these indications misled me, for the big wind did not arrive.

An albatross flying overhead dropped a personal bomb, which hit the mizzen sail fair and square, decorating it with a string of red blobs. Lucky shot! I rove a new tiller line to the steering sail and took the strain on it so that I could adjust the present one, then I did the same with the leeward line. The lengths of the steering lines, and the amount of play or movement of parts of this steering system were most critical, and fine adjustment made all the difference to its effectiveness.

Next day the wind returned to roaring in the rigging, and I dropped all sail except the storm jib and steering sail, content to jog along on course at 4 knots only. Some Mother Carey's Chickens were only six feet away from me when I was working at the stem; I had never seen them so close before. I watched them bouncing off the wave surfaces with their chests, and sometimes hitting the water lightly with first one wing tip and then the other as if they were flicking bits of fluff off a hot plate with their wings.

On November 29 I had sailed for fourteen days since the self-steering bust, and had made good 1,808 miles, an average of 120 miles per day. This was good going because, quite apart from my self-steering difficulties, I was missing one of my best driving sails. Alas, it was not good enough to reach Sydney in the 100 days. I still had 1,057 miles to go and only 6 days of the 100 left. I was depressed because I had had a bad night, unable to sleep through being thoroughly rattled by the radio telephone, and the pressure being exerted on me through it for news, etc. After three months of solitude I felt that it was all too much; that I could not stand it, and could easily go mad with it. All this is weak nonsense, I know, but that is how I felt when I was twisting about in my bunk trying to clear my brain of all the thoughts and images attacking it. I told myself that I must try to be tolerant with the demands being made for air photography, telephone talks, etc., etc.

An hour after midnight on November 30 I was forced out of my bunk by a bad cramp. I always got a cramp if I stretched my legs on waking, but I couldn't stop myself from doing it when still half-asleep. Fortunately, standing upright freed the bound muscles, which were as hard as wood, and very painful. I was always frightened that a muscle would break under the strain. A small drink of sea water usually prevented another attack—maybe I needed salt after losing so much during hard deck work.

That afternoon I sewed up the seam of the mizzen staysail which had given way. It was a delightful sunny day for a change, and warm enough for me to sew in the cockpit. When I set the sail, the steering sail could not control the boat with it up, so I had to haul it down again. Then I set the big 600-foot genoa instead of the 300-foot jib. *Gipsy Moth* was doing 9 knots easily at times, but when the wind piped up the steering sail could not control the boat with that sail set either, and reluctantly I had to drop it again. What was so frustrating was that the wind dropped to near-calm almost to the second as I dropped the sail, and I could have carried it thereafter! If the wind had acted purely out of spite it could not have been more successful. I think there might have been a chance of controlling the boat if the trysail had been dropped, but it was getting dark, and I had a damned radio telephone appointment coming up. So I left the big sail down and rehoisted the 300-footer.

When on the foredeck in the dusk, after I had bagged the big sail, I was startled by what seemed a human scream close to the boat. I swung round to see whatever it could be. It came from an albatross! There were two of them, sitting on the water about ten feet from the boat. They were courting, I think, facing each other, and one had its wings raised in a V with curved sides. It was too poor a light to see more.*

---

*Rex Clements in his book *A Gipsy of the Horn* relates an oddly similar occurrence.

"One dark, moonless night just before we got clear of the 'forties,' there occurred a most uncanny experience.

"It was about four bells in the middle watch, the 'churchyard' watch, as the four hours after midnight is called, that it happened. Suddenly, apparently close aboard on the port hand, there came howling out of the darkness a most frightful, wailing cry, ghastly in its agony and intensity. Not of overpowering volume— a score of men shouting together could have raised as loud a hail—it was the indescribable calibre and agony of the shriek that almost froze the blood in our veins.

"We rushed to the rail, the mate and the men too, and stared searchingly into the blackness to wind'ard. The starbowlines, who a moment before had been sleeping the sleep of tired men in their bunks below, rushed out on deck. Shipwreck would hardly bring foremast Jack out before he was called, but that cry roused him like the last summons. If ever men were 'horror-struck' we were.

"Even the old man was awakened by it and came up on deck. Everyone was listening intensely, straining their eyes into the blackness that enveloped us.

"A moment or two passed and then as we listened, wondering and silent, again that appalling scream rang out, rising to the point of almost unbearable torture and dying crazily away in broken whimperings.

"No one did anything, or even spoke.

"Nobody slept much more that night and thankful we were when the grey dawn broke over the tumbling untenanted sea.

"This was all. In bare words it doesn't sound very dreadful, but it made that night a night of terror. For long enough afterwards the echoes of that awful scream would ring in my ears, and even now it sends a shiver through me to think of it.

"Who and what it was that caused it we never learnt."

I wonder if this might also have been an albatross?

At 6.40 in the morning of December 1, the wind backed to the south-east and *Gipsy Moth* came hard on the wind for the first time for about a month. "I expect," I logged, "that it is going to give me a headache before I reach Sydney." How right I was!

Postscript: Francis Chichester completed his voyage on May 28, 1967—nine months and one day after he departed. During that time he had stopped only once, in Sydney. He was knighted by Queen Elizabeth II in 1967 for his achievement.

Englishman Pete Goss was one of the entrants in the 1996–97 Vendée Globe yacht competition—a nonstop single-handed round-the-world race. A hurricane hit, and when Goss heard the dangerous plight of French sailor Raphaël Dinelli, he turned around his fifty-foot *Aqua Quorum* to attempt a rescue, risking his own life in the process.

CLOSE TO THE WIND

PETE GOSS

In the Southern Ocean

The big day dawned on 5 December. The start of the Southern Ocean. We had dawdled through a South Atlantic high and came out the other side into wind generated by Southern Ocean depressions that were driving across our path. Appropriately, this was the wind that carried us across the 40th parallel and we officially entered the notorious Roaring Forties. I saw my first albatross gliding gracefully across the water. These birds bring life to a desolate region.

The temperature dropped like a stone over the next few days and I found myself wearing my Musto thermals throughout the day to keep warm. It was also wet on deck as the boat gathered up her skirts in the ever-increasing winds and pushed-out big speeds. I decided that I would go far south and get right into the depths of the Southern Ocean—not only did I believe that that was where we would perform at our best but it would also reduce the number of miles that we had to sail. I watched our first depression tracking in on the weather-fax and felt a tingle of anticipation as the pressure fell, the wind increased and the swell built up. I ate, checked the boat once more and reduced sail as we pressed further south in a rising wind.

The boat had a feel of impending action. The air became heavier, the cloud base thickened and the heaving ocean took on an oppressive grey hue. As the wind settled from the west I brought the boat up, eased the sails and let her run—and run she did, sitting up on a steady plane as she thundered down the faces of a very big swell. It was great and I stood in the cockpit for a couple of hours and savoured the sailing with Tina Turner belting through my Sony Walkman. I decided to wang up the spinnaker to see what would happen. It was a stupid thing to do really, but I had a couple of months down here so I might as well find out what the boat was comfortable with. It was blowing thirty knots and I hummed and hahed about which sail I should shove up. I set the autopilot on a very broad reach, eased the main and clambered forward to drop the number one headsail. This became a bit of a handful when it went into the water and took a good ten minutes to retrieve. I hanked on the number two—if the shit hit the fan I didn't want to be wrestling with a bigger sail. I rigged the bowsprit, made off the spinnaker lines, took a deep breath and hoisted the spinnaker in its retaining sock.

I went back to the cockpit and, uneasy, mulled over the decision once more—the boat was going well as it was and I questioned whether I should have been doing this at all. My instinct said no and yet this was my first time down here with the boat and the only way I was going to find out what it was all about was to go for it. Perhaps I was influenced by all the old-timers who talk of keeping their spinnaker up down here. There were six hours of daylight left and I decided to treat this as a training run rather than part of the race, bung it up, see what happened, fiddle about with settings and find our feet. If it all went belly up I had six hours of light to sort myself out. I checked every line and detail one last time, stripped off my heavy thermals so that I was more agile, donned my sailing gloves, made my way to the mast and clipped on. I mentally ran through everything again before I untied the sock and started to pull it up the sail. The wind immediately filled the foot, the sock ran away and the check line burned through my fingers. The spinnaker filled with a bang and we started to lay over. I ran aft as *Aqua Quorum* leapt forward and the autopilot struggled on the edge of control as we zigzagged across the wind and waves.

It was bloody hairy now and we drove down a wave at twenty knots and disappeared beneath the water. I eased the spinnaker and the sheet shuddered under the load. That was better, it was a little more comfortable now, but it was relative. We were leaping from wave to wave, the wind was thirty-five knots and gusting. We were going like buggery but I wasn't happy—trouble was just round the corner and I questioned whether I would be able to drop the spinnaker on my own. I told myself not to rush, but to stand and watch, soak up as much information as I could—it would stand me in good stead later.

I got below and made a cup of tea—I needed to get used to life down there with the boat on the edge. I had to learn to relax even when things were marginal. The boat needed to be pushed—it was a race, after all—but I had to resist the urge to leap on deck every time she felt as though she were about to go. She hadn't lost it yet and I should leave her to it. The feeling below was awful. We were screeching along on the edge of control and I had to make a cup of tea and go about daily life. Each time she rolled at speed I felt the bow coming up and I willed the autopilot to put the helm over—it seemed an eternity before it did. It played on my nerves as we yawed from side to side and I made myself shut it out, fill the kettle and get used to it.

I saw that there was a message on the satcom (satellite communication system) and called it up. It was from Amelia Lyon. I hadn't forgotten the article for so and so, had I? They were getting twitchy, the deadline was in four hours' time. Shit! The message had been sitting there for the last hour. Writing an article was the last thing I wanted to do. I bashed away at the laptop but I couldn't concentrate. *Aqua Quorum* talked to me. "Come on, dickhead, you know you shouldn't have this amount of sail up. There are two months of this and if you push me this hard we'll never finish the race." Bollocks, I thought. We're here to race and race we will. By the end of the Southern Ocean this will feel normal.

Suddenly we were on the back of a big wave and accelerating like fury, the wave was steep and we started to come up. The boat heeled, I could hear water rushing across the side deck as we lay over. The log climbed . . . twenty . . . one . . . two . . . three. I looked aft and saw that the helm was hard over. I marvelled at the power of the autopilot and knew that if we pulled out of this and the rudders bit, she would drive herself into a crash gybe. I braced myself and reflected on the lesson that I was about to be taught. Prat. The hull was bouncing and banging across the water. At this speed it felt as if I were driving down a dirt track in a car with no suspension. I could feel the shocks running up through my legs and bent my knees slightly to absorb the impact. The noise was deafening and the moment was bloody marvellous. The wake disappeared over the top of the wave, narrowing at the crest like a country lane over a hill; the spray off the hull cascaded out to the sides. We suddenly decelerated at the bottom of the wave, the brakes were slammed on and the boat submerged.

I braced myself for the worst and mentally ran through the setup—halyards in use, winch handle location, runner, preventer, knife in pocket and so on. We galloped off to leeward. The back of the mainsail curled, the keel was now on the wrong side and we sagged to windward. The autopilot whirred away and the helm went over. She suddenly felt dead in the water, as if she had accepted the inevitable and decided to give up. The main half gybed. I gritted my teeth, this was going to be a belter. Where was the camera? Missed the last one on the Transat, but this time it was handy in a bag by the hatch. There was a crack. I looked up from freeing the camera to see the main slam back in place. Come on, *Aqua Quorum*, you can do it.

The bow lifted and it felt as if a couple of tons had been released as she bounced up and we were off again. I couldn't believe she had managed to pull out of it as I leapt on deck and eased the sheet, thinking, I might just get away with this. The spinnaker flogged, shaking the boat as if it were a toy. I scanned the horizon and saw a big cloud on the way. I had to get the spinnaker down before it arrived. As I ran forward the wind seemed even stronger up there. I braced myself against the mast, which was banging around like a child's fishing rod, and pulled on the spinnaker sock which snuffed out about six feet of sail before it filled again and was forced back up to the head. The rope burned my hands. A glance over my shoulder was enough—I pulled like a bastard, the cloud was looming larger by the minute. We careered off down another wave and I found myself up to my knees in rushing water. The boat lay

over and started to go into another gybe—this was going to be
a shitty one. The spinny suddenly collapsed behind the main.
"Go go go go!" As the sock came down hand over hand,
something tugged at my feet. I glanced down and saw that the
lazy line from the sock had wrapped itself round my leg. Time
stopped. The boat was coming up for another run, the spinnaker was about to be slammed full of wind and I was going
to be strung up with a large sail lashed to my ankle in a tidy
gale. For the first time in the race I was scared. I daren't let go
of the sock line. I had half the sail tamed and yet I needed
both hands to untie the other end round my leg. Shit! I just
couldn't free it. The main filled. I watched the brightly coloured
spinny flutter gaily out from behind the shelter of the main,
swallowed and waited for a lot of discomfort.

The spinnaker filled with a crash and the sock line whipped
taut in my hand. I was lifted off my feet and came up short as
my safety line tightened. I could feel every sinew and tendon
stretching as my body took up the strain. I tensed the muscles
across my back and shoulders. My duff elbow hurt but it was
the thought of my shoulder coming out of its socket as I dangled in mid-air that worried me. There was no way, however
much it hurt, that I was letting go of the line and unleashing
the spinnaker—the consequences were unimaginable. I shut
my eyes and shouted "bastard" at the top of my voice, and
started to feel breathless as the strain took its toll. My right
hand fumbled for the knife I always carried in my left pocket,
but I couldn't reach it. My grip was weakening and I could
feel the line start to run. I had to do something. Dump the halyard—break every rule and dump the halyard. Heaven knows
what would happen but it couldn't be worse. The jammer
was just out of my reach. I concentrated my gaze on it, even
the burning in my left hand was forgotten. The boat came up,
the sail really pulled now and started to run away. I was losing

the fight. The boat lurched and at last the tip of my index finger touched the jammer and I managed to hook it free. The halyard ran—thank heavens I always flake my lines out to avoid tangles. I hit the deck and ripped the line from my leg—I had to get it off before the dumped sail filled with water. I was free. I leapt up to jam the halyard, hoping to save the sail yet. We came up to the wind and stopped with the sail filling beyond the masthead as we lay over. It shook the boat like a rag doll. I dumped the tack, ran aft and winched in on the sheet. It was enough to kill the sail. Good old *Aqua Quorum* came up and ran off downwind with ease. The spinny was sheltered behind the main now and she was quite happy with such a reduction in sail area. It was as if she was saying "told you so."

I dragged the spinny in under the boom, taking care to ensure that I didn't get caught up in it. Wrapping a load of sail ties round it, I dumped it below and closed the hatch—it felt as though I had imprisoned a dangerous criminal who had been running amok. Then it was back to business, a quick stretch, nothing broken, although my shoulder would be tender for a while. I slapped a reef in, tidied the deck and checked that everything was as it should be. I rigged up the pole and prepared to goosewing the number two; I had to keep driving the boat and I now knew when the spinny was a bad idea. I hoisted the number two under the main, returned to the cockpit and winched it across to the windward side. The boat loved it and flew along. It was time for a cuppa. I had been on deck for a good eight hours and felt very tired and cold.

The warmth and light of the stove were great company. I put my heavy thermals on and stuffed a ready-cooked meal into the kettle. It's a great system. I poured the boiling water into my pint cup with four sugars in it, dragged the bag out, cut the top off and dived into a meal of beef stew with dumplings and a handful of cream crackers. Just what the doctor ordered. I polished it off quickly, food didn't stay warm down there for very long. I banged a fix on the chart and was relieved to see that we had made a good run despite the day's antics and turned in feeling pretty pleased with myself. I had learned a good deal that day. How she pulled out of some of those broaches I shall never know. Good old Ade, and well done Cetrek, was all I could say.

I lay back, braced my feet on the end of the bunk so that I didn't slide off it every time we decelerated at the bottom of a wave and wedged myself in. I had my hat, gloves, thermals and Walkman on inside my best sleeping bag. Warmth worked its way back into my bones and with it a heavy weariness. The Walkman was essential because it drowned out much of the noise of the boat as she thundered along. My tastes are varied—Tina Turner, Vivaldi, ABBA, Queen, country and western, anything that grabs me. I was also very lucky to have a load of tapes made up for me by radio reporter Dennis Skillicorn. He had spent hours recording his best interviews from the past forty years for me. There are thousands of them and they are fascinating. An old tramp on the Isle of Wight, Lord Mountbatten, Blondie Hasler's Cockleshell Heroes, an old farm labourer, a poacher, the list goes on and on.

I dropped into a deep sleep and woke with a start two hours later, rolled out of my bunk and dropped into my Mustos, which were hanging nearby ready for action. It was dark, cold and wet and the prospect of going on deck wasn't at the top of my list but it was something that had to be done. I checked the voltameter, which looked good, and flicked the decklight on. A burst of light opened up our little world—I patted the boat, good girl, keep it up. Clipped on with hood up, I eased my way through the hatch and into the cockpit. I glanced at the instruments and watched the waves for a few moments. It was obvious what had woken me—the wind had started to go round and a gybe would be called for some time during the night. I could have done it then but I wanted to push further south and opted to change course instead. I clambered about the deck; a sail tie had come undone but otherwise all seemed well. I shone my spotlight into the rigging, it looked great. I adjusted the course by ten degrees and spent a few minutes with her to make sure that she was happy with this new heading, taking pleasure in watching her surf off under the decklight. It seemed to heighten the experience. Wind, spray, noise, rain and waves got their moment as they swept on- and off-stage, entering the spotlight at random and becoming larger than life in their moment of glory. Sheets of spray, thrown up by the bow, seemed solid in the harsh light but were cut off as soon as they ventured beyond its circle. I spent an hour glorying in it as I let her settle down.

It was time for tea. I shook off my Musto jacket. *Aqua Quorum* is a wet boat and being on deck when she was really tramping was like standing under a pressure hose, and yet I always remained dry. I first used Musto gear during the *Cornish Meadow* Transat when I slept on deck all the way. I have used it ever since and feel privileged to have done my bit in passing back ideas for improvement. Keith Musto decided a few years ago that the material Gore-Tex was the way to go and, with his son Nigel, developed a new benchmark in offshore clothing, the HPX System. Gore-Tex is absolutely waterproof and yet able to breathe, thus venting condensation. It is very light and supple and lets me spend my days sitting about in water while remaining dry and warm.

It was two in the morning but this meant nothing now that my twenty-four-hour body clock was up and running. I munched a slice of Mum's fruit cake, swigged back the last of a cup of tea, and pissed in the keel box, checking the colour of my urine. It is easy for a single-hander to become dehydrated at sea without realising it. Golden urine is a sure sign of this problem, which can creep up just as readily in cold climes as it can in the tropics. I drink tea as a pastime—it is a ritual, a moment for reflection or a time of contemplation before a job that needs to be done. It's no good getting to the end of the boom and finding that the job requires a tool that is sitting below. Better to think it through first and make sure you have it before starting. I have saved myself many wasted hours and energy by cups of tea.

I could make out a big squall in the distance and there was no point in going to bed. I wedged myself in front of the chart table and wrote an article for the *Daily Telegraph* back in London. I was a bit reticent when Amelia fixed up a series of articles for me to write as the race progressed. I had never written before and the prospect seemed a bit daunting. But I found I enjoyed it and could bash out a rough feature in an hour and a half. Even Tracey liked the articles, and if anyone is honest, she is. The cloud passed over and I could see another coming up. I was going to have to sleep at some time and pondered whether to get my head down regardless. I tried dozing in the chair, but it just didn't work. I was still not able to relax down there as the boat thundered on.

I kept pushing south and was soon the southernmost boat in the fleet. It was bloody freezing with driving snow and became difficult to work on deck. My feet developed chilblains. Philippe Jeantot kept reminding me that it was a particularly bad year for icebergs. I was fatalistic. I hadn't seen any ice yet and my instincts told me that there was nothing to worry about. I kept a lookout but stuck to my usual laid-back approach—if a berg had my name on it then I would hit it. I was wearing full thermals, hat and gloves below by now, there was bitter snow on deck, and sail changes were particularly painful to the hands. There was a strong smell of diesel and I traced the problem to the sail locker. *Aqua Quorum* has a large diesel tank which is supplemented by plastic jerry cans. I discovered that the tops were made of a different plastic from the can itself—they were contracting at different rates in the cold and the tops had split, leaking diesel on the sails. It was these little details that I found so interesting. Like the chance discovery that pressurised canisters for inflating life rafts were unable to work in those temperatures—they froze as they decompressed—and a different gas was needed.

The race was not going to plan. I had dropped a touch too far south in my haste to get down quickly and was starting to pick up adverse winds while Raphaël Dinelli and Patrick de Radigues were storming away to the north of us. I was a bit put out by this and made sure that it didn't happen again. I heard something rattle and bang along the hull. Ice! Shitty death! I was up on deck like a shot. It wasn't a big piece but it could have been the precursor to a decent-sized berg. It was hard to see in the blasts of snow. I turned on the radar but all seemed fine. It took a while for the hairs to settle down on the back of my neck, though. The desolation of that place was suddenly underlined. I couldn't see any point in slowing down—better to sail like the devil and push through the area quickly.

The longer I was away the more I missed my family. Tracey's faxes were a daily lifeline. The BT Inmarsat system was so good and immediate that we could have a written conversation. I spent a lot of time working on next year's business and sorting out details that were left undone in the frantic last-minute preparations at the start. Nick Booth and his wife, Sarah, were making progress with the *British Steel* refit and I felt sure that with the two boats we would be able to keep in front of the overdraft. I had managed to sell a couple of days' hospitality on *Aqua Quorum* while I had been racing. It wasn't a chore, in fact it was nice to have something to work on outside the routine of the race.

People tend to think that a race like this is an endless series of adventures. The reality is that it is eighty per cent hard graft and twenty per cent excitement. The outside world focuses on the thrills, but they don't hear about the three grinding weeks of gale after gale. Three weeks' hard work boils down to a series of plots on the chart, that's it, nothing more. A disaster becomes a highlight, a break from the routine, something to write home about.

We emerged from the cold spell one morning to be welcomed by a crisp, sunny day with a northerly breeze. My spirits soared, the headwinds were behind us and I intended to drive myself to the bone until I caught up with Raphaël and Patrick, who were now many miles ahead. I knew we could do it. I spent the day working on the boat and paid particular attention to the sail locker. It took hours to clean up the mess caused by the leaks—a little diesel goes a long way. The decks were as slippery as hell and no amount of scrubbing would take off the greasy film. I just had to be careful as I moved around. It played havoc with my elbow as I slid about. No matter how hard I tried I had to use both hands to stop myself slipping over. It was starting to swell more and the relentless, throbbing pain stopped me sleeping.

I stuck my head out the forehatch with yet another bucket of dirty water, and a growler—a piece of iceberg about the size of a house—quietly slipped by with the sun reflecting off its many faces and making it look like a giant jewel. I hadn't seen anything solid outside the boat for ages and I stood watching it glide away and wondered how many others I had just missed. Back to work, there was another depression on the way and I wanted the boat tiptop.

The pressure dropped and the wind rose. This felt like our

first proper depression, a classic Southern Ocean version
rather than the patchy things we had had to endure so far. We
crossed the 50th parallel, really in among it now and feeling
good. It was not so cold now; in fact, I had been through the
coldest part of the race during the past few days when the
jerry can caps had split. I'll not forget it either, bloody grim,
the warmest place on the boat was below—and that was zero
degrees.

The wind picked up and we had a steady forty knots blowing. I had been progressively shortening sail and we were
down to two reefs, staysail and the number two. *Aqua Quorum*
was going like a bat out of hell and felt comfortable, despite a
horrible little cross sea that kept trying to throw her off
course. Apart from these odd moments I felt happy with
progress and was able to get on with life below. I cooked up
the biggest curry yet and shovelled some sugar into it. My
sugar level felt low and I knew it was going to be a long night.
I threw the pan into the cockpit—it was like a dishwasher out
there, water flying everywhere as we bounced our way down
the waves on a permanent plane. The white spray against the
darkness was fantastic and I spent a couple of minutes looking
aft at the wake as we roared off into the night. Time for a kip;
I had been up too long and hadn't slept for a good eighteen
hours.

I hung up my Mustos in readiness—I didn't expect to be
down for long—and zipped my aching body into my sleeping
bag. The feeling was fantastic and I grinned into the darkness.
I was really enjoying things now, loving the rough and tumble
and the fact that it was all down to me and my wits. I banged
some Tina Turner into my Walkman, settled down and
waited for sleep to overcome the noise and motion. I woke up
and checked the instruments every twenty minutes or so
and popped up on deck every now and then. The wind was

starting to go round and I would need to gybe the boat some time during the night. I didn't like the cross sea, it was giving the boat a hard time, the wind had gone up a bit but I decided to hold on to what sail I had up. We were going like a rocket.

I was woken by a dull thump on the side of the hull and felt the boat yaw to the left and accelerate down a wave. Shit, shit, shit, she was going to crash gybe, I just knew it. The boat heeled to leeward as the wind came further aft and I clawed away at the zip on my sleeping bag which had jammed. I couldn't free it. I heard the battens slam back in place, they had half gybed, bending double before crashing back. We hit the bottom of the wave and round she went. I gave up on the zip, shut my eyes and gritted my teeth. Crash! Over she went, my face was pressed against the hull and I was thrown out of my bunk. It was bloody freezing. Poor old *Aqua Quorum* was flat on her side and beam on to the wind. The keel was on the wrong side and I pictured the main across the runner, pinning the boat down. It was quiet now apart from the wind whistling over us and waves breaking on to the hull.

Take your time, I told myself, we've been here before. It was familiar ground. I worked the zip free, turned on the cabin light and found that my trousers had fallen into the water. I couldn't believe my bad luck, I had managed to keep the inside of them dry for months. Still, at least they would dry out as I wore them. I threw on the decklight and began a by now well-rehearsed sequence of actions. I used the opportunity to lean well out and check the keel. I decided not to perform a jig on it as I did in the Transat—it was pitch black and I didn't feel quite so cocky down here. I flaked out the number two halyard and dumped it, threw off the main halyard and wrestled the sail down the mast. She was coming up now, reacting in the kind and predictable manner that I had come to expect. The rudders suddenly bit and we accelerated off downwind again. The autopilot caught and she settled down on course.

The wind had gone round a bit—not too much, but the combination of that and a larger than usual cross sea was enough to cause the gybe. I sorted out the runners, swung the keel over, gybed the boat properly, heaved the number two on deck and lashed it down. A couple of hanks had ripped out. I put in another reef and spent a further two hours on deck squaring everything away. Below was a mess and I sorted that out, made a cup of tea and rolled into bed absolutely exhausted. We could have had a little more sail up but the time had come for some rest. I would have a big breakfast and resume work at daybreak. We'd done enough damage for one night, thank you very much.

I had an hour's deep sleep and bounced out of bed refreshed. In normal society, everything is geared to that eight-hour sleep. Transport, shopping, radio, television—it goes on and on, ruling your life, confining you like a straitjacket. At sea my sleep pattern varies with the weather and although I feel tired for much of the time I am not debilitated. Physically I feel lean and mean. My pain barrier rises considerably and a knock that would have hurt like buggery ashore is shrugged off as if it were nothing. There is the odd day when my limbs feel heavy, my eyes are gritty and I catch myself gazing into space in a kind of exhausted trance. Then I know it's time to have a good curry and follow it up with a decent kip.

I was very tired after the capsize but I spent the day mending the damage that it caused. All the battens in the main had broken and I took the opportunity to go over the sail with a needle and thread, touching up where necessary. The number two took an hour to repair and the rest of the day was spent sorting out below and writing an article that was well overdue.

I managed to keep the boat on the boil, though, and ended the day with a serious look at how I was running my race. I took a glance at the chart to see that we hadn't even scratched the surface of the Southern Ocean and we had already suffered a lot of damage. If I wanted to stay in the race I would have to adapt to the environment and modify my pace.

Head down, I ignored my elbow, which did a lot of work during the capsize and was aching like a bastard, and got on with the job. *Aqua Quorum* was performing like a dream: each time the race positions came in I saw that we had pulled decent miles out of the opposition. I ate, slept, worked and kept the boat up to speed, driving her hard but not so hard that we sustained damage. A sixth sense picked up the warning signals and we didn't get caught out again.

The one thing I always insist on is reassuring Tracey that all is well. However, I was very tired after the last capsize and, although I informed the race organisers of the incident during the daily chat show, I forgot to fax the news to Tracey that night. The incident quickly hit the press and sounded worse than it was. The first a worried Tracey heard of it was a call from a journalist. I was not pleased with this slip-up on my part.

We were really pulling our way up the fleet now. I was caught in a high shortly after the capsize and two records were set that day. Christophe Auguin had a record run of 375 nautical miles—and I got the record for the least. Fourteen comes to mind. That was all behind us now, and we were the fastest boat in the fleet for a full seven days, which was topped by a blistering twenty-four-hour run of just over 344 miles on 20 December. Philippe Jeantot informed me that this was a new record. I was well chuffed because I knew that the boat was capable of doing even better.

I was overjoyed to see that our wild dash had put us back

up with Raphaël and Patrick. I knew we could do it and spent a few hours pondering the weather information. My next target was to catch up with Eric Dumont on *Café Legal*. It was a tall order but I believed that we could do it. He had had some problems and did not seem to be on the pace as much as he should. I decided to keep pushing on—our performance hadn't cost us too much in terms of damage and I felt we had at last found our pace. The only cloud on the horizon was that Catherine had had a rough time with a bad knockdown and suffered a lot of damage. She was now a long way behind. I felt for her and hoped that she would be able to find her stride again. I was sure that she would become the first woman to finish the Vendée. She had the depth of character to overcome her problems and see it through to the end. I wished her well on the radio and acted as a link between her and the shore. It was the last radio call I would make before mine packed up.

The radio had died on me. It had received a good soaking in the capsize and, although it kept going for a couple of days, it was now silent. Never mind, I was quite happy out here and the less outside influence there was the better. It was as if the radio was my last link with society and I was unable to settle into this life of total self-reliance until my last crutch had been knocked away. The BT Inmarsat system did not have this effect—I called up its messages when I was ready for them, it was communication on my terms. Happy solitude.

The shallow bank of the Kerguelen Ridge presented a tactical dilemma. If it is blowing there, the Southern Ocean waves can build up into a raging mess. I had a taste of it during the British Steel Challenge and had no wish for a repeat performance. Put simply, the bank has an island at either end, Kerguelen to the north and Heard Island to the south. My track would take me slap bang between the two. I didn't like it and decided to duck further south in order to avoid the area completely. I might lose a few miles but Raphaël and Patrick were welcome to them in this case. As it happened the dogleg cost us little and I was glad to see that the others had cleared the area without mishap.

It was 22 December, my thirty-fifth birthday. I was fifty-five degrees south, the Kerguelens were well behind us and I felt great. It was time for a treat. I warmed up a bucket of water and had a shower in the cockpit under the cuddy. I put the heater on for an hour to dry the cabin, stood naked in the accommodation to let the warm air get to my skin and checked myself over. Loads of bruises, elbow hurting, but otherwise in good shape. No rashes or sores, the diet was obviously working. I slipped into a clean set of thermals—absolute luxury—and celebrated by trimming my moustache. The beard, if you could call it that, would stay because it stopped wet, salty clothing from chafing my neck.

Thirty-five years. I couldn't believe how quickly it had gone, it had been great. I had managed to fit a fair bit in so far and couldn't wait to grab the next thirty-five by the horns. Tracey and the kids sent a lovely fax, they had baked a birthday cake and eaten it for me. The race was going our way, we were catching the opposition and here I was fulfilling a lifelong dream. What a lucky man I was.

The next two days passed without a hitch and I carried out some routine maintenance and eased up on myself a little. I found that I was tired after working so hard to catch up with and pass Raphaël and Patrick. I spent the odd extra hour or so in bed and made sure that I ate well. When I looked at the chart I was awed by the scale of this race—I had already packed in adventure after adventure and yet the halfway mark was still days away. Nevertheless I felt good—*Aqua Quorum* was bedded in and I knew that we would keep on improving our performance as we went on.

A Close Encounter

Christmas Day 1996 began with a bright blue sky and a crisp, refreshing, twenty-knot wind from the north. My position was about 1,400 miles south of Perth, Western Australia. Perfect. I had been making good speed all night under the number two, staysail and one reef in the main as we surged along over the large northerly swell that had set in. It would have been idyllic if it hadn't been for the barometric pressure, which was dropping fast. A fall of thirty-six millibars in twenty-four hours, and most of that had been in the last twelve. The forecast looked horrifying—the isobars on the weather chart were so close together that they seemed to merge into a solid black line. I had a deep sense of impending doom and felt very uneasy—I couldn't settle, couldn't relax. I had seen livestock back in the West Country bunch together and move restlessly about the field before a bad storm; I could relate to the feeling, except I was on my own. I had experienced many severe blows over the years but this one, for some reason, held a heavy sense of foreboding. I could almost taste it in the air.

Thoughts of Christmas were pushed to one side. I tried to ignore the feeling of uneasiness but it followed me around the boat as I checked that everything was as it should be. Fear was not an emotion which I associated with the sea. Of course, I respected the ocean but for me it was no longer an alien environment, it had become my way of life over the years and I was comfortable in its presence. I knew that *Aqua Quorum* and I were up to the job—it was the waiting for what were bound to be pretty grim conditions that brought on the whispers, the anxieties. It was time to have a cuppa, get busy, apply logic. Once the storm arrived the rest would be easy.

I could feel it now. I togged up and got on deck. The wind started to back—within three hours it had gone round to the southwest and was rising at an alarming rate. I could only just keep up. No sooner had I gybed and sorted everything out than the number two needed dropping. And I mean dropping, it was over the side and in the sea. Damn! It was a real struggle to drag it on to the deck as we hurtled along. I folded it up and left it lashed there. I knew it should have gone below but I just didn't have time—the wind was rising faster than I had ever experienced. I clambered back to the mast, put the third reef in and still the wind rose. Hell's teeth! I reduced the sail area and immediately it was too much and needed reducing further. I could sense the autopilot struggling to cope as we hurtled along. No time to tidy the reefing lines. I flaked out the staysail halyard and freed the clutch; couldn't afford niceties. The sail flogged like a bastard as we careered off down an odd sea, often submerged. It was hard work to manage the most basic of jobs and my elbow was playing up, too.

I whipped off the staysail and shoved it below taking loads of water with it—so much of the stuff was sweeping the decks that it was hard to judge a good moment. I made the staysail halyard off on the storm jib, thankful that I had already hanked it on in readiness for the occasion, made my way back to the mast and tried to pull it up. It was no good, the wind was too strong. I had to winch it all the way. It felt very hot inside my Musto oilies, I'd been hard at it for a couple of hours now. I went back to the cockpit for a breather to find that the wind was up to forty-five knots and rising. Fuck me—and it was only just beginning. The hair stood up on the back of my neck.

I forgot about taking a breather. I had to get the main down and get it down quickly. Up to the mast, I flaked out the halyard, checked everything over; if it went wrong now I'd have a hell of a job getting it back under control. Not happy with the sheet, I nipped back, winched it in a bit and eased the halyard. The sail fell away and jammed on the spreaders, pinned by gusts of goodness knows what strength. It was a real old struggle and I had to work between the gusts that were whipping the water into a white frenzy. I tied it off with enough rope to moor the *Queen Mary*, removed the halyard, made it off on the end of the boom and took it up tight. I then rigged up a couple of lines from the end of the boom to either side of the cockpit and winched them up bar tight.

I worked my way round the boat, tidying everything away and making sure that all was shipshape. I pulled both dagger boards up and added a line to stop them falling out if we got rolled upside down. I tied off the blades on the wind genera-tor as the automatic brake didn't seem man enough in these conditions. I knew the number two sail should be removed from the deck and stowed below but decided to leave it—the bow was under water most of the time now and discretion was the better part of valour in this case.

I had to crawl on hands and knees back to the cockpit. The wind was still rising and I felt as though I were a passenger in a car, with the driver pressing hard on the accelerator with no regard for a rapidly approaching corner. I rolled from my knees into the cockpit and clipped on my additional safety line before releasing the other. The wind was a screaming banshee lashing the ocean into a frenzy of spume and spray that felt like a shotgun blast on my hands and face. It had settled at a vicious fifty knots, topped up with regular gusts that blasted their way through us at sixty knots, flattening the sea as they passed. Still the storm hadn't settled—it continued to rise.

I stumbled below and for the first time in my life fitted the washboards in anger. I shook off the worst of the water, grabbed a Mars bar and once again called up the weather chart. There was nowhere to go, the best thing was just to run before it and hope the storm dissipated before inflicting too much damage. Looking at the chart I suspected that Raphaël and Patrick might be experiencing even worse conditions and I silently wished them well—we were all caught up in something far greater than we had ever experienced before. The energy of the storm was incredible—they were hurricane conditions. The hull hummed and shook as we surfed off down a wave at twenty-seven knots. I braced myself for the impact at the bottom and we dropped for what seemed an eternity before the crash came. The wind in the rigging rose and fell from a high-pitched screech to a low and sorrowful moan that worked its way into my soul.

I clambered back on deck and marvelled at the conditions as we flew along under the storm jib alone. The sail was little more than the size of a tablecloth and yet the sheet was tight and as unyielding as a steel rod. It resonated when I hit it with a winch handle. There was a roar as a big sea broke behind us. I ducked beneath the canopy and held on for grim death as good old *Aqua Quorum* accelerated out of it. This was fantastic. I grabbed the camera and fired off a few shots for the kids. I had never managed to take a good wave shot in all my years at sea. The lens somehow flattened them out, but I suspected that these monsters might be impressive. And still the wind rose.

My main concern was the waves. A large and menacing sea had been whipped up from the southwest and was being made worse by a northerly swell which would take a while to dissipate. Individually they presented nothing more than one would expect—it was when they combined that they erupted into an unpredictable brute of tumbling water. At times we were planing across the face of a northerly swell, leaning to windward on the occasional steep face when a southwesterly sea slammed into us. The transom was lifted by the combined force of the two waves and we turned and dropped dangerously into a pit. I spent a while finding the best line, set the autopilot and tumbled below. There was no steering out of the bad ones. I was better off shut below in the safety of the hull.

I was worried. I felt my control of the situation ebbing away as the conditions deteriorated. Unusually, the first knockdown was to windward. Two waves erupted on my port quarter, *Aqua Quorum* slewed round until she was dead downwind, the keel on full power pulled her over and the wave did the rest as we accelerated into what felt like a brick wall. I was braced against the chart table, hands against the cabin roof, feet on the floor in a star position, and I watched through the skylight as the spreaders dragged in the water. They pulled her back to windward, she was up, the storm jib filled and she was off again. Water poured into the cockpit and cascaded below.

I considered going to bare poles to slow the boat's headlong rush but instinct told me that speed, alarming as it may have been, was the one defence I had. We hurtled into a hole at forty-five degrees and stopped dead. I waited for the seemingly inevitable pitchpole as we went completely under. The cabin went dark as the sea cut out the light. I was thrown against the chart table and looked out of the back of the boat at the sky as gallons of water poured into the accommodation from the cockpit. The flare box hit me on the shin and the pain gave me something to focus on, dispelling the fear as *Aqua Quorum* struggled to recover. The rudders were out of the water and I held on and hoped. There is always one bad blow on any long race and you know that if you get through it you will make the finish. I had no doubt that this was the one.

There was a tremendous crash and *Aqua Quorum* was
knocked down again. I was thrown across the cabin as the
boat groaned under the strain. Through the din I heard the
satcom system bleeping away. I couldn't believe it was still
able to work on what had practically become a yellow submarine. I struggled across to the chart table and called up the
message. Mayday, mayday, mayday. It was a distress call
being passed on by Marine Rescue and Control Centre
(MRCC) Australia. The vessel in trouble was the yacht *Algimouss*. Poor sods. I wondered who they were and hoped I
wouldn't be joining them. I assumed that she was somewhere
near the Australian coast. I extricated a chart from the mess,
plotted their position and did a double take. They were about
160 miles away. Who the hell would be daft enough to be
down here? It never occurred to me that it might be one of us.
The name *Algimouss* meant nothing to me as race communications had used the name of the skipper rather than the name
of the boat.

The satcom bleeped again. This time the message was
from Philippe Jeantot. The mayday *was* from one of us. *Algimouss* was Raphaël Dinelli's boat and he was in trouble.
Philippe asked if I could help. I took another look at the chart
and realised that things were pretty bad: not only was
Raphaël 160 miles away from me but he was also to windward in atrocious conditions. But I had to go, I knew that. It
was that simple; the decision had been made for me a long
time ago by a tradition of the sea. When someone is in trouble
you help.

However, I needed a minute to grasp the enormity of it.
How could we make headway in this weather? Would *Aqua
Quorum* hold together? The reality of what lay ahead grabbed
at my guts. It was a cold and clammy grasp. Having made the
decision I sat down to contemplate the consequences. It was

only for thirty seconds, a minute—I'm not sure. I thought about what I was about to put on the line: my family, my boat, my life. In my own little world it was a profound moment that I shall never forget. To me, and I am sure it is different for everyone, if you keep chipping away at life you will eventually get to a clear and simple crossroads. I knew I had to stand by my morals and principles. Not turning back, whatever the stakes, would have been a disservice to myself, my family and the spirit of the sea. I fired off a quick fax to Philippe and expressed my doubts as to our ability to make our way back to Raphaël—but I was going anyway.

I ventured on deck and the fight began. I had to think of it as a fight. I shouted at the wind and waves, and the anger helped to strengthen my resolve. We had to gybe. Oddly it was easy and went like clockwork. I brought *Aqua Quorum* up to face the wind, feeling the full force of the hurricane, as the wind across the deck immediately increased by the twenty-five-knot speed that I had been travelling downwind. The first gust put the guardrail under and the lower spreaders touched the water. I couldn't believe the energy that was whistling past. I winched in the storm jib hard, put the helm down again and waited to see what would happen. *Aqua Quorum* was game, it was as if she knew what was at stake. The mast slowly came upright and she began to move to windward. I couldn't believe that she was making about eight knots—sometimes more—as she climbed steeply to the wild, toppling crests at the apex of each huge wave, before accelerating down the fifty-foot slope on the other side and into the next trough. It wasn't quite the course I needed—eighty degrees to the wind was the best we could do—but it was a start, and the wind would ease soon. It had to.

Meanwhile it screamed deafeningly through the rigging, sounding like a jet taking off, as *Aqua Quorum* gamely struggled away. It was impossible to breathe if I faced windward—the breath was sucked from my lungs—and I couldn't open my eyes.

Now that we were committed, I knew that we would do it somehow. The things I learned with the Royal Marines took over: be professional at all times, never give up and make intelligent use of everything to hand. I had asked a lot of my boats in the past, but never this much. I decided to take no prisoners. *Aqua Quorum* would do it or she would break up in the attempt; a man was out there and there could be no half measures. Night closed and we struggled on. The huge, breaking seas and the waves were horrifying.

I had to fire off a fax to Tracey as I didn't want her to hear about all this from someone else. I made the mistake of telling her not to worry which was something I had never done before. She told me later that it was the only time during the race that she became really concerned.

25 DEC 1996 15:56 FROM INMC VIA SENTOSA LES

Hi Tracey, Happy Xmas—I am in bad storm 60knts wind but fine, I stress fine. Another competitor is in distress & I am trying to make my way back to rescue him, I stress I am fine & storm may just be easing so don't worry. Wanted you to know before press start baying. Can't tell you how much I love you. Hope the Xmas meal/day has been good. Love to all. Pete XXXXX

FROM 423420410=AQUA X 25-DEC-1996 15:56:42 MSG214085 SENTOSA C IOR

Below it was an indescribable mess: water slopped about and a litre bottle of cooking oil had burst. Everything was coated with the stuff and it was slippery. I slithered and slid about—it was getting as dangerous below as it was on deck. My infected elbow took a bad blow and would cause problems from then on. A wave swept the deck with such ferocity that all the rope clutches opened. God, what next?

I crawled into the cockpit and we were knocked down again, this time beyond ninety degrees, and I felt myself falling out of the boat. *Aqua Quorum* came up, a spinnaker pole had burst its lashings at one end, the head car metal fitting at the top of the mainsail had broken, and both the mainsail and the number two, which were lashed to the deck, were ripped. I decided not to venture beyond the mast.

I was wet and very cold as I hadn't had the chance to put on my full thermals. I was also hungry. I got below, grabbed some food and shoved it down. Raphaël needed someone in good shape. Come on, keep going, take charge. I could feel the first signs of hypothermia coming on, being soaked through and not wearing my heavy thermals. I put the kettle on and dragged my warmest thermals over the wet ones. A big wave hit the boat and the kettle hit the deckhead. I refilled it and flashed up the stove again. This time I held the kettle down but with the next big wave both the kettle and I hit the deckhead. I crawled into my sleeping bag and tied myself into the bunk before dropping into semiconsciousness. The tea would have to wait.

I awoke with a jolt as we were knocked down again. We were being knocked down every half hour or so now. I was disorientated, tired and confused in the darkness. The cabin filled with a nauseating smell. My stores under the chart table had broken free and an aerosol can of oil was emptying itself. There were big sparks coming from under the table—the can had wedged itself across the live generator terminals and was causing a short circuit. A fire was all I needed.

The wind had lost its edge; I felt the worst was behind us. Hold on, Raphaël. We had eighty miles to go and I could make the course. I updated Philippe, gulped some water, ate what I could and went back to my sleeping bag. I had to conserve energy because I felt my limits were not far off. I thought of Raphaël out there and wondered how he could possibly survive. The wind was easing, we had got through round one, and I needed to make good use of my time in the corner before round two began. I worked as fast as I could; the wind was down to thirty-five knots now and I needed more sail up. I checked the deck and stowed the torn number two. I tackled the repair to the mainsail, drilling holes for the needle to save time. It took two and a half hours, every minute dragging. Raphaël would be in a bad way by now—he had to be. I talked my way through possible first aid treatment as I sewed.

Job done, I went below and stowed the sailmaker kit, put a quick cup of tea on and . . . vrooooom . . . it was a Royal Australian Air Force rescue plane. They told me over the VHF radio that they had dropped Raphaël two life rafts, he seemed well and was in an immersion suit. His yacht *Algimouss* was submerged. I took her position and asked if there were any other vessels involved in the rescue. "No, sir, we're pinning our hopes on you," came the reply. Fine. We'd do it.

Round two began as the aircraft's engines faded into the distance. I spent a quiet few minutes working out my next actions as *Aqua Quorum* continued to bash her way to windward. I needed a new strategy because the fight had changed. My opponent was wily and I must adapt. More thought was required now and instinct and determination were not enough. I broke the way ahead into clearly defined chunks and mentally walked the course a few times. I felt as though I was actually there, each time throwing in a new problem and coming up with a practical solution. Every visualised run culminated in a successful rescue.

Phase one was a simple yacht race to Raphaël's general

location. Phase two would take a little more effort to crack. It was a big area and it would be like looking for a needle in a haystack, particularly as it would be getting dark. Phase three would be the pick-up. This could present all sorts of complications. No worries though. I had plenty of time for some more reruns of this phase. First of all I needed information and so I faxed Philippe and asked for a detailed twelve-hour weather forecast for my area. Philippe played a vital role throughout the operation.

Very soon a special forecast came through from Météo France: a front would arrive in the afternoon, the wind would head me all day, visibility would reduce and winds of forty knots were expected. This would add a good four hours to the passage and make it very hard to find Raphaël. There was no room to manoeuvre. I just had to get on deck and sail like the devil. The rest of the day was spent concentrating on the boat speed—nothing dramatic, just sailing—and it was a relief, apart from the frustrations of being headed off the course by the hour. I continually got updates on Raphaël's position and drift. MRCC Australia confirmed that an RAAF plane would aid the rescue in the morning. This gave me great comfort for we had a safety net if I couldn't find him in the dark.

Provided Raphaël could cope with the cold I felt we had him. I was now twenty miles directly downwind of him and started short-tacking up his drift line. It began to get dark. This could actually be a blessing if the raft had a light as it would make him easier to spot. The wind just would not settle and the autopilot found it hard to keep as close to the wind as I would have liked in the confused seas, so I went back to the helm. Some five hours later, we were five miles downwind of where Raphaël should be, given his drift. I slowed *Aqua Quorum* down and popped up the mast to the first set of spreaders to try and catch a glimpse of him. In those seas, I needed a lot of luck.

I went below and saw that another message had come in. It was a position update and it had changed considerably. We had overshot the mark by seven miles. Philippe also informed me that he had seen a photograph taken from the RAAF plane. *Algimouss* had been dismasted and was submerged. There was nothing to be seen apart from the life raft and he thought the yacht may have sunk by now anyway. There was no point in looking for a mast. The needle in the haystack got smaller.

I sailed back to the exact position I had been given and, as I was to windward, I dropped the main and zigzagged down his drift line under storm jib, keeping the speed down to between three and five knots. It was very dark and the front had arrived. A sense of desperation set in as the wind rose and visibility fell. I stood on the bow, blasting the foghorn and firing rocket flares. If only I could attract Raphaël's attention, he could then let off a flare and we would have cracked it. "Come on, Raphaël. Wake up," I shouted into the darkness. There was no response, just an enveloping greyness that soaked up my attempts to penetrate it.

I reached the end of his projected drift line. He was here, I knew it. I could feel it and yet emptiness pervaded. Come on, come on, we didn't tackle that storm for this. Give us a break, Neptune, surely we deserved one now. I decided to carry on the run until I had doubled his drift. We had to exhaust each avenue. Nothing.

Right. We turned round, got the main up and worked back. We'd bloody well do this all night if we had to. You'll never grind us down, damn you. The main kept jamming in the lazy jacks. My elbow ached and there was no strength. I had to be methodical. Persistence would pay. I nipped below and another position came in. It had changed and the drift was different. All that for nothing. I started to replot the position, but there were now two charts swimming before my eyes as if I were drunk. I just couldn't work it out. The first plot put him a crushing sixty miles away. Whoa, hang on, that wasn't right. I went on deck and stuck my head in a bucket of water. It was the first time I was thankful that the Southern Ocean was cold. I went back to the chart table and started again. It made sense now. He was six miles away and the plot was quite recent. Dawn had arrived. I rammed down some cold beans, a mug of cold water, and went back to concentrating on boat speed. It seemed an eternity before we arrived at the new waypoint and the show started again.

Slowly, slowly. Concentrate, don't miss him. Come on, Raphaël, bang off a flare or something. You have got to help yourself now. I am not enough. I tried the Navico hand-held VHF in desperation. It is waterproof and I could use it on deck. I got a response. "*Aqua Quorum, Aqua Quorum.* This is Rescue 252. We have started our descent and should be with you in four minutes." Thanks, guys. The relief was heady. Soon the RAAF plane flew past. They had a visual. He was three miles away and they would drop a smoke flare by him. I still couldn't see him. They turned and flew back towards me. As they passed over Raphaël they flashed their lights. I took the best bearing of my life. They informed me there were two life rafts, Raphaël was in the first and he had waved at them. Good lad, he must have the constitution of an ox. Phase three suddenly became simple.

I dropped the main, felt the wind and . . . there he was! As the life raft came into sight I judged the best approach. Port side. I had grablines all round the boat and a long line with two fenders on it aft just in case I overshot. Fifty, forty, thirty, twenty metres. It was going to be a good one. Thank heavens for all the practice. I ran forward and threw off the headsail halyard. Raphaël gripped the grabline. Got him!

Wow, a true professional here. He insisted on passing me three distress beacons and a box of stores. There was a bottle of champagne. Oh go on, then, seeing as you've brought a drink. We both heaved and he was on deck. Just like that. The best Christmas present I've ever had, all wrapped up in an immersion suit.

My new passenger lay facedown on the deck and tried to move, but he was too stiff and cold. It was hardly surprising— he had spent two days waiting for me to rescue him. I gently turned him over to reveal a nose and two very inflamed eyes surrounded by thick, yellowish wax. A feeble "thank you" could be heard from inside the immersion suit. All I could see was his eyes and I shall never forget them. I had no idea that a pair of eyes could convey such a depth of relief and gratitude. I was cheered to see that Raphaël could converse and that he tried to help himself—the last thing I wanted was a medical case. I dragged him back to the cockpit by his ankles; his feet were agonisingly painful because of the cold, and he couldn't walk. We worked together to get him under the cockpit over-hang. I nipped up to the foredeck and raised the storm jib to steady the violent roll of *Aqua Quorum* in the swell. I set the autopilot and got back to Raphaël.

His survival suit was inflexible and encrusted with salt, and it took five minutes to undress him. His hands and feet were in the worst condition: cold, colourless and useless. Skin came away on contact and I wondered if there would be long-term damage. The next step was to get him below through the small hatch, which was difficult to negotiate at the best of times. He was very stiff—it was as though rigor mortis was set-ting in—and it took a couple of attempts before he tumbled through. Now he was below in my cramped, wet little hell hole. It was a palace to him and he smiled weakly. I gave him a quick clean with wet-wipes and towelled him down—no major injuries, just bruising.

I put a dry set of thermals on him, pulled a woolly hat over his head and eased him into my best sleeping bag. He couldn't straighten out so I propped him in a sitting position against my kitbag and put a support under his knees. Every movement was slow and painful for him. I bunged on the kettle and informed the RAAF plane of the casualty's condition and thanked them for their help. They asked my intentions. Crumbs, I hadn't thought that far. I'd probably drop him off in Hobart. I asked the RAAF what I should do with the life raft. Leave it, they said. I went on deck and cast it off—it would probably bob around the Southern Ocean for ever. The kettle was boiling and I made a very sweet cup of tea in a cyclist's drinking bottle; I had it on board for just such an occasion as it has a nipple on the top and you can't spill the contents. I helped Raphaël slowly and painfully wrap his frozen hands round it. He took a sip and a look of pleasure lit up a face haggard beyond its twenty-eight years. He told me later that it was as though he had landed in England.

I filled my grandmother's old hot-water bottle and placed it under his feet. As Raphaël began to warm up he started to talk in a mixture of broken English and French, which I found hard to understand. He wanted to share his ordeal, repeating himself many times during the telling of how he fought off death for forty-eight hours. I told him that he was a very lucky man to have survived. It was strange to have another human on board after so long by myself. It was both a pleasure and an intrusion. I had a bizarre urge to start tidying up. *Aqua Quorum* could certainly do with it. What a boat! I felt a great surge of pride at the fantastic job she had done.

Raphaël was very weak and stiff and unable to get out of

his bunk without help. His body had seized up after days of being huddled in a life raft in icy temperatures. Going to the toilet was a major task—I had to carry him to the bucket and support him there. The race doctor was a great help during this time, prescribing medication and giving advice. I administered muscle-relaxant drugs and gave Raphaël physiotherapy in the form of stretching. It exhausted him but improved his mobility, and after five days he could get out of his bunk unaided. When he slept, the roll of the boat seemed to bring back memories of his ordeal and he had the odd nightmare.

The fax continued to pour out an endless stream of messages. Many were from Raphaël's family and he did his best to translate them for me. His parents said that I was now part of the Dinelli family and a fax from his elder brother in Paris said: "We have another brother now in Pete." I was very touched by the warmth of those messages.

Four days after the rescue Raphaël proposed by fax to his girlfriend Virginie on her birthday. I think that perhaps his close brush with death on the deck of *Algimouss* made him realise what was important in his life. She faxed back her acceptance and suggested that I be best man. I was honoured. It was time to have a go at the champagne. The satcom had endless messages for us and demands for our story poured in from the press. It appeared that our little adventure had caused quite a stir. For the moment I only communicated with the race doctor, Jean-Yves, about Raphaël's condition. I was also concerned with trying to get the damage on board sorted out before I arrived in Hobart. I wanted a quick turnaround so that I could get on with the race, having lost many miles and a lot of time. I was told that the race committee would give me an allowance for the time lost during the rescue, but I felt it was all a bit hypothetical.

Apart from a quick handshake at the start of the race, I
didn't really know Raphaël, but we hit it off immediately. I
was to discover over the next days that we were kindred spirits. I have since been told that it is unusual for the relationship
between a casualty and the rescuer to be a successful one
because of complex feelings of guilt, gratitude and debt. Not
so with us. We felt we were facing the same foe. Any one
of the competitors could have been in the path of the freak
wave that capsized Raphaël and destroyed *Algimouss*. There
but for the grace of God . . .

However, all I really wanted to do once I had him sorted
out and in a sleeping bag was to grab some sleep myself—I was
already tired when we went into the storm, and by the time of
the actual pick-up two days later I was exhausted. The trouble
was that Raphaël was on a survivor's high and kept rabbiting
away. I just couldn't shut him up.

At first he kept repeating aspects of his rescue over and over
again and it took a while to piece his ordeal together. His was a
tale of quite extraordinary determination. There is no way that
he should have survived for the length of time that he did. He
had accepted that he was probably going to die, but he never
gave up and kept pushing death before him, day by day, hour
by hour, minute by minute. The man is a giant.

Raphaël had been overtaken by an intense storm. The
wind was blowing at hurricane strength—sixty-five knots and
over—and increasing in the gusts to eighty knots. His boat was
surfing on waves as high as a sixty-foot, six-storey building. It
was too dangerous on deck and he was sheltering down
below and trying to control the headlong rush of *Algimouss*
with his autopilot. It was hopeless. He was trapped inside the
upturned hull of *Algimouss* after being capsized by a huge wave
which crashed across the boat, flipping it on its side and turning it upside down. He was strapped below in his seat with

everything flying everywhere. He worked his way free and activated his satellite emergency radio beacons, praying that someone would hear his mayday. The mast broke and was pile-driving through the hull—water poured in through the holes it made. After freeing himself, he spent the next three hours in the galley with the water rising up to his thighs. The diesel tanks were leaking and the fumes were making him violently sick.

The mast eventually freed itself from the tangled rigging, passed through the side of the hull and the boat righted itself. He clambered into the cockpit, which was awash, clipped himself to the submerged hull, faced the fifty-foot seas and fought it out. Each wave that struck choked and froze him, the icy water working its way down inside his survival suit. He could feel his body locking up with the cold, and started dancing on the flooded deck to keep his circulation going. "I must have looked like a madman," he said later.

He had nothing to eat or drink as he clung on there for twenty-four hours. Huge waves were running and each time they swept the boat he could feel her starting to give up and begin to settle lower under his feet for her final trip to the bottom. He talked to her, shouted at her, and again and again she dragged herself back to the surface. He thought about Virginie and their daughter Philippine. He made plans for the future, determined to be positive. The ropes which attached his life raft to the hull parted in the savage winds, and he was forced to watch his last hope of survival blow away.

He held out through that night and thought that all was lost until the RAAF, who played such a brave and vital part in his rescue, turned up and dropped him another life raft. He clambered on board, taking with him some food and a bottle of champagne which had washed to the surface. Inside the life raft was a message in French saying that Pete Goss and *Aqua*

Quorum were ten hours away, due south. Five minutes later *Algimouss* finally succumbed to the Southern Ocean and sank beneath the waves to begin her long journey, 3,500 metres down to the sea bed. Then began the struggle for survival in the life raft until we finally arrived on the scene.

Postscript: Pete Goss went on to become a national figure who was awarded France's highest award, the Legion of Honor, for his heroism in saving the life of Raphaël Dinelli. He continues to sail competitively and has to date completed six transatlantic and one other round-the-world race.

Thor Heyerdahl's famous Kon-Tiki Expedition in 1947 was inspired by both legend and archaeological evidence that the Incas of South America had sailed all the way to Polynesia. After building a raft of balsa wood and other native materials in Peru, Heyerdahl and his crew pushed off for the 4,300-mile journey across the Pacific. Their only accommodations to the modern world were canned food and water and a radio.

KON-TIKI

Across the Pacific by Raft

THOR HEYERDAHL

Across the Pacific

When the sea was not too rough, we were often out in the little rubber dinghy taking photographs. I shall not forget the first time the sea was so calm that two men felt like putting the balloon-like little thing into the water and going for a row. They had hardly got clear of the raft when they dropped the little oars and sat roaring with laughter. And, as the swell lifted them away and they disappeared and reappeared among the seas, they laughed so loud every time they caught a glimpse of us that their voices rang out over the desolate Pacific. We looked around us with mixed feelings and saw nothing comic but our own hirsute faces; but as the two in the dinghy should be accustomed to those by now, we began to have a lurking suspicion that they had suddenly gone mad. Sunstroke, perhaps. The two fellows could hardly scramble back on board the *Kon-Tiki* for sheer laughter, and, gasping, with tears in their eyes they begged us just to go and see for ourselves.

Two of us jumped down into the dancing rubber dinghy and were caught by a sea which lifted us clear. Immediately we sat down with a bump and roared with laughter. We had to scramble back on the raft as quickly as possible and calm the last two who had not been out yet, for they thought we had all gone stark staring mad.

It was ourselves and our proud vessel which made such a completely hopeless, lunatic impression on us the first time we saw the whole thing at a distance. We had never before had an outside view of ourselves in the open sea. The logs of timber disappeared behind the smallest waves, and, when we saw anything at all, it was the low cabin with the wide doorway and the bristly roof of leaves that bobbed up from among the seas. The raft looked exactly like an old Norwegian hayloft lying helpless, drifting about in the open sea—a warped hayloft full of sunburned bearded ruffians. If anyone had come paddling after us at sea in a bathtub, we should have felt the same spontaneous urge to laughter. Even an ordinary swell rolled halfway up the cabin wall and looked as if it would pour in unhindered through the wide open door in which the bearded fellows lay gaping. But then the crazy craft came up to the surface again, and the vagabonds lay there as dry, shaggy, and intact as before. If a higher sea came racing by, cabin and sail and the whole mast might disappear behind the mountain of water, but just as certainly the cabin with its vagabonds would be there again next moment. The situation looked bad, and we could not realize that things had gone so well on board the zany craft.

Next time we rowed out to have a good laugh at ourselves we nearly had a disaster. The wind and sea were higher than we supposed, and the *Kon-Tiki* was cleaving a path for herself over the swell much more quickly than we realized. We in the dinghy had to row for our lives out in the open sea in an attempt to regain the unmanageable raft, which could not stop and wait and could not possibly turn around and come back. Even when the boys on board the *Kon-Tiki* got the sail down, the wind got such a grip on the bamboo cabin that the raft drifted away to westward as fast as we could splash after her in the dancing rubber dinghy with its tiny toy oars. There was only one thought in the head of every man—we must not be separated. Those were horrible minutes we spent out on the sea before we got hold of the runaway raft and crawled on board to the others, home again.

From that day it was strictly forbidden to go out in the rubber dinghy without having a long line made fast to the bow, so that those who remained on board could haul the dinghy in if necessary. We never went far away from the raft, thereafter, except when the wind was light and the Pacific curving itself in a gentle swell. But we had these conditions when the craft was halfway to Polynesia and the ocean, all dominating, marched itself round the globe toward every point of the compass. Then we could safely leave the *Kon-Tiki* and row away into the blue space between sky and sea.

When we saw the silhouette of our craft grow smaller and smaller in the distance, and the big sail at last shrunken to a vague black square on the horizon, a sensation of loneliness sometimes crept over us. The sea curved away under us as blue upon blue as the sky above, and where they met all the blue flowed together and became one. It almost seemed as if we were suspended in space. All our world was empty and blue; there was no fixed point in it but the tropical sun, golden and warm, which burned our necks. Then the distant sail of the lonely raft drew us to it like a magnetic point on the horizon. We rowed back and crept on board with a feeling that we had come home again to our own world—on board and yet on firm, safe ground. And inside the bamboo cabin we found shade and the scent of bamboos and withered palm leaves. The sunny blue purity outside was now served to us in a suitably large dose through the open cabin wall. So we were accustomed to it and so it was good for a time, till the great clear blue tempted us out again.

It was most remarkable what a psychological effect the shaky bamboo cabin had on our minds. It measured eight by fourteen feet, and to diminish the pressure of wind and sea, it was built low so that we could not stand upright under the ridge of the roof. Walls and roof were made of strong bamboo canes, lashed together and guyed, and covered with a tough wickerwork of split bamboos. The green and yellow bars, with fringes of foliage hanging down from the roof, were restful to the eye as a white cabin wall never could have been, and, despite the fact that the bamboo wall on the starboard side was open for one third of its length and roof and walls let in sun and moon, this primitive lair gave us a greater feeling of security than white-painted bulkheads and closed portholes would have given in the same circumstances.

We tried to find an explanation for this curious fact and came to the following conclusion. Our consciousness was totally unaccustomed to associating a palm-covered bamboo dwelling with sea travel. There was no natural harmony between the great rolling ocean and the drafty palm hut which was floating about among the seas. Therefore, either the hut would seem entirely out of place in among the waves, or the waves would seem entirely out of place round the hut wall. So long as we kept on board, the bamboo hut and its jungle scent were plain reality, and the tossing seas seemed rather visionary. But from the rubber boat, waves and hut exchanged roles.

The fact that the balsa logs always rode the seas like a gull, and let the water right through aft if a wave broke on board, gave us an unshakable confidence in the dry part in the middle of the raft where the cabin was. The longer the voyage lasted, the safer we felt in our cozy lair, and we looked at the white-crested waves that danced past outside our doorway as if they were an impressive movie, conveying no menace to us at all. Even though the gaping wall was only five feet from the unprotected edge of the raft and only a foot and a half above the water line, yet we felt as if we had traveled many miles away from the sea and occupied a jungle dwelling remote from the sea's perils once we had crawled inside the door. There we could lie on our backs and look up at the curious roof which twisted about like boughs in the wind, enjoying the jungle smell of raw wood, bamboos, and withered palm leaves.

Sometimes, too, we went out in the rubber boat to look at ourselves by night. Coal-black seas towered up on all sides, and a glittering myriad of tropical stars drew a faint reflection from plankton in the water. The world was simple—stars in the darkness. Whether it was 1947 B.C. or A.D. suddenly became of no significance. We lived, and that we felt with alert intensity. We realized that life had been full for men before the technical age also—in fact, fuller and richer in many ways than the life of modern man. Time and evolution somehow ceased to exist; all that was real and that mattered were the same today as they had always been and would always be. We were swallowed up in the absolute common measure of history— endless unbroken darkness under a swarm of stars.

Before us in the night the *Kon-Tiki* rose out of the seas to
sink down again behind black masses of water that towered
between her and us. In the moonlight there was a fantastic
atmosphere about the raft. Stout, shining wooden logs fringed
with seaweed, the square pitch-black outline of a Viking sail, a
bristly bamboo hut with the yellow light of a paraffin lamp
aft—the whole suggested a picture from a fairy tale rather than
an actual reality. Now and then the raft disappeared completely behind the black seas; then she rose again and stood
out sharp in silhouette against the stars, while glittering water
poured from the logs.

When we saw the atmosphere about the solitary raft, we
could well see in our mind's eye the whole flotilla of such vessels, spread in fan formation beyond the horizon to increase
the chances of finding land, when the first men made their
way across this sea. The Inca Tupak Yupanqui, who had
brought under his rule both Peru and Ecuador, sailed across
the sea with an armada of many thousand men on balsa rafts,
just before the Spaniards came, to search for islands which
rumor had told of out in the Pacific. He found two islands,
which some think were the Galapagos, and after eight
months' absence he and his numerous paddlers succeeded in
toiling their way back to Ecuador. Kon-Tiki and his followers
had certainly sailed in a similar formation several hundred
years before, but, having discovered the Polynesian islands,
they had no reason for trying to struggle back.

When we jumped on board the raft again, we often sat
down in a circle round the paraffin lamp on the bamboo deck
and talked of the seafarers from Peru who had had all these
same experiences fifteen hundred years before us. The lamp
flung huge shadows of bearded men on the sail, and we
thought of the white men with the beards from Peru whom
we could follow in mythology and architecture all the way

from Mexico to Central America and into the northwestern area of South America as far as Peru. Here this mysterious civilization disappeared, as by the stroke of a magic wand, before the coming of the Incas and reappeared just as suddenly out on the solitary islands in the west which we were now approaching. Were the wandering teachers men of an early civilized race from across the Atlantic, who in times long past, in the same simple manner, had come over with the westerly ocean current and the trade wind from the area of the Canary Islands to the Gulf of Mexico? That was indeed a far shorter distance than the one we were covering, and we no longer believed in the sea as a completely isolating factor.

Many observers have maintained, for weighty reasons, that the great Indian civilizations, from the Aztecs in Mexico to the Incas in Peru, were inspired by sporadic intruders from over the seas in the east, while all the American Indians in general are Asiatic hunting and fishing peoples who in the course of twenty thousand years or more trickled into America from Siberia. It is certainly striking that there is not a trace of gradual development in the high civilizations which once stretched from Mexico to Peru. The deeper the archaeologists dig, the higher the culture, until a definite point is reached at which the old civilizations have clearly arisen without any foundation in the midst of primitive cultures.

And the civilizations have arisen where the current comes in from the Atlantic, in the midst of the desert and jungle regions of Central and South America, instead of in the more temperate regions where civilizations, in both old and modern times, have had easier conditions for their development.

The same cultural distribution is seen in the South Sea islands. It is the island nearest to Peru, Easter Island, which bears the deepest traces of civilization, although the insignifi-

cant little island is dry and barren and is the farthest from Asia
of all the islands in the Pacific.

When we had completed half our voyage, we had sailed
just the distance from Peru to Easter Island and had the legendary island due south of us. We had left land at a chance
point in the middle of the coast of Peru to imitate an average
raft putting to sea. If we had left the land farther south, nearer
Kon-Tiki's ruined city Tiahuanaco, we should have got the
same wind but a weaker current, both of which would have
carried us in the direction of Easter Island.

When we passed 110° west, we were within the Polynesian
ocean area, inasmuch as the Polynesian Easter Island was
now nearer Peru than we were. We were on a line with the
first outpost of the South Sea islands, the center of the oldest
island civilization. And when at night our glowing road guide,
the sun, climbed down from the sky and disappeared beyond
the sea in the west with his whole spectrum of colors, the
gentle trade wind blew life into the stories of the strange mystery of Easter Island. While the night sky smothered all concept of time, we sat and talked and bearded giants' heads were
again thrown upon the sail.

But far down south, on Easter Island, stood yet larger
giants' heads cut in stone, with bearded chins and white
men's features, brooding over the secret of centuries.

Thus they stood when the first Europeans discovered the
island in 1722, and thus they had stood twenty-two Polynesian generations earlier, when, according to native tradition,
the present inhabitants landed in great canoes and exterminated all men among an earlier population found on the
island. The primitive newcomers had arrived from the islands
farther west, but the Easter Island traditions claim that the
earliest inhabitants, and the true discoverers of the island, had
come from a distant land *toward the rising sun*. There is no land

in this direction but South America. With the early extermination of the unknown local architects, the giant stone heads on Easter Island have become one of the foremost symbols of the insoluble mysteries of antiquity. Here and there on the slopes of the treeless island their huge figures have risen to the sky, stone colossi splendidly carved in the shape of men and set up as a single block as high as a normal building of three or four floors. How had the men of old been able to shape, transport, and erect such gigantic stone colossi? As if the problem was not big enough, they had further succeeded in balancing an extra giant block of red stone like a colossal wig on the top of several of the heads, thirty-six feet above the ground. What did it all mean, and what kind of mechanical knowledge had the vanished architects who had mastered problems great enough for the foremost engineers of today?

If we put all the pieces together, the mystery of Easter Island is perhaps not insoluble after all, seen against a background of raftsmen from Peru. The old civilization has left on this island traces which the tooth of time has not been able to destroy.

Easter Island is the top of an ancient extinct volcano. Paved roads laid down by the old civilized inhabitants lead to well-preserved landing places on the coast and show that the water level round the island was exactly the same then as it is today. This is no remains of a sunken continent but a tiny desolate island, which was as small and solitary when it was a vivid cultural center as it is today.

In the eastern corner of this wedge-shaped island lies one of the extinct craters of the Easter Island volcano, and down in the crater lies the sculptors' amazing quarry and workshop. It lies there exactly as the old artists and architects left it hundreds of years ago, when they fled in haste to the eastern extremity of the island where, according to tradition, there

was a furious battle which made the present Polynesians vic-
tors and rulers of the island, whereas all grown men among
the aboriginals were slain and burned in a ditch. The sudden
interruption of the artists' work gives a clear cross section of
an ordinary working day in the Easter Island crater. The
sculptors' stone axes, hard as flint, lie strewn about their
working places and show that this advanced people was as
ignorant of iron as Kon-Tiki's sculptors were when they were
driven in flight from Peru, leaving behind them similar gigantic stone statues on the Andes plateau. In both places the
quarry can be found where the legendary white people with
beards hewed blocks of stone thirty feet long or more right
out of the mountainside with the help of axes of still harder
stone. And in both places the gigantic blocks, weighing many
tons, were transported for many miles over rough ground
before being set up on end as enormous human figures, or
raised on top of one another to form mysterious terraces and
walls.

Many huge unfinished figures still lie where they were
begun, in their niches in the crater wall on Easter Island, and
show how the work was carried on in different stages. The
largest human figure, which was almost completed when the
builders had to flee, was sixty-six feet long; if it had been finished and set up, the head of this stone colossus would have
been level with the top of an eight-floor building. Every separate figure was hewn out of a single connected block of stone,
and the working niches for sculptors round the lying stone figures show that not many men were at work at the same time
on each figure. Lying on their backs with their arms bent and
their hands placed on their stomachs, exactly like the stone
colossi in South America, the Easter Island figures were completed in every minute detail before they were removed from
the workshop and transported to their destinations round about

on the island. In the last stage inside the quarry the giant was attached to the cliff side by only a narrow ridge under his back; then this too was hewn away, the giant meanwhile being supported by boulders.

Large quantities of these figures were just dragged down to the bottom of the crater and set up on the slope there. But a number of the largest colossi were transported up and over the wall of the crater, and for many miles round over difficult country, before being set up on a stone platform and having an extra stone colossus of red tuff placed on their heads. This transport in itself may appear to be a complete mystery, but we cannot deny that it took place or that the architects who disappeared from Peru left in the Andes Mountains stone colossi of equal size which show that they were absolute experts in this line. Even if the monoliths are largest and most numerous on Easter Island, and the sculptors there had acquired an individual style, the same vanished civilization erected similar giant statues in human shape on many of the other Pacific islands, but only on those nearest to America, and everywhere the monoliths were brought to their final site from out-of-the-way quarries. In the Marquesas, I heard legends of how the gigantic stones were maneuvered, and, as these corresponded exactly to the natives' stories of the transport of the stone pillars to the huge portal on Tongatabu, it can be assumed that the same people employed the same method with the columns on Easter Island.

The sculptors' work in the pit took a long time but required only a few experts. The work of transport each time a statue was completed was more quickly done but, on the other hand, required large numbers of men. Little Easter Island was then both rich in fish and thoroughly cultivated, with large plantations of Peruvian sweet potatoes, and experts believe that the island in its great days could have supported a population of seven or eight thousand. About a thousand men were quite enough to haul the huge statues up and over the steep crater wall, while five hundred were sufficient to drag them on further across the island.

Wearproof cables were plaited from bast and vegetable fibers, and, using wooden frames, the multitude dragged the stone colossus over logs and small boulders made slippery with taro roots. That old civilized peoples were masters in making ropes and cables is well known from the South Sea islands and still more from Peru, where the first Europeans found suspension bridges a hundred yards long laid across torrents and gorges by means of plaited cables as thick as a man's waist.

When the stone colossus had arrived at its chosen site and was to be set up on end, the next problem arose. The crowd built a temporary inclined plane of stone and sand and pulled the giant up the less steep side, legs first. When the statue reached the top, it shot over a sharp edge and slid straight down so that the footpiece landed in a ready-dug hole. As the complete inclined plane still stood there, rubbing against the back of the giant's head, they rolled up an extra cylinder of stone and placed it on the top of his head; then the whole temporary plane was removed. Ready-built inclined planes like this stand in several places on Easter Island, waiting for huge figures which have never come. The technique was admirable but in no way mysterious if we cease to underestimate the intelligence of men in ancient times and the amount of time and manpower which they had at their command.

But why did they make these statues? And why was it necessary to go off to another quarry four miles away from the crater workshop to find a special kind of red stone to place on the figure's head? Both in South America and in the Marquesas Islands the whole statue was often of this red stone, and the natives went great distances to get it. Red headdresses for persons of high rank were an important feature both in Polynesia and in Peru.

Let us see first whom the statues represented. When the first Europeans visited the island, they saw mysterious "white men" on shore and, in contrast to what is usual among peoples of this kind, they found men with long flowing beards, the descendants of women and children belonging to the first race on the island, who had been spared by the invaders. The natives themselves declared that some of their ancestors had been white, while others had been brown. They calculated precisely that the last-named had immigrated from elsewhere in Polynesia twenty-two generations before, while the first had come from eastward in large vessels as much as fifty-seven generations back (i.e., ca. 400–500 A.D.). The race which came from the east were given the name "long-ears," because they lengthened their ears artificially by hanging weights on the lobes so that they hung down to their shoulders. These were the mysterious "long-ears" who were killed when the "short-ears" came to the island, and all the stone figures on Easter Island had large ears hanging down to their shoulders, as the sculptors themselves had had.

Now the Inca legends in Peru say that the sun-king Kon-Tiki ruled over a white people with beards who were called by the Incas "big-ears," because they had their ears artificially lengthened so that they reached down to their shoulders. The Incas emphasized that it was Kon-Tiki's "big-ears" who had erected the abandoned giant statues in the Andes Mountains before they were exterminated or driven out by the Incas themselves in the battle on an island in Lake Titicaca.

To sum up: Kon-Tiki's white "big-ears" disappeared from Peru westward with ample experience of working on colossal stone statues, and Tiki's white "long-ears" came to Easter

Island from eastward skilled in exactly the same art, which they at once took up in full perfection so that not the smallest trace can be found on Easter Island of any development leading up to the masterpieces on the island.

There is often a greater resemblance between the great stone statues in South America and those on certain South Sea islands than there is between the monoliths on the different South Sea islands compared with one another. In the Marquesas Islands and Tahiti such statues were known under the generic name *Tiki*, and they represented ancestors honored in the islands' history who, after their death, had been ranked as gods. And therein undoubtedly may be found the explanation of the curious red stone caps on the Easter Island figures. At the time of the European explorations there existed on all the islands in Polynesia scattered individuals and whole families with reddish hair and fair skins, and the islanders themselves declared that it was these who were descended from the first white people on the islands. On certain islands religious festivals were held, the participators in which colored their skins white and their hair red to resemble their earliest ancestors. At annual ceremonies on Easter Island the chief person of the festival had all his hair cut off so that his head might be painted red. And the colossal red-stone caps on the giant statues on Easter Island were carved in the shape which was typical of the local hair style; they had a round knot on the top, just as the men had their hair tied in a little traditional topknot in the middle of the head.

The statues on Easter Island had long ears because the sculptors themselves had lengthened ears. They had specially chosen red stones as wigs because the sculptors themselves had reddish hair. They had their chins carved pointed and projecting, because the sculptors themselves grew beards. They had the typical physiognomy of the white race with a

straight and narrow nose and thin sharp lips, because the
sculptors themselves did not belong to the Indonesian race.
And when the statues had huge heads and tiny legs, with their
hands laid in position on their stomachs, it was because it was
just in this way the people were accustomed to make giant
statues in South America. The sole decoration of the Easter
Island figures is a belt which was always carved round the figure's stomach. The same symbolic belt is found on every
single statue in Kon-Tiki's ancient ruins by Lake Titicaca. It is
the legendary emblem of the sun-god, the rainbow belt. There
was a myth on the island of Mangareva according to which
the sun-god had taken off the rainbow which was his magic
belt and climbed down it from the sky on to Mangareva to
people the island with his white-skinned children. The sun
was once regarded as the oldest original ancestor in all these
islands, as well as in Peru.

We used to sit on deck under the starry sky and retell
Easter Island's strange history, even though our own raft was
carrying us straight into the heart of Polynesia so that we
should see nothing of that remote island but its name on the
map. But so full is Easter Island of traces from the east that
even its name can serve as a pointer.

"Easter Island" appears on the map because some chance
Dutchman "discovered" the island one Easter Sunday. And
we have forgotten that the natives themselves, who already
lived there, had more instructive and significant names for
their home. This island has no less than three names in Polynesian.

One name is Te-Pito-te-Henua, which means "navel of the
islands." This poetical name clearly places Easter Island in a
special position in regard to the other islands farther westward
and is the oldest designation for Easter Island according to the
Polynesians themselves. On the eastern side of the island,

near the traditional landing place of the first "long-ears," is a carefully tooled sphere of stone which is called the "golden navel" and is in turn regarded as the navel of Easter Island itself. When the poetical Polynesian ancestors carved the island navel on the east coast and selected the island nearest Peru as the navel of their myriad islands farther west, it had a symbolic meaning. And when we know that Polynesian tradition refers to the discovery of their islands as the "birth" of their islands, then it is more than suggested that Easter Island of all places was considered the "navel," symbolic of the islands' birthmark and as the connecting link with their original motherland.

Easter Island's second name is Rapa Nui, which means "Great Rapa," while Rapa Iti or "Little Rapa" is another island of the same size which lies a very long way west of Easter Island. Now it is the natural practice of all peoples to call their first home "Great——" while the next is called "New——" or "Little——" even if the places are of the same size. And on Little Rapa the natives have quite correctly maintained traditions that the first inhabitants of the island came from Great Rapa, Easter Island, to the eastward, nearest to America. This points directly to an original immigration from the east.

The third and last name of this key island is Mata-Kite-Rani, which means "the eye (which) looks (toward) heaven." At first glance this is puzzling, for the relatively low Easter Island does not look toward heaven any more than the other loftier islands—for example, Tahiti, the Marquesas, or Hawaii. But Rani, heaven, had a double meaning to the Polynesians. It was also their ancestors' original homeland, the holy land of the sun-god, Tiki's forsaken mountain kingdom. And it is very significant that they should have called just their easternmost island, of all the thousands of islands in the ocean, "the eye which looks toward heaven." It is all the more striking seeing that the kindred name Mata-Rani, which means in Polynesian "the eye of heaven," is an old Peruvian place name, that of a spot on the Pacific coast of Peru opposite Easter Island and right at the foot of Kon-Tiki's old ruined city in the Andes.

The fascination of Easter Island provided us with plenty of subjects of conversation as we sat on deck under the starry sky, feeling ourselves to be participators in the whole prehistoric adventure. We almost felt as if we had done nothing else since Tiki's days but sail about the seas under sun and stars searching for land.

We no longer had the same respect for waves and sea. We knew them and their relationship to us on the raft. Even the shark had become a part of the everyday picture; we knew it and its usual reactions. We no longer thought of the hand harpoon, and we did not even move away from the side of the raft, if a shark came up alongside. On the contrary, we were more likely to try and grasp its back fin as it glided unperturbed along the logs. This finally developed into a quite new form of sport—tug of war with shark without a line.

We began quite modestly. We caught all too easily more dolphins than we could eat. To keep a popular form of amusement going without wasting food, we hit on comic fishing without a hook for the mutual entertainment of the dolphins and ourselves. We fastened unused flying fish to a string and drew them over the surface of the water. The dolphins shot up to the surface and seized the fish, and then we tugged, each in our own direction, and had a fine circus performance, for if one dolphin let go, another came in its place. We had fun, and the dolphins got the fish in the end.

Then we started the same game with the sharks. We had either a bit of fish on the end of a rope or often a bag with scraps from dinner, which we let out on a line. Instead of turning on its back, the shark pushed its snout above the water and swam forward with jaws wide to swallow the morsel. We could not help pulling on the rope just as the shark was going to close its jaws again, and the cheated animal swam on with an unspeakably foolish, patient expression and opened its jaws again for the offal, which jumped out of its mouth every time it tried to swallow it. It ended by the shark's coming right up to the logs and jumping up like a begging dog for the food, which hung dangling in a bag above its nose. It was just like feeding a gaping hippopotamus in a zoological gardens, and one day at the end of July, after three months on board the raft, the following entry was made in the diary:

We made friends with the shark which followed us today. At dinner we fed it with scraps which we poured right down into its open jaws. It has the effect of a half fierce, half good-natured and friendly dog when it swims alongside us. It cannot be denied that sharks can seem quite pleasant so long as we do not get into their jaws ourselves. At least we find it amusing to have them about us, except when we are bathing.

One day a bamboo stick, with a bag of sharks' food tied to a string, was lying ready for use on the edge of the raft when a sea came and washed it overboard. The bamboo stick was already lying afloat a couple of hundred yards astern of the raft, when it suddenly rose upright in the water and came rushing after the raft by itself, as if it intended to put itself nicely back in its place again. When the fishing rod came swaying nearer us, we saw a ten-foot shark swimming right under it, while the bamboo stick stuck up out of the waves like a periscope. The shark had swallowed the food bag without biting off the line. The fishing rod soon overtook us, passed us quite quietly, and vanished ahead.

But, even if we gradually came to look upon the shark

with quite other eyes, our respect for the five or six rows of razor-sharp teeth which lay in ambush in the huge jaws never disappeared.

One day Knut had an involuntary swim in company with a shark. No one was ever allowed to swim away from the raft, both on account of the raft's drift and because of sharks. But one day it was extra quiet and we had just pulled on board such sharks as had been following us, so permission was given for a quick dip in the sea. Knut plunged in and had gone quite a long way before he came up to the surface to crawl back. At that moment we saw from the mast a shadow bigger than himself coming up behind him, deeper down. We shouted warnings as quietly as we could so as not to create a panic, and Knut heaved himself toward the side of the raft. But the shadow below belonged to a still better swimmer, which shot up from the depths and gained on Knut. They reached the raft at the same time. While Knut was clambering on board, a six-foot shark glided past right under his stomach and stopped beside the raft. We gave it a dainty dolphin's head to thank it for not having snapped.

Generally it is smell more than sight which excites the sharks' voracity. We have sat with our legs in the water to test them, and they have swum toward us till they were two or three feet away, only quietly to turn their tails toward us again. But, if the water was in the least bloodstained, as it was when we had been cleaning fish, the sharks' fins came to life and they would suddenly collect like bluebottles from a long way off. If we flung out shark's guts, they simply went mad and dashed about in a blind frenzy. They savagely devoured the liver of their own kind and then, if we put a foot into the sea, they came for it like rockets and even dug their teeth into the logs where the foot had been. The mood of a shark may vary immensely, the animal being completely at the mercy of its own emotions.

The last stage in our encounter with sharks was that we began to pull their tails. Pulling animals' tails is held to be an inferior form of sport, but that may be because no one has tried it on a shark. For it was, in truth, a lively form of sport.

To get hold of a shark by the tail we first had to give it a real tidbit. It was ready to stick its head high out of the water to get it. Usually it had its food served dangling in a bag. For, if one has fed a shark directly by hand once, it is no longer amusing. If one feeds dogs or tame bears by hand, they set their teeth into the meat and tear and worry it till they get a bit off or until they get the whole piece for themselves. But, if one holds out a large dolphin at a safe distance from the shark's head, the shark comes up and smacks his jaws together, and, without one's having felt the slightest tug, half the dolphin is suddenly gone and one is left sitting with a tail in one's hand. We had found it a hard job to cut the dolphin in two with knives, but in a fraction of a second the shark, moving its triangular saw teeth quickly sideways, had chopped off the backbone and everything else like a sausage machine.

When the shark turned quietly to go under again, its tail flickered up above the surface and was easy to grasp. The shark's skin was just like sandpaper to hold on to, and inside the upper point of its tail there was an indentation which might have been made solely to allow for a good grip. If we once got a firm grasp there, there was no chance of our grip's not holding. Then we had to give a jerk, before the shark could collect itself, and get as much as possible of the tail pulled in tight over the logs. For a second or two the shark realized nothing, but then it began to wriggle and struggle in a spiritless manner with the fore part of its body, for without the help of its tail a shark cannot get up any speed. The other fins are only apparatus for balancing and steering. After a few desperate jerks, during which we had to keep a tight hold of the tail, the surprised shark became quite crestfallen and apathetic, and, as the loose stomach began to sink down toward the head, the shark at last became completely paralyzed.

When the shark had become quiet and, as it were, hung stiff awaiting developments, it was time for us to haul in with all our might. We seldom got more than half the heavy fish up out of the water; then the shark too woke up and did the rest itself. With violent jerks it swung its head round and up on to the logs, and then we had to tug with all our might and jump well out of the way, and that pretty quickly, if we wanted to save our legs. For now the shark was in no kindly mood. Jerking itself round in great leaps, it thrashed at the bamboo wall, using its tail as a sledge hammer. Now it no longer spared its iron muscles. The huge jaws were opened wide, and the rows of teeth bit and snapped in the air for anything they could reach. It might happen that the war dance ended in the shark's more or less involuntarily tumbling overboard and disappearing for good after its shameful humiliation, but most often the shark flung itself about at random on the logs aft, till we got a running noose round the root of its tail or till it had ceased to gnash its devilish teeth forever.

The parrot was quite thrilled when we had a shark on deck. It came scurrying out of the bamboo cabin and climbed up the wall at frantic speed till it found itself a good, safe lookout post on the palm-leaf roof, and there it sat shaking its head or fluttered to and fro along the ridge, shrieking with excitement. It had at an early date become an excellent sailor and was always bubbling over with humor and laughter. We reckoned ourselves as seven on board—six of us and the green parrot. The crab Johannes had, after all, to reconcile itself to being regarded as a cold-blooded appendage. At night the parrot crept into its cage under the roof of the bamboo cabin, but in the daytime it strutted about the deck or hung on to guy ropes and stays and did the most fascinating acrobatic exercises.

At the start of the voyage we had turnbuckles on the stays of the mast but they wore the ropes, so we replaced them with ordinary running knots. When the stays stretched and grew slack from sun and wind, all hands had to turn to and brace up the mast, so that its mangrove wood, as heavy as iron, should not bump against and cut into the ropes till they fell down. While we were hauling and pulling, at the most critical moment the parrot began to call out with its cracked voice: "Haul! Haul! Ho, ho, ho, ho, ha ha ha!" And if it made us laugh, it laughed till it shook at its own cleverness and swung round and round on the stays.

At first the parrot was the bane of our radio operators. They might be sitting happily absorbed in the radio corner with their magic earphones on and perhaps in contact with a radio "ham" in Oklahoma. Then their earphones would suddenly go dead, and they could not get a sound however much they coaxed the wires and turned the knobs. The parrot had been busy and bitten off the wire of the aerial. This was specially tempting in the early days, when the wire was sent up with a little balloon. But one day the parrot became seriously ill. It sat in its cage and moped and touched no food for two days, while its droppings glittered with golden scraps of aerial. Then the radio operators repented of their angry words and the parrot of its misdeeds, and from that day Torstein and Knut were its chosen friends and the parrot would never sleep anywhere but in the radio corner. The parrot's mother tongue was Spanish when it first came on board; Bengt declared it took to talking Spanish with a Norwegian accent long before it began to imitate Torstein's favorite ejaculations in full-blooded Norwegian.

We enjoyed the parrot's humor and brilliant colors for two

months, till a big sea came on board from astern while it was on its way down the stay from the masthead. When we discovered that the parrot had gone overboard, it was too late. We did not see it. And the *Kon-Tiki* could not be turned or stopped; if anything went overboard from the raft, we had no chance of turning back for it—numerous experiences had shown that.

The loss of the parrot had a depressing effect on our spirits the first evening; we knew that exactly the same thing would happen to ourselves if we fell overboard on a solitary night watch. We tightened up on all the safety regulations, brought into use new lifelines for the night watch, and frightened one another out of believing that we were safe because things had gone well in the first two months. One careless step, one thoughtless movement, could send us where the green parrot had gone, even in broad daylight.

We had several times observed the large white shells of cuttlefish eggs, lying floating like ostrich eggs or white skulls on the blue swell. On one solitary occasion we saw a squid lying wriggling underneath. We observed the snow-white balls floating on a level with ourselves and thought at first that it would be an easy matter to row out in the dinghy and get them. We thought the same that time when the rope of the plankton net broke so that the cloth net was left behind alone, floating in our wake. Each time we launched the dinghy, with a rope attached, to row back and pick up the floating object. But we saw to our surprise that the wind and sea held the dinghy off and that the line from the *Kon-Tiki* had so violent a braking effect in the water that we could never row right back to a point we had already left. We might get within a few yards of what we wanted to pick up, but then the whole line was out and the *Kon-Tiki* was pulling us away westward. "Once overboard always overboard" was a lesson that was gradually branded into our consciousness on board. If we wanted to go with the rest, we must hang on till the *Kon-Tiki* ran her bow against land on the other side.

The parrot left a blank in the radio corner, but, when the tropical sun shone out over the Pacific next day, we soon became reconciled to his loss. We hauled in many sharks the next few days, and we constantly found black curved parrots' beaks, or so we thought, among tunnies' heads and other curiosities in the shark's belly. But on closer examination the black beaks always proved to belong to assimilated cuttlefish.

The two radio operators had had a tough job in their corner since the first day they came on board. The very first day, in the Humboldt Current, sea water trickled even from the battery cases so that they had to cover the sensitive radio corner with canvas to save what could be saved in the high seas. And then they had the problem of fitting a long enough aerial on the little raft. They tried to send the aerial up with a kite, but in a gust of wind the kite simply plunged down into a wave crest and disappeared. Then they tried to send it up with a balloon, but the tropical sun burned holes in the balloon so that it collapsed and sank into the sea. And then they had the trouble with the parrot. In addition to all this, we were a fortnight in the Humboldt Current before we came out of a dead zone of the Andes in which the short wave was as dumb and lifeless as the air in an empty soapbox.

But then one night the short wave suddenly broke through, and Torstein's call signal was heard by a chance radio amateur in Los Angeles who was sitting fiddling with his transmitter to establish contact with another amateur in Sweden. The man asked what kind of set we had, and, when he got a satisfactory answer to his question, he asked Torstein who he was and where he lived. When he heard that Torstein's abode was a bamboo cabin on a raft in the Pacific, there were several peculiar clickings until Torstein supplied more details. When the man on the air had pulled himself together, he told us that his name was Hal and his wife's name Anna and that she was Swedish by birth and would let our families know we were alive and well.

It was a strange thought for us that evening that a total stranger called Hal, a chance moving-picture operator far away among the swarming population of Los Angeles, was the only person in the world but ourselves who knew where we were and that we were well. From that night onward Hal, alias Harold Kempel, and his friend Frank Cuevas took it in turns to sit up every night and listen for signals from the raft, and Herman received grateful telegrams from the head of the U.S. Weather Bureau for his two daily code reports from an area for which there were extremely few reports and no statistics. Later Knut and Torstein established contact with other radio amateurs almost every night, and these passed on greetings to Norway through a radio "ham" named Egil Berg at Notodden.

When we were just a few days out in mid-ocean, there was too much salt water for the radio corner, and the station stopped working altogether. The operators stood on their heads day and night with screws and soldering irons, and all our distant radio fans thought the raft's days were ended. But then one night the signals LI 2 B burst out into the ether, and in a moment the radio corner was buzzing like a wasp's nest as several hundred American operators seized their keys simultaneously and replied to the call.

Indeed one always felt as if one were sitting down on a wasp's nest if one strayed into the radio operators' domain. It was damp with sea water, which forced its way up along the woodwork everywhere, and, even if there was a piece of raw rubber on the balsa log where the operator sat, one got electric shocks both in the hinder parts and in the fingertips if one touched the Morse key. And, if one of us outsiders tried to steal a pencil from the well-equipped corner, either his hair stood straight up on his head or he drew long sparks from the stump of the pencil. Only Torstein and Knut and the parrot could wriggle their way about in that corner unscathed, and we put up a sheet of cardboard to mark the danger zone for the rest of us.

Late one night Knut was sitting tinkering by lamplight in the radio corner when he suddenly shook me by the leg and said he had been talking to a fellow who lived just outside Oslo and was called Christian Amundsen. This was a bit of an amateur record, for the little short-wave transmitter on board the raft with its 13,990 kilocycles per second did not send out more than 6 watts, about the same strength as a small electric torch. This was August 2, and we had sailed more than sixty degrees round the earth, so that Oslo was at the opposite end of the globe. King Haakon was seventy-five years old the day after, and we sent him a message of congratulations direct from the raft; the day after that Christian was again audible and sent us a reply from the King, wishing us continued good luck and success on our voyage.

Another episode we remember as an unusual contrast to the rest of the life on the raft. We had two cameras on board, and Erik had with him a parcel of materials for developing photographs on the voyage, so that we could take duplicate snapshots of things that had not come out well. After the whale shark's visit he could contain himself no longer, and one evening he mixed the chemicals and water carefully in exact accordance with the instructions and developed two films. The negatives looked like long-distance photographs— nothing but obscure spots and wrinkles. The film was ruined. We telegraphed to our contacts for advice, but our message was picked up by a radio amateur near Hollywood. He telephoned a laboratory, and soon afterward he broke in and told us that our developer was too warm; we must not use water above 60° or the negative would be wrinkled.

We thanked him for his advice and ascertained that the very lowest temperature in our surroundings was that of the ocean current itself, which was nearly 80°. Now Herman was a refrigerating engineer, and I told him by way of a joke to get the temperature of the water down to 60°. He asked to have the use of the little bottle of carbonic acid belonging to the already inflated rubber dinghy, and after some hocus-pocus in a kettle covered with a sleeping bag and a woolen vest suddenly there was snow on Herman's stubbly beard, and he came in with a big lump of white ice in the kettle.

Erik developed afresh with splendid results.

Even though the ghost words carried through the air by short wave were an unknown luxury in Kon-Tiki's early days, the long ocean waves beneath us were the same as of old and they carried the balsa raft steadily westward as they did then, fifteen hundred years ago.

The weather became a little more unsettled, with scattered rain squalls, after we had entered the area nearer the South Sea islands and the trade wind had changed its direction. It had blown steadily and surely from the southeast until we were a good way over in the Equatorial Current; then it had veered round more and more toward due east. We reached our most northerly position on June 10 with latitude 6°19' south. We were then so close up to the Equator that it looked as if we should sail above even the most northerly islands of the Marquesas group and disappear completely in the sea without finding land. But then the trade wind swung round farther, from east to northeast, and drove us in a curve down toward the latitude of the world of islands.

It often happened that wind and sea remained unchanged for days on end, and then we clean forgot whose steering watch it was except at night, when the watch was alone on deck. For, if sea and wind were steady, the steering oar was lashed fast and the *Kon-Tiki* sail remained filled without our attending to it. Then the night watch could sit quietly in the cabin door and look at the stars. If the constellations changed their position in the sky, it was time for him to go out and see whether it was the steering oar or the wind that had shifted.

It was incredible how easy it was to steer by the stars when we had seen them marching across the vault of the sky for weeks on end. Indeed, there was not much else to look at at night. We knew where we could expect to see the different constellations night after night, and, when we came up toward the Equator, the Great Bear rose so clear of the horizon in the north that we were anxious lest we should catch a glimpse of the Pole Star, which appears when one comes from southward and crosses the Equator. But as the northeasterly trade wind set in, the Great Bear sank again.

The old Polynesians were great navigators. They took bearings by the sun by day and the stars by night. Their knowledge of the heavenly bodies was astonishing. They knew that the earth was round, and they had names for such abstruse conceptions as the Equator and the northern and southern tropics. In Hawaii they cut charts of the ocean on the shells of round bottle gourds, and on certain other islands they made detailed maps of plaited boughs to which shells were attached to mark the islands, while the twigs marked particular currents. The Polynesians knew five planets, which they called wandering stars, and distinguished them from the fixed stars, for which they had nearly two hundred different names. A good navigator in old Polynesia knew well in what part of the sky the different stars would rise and where they would be at different times of the night and at different times of the year. They knew which stars culminated over the different islands, and there were cases in which an island was named after a star which culminated over it night after night and year after year.

Apart from the fact that the starry sky lay like a glittering giant compass revolving from east to west, they understood that the different stars right over their heads always showed them how far north or south they were. When the Polynesians had explored and brought under their sway their present domain, which is the whole of the sea nearest to America, they maintained traffic between some of the islands for many generations to come. Historical traditions relate that, when the chiefs from Tahiti visited Hawaii, which lay more than 2,000 sea miles farther north and several degrees farther west, the helmsman steered first due north by sun and stars, till the stars right above their heads told them that they were on the latitude of Hawaii. Then they turned at a right angle and steered due west till they came so near that birds and clouds told them where the group of islands lay.

Whence had the Polynesians obtained their vast astronomical knowledge and their calendar, which was calculated with astonishing thoroughness? Certainly not from Melanesian or Malayan peoples to the westward. But the same old vanished civilized race, the "white and bearded men," who had taught Aztecs, Mayas, and Incas their amazing culture in America, had evolved a curiously similar calendar and a similar astronomical knowledge which Europe in those times could not match. In Polynesia, as in Peru, the calendar year had been so arranged as to begin on the particular day of the year when the constellation of the Pleiades first appeared above the horizon, and in both areas this constellation was considered the patron of agriculture.

In Peru, where the continent slopes down toward the Pacific, there stand to this day in the desert sand the ruins of an astronomical observatory of great antiquity, a relic of the same mysterious civilized people which carved stone colossi, erected pyramids, cultivated sweet potatoes and bottle gourds, and began their year with the rising of the Pleiades. Kon-Tiki knew the movement of the stars when he set sail upon the Pacific Ocean.

On July 2 our night watch could no longer sit in peace studying the night sky. We had a strong wind and nasty sea after several days of light northeasterly breeze. Late in the night we had brilliant moonlight and a quite fresh sailing wind. We measured our speed by counting the seconds we took to pass a chip, flung out ahead on one side of us, and found that we were establishing a speed record. While our average speed was from twelve to eighteen "chips," in the jargon current on board, we were now for a time down to "six chips," and the phosphorescence swirled in a regular wake astern of the raft.

Four men lay snoring in the bamboo cabin while Torstein sat clicking with the Morse key and I was on steering watch. Just before midnight I caught sight of a quite unusual sea which came breaking astern of us right across the whole of my disturbed field of vision. Behind it I could see here and there the foaming crests of two more huge seas like the first, following hard on its heels. If we ourselves had not just passed the place, I should have been convinced that what I saw was high surf flung up over a dangerous shoal. I gave a warning shout, as the first sea came like a long wall sweeping after us in the moonlight, and wrenched the raft into position to take what was coming.

When the first sea reached us, the raft flung her stern up sideways and rose up over the wave back which had just broken, so that it hissed and boiled all along the crest. We rode through the welter of boiling foam which poured along both sides of the raft, while the heavy sea itself rolled by under us. The bow flung itself up last as the wave passed, and we slid, stern first, down into a broad trough of the waves. Immediately after, the next wall of water came on and rose up, while we were again lifted hurriedly into the air and the clear water masses broke over us aft as we shot over the edge. As a result the raft was flung right broadside on to the seas, and it was impossible to wrench her round quickly enough.

The next sea came on and rose out of the stripes of foam like a glittering wall which began to fall along its upper edge just as it reached us. When it plunged down, I saw nothing else to do but hang on as tight as I could to a projecting bamboo pole of the cabin roof; there I held my breath while I felt that we were flung sky-high and everything round me carried away in roaring whirlpools of foam. In a second we and the *Kon-Tiki* were above water again and gliding quietly down a gentle wave back on the other side. Then the seas were normal again. The three great wave walls raced on before us, and astern in the moonlight a string of coconuts lay bobbing in the water.

The last wave had given the cabin a violent blow, so that Torstein was flung head over heels into the radio corner and the others woke, scared by the noise, while the water gushed up between the logs and in through the wall. On the port side of the foredeck the bamboo wickerwork was blown open like a small crater, and the diving basket had been knocked flat up in the bow, but everything else was as it had been. Where the three big seas came from, we have never been able to explain with certainty, unless they were due to disturbances on the sea bottom, which are not so uncommon in these regions.

Two days later we had our first storm. It started by the

trade wind dying away completely, and the feathery white trade-wind clouds, which were drifting over our heads up in the topmost blue, being suddenly invaded by a thick black cloud bank which rolled up over the horizon from southward. Then there came gusts of wind from the most unexpected directions, so that it was impossible for the steering watch to keep control. As quickly as we got our stern turned to the new direction of the wind, so that the sail bellied out stiff and safe, just as quickly the gusts came at us from another quarter, squeezed the proud bulge out of the sail, and made it swing round and thrash about to the peril of both crew and cargo. But then the wind suddenly set in to blow straight from the quarter whence the bad weather came, and, as the black clouds rolled over us, the breeze increased to a fresh wind which worked itself up into a real storm.

In the course of an incredibly short time the seas round about us were flung up to a height of fifteen feet, while single crests were hissing twenty and twenty-five feet above the trough of the sea, so that we had them on a level with our masthead when we ourselves were down in the trough. All hands had to scramble about on deck bent double, while the wind shook the bamboo wall and whistled and howled in all the rigging.

To protect the radio corner we stretched canvas over the rear wall and port side of the cabin. All loose cargo was lashed securely, and the sail was hauled down and made fast around the bamboo yard. When the sky clouded over, the sea grew dark and threatening, and in every direction it was white-crested with breaking waves. Long tracks of dead foam lay like stripes to windward down the backs of the long seas; and everywhere, where the wave ridges had broken and plunged down, green patches like wounds lay frothing for a long time in the blue-black sea. The crests blew away as they broke, and the spray stood like salt rain over the sea. When the tropical rain poured over us in horizontal squalls and whipped the surface of the sea, invisible all round us, the water that ran from our hair and beards tasted brackish, while we crawled about the deck naked and frozen, seeing that all the gear was in order to weather the storm.

When the storm rushed up over the horizon and gathered about us for the first time, strained anticipation and anxiety were discernible in our looks. But when it was upon us in earnest, and the *Kon-Tiki* took everything that came her way with ease and buoyancy, the storm became an exciting form of sport, and we all delighted in the fury round about us which the balsa raft mastered so adroitly, always seeing that she herself lay on the wave tops like a cork, while all the main weight of the raging water was always a few inches beneath. The sea had much in common with the mountains in such weather. It was like being out in the wilds in a storm, up on the highest mountain plateaus, naked and gray. Even though we were right in the heart of the tropics, when the raft glided up and down over the smoking waste of sea, we always thought of racing downhill among snowdrifts and rock faces.

The steering watch had to keep its eyes open in such weather. When the steepest seas passed under the forward half of the raft, the logs aft rose right out of the water, but the next second they plunged down again to climb up over the next crest. Each time the seas came so close upon one another that the hindmost reached us while the first was still holding the bow in the air. Then the solid sheets of water thundered in over the steering watch in a terrifying welter, but next second the stern went up and the flood disappeared as through the prongs of a fork.

We calculated that in an ordinary calm sea, where there were usually seven seconds between the highest waves, we took in about two hundred tons of water astern in twenty-four

hours. But we hardly noticed it because it just flowed in quietly round the bare legs of the steering watch and as quietly
disappeared again between the logs. But in a heavy storm
more than ten thousand tons of water poured on board astern
in the course of twenty-four hours, seeing that loads varying
from a few gallons to two or three cubic yards, and occasionally much more, flowed on board every five seconds. It sometimes broke on board with a deafening thunderclap, so that
the helmsman stood in water up to his waist and felt as if he
were forcing his way against the current in a swift river. The
raft seemed to stand trembling for a moment, but then the cruel
load that weighed her down astern disappeared overboard
again in great cascades.

Herman was out all the time with his anemometer measuring the squalls of gale force, which lasted for twenty-four
hours. Then they gradually dropped to a stiff breeze with
scattered rain squalls, which continued to keep the seas boiling round us as we tumbled on westward with a good sailing
wind. To obtain accurate wind measurements down among
the towering seas Herman had to make, whenever possible,
his way up to the swaying masthead, where it was all he could
do to hold on.

When the weather moderated, it was as though the big fish
around us had become completely infuriated. The water
round the raft was full of sharks, tunnies, dolphins, and a few
dazed bonitos, all wriggling about close under the timber of
the raft and in the waves nearest to it. It was a ceaseless life-
and-death struggle; the backs of big fishes arched themselves
over the water and shot off like rockets, one chasing another
in pairs, while the water round the raft was repeatedly tinged
with thick blood. The combatants were mainly tunnies and
dolphins, and the dolphins came in big shoals which moved
much more quickly and alertly than usual. The tunnies were

the assailants; often a fish of 150 to 200 pounds would leap high into the air holding a dolphin's bloody head in its mouth. But, even if individual dolphins dashed off with tunnies hard on their heels, the actual shoal of dolphins did not give ground, although there were often several wriggling round with big gaping wounds in their necks. Now and again the sharks, too, seemed to become blind with rage, and we saw them catch and fight with big tunnies, which met in the shark a superior enemy.

Not one single peaceful little pilot fish was to be seen. They had been devoured by the furious tunnies, or they had hidden in the chinks under the raft or fled far away from the battlefield. We dared not put our heads down into the water to see.

I had a nasty shock—and could not help laughing afterward at my own complete bewilderment—when I was aft, obeying a call of nature. We were accustomed to a bit of a swell in the water closet, but it seemed contrary to all reasonable probabilities when I quite unexpectedly received a violent punch astern from something large and cold and very heavy, which came butting up against me like a shark's head in the sea. I was actually on my way up the mast stay, with a feeling that I had a shark hanging on to my hindquarters, before I collected myself. Herman, who was hanging over the steering oar doubled up with laughter, was able to tell me that a huge tunny had delivered a sideways smack at my nakedness with his 160 pounds or so of cold fish. Afterward, when Herman and then Torstein were on watch, the same fish tried to jump on board with the seas from astern, and twice the big fellow was right up on the end of the logs, but each time it flung itself overboard again before we could get a grip of the slippery body.

After that a stout bewildered bonito came right on board

with a sea, and with that, and a tunny caught the day before, we decided to fish, to bring order into the sanguinary chaos that surrounded us.

Our diary says:

A six-foot shark was hooked first and hauled on board. As soon as the hook was out again, it was swallowed by an eight-foot shark, and we hauled that on board. When the hook came out again, we got a fresh six-foot shark and had hauled it over the edge of the raft when it broke loose and dived. The hook went out again at once, and an eight-foot shark came on to it and gave us a hard tussle. We had its head over the logs when all four steel lines were cut through and the shark dived into the depths. New hook out, and a seven-foot shark was hauled on board. It was now dangerous to stand on the slippery logs aft fishing, because the three sharks kept on throwing up their heads and snapping, long after one would have thought they were dead. We dragged the sharks forward by the tail into a heap on the foredeck, and soon afterward a big tunny was hooked and gave us more of a fight than any shark before we got it on board. It was so fat and heavy that none of us could lift it by the tail.

The sea was just as full of furious fish backs. Another shark was hooked but broke away just when it was being pulled on board. But then we got a six-foot shark safely on board. After that a five-foot shark, which also came on board. Then we caught yet another six-foot shark and hauled it up. When the hook came out again, we hauled in a seven-foot shark.

Wherever we walked on deck, there were big sharks lying in the way, beating their tails convulsively on the deck or thrashing against the bamboo cabin as they snapped around them. Already tired and worn out when we began to fish after the storm, we became completely befuddled as to which sharks were quite dead, which were still snapping convulsively if we went near them, and which were quite alive and were lying in ambush for us with their green cat's eyes. When we had nine big sharks lying round us in every direction, we were so weary of hauling on heavy lines and fighting with the twisting and snapping giants that we gave up after five hours' toil.

Next day there were fewer dolphins and tunnies but just as many sharks. We began to fish and haul them in again but soon stopped when we perceived that all the fresh shark's blood that ran off the raft only attracted still more sharks. We threw all the dead sharks overboard and washed the whole deck clean of blood. The bamboo mats were torn by shark teeth and rough sharkskin, and we threw the bloodiest and most torn of them overboard and replaced them with new golden-yellow bamboo mats, several layers of which were lashed fast on the foredeck.

When we turned in on these evenings in our mind's eye we saw greedy, open shark jaws and blood. And the smell of shark meat stuck in our nostrils. We could eat shark—it tasted like haddock if we got the ammoniac out of the pieces by putting them in sea water for twenty-four hours—but bonito and tunny were infinitely better.

That evening, for the first time, I heard one of the fellows say that it would soon be pleasant to be able to stretch oneself out comfortably on the green grass on a palm island; he would be glad to see something other than cold fish and rough sea.

The weather had become quite quiet again, but it was never as constant and dependable as before. Incalculable, violent gusts of wind from time to time brought with them heavy showers, which we were glad to see because a large part of our water supply had begun to go bad and tasted like evil-smelling marsh water. When it was pouring the hardest, we collected water from the cabin roof and stood on deck naked, thoroughly to enjoy the luxury of having the salt washed off with fresh water.

The pilot fish were wriggling along again in their usual places, but whether they were the same old ones which had returned after the blood bath, or whether they were new followers taken over in the heat of the battle, we could not say.

On July 21 the wind suddenly died away again. It was oppressive and absolutely still, and we knew from previous experience what this might mean. And, right enough, after a few violent gusts from east and west and south, the wind freshened up to a breeze from southward, where black, threatening clouds had again rushed up over the horizon. Herman was out with his anemometer all the time, measuring already fifty feet and more per second, when suddenly Torstein's sleeping bag went overboard. And what happened in the next few seconds took a much shorter time than it takes to tell it.

Herman tried to catch the bag as it went, took a rash step, and fell overboard. We heard a faint cry for help amid the noise of the waves, and saw Herman's head and a waving arm as well as some vague green object twirling about in the water near him. He was struggling for life to get back to the raft through the high seas which had lifted him out from the port side. Torstein, who was at the steering oar aft, and I myself, up in the bow, were the first to perceive him, and we went cold with fear. We bellowed "Man overboard!" at the top of our lungs as we rushed to the nearest life-saving gear. The others had not heard Herman's cry because of the noise of the sea, but in a trice there was life and bustle on deck. Herman was an excellent swimmer, and, though we realized at once that his life was at stake, we had a fair hope that he would manage to crawl back to the edge of the raft before it was too late.

Torstein, who was nearest, seized the bamboo drum round which was the line we used for the lifeboat, for this was within his reach. It was the only time on the whole voyage that this line got caught up. Herman was now on a level with the stern of the raft but a few yards away, and his last hope was to crawl to the blade of the steering oar and hang on to it. As he missed the end of the logs, he reached out for the oar blade, but it slipped away from him. And there he lay, just where experience had shown we could get nothing back. While Bengt and I launched the dinghy, Knut and Erik threw out the life belt. Carrying a long line, it hung ready for use on the corner of the cabin roof, but today the wind was so strong that when it was thrown it was simply blown back to the raft. After a few unsuccessful throws Herman was already far astern of the steering oar, swimming desperately to keep up with the raft, while the distance increased with each gust of wind. He realized that henceforth the gap would simply go on increasing, but he set a faint hope on the dinghy which we had now got into the water. Without the line, which acted as a brake, it would perhaps be possible to drive the rubber raft to meet the swimming man, but whether the rubber raft would ever get back to the *Kon-Tiki* was another matter. Nevertheless, three men in a rubber dinghy had some chance; one man in the sea had none.

Then we suddenly saw Knut take off and plunge headfirst into the sea. He had the life belt in one hand and was heaving himself along. Every time Herman's head appeared on a wave back Knut was gone, and every time Knut came up Herman was not there. But then we saw both heads at once; they had swum to meet each other and both were hanging on to the life belt. Knut waved his arm, and, as the rubber raft had meanwhile been hauled on board, all four of us took hold of the line of the life belt and hauled for dear life, with our eyes fixed on the great dark object which was visible just behind the two men. This same mysterious beast in the water was pushing a big greenish-black triangle up above the wave crests; it almost gave Knut a shock when he was on his way over to Herman. Only Herman knew then that the triangle did not belong to a shark or any other sea monster. It was an inflated corner of Torstein's watertight sleeping bag. But the sleeping bag did not remain floating for long after we had hauled the two men safe and sound on board. Whatever dragged the sleeping bag down into the depths had just missed a better prey.

"Glad I wasn't in it," said Torstein and took hold of the steering oar where he had let it go.

But otherwise there were not many wisecracks that evening. We all felt a chill running through nerve and bone for a long time afterward. But the cold shivers were mingled with a warm thankfulness that there were still six of us on board.

We had a lot of nice things to say to Knut that day— Herman and the rest of us, too.

But there was not much time to think about what had already happened, for as the sky grew black over our heads the gusts of wind increased in strength, and before night a new storm was upon us. We finally got the life belt to hang astern of the raft on a long line, so that we had something behind the steering oar toward which to swim if one of us should fall overboard again in a squall. Then it grew pitch dark around us as night fell and hid the raft and the sea. Bouncing wildly up and down in the darkness, we only heard and felt the gale howling in masts and guy ropes, while the gusts pressed with smashing force against the springy bamboo cabin till we thought it would fly overboard. But it was covered with canvas and well guyed. And we felt the *Kon-Tiki* tossing with the foaming seas, while the logs moved up and down with the movement of the waves like the keys of an instrument. We were astonished that cascades of water did not gush up through the wide chinks in the floor, but they only acted as a regular bellows through which damp air rushed up and down.

For five whole days the weather varied between full storm and light gale; the sea was dug up into wide valleys filled with the smoke from foaming gray-blue seas, which seemed to have their backs pressed out long and flat under the onset of the wind. Then on the fifth day the heavens split to show a glimpse of blue, and the malignant black cloud cover gave place to the ever victorious blue sky as the storm passed on. We had come through the gale with the steering oar smashed and the sail rent; the centerboards hung loose and banged about like crowbars among the logs, because all the ropes which had tightened them up underwater were worn through. But we ourselves and the cargo were completely undamaged.

After the two storms the *Kon-Tiki* had become a good deal weaker in the joints. The strain of working over the steep wave backs had stretched all the ropes, and the continuously working logs had made the ropes eat into the balsa wood. We thanked Providence that we had followed the Incas' custom and had not used wire ropes, which would simply have sawed the whole raft into matchwood in the gale. And, if we had used bone-dry, high-floating balsa at the start, the raft would long ago have sunk into the sea under us, saturated with sea water. It was the sap in the fresh logs which served as an impregnation and prevented the water from filtering in through the porous balsa wood.

But now the ropes had become so loose that it was dangerous to let one's foot slip down between two logs, for it could be crushed when they came together violently. Forward and aft, where there was no bamboo deck, we had to give at the knees when we stood with our feet wide apart on two logs at the same time. The logs aft were as slippery as banana leaves with wet seaweed, and, even though we had made a regular path through the greenery where we usually walked and had laid down a broad plank for the steering watch to stand on, it was not easy to keep one's foothold when a sea struck the raft. On the port side one of the nine giants bumped and banged against the crossbeams with dull, wet thuds both by night and by day. There came also new and fearful creakings from the ropes which held the two sloping masts together at the mast-head, for the steps of the masts worked about independently of each other, because they rested on two different logs.

We got the steering oar spliced and lashed with long billets of mangrove wood, as hard as iron, and with Erik and Bengt as sailmakers Kon-Tiki soon raised his head again and swelled his breast in a stiff bulge toward Polynesia, while the steering oar danced behind in seas which the fine weather had made soft and gentle. But the centerboards never again became quite what they had been; they did not meet the pressure of the water with their full strength but gave way and hung, dangling loose and unguyed, under the raft. It was useless to try to inspect the ropes on the underside, for they were completely overgrown with seaweed. On taking up the whole bamboo deck we found only three of the main ropes broken; they had been lying crooked and pressed against the cargo, which had worn them away. It was evident that the logs had absorbed a great weight of water but, since the cargo had been lightened, this was roughly canceled out. Most of our provisions and drinking water were already used up, likewise the radio operators' dry batteries.

Nevertheless, after the last storm it was clear enough that we should both float and hold together for the short distance that separated us from the islands ahead. Now quite another problem came into the foreground—how would the voyage end?

The *Kon-Tiki* would slog on inexorably westward until she ran her bow into a solid rock or some other fixed object which would stop her drifting. But our voyage would not be ended until all hands had landed safe and sound on one of the numerous Polynesian islands ahead.

When we came through the last storm, it was quite uncertain where the raft would end up. We were at an equal distance from the Marquesas Islands and the Tuamotu group, and in a position which meant that we could very easily pass right between the two groups of islands without having a glimpse of one of them. The nearest island in the Marquesas group lay three hundred sea miles northwest, and the nearest island in the Tuamotu group lay three hundred sea miles southwest, while wind and current were uncertain, with their general direction westerly and toward the wide ocean gap between the two island groups.

The island which lay nearest to the northwest was no other than Fatu Hiva, the little jungle-clad mountainous island where I had lived in a hut built on piles on the beach and heard the old man's vivid stories of the ancestral hero Tiki. If the *Kon-Tiki* stood in to that same beach, I should meet many acquaintances, but hardly the old man himself. He must have departed long ago, with a fair hope of meeting the real Tiki again. If the raft headed in toward the mountain ranges of the Marquesas group, I knew the few islands in the group were a long way apart and the sea thundered unchecked against perpendicular cliffs where we should have to keep our eyes open while steering for the mouths of the few valleys, which always ended in narrow strips of beach.

If, on the contrary, she headed down toward the coral reefs

of the Tuamotu group, there the numerous islands lay close together and covered a wide space of sea. But this group of islands is also known as the Low or Dangerous Archipelago, because the whole formation has been built up entirely by coral polyps and consists of treacherous submerged reefs and palm-clad atolls which rise only six or ten feet above the surface of the sea. Dangerous ring-shaped reefs fling themselves protectingly round every single atoll and are a menace to shipping throughout the area. But, even if coral polyps built the Tuamotu atolls while the Marquesas Islands are remains of extinct volcanoes, both groups are inhabited by the same Polynesian race, and the royal families in both regard Tiki as their primeval ancestor.

As early as July 3, when we were still 1,000 sea miles from Polynesia, Nature herself was able to tell us, as she was able to tell the primitive raftsmen from Peru in their time, that there really was land ahead somewhere out in the sea. Until we were a good thousand sea miles out from the coast of Peru we had noted small flocks of frigate birds. They disappeared at about 100° west, and after that we saw only small petrels which have their home on the sea. But on July 3 the frigate birds reappeared, at 125° west, and from now onward small flocks of frigate birds were often to be seen, either high up in the sky or shooting down over the wave crests, where they snapped up flying fish which had taken to the air to escape from dolphins. As these birds did not come from America astern of us, they must have their homes in another country ahead.

On July 16 Nature betrayed herself still more obviously. On that day we hauled up a nine-foot shark, which threw up from its stomach a large undigested starfish which it had recently brought from some coast out here in the ocean.

And the very next day we had the first definite visitor straight from the islands of Polynesia.

It was a great moment on board when two large boobies were spotted above the horizon to westward and soon afterward came sailing in over our mast, flying low. With a wing-spread of five feet they circled round us many times, then folded their wings and settled on the sea alongside us. Dolphins rushed to the spot at once and wriggled inquisitively round the great swimming birds, but neither party touched the other. These were the first living messengers that came to bid us welcome to Polynesia. They did not go back in the evening but rested on the sea, and after midnight we still heard them flying in circles round the mast, uttering hoarse cries.

The flying fish which came on board were now of another and much larger species; I recognized them from fishing trips I had taken with the natives along the coast of Fatu Hiva.

For three days and nights we made straight toward Fatu Hiva, but then a strong northeast wind came on and sent us down in the direction of the Tuamotu atolls. We were now blown out of the real South Equatorial Current, and the ocean currents were no longer behaving dependably. One day they were there; another day they were gone. The currents could run like invisible rivers branching out all over the sea. If the current was swift, there was usually more swell and the temperature of the water usually fell one degree. It showed its direction and strength every day by the difference between Erik's calculated and his measured position.

On the threshold of Polynesia the wind said "Pass," having handed us over to a weak branch of the current which, to our alarm, had its course in the direction of the Antarctic. The wind did not become absolutely still—we never experienced that throughout the voyage—and when it was feeble we hoisted every rag we had to collect what little there was. There was not one day on which we moved backward toward America; and our smallest distance in twenty-four hours was 9 sea miles, while our average run for the voyage as a whole was 42½ sea miles in twenty-four hours.

The trade wind, after all, had not the heart to fail us right in the last lap. It reported for duty again and pushed and shoved at the ramshackle craft which was preparing her entry into a new and strange part of the world.

With each day that passed, larger flocks of sea birds came and circled over us aimlessly in all directions. One evening, when the sun was about to sink into the sea, we noticed that the birds had received a violent impetus. They were flying away in a westerly direction without paying any attention to us or the flying fish beneath them. From the masthead we could see that, as they came over, they all flew straight on on exactly the same course. Perhaps they saw something from up above which we did not see. Perhaps they were flying by instinct. In any case they were flying with a plan, straight home to the nearest island, their breeding place.

We twisted the steering oar and set our course exactly in the direction in which the birds had disappeared. Even after it was dark, we heard the cries of stragglers flying over us against the starry sky on exactly the same course as that which we were now following. It was a wonderful night; the moon was nearly full for the third time in the course of the *Kon-Tiki*'s voyage.

Next day there were still more birds over us, but we did not need to wait for them to show us our way again in the evening. This time we had detected a curious stationary cloud above the horizon. The other clouds were small feathery wisps of wool which came up in the south and passed across the vault of the sky with the trade wind till they disappeared over the horizon in the west. So I had once come to know the drifting trade-wind clouds on Fatu Hiva, and so we had seen them over us night and day on board the *Kon-Tiki*. But the lonely cloud on the horizon to the southwest did not move; it just rose like a motionless column of smoke while the trade-wind clouds drifted by. The Polynesians knew land lay under such clouds. For, when the tropical sun bakes the hot sand, a stream of warm air is created which rises up and causes its vapor content to condense up in the colder strata of air.

We steered on the cloud till it disappeared after sunset. The wind was steady, and with the steering oar lashed tight the *Kon-Tiki* kept to her course unaided. The steering watch's job was now to sit on the plank at the masthead, shiny with wear, and keep a lookout for anything that indicated land.

There was a deafening screaming of birds over us all that night. And the moon was nearly full.

—Translated by F. H. Lyon

Postscript: After a hundred and one days at sea, Thor Heyerdahl and his crew crashed into a reef at Raroia in the Tuamotu Islands, proving that prehistoric peoples could indeed have traveled from South America to Polynesia. His account of the journey was translated in over forty languages, and the film documentary was presented with an Academy Award in 1952.

The treacherous waters of the Southern Ocean between Antarctica and South America are considered by most sailors to be the ultima Thule of conditions. And the Vendée Globe solo nonstop round-the-world race is considered by many to be the most extreme of extreme sports. Derek Lundy masterfully recounts the drama of the 1996–97 race, and it is a captivating story of rescue—and of disappearance.

GODFORSAKEN SEA

Racing the World's Most Dangerous Waters

DEREK LUNDY

Until Christmas Day 1996, the race had been a typically robust version of previous Vendée Globe and BOC races. If anything, it had been easier on the competitors than most of the earlier events. None of the collisions with flotsam or ice in this Vendée Globe had put the sailors' lives on the line. It was true that the Southern Ocean had behaved as usual—its chain of low-pressure systems moving relentlessly along the racers' path. Storm- and often hurricane-force wind had piled waves up to heights of fifty or sixty feet. At times, the boats had surfed down wave faces at thirty knots, almost out of control. They had struggled through the dangerous and chaotic cross-seas that followed quick changes in wind direction and had been

knocked down often. For several weeks, the skippers endured
this trial by wind and cold, ice and breaking waves, skirting
the edge of catastrophe as they threaded their way through the
great wilderness of the southern seas.

True, it was still a long way to Cape Horn. The greater
extent of the Southern Ocean still lay ahead for most of the
boats. There was a lot of time left for something to happen. At
some point in every one of these races, most often in the
Southern Ocean, a sailor's life becomes problematic, hangs by
a thread. Sometimes, a life is snuffed out: by inference at first,
as contact is suddenly ended; later with certainty, as enough
silent time goes by or the searchers find a boat, drifting and
unmanned. Some names: Jacques de Roux (1986), Mike Plant
(1992), Nigel Burgess (1992), Harry Mitchell (1995)—a few of
the ones who have been wiped off the planet. Who knew
exactly how? What were the circumstances? An unendurable
rogue wave capsizing the boat? Ice? Or a sudden, treacherous
slip over the side and into the sea, followed by a final minute
or two treading the frigid water, watching the boat (with
acceptance? anger? terror?) intermittently visible on the wave
crests, surfing farther and farther away, its autopilot functioning perfectly.

There hadn't been any of that yet in this Vendée Globe. But
the dragons were certainly there. The "quakin' and shakin'"
was about to begin. During the twelve days of Christmas, the
race changed utterly.

The strength of the storm was a surprise. Catherine Chabaud,
sailing four hundred miles behind Raphaël Dinelli, was getting the weather first as it swept from west to east. She radioed
to him and the other sailors ahead of her a description of the
strength and direction of the wind in the low-pressure systems
that overtook her, one after the other. This time—seven weeks

into the race, just before Christmas—she advised Dinelli to expect a low during the night, with the usual quick wind rotation from northwest to southwest, blowing at around forty to forty-five knots, as the cold front crossed over. It was nothing special—a typical Southern Ocean low of moderate intensity.

What happened instead was unusual and terrifying.

As the low-pressure system began its pass over Dinelli, a warmer high-pressure air mass crowded down from the north. The two systems squeezed together. The cold air of the low slid in under the warmer air of the high and pushed it up. The air already blowing into the center of the low increased in velocity, shooting up and spiraling out higher in the atmosphere. As more air was displaced from the sea's surface, the air pressure there dropped even further. Wind is the flow of air from areas of high to low pressure down the pressure slope, or gradient. It's exactly the same process as water flowing from higher to lower elevations. The steeper the slope, the faster the air moves, and the stronger the wind. As the low approached, its pressure gradient grew ominously steeper.

When the system overtook Dinelli's position, the wind increased until it was blowing close to hurricane strength—sixty-four knots and over—and gusting to eighty knots. It quickly whipped up the constant swell of the Southern Ocean into huge seas. Dinelli's boat started surfing on waves that grew to between fifty-five and sixty-five feet—like fast-moving, always-toppling six-story concrete buildings. It was apocalyptic sailing.

Dinelli couldn't stay on deck because it was too dangerous. From inside the damp, frigid cabin, trying to make sense of the shape and steepness of the waves, he did his best to direct the onrushing boat by manipulating his autopilot. But control was impossible. *Algimouss* capsized, violently inverting in a few seconds. The tremendous shock compressed the mast so that

it pierced the deck; the boom smashed through one of the
large cabin windows and water flowed in. It was Christmas
Day morning.

Dressed in a survival suit that had got torn in the capsize,
Dinelli wedged himself into a corner of his upside-down
cabin. Bit by bit, the water displaced the trapped air in the
hull. During the capsize, the mast had snapped off a few
feet above deck level. The standing rigging held it more or
less in place, and it acted as a kind of keel, holding *Algimouss*
stably inverted. After three hours or so, however, wrenched
by the boat's furious rolling and pitching, the mast broke
away completely. Freed of the resistance of mast and rigging,
the three-ton bulb of ballast at the end of the keel regained its
leverage, and the boat rolled upright again—sluggishly,
because of the weight of water inside. As it did so, Dinelli,
mostly underwater, half swam, half walked his way off the
cabin top and down the sides until he was standing on the floor
again. Now he could activate his satellite emergency radio
beacons. He hadn't set them off sooner because the signal
wouldn't have been able to penetrate the boat's upside-down
carbon-fiber hull.

Within a couple of hours of righting itself, the boat had
almost completely filled with water. The waves slammed in
through the table-sized hole in the deck with such force that
they broke the hull's watertight bulkheads. Each Vendée
Globe sixty-footer was required to have three of these, dividing the boat's interior into compartments that could be sealed
off, limiting the amount of inflowing water. But no material
could withstand the force of these seas. Soon the deck was at
water level. Each enormous wave seemed determined to sink
the boat.

Dinelli climbed onto the deck and tethered himself to the
stump of the mast, struggling to stay on his feet as the boat

lurched and plunged. The waves crashed over him continuously. His torn survival suit soon filled with water. The hull of *Algimouss* was completely submerged, its deck barely visible in the foam of breaking seas. Alternately soaked by waves of frigid Southern Ocean water and blasted by a windchill well below zero, Dinelli felt his body temperature begin to drop.

He stood on the deck of his boat for the rest of Christmas Day, through the high-latitude austral summer night, and all the next day, the wind never dropping below gale force. Adrift in the Southern Ocean at almost fifty degrees latitude, twelve hundred miles south of Australia, closer to Antarctica, he was as alone and exposed as any human on earth could possibly be. As the second night approached, the twenty-eight-year-old sailor was exhausted and hypothermic. He knew without any doubt that he would not be able to survive until the next morning. Death was very close.

To understand this story, you have to understand the Southern Ocean and what it means to sail through it in a small sailboat.

The vast sea area of the Southern Ocean is really the extreme southern portion of the Pacific, Indian, and South Atlantic oceans. Its official demarcation is forty degrees south latitude. It includes the latitudes sailors long ago nicknamed the roaring forties, the furious fifties, and the screaming sixties. It's an area of almost constant high wind and frequent gales, often exceeding hurricane strength. In storms, the waves build and build until they reach almost unimaginable heights. The highest wave ever reliably recorded—120 feet high—was encountered there. The waves of the Southern Ocean roll around the world unimpeded by land. Icebergs and smaller "growlers" drift through the frigid water. Over the centuries, it has been a sailors' graveyard—square-rigger seamen called the Southern Ocean path to Cape Horn "Dead Men's Road." It embodies what Melville called "that sense of the full awfulness of the sea."

The Southern Ocean contains that point on earth that is farthest from any land. It's about 1,660 miles equidistant from Pitcairn Island, the *Bounty* mutineers' last refuge, and Cape Dart on Antarctica. Many of the Vendée Globe boats sail close by it, or even, by chance, right through it, as they make for Cape Horn. Only a few astronauts have ever been farther from land than a person on a vessel at that position. But that doesn't begin to describe the remoteness of this part of the planet. Some sailors call a large area of the Southern Ocean "the hole." It's too far away for even long-range aircraft to get to—assuming they want to return to land. On maps made when large chunks of territory had still not been penetrated by Europeans, cartographers would label the vast, unknown spaces *Hic sunt dracones*—"Here are dragons." This confident prophecy of unpredictable and fearsome dangers still applies to the Southern Ocean.

It's difficult for us to grasp the idea that parts of our planet remain in an almost primordial state of wildness and isolation. There are only a few places left on earth where merely getting across them is an achievement: Antarctica, whether on foot or snowmobile; the Sahara off its beaten and braided tracks; the Southern Ocean in a sailboat. The wildernesses of ice or sand or water are terrible places where nature retains power over humans to terrify and to diminish—a power it had everywhere until very recently in our history.

Two round-the-world races for single-handed sailors take competitors through the heart of the Southern Ocean. The Around Alone race (formerly the BOC Challenge) takes place in four separate legs. The boats make three scheduled stops along the way and can also take unscheduled refuge, without disqualification, to make repairs or find replacements for broken gear. In the Vendée Globe, however, the competitors must sail nonstop and completely unassisted. It is the most extreme of long-distance sailing races. According to the disarmingly simple rules, the race was created "to answer the needs of sailors eager to reach their uttermost limits." There are no complex handicaps or arcane racing rules like those in shorter competitions. In the Vendée Globe, the winner is the first to cross the finish line—one person, one boat, first home.

For the competing skippers, the Southern Ocean is the heart of the matter. It makes up almost half of the total race distance of twenty-seven thousand miles and requires six to eight weeks of formidable effort to get through—if nothing goes wrong. The other sections of the race pose their own challenges and involve real dangers, but most are manageable. When they sail into the Southern Ocean, the sailors enter a realm of contingency: wind and sea conditions there can destroy even the best boat and the skipper unlucky enough to encounter them. The racers often find themselves in survival conditions—overpowering wind and sea become the master, and the sailor can only hang on and hope for the best. The race is really divided into three parts: the Atlantic, the Southern Ocean, the Atlantic. That middle section is the killer.

"After that, it's a holiday," said one Vendée Globe skipper, Christophe Auguin.

In the Southern Ocean, the fragile lines that connect the sailor to humanity are stretched to the limit. Sometimes they break. The sailors in these races depend for help on their connections with one another far more than on any remote and uncertain source of aid from land. Some skippers have been lifted almost literally out of the sea by fellow racers. Most wouldn't have survived long enough to be picked up by diverted ships or to be reprieved by lifesaving equipment dropped from planes—if they happened to be within reach of them. And in some races, a boat and sailor have just disappeared without word or trace.

Yet the racers are tied into the worldwide network of satellite and computer communication. Onboard computers coordinate satellite-based navigation, communication, and weather-forecasting systems. They can fax, e-mail, talk on long- or short-range radios, get detailed weatherfax charts whenever they want. Even in the Southern Ocean, where weather forecasts are sketchy and unreliable, the sailors can often see the weather that's on its way to clobber them. Sometimes, they can even avoid the worst of it.

Their navigation and safety equipment is sophisticated and powerful, and their systems are backed up as if they were on Apollo flights to the moon. The boats' cabins look like electronics stores. The skippers are in constant contact with race headquarters in France or the United States. The race directors, in turn, always know where each boat is, within a few miles or less—a constant radio signal (from an ARGOS transmitter) is broadcast from each boat to satellite receivers. When trouble comes—if a boat's rolled over by a Southern Ocean graybeard, dismasted, and waterlogged—the hypothermic and exhausted sailor can activate emergency position-indicating radio beacons (EPIRBs), which notify the satellites. The EPIRBs were the most revolutionary devices the boats carried, and they have changed dramatically the odds of rescue when a sailor gets into serious trouble. They are small and portable—one of the newer ones, for example, is the size of a large flashlight and weighs less than three pounds—and there are several different types. They were the devices the sailors hoped never to use, although in this race, they were destined to be used with some regularity. When an EPIRB is activated, race headquarters and marine-rescue centers know within a few minutes that the dragons have struck. Search-and-rescue operations begin right away.

But getting help to a boat's exact-known location can take days. If none of the other competitors can reach the spot, it may be impossible to get to an injured boat for a week or more—until a dispatched warship or diverted freighter can struggle through. Cargo ships make their regular way across the Southern Ocean—tankers, bulk cargo or container ships bound both ways round the Horn—but they stick to narrow routes and are few and far between. And sometimes these big ships can't search properly because even they may be endangered by making search maneuvers in heavy seas.

In any event, an EPIRB has to be on the sea surface for the transmission to work. It won't penetrate hull material or several feet of water. If the boat stays upside down—as Dinelli's did—the sailor must find a way of floating the beacon out of the cabin to the surface while still keeping it attached to the boat. The newest and most accurate EPIRBs have a battery life of thirty-six to seventy-two hours or so, depending on the temperature. The colder it is, the shorter their operating time. After they quit, the boat's position becomes a matter of drift analysis—guesswork based on the vagaries of wind and wave action.

In early January 1997, thirteen Vendée Globe solo sailors were strung out across six thousand miles of the Southern Ocean, stretching from south of Australia almost to Cape Horn. The sailors had already been at sea for more than two months. Of the sixteen starters, only ten were still officially in the race. Three more kept sailing but had been disqualified for stopping in one port or another along the way to make repairs to their boats—strictly prohibited by the race rules. Dinelli had been sailing as an unofficial entrant because he hadn't had time to make the two-thousand-mile sail required to qualify for the Vendée Globe. Two racers had withdrawn soon after the start on November 3 of the previous year because of damage suffered in a storm in the Bay of Biscay.

Deep in the Southern Ocean, the skippers had lived for weeks in wet foul-weather gear in cold cabins dripping with condensation or wet with seawater that found a way in. The widely spaced boats were dealing with various weather conditions, none of them pleasant. At best, some were running uncomfortably, but not dangerously, before the gale-force depressions that travel unceasingly across the high southern latitudes. For other boats, there wasn't enough wind to enable them to handle the sea conditions—big seas persist for some time after the weather that created them has moderated. The boats were faltering in waves that struck anarchically from all directions without the governing discipline of strong wind.

Other skippers found themselves in particularly severe low-pressure systems—storms that made our Virgin Islands "yachtsman's gale" seem like the briefest and most benign of squalls. They were struggling to control their boats as they surfed at breakneck speeds of twenty-five knots or more down waves like steep hills in winds of near-hurricane strength.

In just those conditions, during the night of January 4, two of the sixty-foot-long Vendée Globe boats capsized. They were sailing fourteen hundred miles southwest of the Australian Cape Leeuwin at about fifty-one degrees south latitude—just inside the border of the furious fifties. The boats were within forty miles of each other, near the back of the strung-out fleet.

Aboard *Exide Challenger* (a sophisticated ketch—a two-masted rig), Tony Bullimore heard a loud bang. He could hear it even over the shrill tumult of his boat's rush through the storm. The carbon-fiber keel, fatally fatigued by the boat's unending motion, had suddenly snapped off, plunging down to the ocean floor—in this sea area, the relatively shallow southeast Indian Ridge, five hundred fathoms down. Suddenly deprived of its four and a half tons of ballast, the now top-heavy boat flipped over with shocking speed—two or three seconds. Just before it happened, the fifty-seven-year-old Bullimore had been standing wedged in his cabin, drinking a mug of tea he'd managed to brew up on his gimballed one-burner stove and smoking one of his roll-your-own cigarettes. As the boat flipped, he rolled around with it and found himself standing on the cabin top, which was now the floor.

The abruptness of the event astonished him. He looked down through the big cabin windows, which were now acting as the bottom of the hull, and saw seawater rushing past, like a fast-flowing river under his feet. The howl of the wind passing at seventy knots around the boat's two masts and rigging had stopped. In fact, it was almost quiet—although the boat was still rocking and rolling.

His mug of tea had disappeared, but he still had his cigarette in hand. He stood on the inside cabin top of his upside-down boat, took a few draws on the cigarette, and phlegmatically considered the situation. There wasn't much he could do, he thought. He went through the pluses and minuses of his position, trying to think through how he could survive. He had to try to get an EPIRB signal out to the world. Maybe he could use his tools to cut a hole in the hull. He became aware of the boat's heavy boom, mixed up with the tangle of mast and rigging below the boat. Swinging around in the underwater turbulence, it was tapping on one of the big cabin windows.

Suddenly, in one violent lurch, the boom smashed the window. The sea roared in like Niagara Falls. The electric lights, which had stayed on since the capsize, now went dead. Within seconds, the dark cabin filled with water whose temperature was close to zero degrees Celsius, leaving only a few feet of air near the top, which was really the cabin floor. Bullimore quickly became very cold. He waded through the chest-high water, found his survival suit, stripped off his foul-weather gear—which only protected him from rain, spray, and the occasional breaking wave—and managed to pull the suit on over his cold and sodden underclothes. The insulated waterproof survival suit was designed to stave off hypothermia, but it was a model that left his hands and feet exposed, and all he could do was stuff his already frozen feet back into his soaked seaboots.

His food and drinking water were gone, except for some chocolate and several tiny sachets of water—a cup or so. Like most of the equipment in the cabin, his food and water had been sucked out through the smashed window by the powerful vacuum of departing waves.

There was no need now to cut a hole in the hull to release an EPIRB signal; the boom had done it for him. He activated one of his ARGOS-type EPIRBs and tied it to a piece of line. (The ARGOS position transmitter became an EPIRB when switched to alarm mode.) Plunging down into the freezing water in the cabin, he pushed it through the broken window and floated it up to what he hoped was the surface of the sea, but it could easily have become entangled in the mess of rigging and debris outside. Bullimore wasn't sure that his distress transmission was in fact getting out.

Whether *Exide Challenger* would stay afloat depended on his watertight bulkheads, in particular on the forward bulkhead, which was keeping water out of the boat's bow section.

In case they didn't hold, he needed his life raft, which was secured in the cockpit. Several times, his eyes and ears seared by the cold, he dove down and through the companionway hatch to cut it free. But it was too bulky to move, pinned against the bottom of the inverted cockpit by its own buoyancy. On his last dive, the hatch was caught by a surge of wave water and slammed shut on his hand. It chopped off his left index finger at the lower knuckle. In the icy water, the stub soon stopped bleeding and the cold numbed the fiery pain.

Bullimore crawled onto a narrow shelf high up under his new ceiling, where it was relatively dry for now. But the water was rising and it soon began to wash over him periodically in this last refuge. He felt desperately cold and tired. He knew that the Australians were his best hope for rescue, but it would take them at least four or five days to get to him. That is, if the EPIRB had made it to the surface—if its signal was getting through to anyone at all.

First, Thierry Dubois's *Pour Amnesty International* was dismasted. In wind that never fell below sixty-five knots (hurricane force) and in fifty-five- to sixty-foot-high seas, the boat capsized. It righted immediately, but its mast had buckled and broken into three pieces. Waves repeatedly smashed the two mast sections in the water up against the hull, threatening to hole it. Dubois had to use a hacksaw to cut through the rigging and free the remains of the mast from the boat. While he was below getting warm, getting his breath back, his boat was rolled again through 360 degrees by a huge, steep wave. Still Dubois did not activate an EPIRB. Instead, he jury-rigged (improvise from broken or spare material on board) a mast and a sail. In the tradition of the self-sufficient mariner, he was determined to reach an Australian port under his own power.

The following day, as he slept below, exhausted, and at

almost the same time as Bullimore's capsize, another big wave turned the boat over. This time, it stayed upside down, drifting haphazardly among the long, wild Southern Ocean rollers. Now he set off his emergency beacon.

After two hours or so, the boat showed no sign of righting itself. In spite of its keel's weight, and even without the countervailing underwater resistance of its mast, Dubois's boat seemed comfortably stable upside down. Dressed in his survival suit, he squeezed through a small escape hatch in the transom (the vertical, or near-vertical, part of the stern). After several attempts at crawling up onto the slick, curved surface of the overturned hull, he managed to take advantage of a wave that washed him up onto it. He clung to one of the boat's two long, narrow rudders. The wind was still blowing at more than fifty knots. Enormous Southern Ocean seas, as high as the boat was long, towered over the exposed man and machine. The closest fellow racer was twelve hundred miles to the east and couldn't possibly sail back that far against gale-force winds and seas. At the tail end of the fleet, Dubois and Bullimore were particularly isolated. An Australian ship or a passing freighter were their only chances.

As he tried to balance himself on the overturned hull's rolling, slippery surface, in the extreme windchill of the storm-force winds, the waves periodically inundating him, Dubois believed that his life was over. The only uncertainty was how many hours, perhaps minutes, he had left.

In about 1805, Adm. Sir Francis Beaufort, of the British Royal Navy, drew up a scale that related wind strength to sea conditions. The navy adopted the Beaufort Wind Scale as part of its standard navigational repertoire in 1830. In modified form, it has since become a tool used almost universally by mariners. Its descriptions of wild weather are terse and clinical, but they provide a handy scale of relativity for appreciating what wind does to the sea. The sixty-five- to seventy-knot winds that Bullimore and Dubois experienced were just above the sixty-four-knot (seventy-three miles, or one hundred eighteen kilometers, per hour) threshold of force 12—hurricane force, the highest category on the scale. At sea, wrote Beaufort, "air filled with foam; sea completely white with driving spray; visibility greatly reduced." Sea state is described as "phenomenal," with mean wave heights of more than forty-four feet. Of the wind's effects as observed on land, the admiral noted, "Very rarely experienced on land; usually accompanied by widespread damage."

An adult human finds it very difficult to walk into a seventy-knot wind. It can blow over the unwary pedestrian. While one is facing the wind, breathing is difficult. At sea, water driven by a wind of that velocity is painful and can damage an unprotected eye. In hurricane-force winds, sailors must often wear diver's face masks or goggles. On deck, the sailor must crawl from one handhold to the next.

If the wind seems bent on manslaughter, the waves generated by hurricane-force winds in the Southern Ocean are homicidal. That day, Bullimore and Dubois (and Dinelli ten days earlier) had fought seas that were the height of a five-story building, with some as much as 50 percent higher than that—almost an eight-story building. But there's more to it than the height of the waves. Wave energy moves through water surprisingly fast. The speed at which a wave travels depends on its length—the distance between wave crests. The greater the length, the faster the wave. For example, waves whose crests are ten yards apart will move at eight knots; those one hundred yards apart, at twenty-five knots. But the Southern Ocean waves, with literally all the space in the world to form and build, are very long—the crests often two

BEAUFORT WIND SCALE

| Beaufort number or force | Wind speed | | | | World Meteorological Organization (1964) | Estimating wind speed |
	knots	mph	meters per second	km per hour		Effects observed far from land
0	under 1	under 1	0.0–0.2	under 1	Calm	Sea like mirror.
1	1–3	1–3	0.3–1.5	1–5	Light air	Ripples with appearance of scales; no foam crests.
2	4–6	4–7	1.6–3.3	6–11	Light breeze	Small wavelets; crests of glassy appearance, not breaking.
3	7–10	8–12	3.4–5.4	12–19	Gentle breeze	Large wavelets; crests begin to break; scattered whitecaps.
4	11–16	13–18	5.5–7.9	20–28	Moderate breeze	Small waves, becoming longer; numerous whitecaps.
5	17–21	19–24	8.0–10.7	29–38	Fresh breeze	Moderate waves, taking longer form; many whitecaps; some spray.
6	22–27	25–31	10.8–13.8	39–49	Strong breeze	Larger waves forming; whitecaps everywhere; more spray.
7	28–33	32–38	13.9–17.1	50–61	Near gale	Sea heaps up; white foam from breaking waves begins to be blown in streaks.
8	34–40	39–46	17.2–20.7	62–74	Gale	Moderately high waves of greater length; edges of crests begin to break into spindrift; foam is blown in well-marked streaks.
9	41–47	47–54	20.8–24.4	75–88	Strong gale	High waves; sea begins to roll; dense streaks of foam; spray may reduce visibility.
10	48–55	55–63	24.5–28.4	89–102	Storm	Very high waves with overhanging crests; sea takes white appearance as foam is blown in very dense streaks; rolling is heavy and visibility is reduced.
11	56–63	64–72	28.5–32.6	103–117	Violent storm	Exceptionally high waves; sea covered with white foam patches; visibility still more reduced.
12	64 and over	73 and over	32.7 and over	118 and over	Hurricane	Air filled with foam; sea completely white with driving spray; visibility greatly reduced.

hundred yards apart or more. A wave of that length will travel
at close to thirty-five knots.

To get an idea of the stresses that Bullimore and Dubois,
and their boats, experienced, nonsailors might try to visualize
a never-ending series of five- or six-story buildings, with sloping sides of various angles and with occasional buildings half
as high again, moving toward them at about forty miles an
hour. Some of the time, the top one or two stories of the buildings will collapse on top of them. The concussive effect of
seawater isn't much different from that of concrete. Add the
isolation and the noise—the boom and roar of the waves,
the deafening, unearthly, unnerving scream of wind around
the obstructions of mast and rigging—and the picture should
become clearer.

To understand the Southern Ocean, you also have to understand Cape Horn.

In form and function, it serves the mundane purpose of
capes everywhere: a promontory, or headland, dividing
one body of water from another. But the Horn is unique. It's
very far south, at fifty-seven degrees latitude. To go around it,
vessels must plunge down, deep into the Southern Ocean.
From Cape Horn, Antarctica is only six hundred miles away.
Untrammeled in their progression around the globe, the
Southern Ocean lows get squeezed together in the bellows of
the Drake Passage between the Horn and Antarctica. Sometimes the systems get more complicated, and therefore more
hazardous, as they meet the local weather coming off the
nearby land masses. Williwaws sweep down the alpine valleys
and far out to sea. The bottom comes up very quickly on the
lip of the continental shelf. Waves shorten and steepen in the
shallower water.

Cape Horn is the real, and certainly the psychological,

turning point of any voyage or race through the Southern Ocean. Actually a high rocky island just off the tip of the continent, it has a singular and mythological weight for sailors as a symbol of pain, hardship, and death. In the days of the square-riggers, ships would sometimes spend weeks trying to round it from east to west, against the prevailing wind, seas, and current. Bligh's *Bounty* struggled to round the Horn for twenty-nine days before giving up and running off to the east. It eventually reached the South Pacific by way of the Indian Ocean and through the narrow straits off southeast Asia. Bligh's crew, with cruel and unconscious hypocrisy, never forgave him either for the hardships and terrors of that month or for turning tail at the end of it.

In *Two Years Before the Mast*, Richard Henry Dana describes his ship's ordeal in the frigid southern winter of 1836, as it tried to round the Horn from west to east with a cargo of California hides. This was supposed to be the easy way round, with its following winds. But it took them two weeks in head winds, uncharacteristic calms, and easterly gales. They were often blocked by ice fields. When they finally reached it, the Horn was a dismal and desolate sight, Dana wrote. But it was also a welcome vision to the frozen and exhausted crew. It was a signal that they might finally "bid defiance to the Southern Ocean."

My great-grandfather saw the Horn once as the grain-carrying square-rigger on which he was an able seaman surged past it on the way to Liverpool. He told my grandmother only that it looked to him like a small jagged mound in the sea, and that he hated and feared it.

For the pathologically adventurous sailor, rounding the Horn is the height of achievement, although doing it may be a short-lived triumph—exactly because it means so much. The Argentine single-hander Vito Dumas sailed from Chile to

Buenos Aires in 1934 and was welcomed as a hero. But Dumas's mind was not with the adoring crowds. His great moment had come and gone, he wrote later. All he could hope for was that somewhere, "at another distant point in the sea, I could find another Cape Horn."

Its ambiguous attractions are still potent. In 1985, father and son David and Daniel Hays sailed around Cape Horn in the smallest boat that any Americans had ever sailed there—an English-designed twenty-five-footer. They were lifelong sailors for whom the Horn was "the big one." In *My Old Man and the Sea*, David, the father, describes sailing as "an incontrovertible act of truth." Because the water had given him that gift, he thought he owed something back. To repay it, he had to take from the sea, not just the summertime pleasures of the coast, but all that it would give. And that, without question, was the Horn. When they rounded the cape months later, in a gale, of course, father and son thought simultaneously of the only possible toast for their finger each of Kahlúa: "To the men who died here."

For sailors, Cape Horn has become a comprehensive metaphor—it's their Waterloo, Ithaca, Jerusalem, all bound together. Bernard Moitessier, the long-distance solitary sailor and romantic—and one of the forefathers of single-handed sailing—wrote: "A sailor's geography is not always that of the cartographer, for whom a cape is a cape, with a latitude and longitude. For the sailor, a great cape is both a very simple and an extremely complicated whole of rocks, currents, breaking seas and huge waves, fair winds and gales, joys and fears, fatigue, dreams, painful hands, empty stomachs, wonderful moments, and suffering."

The Vendée Globe sailors look ahead to Cape Horn as a marker of their return to the world, to civilization. Christophe Auguin, a few days away from rounding the Horn in the

Vendée Globe, exclaimed how much he was yearning for "*la sortie d'enfer*"—the exit from hell.

On January 6, two days after Bullimore and Dubois had capsized, Gerry Roufs sent one of his regular e-mail transmissions to his Web site. He described the hurricane he had had to contend with a week earlier. Not just a Southern Ocean storm with hurricane-force wind, but an actual cyclonic storm, "Fergus" had veered off the usual paths of South Pacific cyclones and ripped its way south past fifty-five degrees latitude. In the usual Southern Ocean storms out of the west, it's easy for the Vendée Globe boats to adopt storm tactics—running off before the wind and keeping their sterns directly into the waves—as they race east toward Cape Horn. But caught in an area where Fergus's circling winds were blowing from the south, Roufs had had to turn *Groupe LG2*'s tail to the ferocious seas and head off course to the north until the storm passed over. He was still sailing second in the race, but his forced diversion had lost him a lot of ground on the leader, Christophe Auguin.

"It's one thing to settle down comfortably to a series of depressions that move around between the 40s and 50s," he wrote. "But how do you avoid a strong depression coming from the north and whose centre falls smack-dab right on top of you? And then it's practically Noah's Ark. Fierce storm, sea very dangerous that could easily capsize the boat. . . . I had to fly before 55 to 62 knot winds. For landlubbers: at this stage, children under 12 would fly away!"

In a storm like Fergus, "the race's importance takes second place. You could say it's a question of survival," he said.

He had heard about the other sailors' distress signals. It made him think again about how dangerous the Southern Ocean was. The longer you were there, the greater the chances of disaster. It was at once beautiful and terrifying.

"But I've been here long enough. . . . At an average speed of ten knots, the Horn ought to appear on the horizon in a week and a half or less. . . . As for the boat, it's my best friend because it's my ticket out of here. . . . The only thing that bothers me is that a breaker filled the cockpit and washed away my two buckets even though they were secure."

Roufs's boat was no different from the other racing machines, loaded down with technology but with rudimentary accommodation. He had lost his toilet and his sink in one cruel blow.

The day after this message, Roufs and the Frenchwoman Isabelle Autissier (the other woman in the race besides Catherine Chabaud), sailing about thirty miles apart, were overtaken by an extreme storm, this time just an intense version of the usual Southern Ocean low-pressure system. It developed very quickly, the wind rising from thirty-five to seventy knots in three hours or so. Because the wind had not had time to stretch out the forty- to fifty-foot-high waves, they were relatively steep and close together, particularly dangerous seas for small boats. For Autissier, the most impressive thing was that she couldn't distinguish the waves from the sky or clouds.

"The air was full of sea and the clouds were so close to the sea that everything was gray," she told me. "It was like a huge gray mass—white and gray because of the waves. It was very terrible, terrifying."

During the course of the day, Autissier's boat was knocked down (flattened by a wave so that the mast was horizontal to the water) six times. Twice, the top of her eighty-foot mast was driven beneath the water's surface. On one of those occasions, Autissier broke one of her fingers as she was flung against the cabin top of the almost upside-down boat.

It was during this severe storm, thirty hours after he sent

his e-mail, that the ARGOS radio position beacon on Roufs's boat suddenly stopped transmitting. One second it was beeping away, relaying his constantly changing position. The next second, there was complete silence. Perhaps it was only the ARGOS itself. Roufs might not notice that it had shut down. He was far out in the Southern Ocean—in the hole. No shore-based plane or ship could reach his position. Only other vessels at sea might be within striking distance of him if something had in fact gone wrong.

The following day, Autissier, who was still sailing close to Roufs, reported that she had not been able to make radio contact with him. It might only be that his electrical system had failed and that he was continuing to sail along, out of contact with the world. But winds in the area were hurricane strength. Autissier herself was struggling to survive. Roufs's boat remained silent. No EPIRB signals from *Groupe LG2* had been received by any of the monitoring satellites. Nevertheless, at race headquarters in Rennes, in Brittany, a worried Philippe Jeantot, the Vendée Globe director, ordered a search operation for Roufs to begin.

Postscript: Amazingly, Dinelli, Bullimore, and Dubois were all successfully rescued. Roufs's boat was eventually found, but what happened to its owner will forever remain a mystery.

To circumnavigate the world alone and without stopping was
the object of the 1968 *Sunday Times* Golden Globe race. The
Frenchman Bernard Moitessier entered the race with his
twelve-meter, steel-hulled ketch dubbed *Joshua* after Joshua
Slocum, the first sailor to circumnavigate the earth alone. His
joy at simply being on the water is tangible and has inspired
many to go forth to a life at sail.

THE LONG WAY

BERNARD MOITESSIER

Played and Lost . . . Played and Won!

Fifty-nine days into the trip,
the October 19 sight places us about forty miles SW of Cape
Agulhas, the extreme tip of South Africa.

The sky was cloudy all yesterday, with a force 5 NW wind,
shifting to SW during the night. The barometer, already high,
continues to rise. Today it stands at an abnormal 1,027 millibars, a sure sign that the permanent South Atlantic high has
moved well toward *Joshua*'s waters. For several days I have
tried to tune in weather reports on the wavelengths indicated
in the Radio Weather Aids manual, but in vain. Even if I
picked up the dit-dit-dah of the South African Morse code

broadcasts, it would not do any good, as they are transmitted in an international code which is Greek to me.

Greek or not, it is more than likely that with the barometer so high, the wind will shift to the east by tomorrow. Not too strong, I hope!

If I had played by the rules, *Joshua* would have raced south, to get away from the edge of the high pressure system and not risk losing the westerlies. But the die was cast yesterday: I intend to cross the Agulhas Bank close to shore and have a ship report me to Lloyds. With a little luck (lots of luck) *Joshua* may even meet a fishing boat, to whom I could heave a package for the *Sunday Times*.

I have photographed my log twice, page by page, to spread the risks during a flying trans-shipment to the deck of a trawler. I pack the rolls of film in two of the heavy watertight plastic bags Bob and Steve gave me, with the address of the *Sunday Times* and forwarding instructions printed in four languages. I added a few rolls of snap-shots as well: Trinidad with its green roofs, a gannet who could read MIK, the dorado caught as we entered the trades, a burst of flying fish, albatrosses, flocks of little silvery web-footed birds that have kept us company these last days, porpoises playing with *Joshua*—life at sea, so simple and so transparent, with its calms and breaking waves.

I imagine Robert, Steve and Bob's joy at receiving one of these marvel-crammed packages. I can see Françoise's joy as she realizes all's well aboard, that I have not lost weight (she will not know that I have—none of her business). I can just see my children's excitement, shouting all through the house, "*Joshua* is rounding Good Hope!"

Yet it is a hard card to play, this need I feel to reassure family and friends, to give them news, pictures, life—to bestow that infinitely precious thing, the little invisible plant called hope. Logic shouts at me to play the game alone, without burdening myself with the others. Logic would have me run SE, far from land, far from ships, back to the realm of the westerlies where everything is simple if not easy, leaving well to the north the dangerous area of the convergence.

But for many days another voice has been insisting, "You are alone, yet not alone. The others need you, and you need them. Without them, you would not get anywhere, and nothing would be true."

The sun has long since set when my heart starts to pound: the Cape Agulhas lighthouse!

As common as I know it is in this age of modern tables and radio time signals, for me a perfect landfall will always stay wreathed in magic, like an answer from the stars, whom I had earlier asked, "Where am I?" And the stars had answered, "Don't worry, you'll see Cape Agulhas before midnight." Warmth fills my chest at the beacon's little flash, showing between the black of the waves, right where I was looking with binoculars two hours after a star sight. Warmth in my chest and a little chill down my back . . . because this cape is a Great Cape.

Shortly after sundown, the wind had veered to the south, then SSE. Now *Joshua* is sailing closehauled, the beacon clearly visible a hand's-breadth to the left of the jib.

At two in the morning, all the sails are close reefed to a SE force 7 wind. It was to be expected with the barometer so high. Yet I feel inexplicably happy.

The lighthouse is only eight or ten miles ahead when I decide to heave-to on the other tack and wait for daybreak before making up my mind.

All at once, I am very tired. I have to sleep, if only for an hour or two. Strange, how fatigue can cut a man down without warning. You hang on and on . . . and suddenly you collapse. But only when it is all clear ahead.

I light the lamp, and go below to take a nap. All clear: there are no ships where *Joshua* is lying hove-to. They pass either close to land or far offshore, making the most of the current.

Nearly four in the morning! I slept like a log, all my fatigue has lifted. I stretch, yawn, light the stove. A small mug of coffee is followed by a big Ovaltine and three army biscuits spread with butter and orange marmalade. I feel great.

I gybe to get under way without having to touch the sheets, already trimmed for a beat. While I was asleep, the wind eased to force 4 or 5 and shifted to ESE. The beacon is now a finger to the right of the jib.

I keep the reefs in; all signs point to a SE gale. No sense trying to tack into it for days on the Agulhas Bank, with the ships and contrary current. Sailing is a compromise between distance covered and mounting fatigue, for both crew and boat; and fatigue can snowball fast.

Heading south would be no better. Sooner or later, *Joshua* would wind up in the area of current convergence on the steep edge of the Agulhas Bank. That would spell trouble in a gale from any direction.

Best heave-to until the wind returns to the west, a matter of two or three days. Before I do that, though, *Joshua* could easily run before the wind along the coast between Cape Agulhas and the Cape of Good Hope,* and drop in at Walker Bay where the chart shows a little port, which means a few yachts.

---

*Good Hope is in the Atlantic, about thirty miles NW of Cape Agulhas.

It is Sunday, so I am sure to find one out in the bay, and could pass her my bags of film.

Simple! It could even kill two birds with one stone, as the yacht will certainly have news of Loïck, Bill King and Nigel. Their names have not been mentioned once in the BBC overseas broadcasts. Where are they?

The wind picks up at dawn, force 6 around 7 A.M., nearly force 7 an hour later. The cloudless sky is magnificent, the coast is five or six miles off, the sea a bit heavy, but *Joshua* is running downhill.

Three lines of position a few minutes apart confirm my dead reckoning: the entrance to Walker Bay is about twenty miles ahead.

A good force 7 is blowing now; the gale is almost upon us. Spray flies high against the ships making for Cape Agulhas. For those heading north, it is a piece of cake. For *Joshua* too . . . but I am beginning to wonder if I will find a yacht out in Walker Bay in this weather. I have replaced my old MIK flags with a new set.

More and more, I get the impression no yacht is going to put her nose into Walker Bay. The gale should be here any minute, and one of the ships that have been passing for the last hour may have already reported me to Lloyds. The catch is that they will report me as being on course for Europe.

Walker Bay is about fifteen miles ahead now, and I have a sinking feeling that absolutely no yachts will be out; no fishermen either, as it is Sunday. And all the passing freighters can read my MIK flags . . . as I steer North! There is a little one astern, all dingy and black, belching a big plume of smoke that spreads out ahead. She can't be making more than 8 knots, because *Joshua* is doing 7 and she has been trying to catch up for a long time. The freighter will pass close . . .

I quickly go below and write two copies of a message asking the captain to slow down and stay on a straight course, so I can draw level and heave him a package. The message also states that I am continuing toward Australia, regardless of appearances. I roll my two handwritten notes and stuff them in aluminum film cans. Each can is weighted with a bit of lead. If the first message falls in the water, I will still have the carbon copy for a second shot. And the freighter's very low deck will be perfect for eventually transferring the plastic bags, each tightly rolled and tied to make them easy to throw in spite of the wind.

I return to the cockpit with my two projectiles and the slingshot.

The black freighter is twenty-five yards off to my right. Three men are watching me from the bridge. Snap! . . . the message lands on the ship's foredeck. One of the officers twirls a forefinger at his temple, as if to say I must be a little nuts to be shooting at them.

The bridge draws level. I yell "Message! Message!" They just stare at me, bug-eyed. At this range, with lead balls, I could knock their three hats off with three shots. When I was a kid, slingshot practice consisted of hitting a tin can thrown into the air by one of my brothers. And using a slingshot is a little like Ping-Pong—you never lose your touch, even years later. Still, I do not dare shoot the duplicate message right at the bridge, because these film cans are a lot less accurate than lead balls: I might break a window, or hit one of them.

The bridge is almost beyond us: I have to salvage the situation fast. I brandish the package, and make as if to give it to them. An officer acknowledges with a wave and puts the helm over to kick the stern my way. In a few seconds, the main deck is ten or twelve yards off. I toss a package. Perfect!

It is time I pulled away, but I am going to make a serious mistake by throwing the second package instead of racing to the tiller to steer clear. I won up and down the line with my first package; I will lose it all with the second. By the time I dash to the tiller, it is already late. The freighter's stern is still slewing my way. To make matters worse, she has blanketed my sails by passing me to starboard while I was on a starboard tack.

Joshua begins to pull clear, but not fast enough. By a hair, the stern's overhang snags the mainmast. There is a horrible noise, and a shower of black paint falls on the deck; the masthead shroud is ripped loose, then the upper spreader shroud. My guts twist into knots. The push on the mast makes *Joshua* heel, she luffs up toward the freighter . . . and wham!—the bowsprit is twisted 20° or 25° to port. I am stunned.

It is all over, the black monster is past. I gybe quickly and heave-to on the port tack, drifting away from the coast. That is the main thing right now, so I can repair the shrouds without hurrying.

No doubt worried, the freighter has changed course. I wave that all's well, because in coming back to help, she would finish me off!

A trifle often irritates me and can send my spirits tumbling. But when things really get rough, I sometimes seem to become a cold, lucid observer from another world. I did not even read the freighter's name, keeping to the strict essential of saving the mast.

Outside of that, nothing has the slightest importance. I feel neither anger nor weariness nor fear. I did not mutter, "The beautiful trip is over, you can never continue non-stop with so much damage; we will have to put in at Cape Town or Saint Helena for repairs." Saving the mast, without thinking beyond that. Afterwards, I will see what else needs to be done. But above all, do not think of the twisted bowsprit, irreparable with what I have on board.

I have played and lost, that's all; it is not the end of the world. A kind of temporary anaesthesia. Later, perhaps, it will hurt. But later is far away.

I had the same reaction, though a hundred times stronger, when I was swept overboard in a gale off Durban as *Marie-Thérèse II* lay hove-to.

I found myself in water made very light by the millions of bubbles of foam from the enormous breaking sea that had capsized my boat. In a flash, I had glimpsed the cabin hatch cover, ripped off its tracks. With an opening like that, and her keel out of water, *Marie-Thérèse II* could only go to the bottom. Yet I felt no despair, no bitterness. I just whispered to myself "This time, old man, your number is up." And I remembered the page on destiny in *Wind, Sand and Stars*, on the absolute need to follow one's fate, whatever its outcome. I, too, was going to end up like Saint-Exupéry's gazelle, whose destiny it was to leap in the sunshine and die one day under a lion's claw. Yet I regretted nothing as I floated in the warm, very light water, making ready to peacefully leave on my last journey.

Marie-Thérèse II had righted herself before shipping a fatal wave through the big opening. I climbed aboard easily, with the hatch cover. Then I pumped for five hours straight, glad to start living again.

The two shrouds have been repaired less than two hours after the collision. I did not have to climb the mast; only the lower cable clamps had slipped.

The spreaders did not bulge, thanks to their flexible mount-ings. For the mast I feel nothing but admiration: at the moment of impact it looked like a fishing rod bent by a big tuna. It confirms the trust I had instinctively felt for the good old telephone pole. All in all, I have had a lot of luck in my misfortune.

The problem of the bowsprit remains; that is more serious. It is 6 ft. 10 in. long, made out of a 3 in. steel pipe about ³⁄₁₆ in. thick, reinforced by a second steel pipe inside. The bowsprit bent very slightly when it was hot-dip galvanized, and it took me nearly an hour's work on the quay to straighten it with the help of a friend.

So I will have to run the jibstay to the stem and do without the benefit of the bowsprit; and more than 20,000 miles yet to go, in a mutilated *Joshua* . . . just thinking about it makes me sick. We will see tomorrow; I am too tired now.

October 21. SE gale. I finally caught the Cape Town weather forecast at news time. *Joshua* lies-to peacefully, with the foam of the breaking waves scintillating in the sun.

I did not get much sleep last night, thinking all the time about the bowsprit. I had the impression that Henry Wakelam was there, close to me. From time to time I mumbled, "Good God, if you were here, you would have already figured a way to straighten it."

Yesterday, as I worked on the shrouds, the problem of the bowsprit hovered in the background, and I felt my friend's breath and presence next to me. I talked to him from time to time; I would ask him not to drop the crescent wrench we were using to tighten the cable clamps. And he helped quietly, without lecturing me, without a word on the real problem. The shrouds were just tinkering, an odd job tossed off with wrench, cable clamps and ¼ in. nuts. It took no particular genius, beyond watching that the wrenches did not fall

overboard when the boat would heel lying hove-to. The real
hurdle would be the bowsprit, on which I did not want to
crystallize my thinking prematurely.

When Henry and I had had to work out a really sticky
problem together, neither of us was allowed to mention it. No
bursting out with "Say, I've got an idea! What do you think of
this? . . ." It was not allowed, because the thing had not matured
enough, and putting forth an idea that was not worked out in
detail wasted the other's time and kept him from letting it
"ripen." Only that evening or the next morning would we talk
about possible solutions. By then the ground had been gone
over in detail, and all we had to do was get to work without
groping, by the shortest path.

October 22. The sea is still heavy in the morning, but the gale is
over. At 2 P.M. the sea is all right again. The wind has dropped
considerably, but there is enough filling the sails to keep
us from rolling. I have prepared a large four-part block and
tackle, with the spare mizzen boom to increase the angle at
which the block pulls. I hinge the spar to the foreward bitt
with a shackle. No, that won't do, another shackle is needed
as a gimbal, so the spar can move both horizontally and verti-
cally.

Good, that should do the trick. The spare staysail halyard
serves as a topping lift. The rig is strong, and swings easily off
the starboard bow. I run a ⅜ in. chain from the tip of the
bowsprit to the outer end of the spar and secure the tackle
opposite, with the line running back to the big starboard
Goïot winch.

Incredible, the power of a tackle on a winch . . . I feel I am
going to start crying, it's so beautiful . . . the bowsprit begins
to straighten out, very, very slowly. I am wild with joy!

Henry old pal, you would be proud of your disciple.

———

By sundown everything is shipshape again; bowsprit straight as before, bobstay and whisker stays tightened. They are ⅜ in. galvanized chain; one stretched several inches in the collision, and I merely cut two links out. With wire rope the damage would have been much harder to repair. The pulpit, which took a real beating, is also back in place, nice and straight, securely bolted and good as new.

Worn out by fatigue and emotion, I fall into bed after swallowing a can of soup for dinner.

The day before yesterday, I had played and lost. Then I saw Henry and all his power. I saw César, as well, the foreman during *Joshua*'s construction, when a steel sheet refused to fit. César used to repeat, "Man is always the strongest." And the sheet wound up in the proper shape.

I am tremendously tired, yet I feel crammed with dynamite, ready to level the whole world and forgive it everything. Today, I played and won. My beautiful boat is there, as beautiful as ever.

Good Hope

On October 24, Joshua *crossed* the longitude of Cape Agulhas, two hundred miles from the coast. She will continue SSE until tomorrow, to gain more offing and leave the zone of convergence well to port.

It is my sixty-third day at sea, with 7,882 miles covered between noon sights, a quarter of the distance from Plymouth to Plymouth by the three capes. The Atlantic is in the wake; ahead, the Indian Ocean. Yet *Joshua* is not actually in the Indian Ocean, despite the theoretical boundaries, but in a kind of no man's land: the waters of Good Hope. They stretch between the longitude of the Cape and that of Durban, some six hundred miles.

———

This area can be dangerous—often worse than the Horn—because of seas raised by the Agulhas Current. Many 25 to 50 ft. yachts remember it. *Atom* was rolled over near the Cape and emerged with her deck flat as a raft. *Awahnee* encountered the most terrible weather of her career in these waters, and she is a veteran of the Horn. Between Durban and Port Elizabeth *Marco Polo, Eve, Adios, Walkabout, Wanda, Marie-Thérèse II* and others were knocked on their beam ends, or hit very hard, by breaking seas kicked up by gales blowing against the Agulhas Current, which reaches 5 knots in places.

According to the *Sailing Directions*, the most dangerous area is off the steep SE edge of the Agulhas Bank, where frequent gales raise an enormous sea, reinforced by the meeting of the warm, salty current from the Indian Ocean and the cold (less salty) Antarctic Current. When you have seen the eddies caused by salinity differences in the Panama locks, one prefers to give a wide berth to similar phenomena when they are on an oceanic scale.

Yesterday there was a gale from the west. Today Radio Cape Town announces that nothing is expected before midnight. I should take advantage of it to get cracking. But I let *Joshua* drag along at 6 knots fully reefed, whereas she would better 7 if I replaced the 54 sq. ft. storm jib with the 161 sq. ft. jib, and raised the big staysail instead of keeping the 38 sq. ft. handkerchief she is carrying now. The fact is, I don't have much resilience left. I got hardly any sleep last night; it was blowing hard, with an occasionally choppy sea that made me suspect a current convergence.

The sky is fairly clear now; the westerly wind varies between force 5 and 6, without any real gusts, and the barometer seems steady at 1,013 millibars. Yet the sea is strange: it

subsides right away when the wind drops to force 5, only to
rise very fast, with big breaking seas as soon as it exceeds
force 6 in the moderate fair-weather squalls. I am also reluctant to hoist the large jib because I would have trouble bringing it in, should the weather worsen again. Last night I had
difficulty keeping the jib under control and raising the storm
jib in its place. My motions were clumsy and inefficient; it
took me three times longer than usual to secure gaskets and
reef points. And my reflexes were dangerously slow: somehow, I got caught with water up to my knees at the end of the
bowsprit, without having seen it coming. The mounting
fatigue and undernourishment of these last days may be to
blame.

Sure, I would like to get out of this lousy place by crowding
on canvas. But if the weather turns mean, as it very quickly
can here, I am much better prepared with shortened sail.
Wiser in my weakened condition. Nothing to worry about,
far from it . . . but I am asking *Joshua* to do her best until I get
back into shape.

Outside are the high latitudes and the sea rumbling a little
under the force 6 westerly wind; inside, the calm and peace
of my little world. I smoke, dreaming before the little globe
my friends on the yacht *Damien* gave me. They went north, I
went south. And it is all the same, since we are at sea in our
boats.

I gaze at the long curve drawn on the globe: *Joshua*'s route
since England, with porpoises and albatrosses, joys and sometimes sorrows.

During Tahiti-Alicante, Françoise and I would draw the
route covered in the same way on the tiny school globe our children had sent us. And we would always wait until *Joshua* had
covered ten degrees of longitude or latitude before extending

the line. To have done it sooner would have brought bad luck, attracting a contrary gale or an endless calm.

I raise the big staysail at sunset, but keep the storm jib. A reef is shaken out of the mainsail and mizzen a little before midnight. The bow wave glows with phosphorescence, and the wake stretches out far astern, full of sparks.

The old-timers in the great days of sail come to mind: for centuries they furrowed the oceans in trade or discovery. But always for the sea. I reflect on what they bequeathed us in nautical documents, where words stand for the sea and sky, where arrows try to tell of currents and winds, of the anguish and joys of those sailors, as if that could be done, as if experience of the great laws of the sea could be passed along, as if the vibrations of the sea could go through you with only words and arrows.

And yet . . . I see myself in Mauritius again, fifteen years ago, studying the *Sailing Directions* and the Pilot Charts for the run from Port Louis to Durban. I would underline in red the ominous portents of an approaching SE gale blowing against the Agulhas Current, in blue the signs propitious to a return or holding of fair weather. Closing my eyes, I tried to see and feel what emanated from the rectilinear arrows, the dry phrases, the whole austere, scientific technicalness, full of hidden things trying to emerge in me.

Once under way for Durban, I felt at times that I had covered the same stage before. The sea had shaken itself free of the morass of words, and I was reliving a journey already made, reading in advance the Indian Ocean's tidings.

The next day's sight shows 164 miles covered. *Joshua* is seventy miles inside the iceberg limit, but she has reached the 40th parallel, and can now head NE to leave the ice area by tomorrow, while staying away from the current convergence.

The sky is covered with a lot of flattened cumulus, real fair-weather clouds for these latitudes, with sometimes large sweeps of blue, almost empty of cirrus. The wind, force 6 since dawn, has veered to WNW. This shift worries me a little, especially as I was not able to get the weather report. But the barometer is steady; that is the main thing. The sea is very beautiful, meaning very heavy. On the other hand, breaking seas are few and generally not too large.

I spent most of last night in the cockpit again, because of the broken red line on the Pilot Chart showing the iceberg limit. This second sleepless night has not tired me. Still, it is about time I got out of here, otherwise my supply of tobacco and coffee will not last the trip! *Joshua* is doing 7 knots; at that rate we should soon be over the line.

I wonder if my apparent lack of fatigue could be a kind of hypnotic trance born of contact with this great sea, giving off so many pure forces, rustling with the ghosts of all the beautiful sailing ships that died around here and now escort us. I am full of life, like the sea I contemplate so intensely. I feel it watching me as well, and that we are nonetheless friends.

I made two serious mistakes today; my first since the beginning of the trip. I had just observed the meridian. Instead of stowing the sextant immediately, as I always do in these latitudes, I just boxed it, and wedged the case in a corner of the cockpit: it was very important that I trim the sails a little before going below—a matter of a few seconds. Actually, it could easily have waited.

I was busy taking up slack in the mizzen preventer when a fairly large breaking sea crowned the rudder. I gauge it out of the corner of my eye, and pull myself up by the shrouds, knees tucked under my chin to avoid getting soaked as the wave flows over the aft cabin and fills the cockpit; the sextant is afloat.

Luckily, I had not snapped on my harness, and am bare-foot and extra mobile. I dive for the sextant before the next roll carries it overboard along with three-quarters of the water flooding the cockpit. I am already in the cabin, both proud and ashamed of my double stunt.

I take the sextant out of its case, wipe it off, and wedge it with pillows on the port berth. "You barely pulled through, old pal." The case has to be rinsed inside to get rid of the salt, which would absorb moisture from the air and soon spoil the silver on the mirrors.

I light the stove to dry the case on an asbestos pad over a low flame, and go on deck to take a second reef in the main and mizzen, and a reef in the staysail. The wind is still WNW, now blowing a steady force 7. For this region it is still a fair-weather sky.

My eyes sting when I go below again. The sextant case, while not exactly burning, is certainly dry now! I turn off the stove, remove boots, harness and oilskins, wipe my hands, face and neck, put on my slippers and roll myself a cigarette. A spot of coffee? Why not! God, it's good to be inside when things are roaring out there.

I am pleased with the way I had shortened sail: quick reflexes, good grip. The staysail came along without any fuss when I reefed it, swallowing 75 sq. ft. at a gulp.

I smoke, musing over the chart. *Joshua* is behaving beauti-fully under so little canvas, with almost no yawing in spite of her speed. Tomorrow we will be far away: 180 miles? 190? The Pilot Chart gives a 1 knot favourable current for the area, so we could well break through the 200 mile ceiling if the wind holds. I am not tired; I have never been tired.

So, *Joshua*, we are taking Good Hope in our stride.

———————

I have not finished my cigarette when an enormous breaking sea hits the port beam and knocks us flat. All the portholes have shattered . . . no, they are intact (at least in my cabin); I can hardly believe it. A muffled torrential roaring and a sound almost like sheet iron under a blacksmith's hammer fill the air.

I open the hatch and stick my head out. The sails are flapping because the boat has luffed. Incredibly enough, the booms are not broken in spite of the preventers.* Luckily I had slacked off the one on the mainsail, just in case we were suddenly hove down on a broad reach. The ⅜ in. nylon preventer on the mizzen had parted. The line was three years old; I should probably have got rid of it long ago . . . but I liked it, and had got used to it during Tahiti-Alicante. Its parting probably saved the boom, but the latter, pushed amidships by the force of the water, neatly snapped off the wind vane shaft. Not serious: half a minute is all it takes to change the vane, thanks to a very simple rig. I have seven spare vanes left, and material to make more if necessary.

I go on deck to connect the steering wheel, and quickly duck below again, soaked by a blast of spray. The aft cabin portholes are intact, a sight that warms my heart. I fill the sails again, steering with the inside wheel, and go back on deck to replace the wind vane with a much smaller one set for running downwind, since *Joshua* was on a broad reach when the breaking sea hit. The only other thing is to replace the mizzen

*Preventer: line running from the boom end forward, and then secured to the boat. In case the boat yaws while sailing downwind, it prevents the boom from swinging to the other side, which could cause damage. Preventers are also useful in light airs to keep the sails from chafing against the shrouds, and also to prevent the mizzen boom hitting the self-steering wind vane on a roll, when the wind is not strong enough to keep the sails constantly filled.

preventer with a new line. Quickly done. This time I give it plenty of slack, as I did for the mainsail.

Everything is shipshape on deck. I can go below to get warm and straighten up the cabin. I pick the globe out of the sink, on the starboard side, and wedge it back in place, to port. The island of Java is a bit scraped.

The sextant . . . I had forgotten it on the port berth, buried in the pillows. Now it looks out at me from the starboard berth. Poor little pal, if this hasn't done you in, there really is a guardian angel for sextants, and morons too. First I leave it in the cockpit, then on the *windward* berth . . . It took an eight foot free fall through the cabin when *Joshua* went over. One of its legs sheared off at the thread, though it is nearly ¼ in. thick. There are three holes in the plywood facing of one of the drawers. The one on the left is at least ¼ in. deep, the right one a bit less, the top one barely visible. They are the holes made by the legs of the sextant when it smashed into the drawer.

Joshua has a second sextant, a big Poulin micrometer drum model, very accurate and easy to read; a light in the handle makes it particularly handy for star sights. The other one (now an amputee) is an old vernier model which I very much like for sun shots in the high latitudes because it is small, light, and easy to handle. I will try to glue the leg back with epoxy cement when I find it. I will also have to adjust the mirrors, which must be out of alignment after such a shock.

By and large *Joshua*, the sextant and I came through all right. But two such serious mistakes, one after the other, are inexcusable, and cause for concern.

Barely an hour later, *Joshua* had another knockdown. This time, I saw nearly all the action.

I was squatting on the inside steering seat, watching the sea
through the little rectangular ports of the metal turret. The
wind had noticeably eased since the first knockdown, to
force 6 at most. But the sea had become strange, with peaceful
areas where it was very heavy, yet regular, with no dangerous breaking waves. In those areas, I could have walked blind-
folded twenty times around the deck. Then, without any
transition, it would turn jerky and rough; high cross-seas over-
lapped to provoke sometimes very powerful breaking waves. It
was probably one of these cross-seas that hit us earlier. Then
Joshua would again find herself in a quiet area for ten minutes
or more, followed by another rough one.

From time to time I stood up on the seat to take a few deep
breaths and get a better feel of the conditions. During the
quiet periods I went out in the cockpit, but without letting go
of the hatch cover handle, ready to dive below.

If I were rounding Good Hope in the same direction again,
I would probably stay between the 41st and the 42nd parallel
(instead of the 40th), to avoid skirting too closely the area
of convergence of warm and cold currents. True, this would
force me much further beyond the red line on the Pilot Chart,
with a longer period of vigilance. Last night's watch for icebergs was enough, but I will hardly need to stand one tonight
as we will be practically clear of the red line. So if I had to do it
over, I might just do the same as now, if the barometer
behaved. Which it is; it has even tended to rise since this
morning.

I went below to suck on a can of condensed milk and roll
myself a cigarette. Then I regained my perch, again watching
the sea through the closed turret. We were crossing another
rough stretch.

An exceptional wave rose astern; it looked like a small
dune. It was not very steep, but seemed twice as high as the

others, if not more. The sea was not breaking yet, and I had the impression that it would not break, that it did not need to.

I jumped to the floor and gripped the chart table with both arms, my chest flat against it and my legs braced. I distinctly felt the surge of acceleration as *Joshua* was thrust forward. Then she heeled a little, seemed to brake, and was slammed down hard. Water spurted through the hatch cover joint, but I am not sure the wave responsible even broke. *Joshua* righted herself in four or five seconds. It took longer than after the first knockdown; a huge force seemed to keep her pressed to the water.

Again, no damage. Mast and spreaders held. The sails did not split. There was plenty of slack in the preventers, fortunately, and nylon can stretch. If things inert to us could do more than grit their teeth, I would have heard some real screaming up there on deck. Even the miraculous little wind vane held, and *Joshua* does not seem to have luffed; she is running downwind again, as if everything were already forgotten. Just the same, I am astonished to see the radar reflector in place on its masthead pivot. It too has already forgotten.

I am almost sorry now that I did not stay glued to the seat to see the whole show, my eyes riveted to the little turret ports . . . but when I saw the dune-like sea I felt *Joshua* could have pitchpoled,* in that case I would have broken my neck on the hatch coaming.

Pitchpoling at force 6 . . . I know very well it is impossible . . . but I feel anything is possible around here.

---

*Pitchpole: to capsize forward, turning end over end. This happened to *Tzu-Hang* and *Sandefjord*. When a boat pitchpoles the shock is frightful. *Tzu-Hang*'s doghouse was ripped right off, as if by a giant sledge hammer. *Joshua* nearly pitchpoled once in a gale during Tahiti-Alicante. She was very heavy at the time.

The wind drops further towards the end of the afternoon. The sea takes on its grandeur of old, tranquil and powerful. I feel the night will be fine, without treachery. I ought to stretch out for an hour before tonight's watch for possible ice; I have been on the go since dawn . . . for many dawns. But the sun will soon set, and I cannot tear myself from my contemplation of the sea and the boat.

I do have to get more sleep, though; catnapping is easy. I should pay more attention to food. I rely on coffee and tobacco to keep me going, and sustain myself by nibbling here and there. I ought to be able to find time for solid sleep and hearty meals. After all, there is not that much to do on a boat, even rounding Good Hope. Or even the Horn. But there is a lot to *feel* in the waters of a great cape. And that takes all the time in the world.

So one forgets oneself, one forgets everything, seeing only the play of the boat with the sea, the play of the sea around the boat, leaving aside everything not essential to that game in the immediate present. One has to be careful, though, not to go further than necessary to the depths of the game. And that is the hard part . . . not going too far.

The weather turns beautiful the very next morning. For two days the wind romps between NW and SW, the barometer is high and the sun burnishes the curve of the long westerly swell. It looks as if the sea too is happy to rest.

I eat with a terrific appetite; at night, I sleep as soundly as possible, and take little snoozes during the day whenever I feel like it. The October 26 sight shows only 117 miles covered, and the next day just 68, partly thanks to current. But calms and light airs are welcome sometimes; we both need them. I work calmly at the odd jobs that make up my universe, without haste: I glue the sextant leg back on with epoxy, adjust the mirrors, replace five worn slide lashings on the mainsail and three on the mizzen, splice the staysail and mizzen halyards (they are Tergal; the jib and mainsail halyards are steel) to freshen the nip on the sheaves.

Flat calm now. I am busy doing a little extra job near the end of the mizzen boom, using my Swedish marlinspike. There is a jerk, I don't know why, and the marlinspike falls overboard . . . I dive instantly, fully dressed. It did not sink very deep thanks to its wooden handle and light wedge-shaped spike. I am happy and proud, bringing it back aboard, because that way *Joshua* will not have shed the least of her feathers since the start. As for me, I dove into the icy water though it did not seem necessary, since there is a spare marlinspike. Yet it was necessary . . . not one feather missing!

Joshua is in full regalia, the shrouds festooned with all the soaked sweaters and wool trousers now drying in the warm sun. Clothes with salt in them get clammy as soon as the air becomes humid. But if one shakes them vigorously when they are good and dry, the salt crystals are dislodged, and the clothes will stay dry (or nearly).

Jean Gau taught me the trick when *Atom* and *Marie-Thérèse II* were together at Durban. He wore impeccable shirts washed in sea water with Teepol detergent, and hung to dry as high as possible, out of range of spray. The wind snapped the cloth, and knocked the crystals out.

Right now, the breeze is too light to snap my heavy woollens, so I lend a hand, shaking furiously, and brushing them from time to time. It works perfectly; you can see the crystals flying. The big green and blue checked blanket had got a little damp, and is soaking up the sun on the warm deck. It will go back on the berth as soft and fluffy as it was at Plymouth.

Joshua is just as fit as when we left England, further lightened by two month's sailing and in better trim to face heavy weather. The sails are like new; I did not have to replace a single Goïot sail hank. They do not even show signs of real wear after 65 days of chafe, not counting the 30 day Toulon–Plymouth run.

Judging from the appearance of the rudder, which I can see very well in calm periods, the bottom must be spotless. The barnacles removed after Trinidad have not grown back, and there are no stains on the antifouling. Me? Very well, thanks.

Jean Knocker, *Joshua*'s designer, gave me three bottles of champagne when he called at Plymouth on *Casarca*. I was to drink one at each cape.

I wanted to wait until *Joshua* had crossed the 30th meridian (160 miles ahead) before opening the first bottle. If I downed it too soon, Good Hope might see me and get angry before I had time to run. Geographically, it is already four hundred miles astern, but the damned cape has a long arm. It could still say, "Come here, little boy, come get your spanking, because you know the two miniature breaking seas the other day were just a joke, so come over here, my pet, and I'll show you breaking seas from Good Hope!"

Tonight, I am almost sure Good Hope has been completely rounded. I slowly warm a big can of fish soup in the pressure cooker. It will stay hot for a long time. To flesh it out, I toss in a handful of cooked rice left over from lunch and a big dab of butter.

The sun sets in a reassuring blaze of red, and the barometer is high, 1,022 millibars. What little breeze was left this afternoon has died, and I heave to for a really quiet night;

sheets aback, helm down and sails fully reefed, ready for any surprises.

Complete rest, no decisions to make. *Joshua* waits for the wind to come back, as do the gulls and albatrosses resting on the sea all around.

Night. There is not much moon, but it is high, and the whole night is lit up, so clear is the air. No cirrus, still no cirrus.*

A burning mug between my hands. I drink the fish soup in little swallows, and the soup becomes blood and warmth within me. Radio Cape Town, which I had not been able to get for the last four days, forecasts no gales on the coasts of South Africa. I knew it: the sea, the sky, the albatrosses, the missing cirrus had already told me. But it is nice to hear it confirmed by that friendly voice.

I like the Cape Town announcer. When he warns of a gale, you can feel the worry in his voice; he gives the warning twice, then repeats it at the end of the forecasts. He is not just talking to hear himself talk, lulling himself with the sound of his own voice. He is communicating with people at sea, and one feels he gives us all he has to give. He brings humanity to his work.

As the westerly gales announced by Cape Town are linked with lows moving from west to east observed in the South Atlantic, I know I can count on at least two more days of good weather, even if a gale reached South Africa tomorrow undetected (*Joshua* is already 430 miles east of Cape Agulhas).

I don't like ceremonies . . . but I really feel like having that champagne! I drink it very, very slowly, and finish the whole bottle in little sips. The fish soup practically boils in my veins. I am terrifically happy. I feel so happy, so much at peace with

*Cirrus clouds form in front of weather disturbances and generally indicate their approach.

the entire universe, that I am laughing and laughing as I go on deck for a perfectly normal urge after all that liquid. But there, I behold a scene so amazing as not to be believed.

There was this guy standing aft; yes, that's right, a guy. He looked happy as could be, and he laughingly said (I repeat word for word), "Hey there, Good Hope, since your arm's so long, it must be mighty handy to scratch your ass, eh?"

It was cause for concern, but he vanished without my seeing him go, while I was picking my way aft to shut him up. I threw the empty bottle overboard, and went below. Just then, I saw the Southern Cross to port, *Joshua* having swung around little by little in the flat calm, unnoticed. So the other guy blasphemed with his back to Good Hope. Nothing serious, thank God!

The stars are twinkling very brightly up there in the night. When I was a kid, an old Indochinese fisherman explained to me why the stars twinkle, and why they twinkle very strongly when the wind is going to come back. But I can't tell that story tonight, I'm too sleepy.

Slept well. The wind has come back, just as the stars promised. The October 28 sight shows 188 miles covered noon to noon. We are sailing at top speed; it is terrific, with the heavy sea shining under the sun. I spend nearly an hour sitting on the pulpit, unable to take my eyes off *Joshua*'s bow slamming through the sea. To think I almost had no bowsprit at all! She would never have done that well, even helped by the current.

I put the rice on to cook at 2 P.M.; despite my hunger, I was unable to tear away from my nearly hypnotic contemplation of *Joshua* plunging into the foam and sun on the sea. The line on the *Damien* globe has lengthened again. Good Hope is in the wake, Leeuwin and the Horn remain.

No . . . only Leeuwin remains. One thing at a time, as in the days when I was building *Joshua.* If I had wanted to build *all* the boat at once, the enormity of the task would have crushed me. I had to put all I had into the hull alone, without thinking about the rest. It would follow . . . with the help of the gods.

Sailing non-stop around the world is the same. I do not think anyone has the means of pulling it off—*at the start.*

Leeuwin remains . . . and all of my faith.

A Saw-tooth Wake

Joshua is sailing due east along the 39th parallel. Now, the iceberg limit is far enough away, about 150 miles south. The weather is still fair—you can't be too choosy in a place like this. But the wind has dropped a lot, with periods of near calms, and there is a swell from the east I don't like. Moreover, the barometer is too high, a sign that the anti-cyclone has moved south. If I wanted to play it by the book, I would stay closer to the 40th parallel, to make sure of not losing the westerlies. I hesitate though, because that's the mistake I made three years earlier, dropping further than necessary to the south; *Joshua* was nearly wiped out by the gale of her career in the Pacific, about 3,000 miles before rounding the Horn.

If the east wind announced by the swell and the barometric rise does not show up in the next two days, I may put a little north in my east, because of the austral spring. Actually, this is conjecture; I don't know what I will do . . . it depends on too many little things, as always at sea.

The first gale of the Indian Ocean hits on October 30, from the SE. The forecast mentions a NE blow on the coast of Natal, soon swinging to the west when it will diminish. Natal is far behind, but it always helps to know what is happening there.

It would be possible to beat, as the wind only reaches force
8 in the gusts. Just the same, I heave *Joshua* to under double
reefed main and mizzen, 54 sq. ft. staysail and the storm jib
aback, with the helm down. Not only is it much less tiring
than diving into the fray on a close reach, but I prefer to
renew cautiously my acquaintance with the Indian Ocean, the
most savage of the three.

The wind becomes NE during the night, without increasing.
I put the tiller almost amidships and trim the staysail sheet
for a close reach, leaving the storm jib aback so as to slowly
jog along ESE. The dead water from our drift no longer
protects us, but the breaking crests remain moderate, as is
usual in an easterly gale. *Joshua* takes two of them without any
fuss.

The wind then backs to north, and finally to NW in the
morning, dropping to force 3. The sea becomes exceedingly
choppy. At one point, the boat took seas simultaneously *fore
and aft*. It is an odd feeling, but is not dangerous. The seas
have become extremely steep, with pyramids of foam at their
peaks, which stay on the backs of the main west and SW
swells. It is very much like the strange sea *Joshua* met just after
the Horn a few years ago, in an almost complete calm. I am
glad some wind now remains to press against the sails. Fairly
big breaking seas once in a great while.

Gradually the bigger breaking waves become less frequent.
The sky turns completely blue to windward, without a cloud
on the horizon. The barometer begins to rise again. What is
left of the wind is still from the NW. But that will change
soon . . . nothing stays the same long in these waters.

I leave the sails close reefed, and do not even change the
headsails, because we would not sail any faster in the enormous

chop. It comes from everywhere at once, and whips the rigging around. Actually, I still don't quite have my old punch. Before Good Hope I would not have stood the storm jib another minute. Since Good Hope, I tend to save my strength.

At the end of the afternoon the entire sea begins a sound. It reminds me of an angry termite colony, when the soldier-termites who escort the workers start clicking their mandibles together by the thousands. The Indochinese termites have such powerful mandibles that the planters in the bush used them to close wounds when there was no doctor available. Here, the entire surface of the sea shivers with the same rustling like dead leaves. Each crest is covered with foam, none breaking dangerously; one could not even call them whitecaps. And all this in a nearly complete calm. I have never seen anything like it. Add a gale on that, and you would see terrific breakers. Thank God, the barometer looks OK!

A few hours later not a sound—just the long swell cut by many secondary wave trains. Not a breath of wind. The sails slat and chafe, so everything has to be sheeted in.

I put the helm alee, and will get under way when *Joshua* starts heeling. Conor O'Brien, whose Indian Ocean crossing I am re-reading, recommends a solid day's rest from time to time, when it does not pay to wear yourself out trimming the sails. O'Brien adds that he himself is too restless to follow the advice, but it suits me just fine. It is nice to be in my bunk. Hardly any motion. The wind will come back.

I think of the little plank I saw alongside this morning, squared off, planed smooth, and perfectly clean, without a speck of seaweed, as if laid there by a mysterious hand. I had given a long, sweeping look around. Nothing. Just the little board, already disappearing in the wake of the gale . . . the sign of a human presence, so close, so fugitive, in waters visited only by seabirds.

Where are Bill King, Nigel, Loïck? I had hoped day after day to get news of them from the BBC or Radio Cape Town after my message to the little black freighter. Not a mention. I am playing alone with the entire sea, alone with the past, the present and the future. Maybe it is better this way . . . but I would like news of my friends.

Loïck is probably a week away from Good Hope, watching the mood of the barometer, wondering whether it would be better to pass close to land, like Vito Dumas and Conor O'Brien, or far off the Agulhas Bank. Is he growing his seeds in the plastic saucers we bought together at Plymouth? Very easy: you take seven saucers, punch a few holes in them, and line them with cloth. Fill with wheat grains, soybeans and watercress seeds. Stack them one on top of the other, and moisten with a little water. After a few days, the sprouts are long enough. Remove the bottom saucer, and boil the sprouts or make a salad. Refill the saucer with fresh seeds, put it on top of the pile and sprinkle, next day, remove the bottom saucer, eat the sprouts, refill with seeds, put it on top, sprinkle, etc., and you have perpetual motion! It is easy, but I find it a bother, and I prefer Ovaltine, which contains barley germ and lots of other good things. I tossed my seed packets overboard after a month at sea, except for a pound bag of soybeans, just in case.

Nigel laughed at our germination experiments: he thought we were going to a lot of trouble for nothing, and he was probably right. Where is Nigel? How far will he get with his trimaran?

And Bill King, where is he? Perhaps far ahead, perhaps behind if he got hung up in the doldrums, perhaps very close if the gods have permitted. It would be a victory for all of us, if

Bill King's trip made it possible to perfect a Eurasian rig that is close to ideal, thanks to its extreme simplicity of handling. It is surprising that I did not hear about anyone on the BBC or elsewhere, since Bill and Nigel have weekly radio contact with their sponsoring newspapers.

Maybe they just chucked it . . . transmitter, batteries, brain-rattling generator, jerry cans of explosive gasoline, heave ho!–the whole bloody lot overboard, for a little peace and quiet.

Nearly midnight. I slept for a few hours, as usual. The rhythm of the sea is not the same as that ashore. At sea I wake up almost automatically around midnight, feeling fresh, and go back to sleep an hour later. This gives me plenty of time for a turn on deck to feel the heart of the night and sense what is around. Then I roll myself a cigarette at the chart table, dreaming before the *Damien* globe.

When I feel really conscientious I fix myself a mug of Ovaltine and munch a biscuit. When I feel less so, I settle for coffee and another cigarette; rolled not too thick, because a package of tobacco has to last three days.

The sea has very quickly become fine again. Barely twelve hours ago it was breaking under a thick overcast. Then it started to boil with cross-seas from the east quadrant when the wind eased. Now the wind is back, force 2 from the west, and the sea is all smiles in the moonlight.

I get under way, shake out the reefs and set the big staysail. I will wait for dawn to replace the storm headsail with the working jib.

The middle of the night is the moment I like best when the weather is nice; it is as if the next food day were beginning then instead of at dawn. But my cigarette and coffee taste a little stale, because I am a bit sick at the thought of *Joshua* doing a knot less than she could in such fine weather. I finally set the working jib and treat myself to an extra spot of coffee before curling up in my bunk.

Ashore, coffee keeps me awake, but not here. And I sleep all I like during the day. People often imagine that sailors are a breed of supermen; that we almost never sleep, spend all our time handling sails, never get a hot meal. If they only knew! The wind has come back. *Joshua* is sailing east in the belt between the 37th and 38th parallels. In theory, she will stay there until she is 2,000 miles from Australia, then put a little south in her easting to round Cape Leeuwin and Tasmania. Conor O'Brien, a model of lucidity and seamanship, adopted that tactic to avoid the area further south, with its high percentage of gales. Vito Dumas, who went far north to the 35th parallel at one point, encountered long periods of calms and light variable winds there.

I hate storms, but calms undermine my spirits. I will have to be careful not to commit any big strategic blunders; I don't feel as tough as I used to. But I know that despite the most painstaking and technical study of the best routes, whether you get wind or not is up to heaven.

A quarter of the Indian Ocean is already astern, and the weather has been fairly nice for the last few days. Huge cloud systems pass overhead from time to time and drop some rain, but the few quarts collected in the buckets under the booms are still brackish. The sails got covered with a thin crust of salt during the days spent lying hove-to west of Good Hope, when the wind was filled with spray and the hot sun dried everything in a few seconds. It will take a hard rain to get rid of the salt.

I am not worried yet—rain is hardly lacking in these latitudes—but I would still like to raise the level of my tank. About fifty gallons are left of the hundred; this means a range of about a hundred days, figuring normal consumption at half a gallon a day.

The days go by, never monotonous. Even when they appear exactly alike they are never quite the same. That is what gives life at sea its special dimension, made up of contemplation and very simple contrasts. Sea, winds, calms, sun clouds, porpoises. Peace, and the joy of being alive in harmony.

Albatrosses, malamocks, Cape pigeons, shearwaters and a species I do not know which I dub Cape robins have been keeping *Joshua* company since the 35th parallel in the Atlantic. They seem to feed on spray and fresh air, skimming the waves without ever dipping their beaks.

Albatrosses and malamocks are loners. The others live in communities, with the smaller birds like the Cape robins making up the densest flocks. *Joshua* passes through groups of more than a hundred of these very little birds, about the size of robins, with silvery plumage, whose quick turns and sideslips remind me of swallows before a storm. Their undersides are white, the tails dark grey, and a big W marks the tops of their wings. They zig-zag along the water, often putting a leg down as if to help them turn. No relation to the tiny black and white petrels, who play in the air as lightly as butterflies. They too often turn by pushing a foot against the water.

Vito Dumas described his tame Cape pigeon as a black bird with lovely white markings. Without that description I would worry sometimes; seen head-on, Cape robins fly just like pigeons, and I read somewhere that big flocks of Cape pigeons are a sure sign of icebergs nearby. Two or three Cape pigeons have been keeping us company since Good Hope. They are exactly as Dumas described them, with large white spots blending into the black of their wings.

The shearwaters are the size of a big gull, and look just like crows sitting on the water. Their even plumage, very dark brown, shows reddish highlights in the sun, but looks black in overcast weather. They glide along without beating their wings, a little hunched over, in groups of eight to fifteen, often abreast. They look as if they were raking the sea as a team, making their lithe, harmonious turns nearly in formation. The same group has been with us a long time. I can recognize one by a feather missing from his left wing.

The most beautiful are the malamocks, a kind of albatross only smaller (6 ft. wingspan) and infinitely more graceful. All the ones I see have nearly the same wardrobe: white belly, neck and tail, with wings of dark grey on top, pearl grey underneath along the leading edge, and very light grey, some-times almost white, along the trailing edge. All display an attractive almond-shaped pattern around the eye, like a vamp's makeup.

Malamocks have real feathers, whereas the albatrosses (wingspan over 9 ft.) seem covered with a woolly down. Each has his personal attire, and it would be impossible to mistake one albatross for another. There is one I always look for when I come on deck: very big, cindery grey underneath and nearly black on top, with a brown spot under his left eye. With malamocks, on the other hand, it would take a sharp eye to pick one out from twenty others, even after a month of daily contact.

The birds here behave in a completely different way from the ones in the tropics. There, everything is gaiety, screaming and diving. I know few sights to compare with forty gannets tumbling from the sky like rockets on a school of sardines. On *Marie-Thérèse II*, between Cape Town and Saint Helena, I danced around the deck echoing their cries, to see them work-ing with such gusto. Often one would leave the group to glide in close to the mizzen for a moment, before going back to his fishing. The wideawakes and tropic birds were friendly too. Even the frigate birds, usually stand-offish, took an interest in my boat.

Here, albatrosses, malamocks, shearwaters, Cape pigeons and the tiny petrels glide along indifferently. *Joshua*, for them, does not exist. Yet she must, because my big cindery albatross is often there, as well as my shearwater with the missing feather. But above all, they seem to be searching for something, something very important in the wind and spray.

Nevertheless, Cape robins are friendly and curious at times, when they show up to pass the time of day. Just for fun, they come over in twos and threes to check on the rigging and play with the eddies in the lee of the sails. They sideslip so nimbly that I can't keep them in the Beaulieu's rangefinder.

I would give a lot to tame a Cape robin. They do not stay long enough, though, and each flock I meet keeps to its own territory.

Though we have almost reached the 37th parallel, the weather keeps changing, sometimes abruptly. It rained or drizzled all last night and finally rinsed the sails, allowing me to collect eight gallons of water. At sunrise a light band far to windward cuts across the low ceiling. An hour later the sky is blue, with little round cumulus and a SW wind announcing fair weather. Towards 11 o'clock I begin to wonder whether the sun will be out for the noon sight and I take an early sight just to be on the safe side, as heavy altocumulus and probably stratus close in very quickly from the west. I still manage to catch the sun at the meridian through the veil of stratus; then it clears. But a little while later the southern horizon is blocked by a very heavy cloudbank showing protuberances and rain. I shook out the reefs this morning; I tie them in again, one each in main and mizzen. No point in reefing the staysail; since I have to stay on deck, it will be simpler to take it down if the wind turns gusty, and raise it again later.

No gusts. Yet the seas build and begin to break without any real increase of wind. Then it starts drizzling and the wind eases to force 4, veering to the SSW. I go below to gulp down a can of Camembert with army biscuits and some custard, as I had not eaten and the clock says 2 P.M. When I go back on deck ten minutes later, I find that the two buckets hung under the booms have more than a gallon of water. I pour my precious gallon into the jerry can, thanking heaven and cursing the unstable weather, as the wind is down to force 3, and the choppy sea is taking its toll of the sails.

I shake out the reefs at 3 P.M., under a sky blanketed from one horizon to the other. Still, the log shows eighteen miles covered since noon; that is 6 knots, for the moment. But miles are hard-won around here. SW force 5 wind again at 3.30 P.M. Same sky, same type of weather. A little nap.

By the next day's sight 160 miles have been covered. Beautiful weather from the SW, wind force 5 to 6, very pronounced seas, all blue and lovely. The cumulus are nice and round, instead of flattened as they usually are here. It rained or drizzled again last night, in spite of the usually dry SW wind, and I got up to collect water from the buckets. They are nearly full again this morning. So I now have more than ten gallons in my jerry cans, which I pour into the tank. The two last months' near-absence of rain had me worried, as did the sails' stubborn saltiness.

I have been feeling tired for a week. Moreover, my back has started acting up, probably due to a weakening of the muscles along the spine, caused by too little exercise and a certain lack of variety in diet. I was already seven pounds underweight when I left Plymouth. A few days ago I managed to weigh myself in a flat calm: another couple of pounds lost in three months . . .

Yes, I feel tired. Occasionally I find myself taking a long look at Mauritius on the chart, not very far north of here. It is the most beautiful place I know, with Saint Helena. But Saint Helena is far, very far away, beyond the Horn and at the other end of the world; I do not even dare think of it. Mauritius, on the other hand, is close, too close, and filled with memories of my Mauritian friends with whom I spent three of the most beautiful years of my life. I feel very weary at times. If I do not get on top of things, *Joshua* will not reach the end of the long ribbon of foam that leads to Plymouth. But now there are moments when I feel a great emptiness inside, when I am no longer sure where to go.

I have started taking Pentavit tablets (vitamin B complex), and will keep at it for a month, because my fatigue may be due to vitamin deficiency. But I will also have to take more interest in cooking: vitamin tablets will never replace a hearty appetite. Above all, start exercising, as I used to do in the old days. And go on deck more often, regardless of weather. Many things are cured by wind and sea, if you stay on deck with them long enough.

Sticking to the 36th parallel may be wise also, to let my feathers grow back in a kinder climate before turning south for Cape Leeuwin and Tasmania. But how far, and how vain, all that seems to me when I really think about it.

Take reefs in, shake them out, take them in, shake them out, live with the sea, live with the birds, live with the present, never looking beyond today, knowing that everything comes with time . . .

Progress is slow, as the weather is very unstable and also because I have decided not to carry maximum sail between sunset and dawn, so as to spend a week with no worries at night. One day we covered 136 miles at the noon sight, 134 the next, then just 29 because of a great calm full of sunshine, then 88 miles, 159 miles, 131 miles, 119 miles, 160 miles, 167 miles . . . a real sawtooth wake.

SE gale on November 10 and 11. I was forced to heave-to on the starboard tack and drift north for 24 hours, to avoid being pushed south. Next day, 145 miles on the 36th parallel, then 162, and 183 in a SSW gale that raised really big breakers. I have to take them nearly astern, losing still more latitude, to avoid serious damage. Then 146 miles on the 15th in a terrifically choppy sea, 150 miles on the 16th . . . and here I am, becalmed on November 17 in 34° 38′ south latitude, with barely 45 miles to the good since last night. For all my careful planning to avoid Vito Dumas's mistake, I fell right into the same trap.

Nonetheless, the line on the *Damien* globe is longer; we are nearly halfway between Good Hope and Tasmania. The sun is glorious, and I am grateful just to rest for the day, watching the calm while my bedding airs on deck.

I go below to straighten the aft cabin, where grapefruit, lemons, garlic and onions are stowed. The garlic will last a century! The lemons have kept perfectly too. Françoise wrapped each of them in a page from the *Reader's Digest*, which is just the right size. I will eat my last grapefruit today. Of the hundred taken aboard three months ago, only five or six went bad.

The little purple Morocco onions that Loïck gave me at Plymouth are still in very good shape; at most, a few sprouts, which are not wasted since I usually put them in my rice. On the other hand, picking through the big white onions again is pointless. They are completely rotten, and I heave the bag overboard.

Seven malamocks and a flock of shearwaters are gliding nearby at that moment. Many of them fly right over the bag of onions without seeing it. I suppose their eyes are focused at the distance that allows them to make out whatever it is they are looking for (just what that is, I wish I knew). Finally, one of them notices the bag and makes a sharp turn to land by it. Only then do the others realize that something interesting might be happening, and they come and land next to the first, one after the other. What the devil are they looking for, among the wave tops? It must be awfully hard to find, for them to fly right past that enormous thing ten times without so much as noticing it. And how about you, old man . . . what are you looking for?

Absolutely flat calm; sunshine everywhere, above and below. Filling a bucket with water for the dishes, I notice that the sea is covered with plankton. It is made up of tiny animals smaller than pinheads, zig-zagging along the calm water. Scooped along the surface, the bucket harvests a good hundred of the living mites; a foot or so deeper it only brings up three or four.

There is also a carpet of pretty, flat jellyfish the size of a penny, that I do not recognize, and a few Portuguese men-o'-war, lovely in the sunlight. They look like blue-tinted oval balloons, capped by a translucent crest for sailing into the wind, when there is any.

The calm becomes a breath of air, nearly transparent, but steady. The wake appears on the smooth sea. Today I would like to see some of the water spiders that fled from *Joshua*'s bow as we were leaving the doldrums in the Atlantic. I wasted two reels trying to film the long-legged insects, whose bodies are no bigger than flies'. They were too quick, impossible to catch in the lens. The boat frightened them moving at 4 knots. It would be easy today; they would keep still in the glitter of the sun.

They were the same water spiders as those in the streams of Europe and Asia. On *Marie-Thérèse* I encountered lots of them in mid–Indian Ocean, very far west of Sumatra. At first I could not believe it, yet there they were, skittering over the sea on their long, curved legs. They do not dive, and are carnivorous, so there must be invisible lives on the surface of the sea. How could they survive, so fragile in appearance, when the waves turn ugly? Yet they managed very well; there were thousands around *Marie-Thérèse*. It was a day of calms. The night before, we had been hove-to.

Two tiny things are swimming alongside. One chases the other, catches it, lets it go, catches it again. They fight, I trap them in the bucket for a closer look. They resemble two miniature cicadas. They do not fight, they procreate. Marvellous, to see life going on, so far from everything and against all odds.

I look for others, while *Joshua* drifts in the light airs, but there are just two of them, no bigger than a baby's fingernail, for the entire sea. Yet they managed to find each other despite the dangers of this great open sea.

When I was a child, my mother told me God had painted the sky blue because blue is the colour of hope. He must have painted the sea blue for the same reason. I feel myself going far back to my childhood in Indochina to the period when I hunted barefoot with my slingshot. It was not so much to kill birds as to listen to the murmurs, the reflections, the imperceptible crackings and the abrupt silences of the forest, full of clues and secret things.

I wipe off my Beaulieu slowly, with affection. Little by little, it has become more than a mere tool. There are only twenty-seven reels left, to finish a trip that has just begun. Will it be possible to bring pictures that say everything, where nothing needs to be explained?

The wind picks up after the noon sight, northerly, force 3 to 4. The barometer has not thrown any fits in the last three days and *Joshua* sails very fast on a sea that is still flat, steering SE so as not to lose the wind. I have added a bonnet under the mainsail boom, an extra staysail and storm jib forward, and a mizzen staysail: 1,075 sq. ft. in all.

I gaze at my boat from the top of the mainmast. Her strength, her beauty, her white sails well set on a well found-boat. The foam, the wake, the eleven porpoises on either side of the bowsprit. They are black-and-white porpoises, the most beautiful I know. They breathe on the fly, almost without breaking the surface, without wavering from the course, towing *Joshua* at nearly 8 knots by invisible bonds. Climbing down to fetch the Beaulieu is out of the question. I would lose everything, and what they give me is too precious; a lens would spoil it all. They leave without my touching them, but the bonds remain.

My big cindery albatross, the malamocks and the shearwaters have resumed their endless quests, level with the waves. They almost all landed during the calm, showing no interest in *Joshua*. I threw them a few pieces of the dorado caught in the trades, which has been drying in the mizzen shrouds for two months at the mercy of the weather, without rotting or smelling bad. It did not interest them either. Just the same, two shearwaters ducked their heads under to watch the little cubes sinking toward the depths.

They are all gliding now, happy as I that the wind has

come back. Their slender, motionless wings flutter at the tips as if feeling the air, sensitive as a blind man's touch. The Cape robins have not been around for a good week; perhaps I went too far north for them. My shearwater with the missing feather is not there either. It is not the first time he has disappeared though, and I know he always comes back.

—Translated by William Rodarmor

Postscript: Seven months later and nearing the finish, Bernard Moitessier suddenly pulled out of the race and sailed on for another three months before ending his 37,455-mile journey, never once touching land.

One of the top three offshore races in the world is the annual run from Sydney, Australia, to Hobart, Tasmania. The 630-mile race takes place the day after Christmas and is considered especially challenging because of wildly unpredictable currents and weather. In 1998 the 115 boats that entered the race were warned of approaching gale-force winds, which resulted in a maritime disaster that will not soon be forgotten.

FATAL STORM

*The Inside Story of the Tragic
Sydney–Hobart Race*

ROB MUNDLE

The Anticipation

A magnificent summer day dawned over Sydney Harbour on December 26, 1998. Steve and Libby Kulmar awoke around 6:30 to the first silver shafts of sunlight dancing on the glassy waters of the harbor off Forty Baskets Beach. Steve noticed that a heavy dew had settled on the lawn during the night. In Sydney that could only mean that a strong northeasterly sea breeze would develop in the afternoon, a breeze that would make for great racing under spinnaker.

As always, Steve's mother had made a boiled fruitcake for the crew. While breakfast was being prepared, Libby cut this moist and dark homemade treat into sections so everyone on board could enjoy two slices each. She was tempted to taste it but resisted out of superstition and tradition. Meanwhile Steve methodically packed his gear, and went to great lengths to ensure everything would stay dry.

Libby's parents, John and Nerolie—"Noo" to everyone— were also up. John planned to go to the club to enjoy the sights and bid farewell to Steve. Then he and Noo would head north to the central coast for a vacation at picturesque Avoca Beach.

"Why don't you come up for a few days while Steve's away?" Noo asked Libby over breakfast.

"Oh, I don't think I'll come up. I think I'm going to have to pick up Steve." Libby's response shocked her after she'd said it. In recalling those comments Libby did not know what prompted her. "I've never ever said anything like that before Steve had gone to do any other ocean race. We've always expected him to finish in Hobart and he has. I can't explain why I said it."

The latest weather forecasts confirmed that nothing had changed. There would be a nice northeasterly for the start, then a south to sou'westerly change during the night—a typical southerly buster for what was shaping up as a typical Hobart race. There was, however, still an element of uncertainty about the intentions of a low lingering off the New South Wales coast and what impact an upper air disturbance might have on conditions in Bass Strait. Roger Badham was already well on his way to the CYC from his home at Coledale, south of Sydney. He had been up almost the entire night analyzing the very latest local and international computer models of the developing weather patterns.

Badham had outlined what he expected to happen, what to watch for and what other potential scenarios might occur. Most of the race's high-profile competitors were relying on him to provide the answers to the mysteries of meteorology— answers that would give them the best possible chance of winning. Badham's briefcase was filled with folders marked with the name of each yacht he was servicing: *Sayonara*, *Brindabella*, *Wild Thing*, *ABN AMRO Challenge*, *B-52*, and many others.

"This is a typical Hobart race—with the southerly change— but this is one of the most difficult in recent years to accurately pinpoint the wind changes due to an intense low that looks set to develop near Tasmania," he said. "The low is associated with an upper cold air trough [and fast-moving fronts] that will produce heaps of breeze south of Tasmania, and things look pretty reasonable on the Tassie coast. Over Bass Strait—well, it depends exactly where the low develops— how close to Tasmania . . . but best guess is not too far south, and the forecast [in the early hours of December 26] is for quite strong winds across Bass Strait on the 27th and slowly moderating winds on the 28th.

"This afternoon/tonight, 26 December: northeasterly sea breeze in the afternoon ahead of a southerly front expected around midnight. This is a sou'westerly change through Bass Strait and a southerly (180°) change along the NSW [New South Wales] coast. This is a trough system, and thunderstorms are likely. Late yesterday, storms gave short wind-squalls of 50 to 60 knots across Victoria—this will be the case again this afternoon, so be prepared. A low in the Tasman looks like being absorbed into the trough/front and sliding down the front to be off Tasmania tomorrow.

"Sunday 27 December: high pressure must wait over the Great Australian Bight while a low-pressure system spins up southeast of Tasmania. The high will ridge along the Victorian coast and north Bass Strait around the New South Wales corner, but if the low really spins up, it will be the cyclonic circulation around this that will dominate Bass Strait."

The one word that stood out was "cyclonic." Americans call it a hurricane.

There was plenty already happening when Badham and his wife, Margaret, arrived at the CYC to deliver the eagerly awaited forecasts. His weather predictions would determine sail inventory for the race, the yacht's course, and tactics for the first twelve hours, and how the yacht might be configured for maximum performance. The docks were jammed with sailors, supporters, spectators, and media. Wheelbarrows laden with supplies, ice, crew bags, and equipment were deftly guided through the crush. High in the forest of masts and what seemed to be the tangle of rigging supporting them, crew members were swinging around like monkeys on strings, scanning for potential problems. Television crews with bulky cameras on their shoulders panned, tilted, and zoomed in and out to capture the prerace atmosphere. Reporters were busy interviewing race personalities.

Tom Sobey, a seventeen-year-old from Albury on the New South Wales–Victoria border, attracted much attention. His efforts the previous day to hitch a ride aboard a race yacht had failed. Undaunted, he decided to give it one more shot on Boxing Day. From 7 A.M. he had walked the docks at the CYC with signs pinned to the front and back of his shirt. The scrawled red writing read CREW AVAILABLE. Sobey had just finished his final year of high school and had come to Sydney on the off-chance he might snaffle a ride to Hobart. Like so many young sailors raised in a world of dinghy racing, Sobey regarded the Hobart as the ultimate event. But 1998 was not his year, and as the fleet set sail, Tom Sobey watched from shore.

As Steve Kulmar was leaving for the CYC on Boxing Day morning, he stopped by his daughter Pip's room, kissed her cheek, and whispered good-bye. A muffled grunt from a head firmly buried in a pillow was Pip's only response. Later, as Steve and the other family members drove toward the Sydney Harbour Bridge, a personal concern unrelated to the race or the weather niggled him. He hated the fact that the yacht was at the crowded club on race day and much preferred it when the preparations were done elsewhere. He didn't enjoy struggling with his bags through a crowd to get to the yacht. But like the weather conditions, this was out of his control.

Sailors, wannabes, socialites, media types, and countless curious spectators had been gathering at the club since early morning. For some, navigating through the throng had become a tricky business. Paul Borge, from Mooloolaba in Queensland, confidently made his way along the dock with a white cane in one hand and a friendly arm to hang on to. He was heading for *Aspect Computing*–the yacht manned by the group competing under the banner "Sailors with Dis-Abilities." Borge had lost his sight two years earlier yet was determined to continue sailing. Also in the *Aspect Computing* crew was twelve-year-old Travis Foley, a dyslexic from Mudgee and the race's youngest competitor.

The smell of breakfast–bacon and eggs cooking on the club's outdoor barbecue, toast, and freshly brewed coffee–filled the air as sailors clad in their colorful T-shirts and shorts mingled with the punters in their best summer attire. In the small parking lot at the side of the club, crew members waited anxiously for representatives from the Bureau of Meteorology to arrive with the official race forecast. On the street, others were paying ten dollars and throwing their excess baggage, cruising sails for the trip home, inflatable dinghies, and spare equipment into the back of the large truck that was heading to Hobart. Excess weight would slow a yacht, so only the bare essentials could be taken on board.

George Snow, property developer and owner of Australia's glamour maxi, *Brindabella*, was having his hand shaken and his back slapped as he struggled through the crowd to his seventy-five-foot racer at the end of the marina.

"Good luck, mate. Make sure you beat those Americans," came a call from the crowd. It was a nice thought, but deep down Snow and his enthusiastic supporter both knew that the odds were against his "old girl" beating the triple world champion *Sayonara*. A few hundred meters to the north, at d'Albora Marinas, *Sayonara*'s owner, the trim, fit, and energetic Larry Ellison, had arrived and was attracting a fair amount of attention. But one of his crew members was stealing the show. Lachlan Murdoch, the twenty-seven-year-old CEO and Chairman of News Corporation in Australia, stood with his fiancée, Sarah O'Hare. Needless to say, the photographers were having a field day.

Sayonara was an impressive piece of yachtbuilding and a beautiful boat. From its sleek white hull and aerodynamic carbon-fiber mast to the crew's crisp white T-shirts—complete with the bold red-and-black *Sayonara* logo—it was arguably one of the finest yachts in the world and was wholly justified in being the odds-on favorite. A spare-no-expense campaigner, Ellison had assembled an experienced and highly accomplished crew. It was headed by New Zealand ace and principal helmsman Chris Dickson, an America's Cup, match racing, and around-the-world racer who had come straight from taking his marriage vows in Auckland. Californian Mark Rudiger, the navigator, had guided Paul Cayard's *EF Language* to a crushing victory in the Whitbread round-the-world race earlier in the year.

Steve Kulmar and family arrived at the club, squeezed their car into the packed temporary parking lot, unloaded gear, then prepared themselves for the annual dock dance, ducking, weaving, and dodging to reach the yacht.

"We'd never been aboard *Sword of Orion*, so we all hopped on and had a bit of a look around," recalls Libby Kulmar. "I hadn't met Glyn [Charles] and some of the crew, so we chatted while they were getting ready."

The family didn't want to stay for the start, preferring to be home in time to watch it live on television. They decided to go to the clubhouse with Steve, but not before Madeline photographed her father with the new waterproof camera he'd been given for Christmas. They met up with friends, Bob and Sue and Matt Fraser. Bob had an update on the weather—the southerly buster was definitely brewing and would likely greet the fleet off the south coast of New South Wales between 2 A.M. and dawn. He confirmed the anticipated wind strength in the change was around 35 knots and added that it might back to the west. The looming low was still an unknown quantity. Kulmar thought they would probably have a quick beam reach for the crossing of Bass Strait. But he was getting impatient. It was time to go. He walked Libby, Maddie, and John back to the car.

"We wanted to get back home, cool off with a swim, then watch the start on television," said Libby. Steve was about to say good-bye to Maddie when she produced a surprise gift for him.

"Dad, I got this in the Christmas stocking. It's a good luck charm for you. I've got one and this one's yours."

She handed him a loop of thin luminous yellow cord. Hanging on it like a pendant was a pink piglet's head, about one third the size of a golf ball. When you squeezed it, the piglet's mouth opened and shut and made a clacking sound.

"You have to wear it," Maddie said.

Steve bent down and Maddie put it over his head.

"Maddie, it's beautiful. Thank you, darling," he said as he kissed her good-bye. He waved as they drove off, and then, with the piglet pendant secured around his neck, battled his way back to *Sword of Orion.*

The CYC was not the only hive of prerace activity Boxing Day morning. All around the harbor, other yacht clubs, marinas, and private docks were buzzing with last-minute preparations. In pretty Mosman Bay, two well-known and well-respected yachting figures were getting their charges set for sea.

Ian Kiernan, better known as "Bik," or "Captain Yucky Poo" to his mates (he earned the latter nickname through his prodigious environmental activities), had in recent years become a household name in Australia. More than a decade earlier Kiernan's love for Sydney Harbour had motivated him to organize the successful "Clean Up the Harbour" community campaign. It soon grew into "Clean Up Australia" and then the United Nations–backed "Clean Up the World" campaign.

"It started with 40,000 people cleaning up Sydney Harbour in 1989," Kiernan recalls. "It has now grown to 40 million people in 120 countries cleaning up the world. I'm proud of every one of them."

Kiernan's yacht, the classic Alan Payne–designed thirty-six-footer *Canon Maris,* had a historic link with the Hobart race. Its original owner, Jack Earl–a man whom Kiernan regarded as a father figure and mentor–was one of the event's founders. That link was strengthened when Earl's grandson, Matthew Tomaszewski, joined the *Canon Maris* crew. Also aboard were Jonathan "Gibbo" Gibson, son of John "Gibbo" Gibson, who was aboard *Winston Churchill,* and Richard "Sightie" Hammond, perhaps the most experienced competitor in the race, who was navigating. And to top it all off, 1998 was *Canon Maris*'s fortieth anniversary.

Canon Maris, a tidy, low-sided little wooden yawl with clean white topsides, a teak deck, and an immaculately varnished cabin, was meticulously maintained and, according to Kiernan, "probably better than the day it was built." A lot of water had passed under its keel since it came into Kiernan's hands in 1970. "I've sailed her twice to the United States, done four Hobarts in her, plus a single-handed Trans Pacific and a single-handed Trans Tasman." If that wasn't enough, Kiernan had also completed a single-handed around-the-world race, and had crewed for Australia in the Admiral's Cup in England and Clipper Cup in Hawaii. He knew this would be a tough race.

"For some reason I just picked it. Regardless, you should always be ready for rough weather. With the boat being forty years old, we always take our race preparation very seriously, but this time we were even more prepared. At the last moment I had a new storm trysail made, and we were attending to all of the issues for a heavy race. I ordered a new life raft and had an EPIRB [emergency position-indicating radio beacon for rescues at sea] fitted to that. All of our crew were provided with full sets of Musto HPX wet-weather gear with flotation vests and integrated safety harnesses. I wanted everyone to be dry and comfortable because on *Canon Maris* we live, eat, sleep, sail, and breathe the race. No one gets out of their sailing gear during the race. Everyone is ready to go on deck at all times. That way there's none of the frigging around with guys saying, 'who's got my seaboots and my safety harness?'"

The six *Canon Maris* crew were at Mosman Bay Marina at 9 A.M., resplendent in their red shirts, white shorts, and the traditional *Maris* beret, a tribute to artist and original owner Jack Earl. *Canon Maris*, *Winston Churchill*, and *Southerly* were set for a veteran's race among themselves. The wager was beers

and rum and Cokes, and the bets would be paid and collected
at a Hobart waterfront hotel.

As *Canon Maris* headed out of the bay the crew enjoyed some
light banter with the team preparing one of the hottest contenders for handicap honors—Syd Fischer's fifty-footer, *Ragamuffin*. Fischer, now at the ripe old age of seventy-three, had,
without question, been Australia's most successful ocean-
racing yachtsman. He had won just about everything that
mattered, including the Hobart race, the six-hundred-mile
Fastnet Race, the Admiral's Cup, and the Kenwood Cup. He
had led the Australian team to victory in the disastrous 1979
Fastnet Race. This was to be Fischer's thirtieth Sydney to
Hobart.

A fleet of yachts, including his 1995 America's Cup race
entrant and of course the mighty "Rags," was docked at the
harborfront doorstep of Fischer's three-level dark-timber resi-
dence. The large room on the lower level was devoted to
yacht-racing memorabilia and photographs covering Fischer's
nearly forty years of offshore competition. Minutes before
Canon Maris glided past, Fischer had assembled the crew—a
powerful blend of experience and raw, young energy—in the
"racing room" so sailing master Grant Simmer could brief
them on race weather and tactics. For twenty-one-year-old
crew member Nathan Ellis, this was his initiation to the classic. Once the briefing was over, the crew moved outside to
make the important final checks.

Immediately adjacent to the CYC, the Royal Australian
Navy's headquarters at Garden Island was also bristling
with prerace activity. The Navy's youth-training vessel, the
144-foot *Young Endeavour*, Britain's bicentennial gift to Australia in 1988, was preparing to go to sea. The classically
proportioned brigantine would again be the radio-relay vessel. The previous week the CYC's chief radio operator Lew

Carter and his team of technicians had installed the bank of radios needed to communicate with the fleet.

It was a symbolic Hobart race for Carter. He had completed sixteen races aboard yachts and had done an additional nine as radio operator, which took him to the magic number of twenty-five. Lew's two volunteer assistants, Michael and Audrey Brown, were also entrusted with a highly demanding job. They would provide strong support for Carter in what is an around-the-clock task. When the trio arrived at Garden Island on Boxing Day and were welcomed aboard by the ship's captain, Lieutenant Commander Neil Galletly, Carter had two concerns.

"I always thought it was going to be a rough year, just by looking at the weather patterns leading up to it, even over a couple of months. I was at the race briefing, and after listening to Ken Batt deliver his forecast I thought he was pretty skeptical about the whole thing. He didn't seem to be able to say what he thought we were going to get. I sensed he glossed over a few things without giving his true opinion. He seemed to have a bet each way."

Carter was also worried about the radios for the race.

"The radios are checked while the ship is at the dock, but I have said for a number of years I considered the procedure insufficient. The radios should be tested at sea, probably a fortnight prior to the race and preferably during some of the club's short ocean races. I think it would be a good idea to incorporate skeds [from *schedule*, a prescheduled news and weather update with fleet 'roll call' and position reports] into those short ocean races to acclimatize ourselves and the yachties again with procedures. It is very difficult to test the radios on *Young Endeavour* at Garden Island. You don't get out properly because there are so many buildings and other areas of interference. I wasn't happy with the radio from the start, right from when we were in Garden Island. I didn't appear to be getting to some of the places I thought we should have been able to contact."

Back at the CYC, the atmosphere was electric. Driving to the club with John "Steamer" Stanley, young Michael "Beaver" Rynan's eyes were like golf balls, his mouth agape as he took in the excitement of the morning of his first Hobart race. The pair made their way to *Winston Churchill* and met up with the rest of the crew. Crisp new boldly striped shirts and shorts were issued and once everything had been readied, most of the crew paraded back along the dock in their new attire to enjoy a few drinks with mates before they put to sea.

Steamer spotted race meteorologist Ken Batt. He sat down with him and showed him some old photographs of *Winston Churchill* in the first Hobart race in 1945. "Ken had some relatives racing on the yacht that year, and I was trying to see if he could identify them." Naturally they also discussed the weather, and Batt confirmed what he had said at the briefing: there was a chance the fleet would be buffeted by winds up to 50 knots and that it was going to be southwest turning west. Steamer thought, "Hang on, this doesn't sound right," but Batt could offer nothing more due to the instability of the pattern.

Meanwhile, Ian Kiernan was easing *Canon Maris* into "the Pond" next to the outdoor bar. Kiernan's wife, Judy, was put ashore to join a spectator boat. The bar was buzzing and among the myriad faces, Kiernan recognized plenty of mates, including Stanley and Mickleborough. "We had to put up with the bloody ragging of Mickleborough and his bloody larrikin *Southerly* crew—'We'll be on the dock with a beer for you, and all that shit,'" recalls Kiernan. "Then I looked across and there was Steamer just sipping on a schooner. I gave him the finger and he knew what it meant: the race was on. He smiled, gave me the Hawaiian Salute—the thumb and the little finger—and continued drinking. Jim Lawler was nearby and I shouted out 'Hi' to him. He was looking just like a bloody prince of a man in his sailing hat. I exchanged calls of 'Good luck' with Gouldy and Richard Winning. They had brought *Winston Churchill*'s performance right up, and we knew they were going to be bloody hard to beat."

The *Canon Maris* crew pushed their yacht away from the dock, Kiernan slipped the engine into gear, eased the throttle forward, turned his charge away from the marina, and powered off toward the start line.

On the way out, Kiernan reminded the crew of what was expected. "Guys, I think we're going to have a heavy and wet-weather race," said Kiernan. "We've all got plenty of experience, but I want to remind you that the executive decisions are made by Dick Hammond and myself. We want your feedback all the time, but we don't want chatter in times of decision. Keep yourselves clipped on. Sail conservatively but quickly and enjoy the bloody race." Hammond confirmed the heavy-weather prognosis and outlined what he expected for the run down the coast that afternoon and when the blow might arrive that night.

Winston Churchill's crew had also decided it was time to move. They returned to the yacht, said good-bye to their support team, including Stephanie Winning and the children, then guided the historic boat into the harbor. Peter Joubert's *Kingurra* had gone out early, for what crewman Peter Meikle recalls was a very good reason.

"Peter always makes us put up the storm jib and the trysail before the start. He does it every year so the old-timers are reacquainted with the settings and any new guys know where it all goes—and learn how not to scratch the varnish. I remember distinctly sailing past a few race boats with lots of people wearing smart, matching shirts. They were all pointing at us, laughing and carrying on. The same blokes would probably be saying later on that what we did should be a compulsory prestart practice."

The team from North Queensland aboard Wayne Millar's yacht, *B-52*, departed the CYC marina and headed out onto the harbor grinning from ear to ear. The forecast northeasterly for the first half-day should allow them to produce their secret weapon—a blooper. The youngest sailors in the race would never have heard of a blooper. To them the word meant an embarrassing mistake, nothing more. A blooper was, in fact, a special offshore racing sail in vogue in the 1970s. It was a lightweight headsail attached to the bow and set outside the leech (trailing edge) of the mainsail when the yacht was sailing directly downwind under spinnaker. In the Hobart race it was deemed illegal for the Grand Prix division, the IMS (International Measurement System) yachts. But as the boys from Townsville discovered, it was quite legal in their division, the CHS (Channel Handicap System) section.

That youthful ignorance had prompted its resurrection. *B-52* crewman and Townsville solicitor John Byrne had discovered the blooper loophole in the CHS rule just before the Hobart. "I mentioned tallboys and bloopers to a group of young sailors, and they looked at me with blank stares," Byrne recalls. "They'd never heard of those sails. For some reason that sparked my interest. I knew the blooper was illegal under the IMS rule, but I wasn't sure about CHS. I checked the rules, then went to the committee in England that controls CHS racing. They agreed it would be legal."

Byrne told Millar of the breakthrough and the pair swiftly contacted North Sails in Sydney, stressing the need for total secrecy. North Sails management researched the project and found that their loft in South Africa still had designs for bloop-ers. The new sail was shipped to Sydney just before the start. Secret tests had showed that speed increased from 8 knots to 9.5—which could produce a gain of eighteen valuable miles over their rivals if it was used effectively in the first twelve hours.

Don Mickleborough's sloop *Southerly*, known as "the Floating Hotel," was probably the least conspicuous yacht on the CYC dock. Built in 1939, she was one of the grand old ladies in the fleet. She boasted the oldest and most experienced crew, with an average age somewhere around sixty and a group total of more than a hundred Hobarts. Mickleborough had done thirty, while Tony Cable topped the list with one more. The sign swinging in the breeze on *Southerly*'s mast revealed this team's attitude toward their younger rivals: OLD AGE AND TREACHERY WILL OVERCOME YOUTH AND SKILL.

Over the years, Mickleborough had become something of a traditionalist. The oldest yacht, he felt, should see "the youngsters"—that is, everyone else—off. Two hours before the start, when most other crews were clambering aboard their yachts as families and friends waved good-bye, the senior citizens from *Southerly* were still firmly ensconced in the bar enjoying perfectly poured beers. They left at 12:15 P.M., forty-five minutes before the start, when they were certain all others had departed. They walked leisurely down the dock to the yacht, laughing and appearing casual and carefree. The dock-lines were cast off and they motored the old girl out into the fray.

It seemed that just about anything that floated was out on the harbor that glorious Boxing Day morning; everything from large luxury vessels to ferries, yachts and powerboats, and even canoes, surf skis, and paddleboards carrying some of the more adventurous. Waterway authorities, water police, and volunteer groups patrolled the boundaries of the course in small boats keeping watch over the no-go zone. At this stage their job was relatively easy, but once the post-start stampede toward the harbor entrance began, they would be tested to their limits.

Sydney's harbor is one of the world's most beautiful. The modern and vibrant city sits superbly on its southern shore some seven miles from the Heads. The famous Opera House with its sail-like roof, and the gunmetal gray "coat hanger"—the Harbour Bridge—recline like a proud guard of honor at the entrance to Circular Quay, the bay that is the city center's maritime doorway. The harbor forms a magnificent natural amphitheater, and the surrounding hills are an appealing mix of bushy parkland and seaside suburbs dotted with a broad spectrum of homes. Ribbons of golden sand, backed by grass-covered picnic grounds, give the city folk, lovers of the outdoor life, excellent access to the water.

Thousands of moorings, marina berths, and private docks are filled with every conceivable type of craft, from multimillion-dollar megayachts to the tiniest of "tinnies"—small aluminum dinghies. On Boxing Day the surrounding homes, hills, and headlands are packed with more than 300,000 people waiting eagerly to witness the spectacular start. On South Head, the rocky bastion marking one side of the port's entrance, the outside broadcast television unit from Network Ten was already on the air. Overhead, between fifteen and twenty media helicopters buzzed like dragonflies.

At the controls of one of them was Gary Ticehurst, chief pilot with the Australian Broadcasting Corporation (ABC) television network in Sydney and a man who had become somewhat of a race legend over the previous sixteen years. Flying helicopters was his first love, and his pet assignment each year was to shadow the Hobart fleet as the aerial camera platform supplying shots to the television news pool. His efforts had resulted in spectacular footage beamed around the world of the 1984 and 1993 events, two of the roughest races on record. In 1993 Ticehurst took part in a number of search operations that located upturned and badly damaged yachts. Each year he would spend up to two months planning the filming and communications strategy—how the signals would be sent back, what frequencies would be used, where he would locate the base to transmit all the signals, and how he would talk to the yachts. Before the start, preparations for the 1998 event had been running smoothly.

"I went out to the ABC and readied the helicopter. The frustration really started because the fuel pump at the ABC failed. We couldn't fuel the chopper and it was less than thirty minutes before we had to be in the air. There was no way the pump was going to be fixed by the time I was due to do the coverage. Eventually we went to Channel 9 and did the shuttle service over there all day. It was tiring but at least we got the chopper going." This was the first of a number of long and tiring days for Ticehurst.

While many yachts stayed near the starting line off Nielsen Park Beach—about three miles up-harbor from the Heads— some of the more serious contenders for line and handicap honors cruised to the harbor entrance. The aim was to let everyone on board get a feel for the conditions developing on the ocean, and to help settle any prerace jitters. They were greeted by a sparkling blue ocean with gently rolling swells from the northeast. Some of the more commercially inclined yachts sailed the five miles inside the harbor up to Manly, turned, set the spinnaker that was plastered with their sponsor's logo, and cruised back to the starting line.

Half an hour before the official 1 P.M. start, most of the 115 contenders had maneuvered themselves into the starting area.

Large, circular Telstra decals on the bow, plus flags fluttering from the stern, identified them as race boats. The yachts left a lattice-like pattern of white wakes on the blue water as they crisscrossed the harbor with only mainsails set. It was the aquatic equivalent of thoroughbreds parading in the ring before the start of the Kentucky Derby. The massive maxis with their towering rigs were the most easily identifiable. Sail number US17 was *Sayonara*, C1 was *Brindabella*, M10 was Grant Wharington's exciting new *Wild Thing*, and 9431 was *Marchioness*, whose crew looked as pleased as punch, for they knew the strengthening northeasterly breeze during the day could give them an edge on the downward run. They also knew that a southerly would hamper their progress—*Marchioness* was far from fast when sailing to windward.

One yacht that stood out was David Witt's *Nokia*, a ketch with a bright blue hull and the sponsor's name written proudly on the side. *Nokia*'s sail number, COK1, revealed that it was the first big boat racing internationally under the Cook Islands flag. Papa Tom stood on deck absorbing the excitement, his long, shiny gray hair flowing in the breeze.

The dark-hulled radio-relay vessel *Young Endeavour*, with its crew of twelve officers and eighteen trainees aged between eighteen and twenty-three, made a magnificent sight as it moved slowly down the harbor past the race yachts and spectator craft. It would wait for the race fleet outside the Heads. Lew Carter didn't take in the scenery; he was in the radio room, still frustrated by poor communications.

"I found it difficult to contact some of the yachts. We probably kidded ourselves [about the problem] at the time, thinking 'it's only because of where we are.' Then, when we got outside the Heads we still had problems. I noticed that the squelch button on the radio wasn't working at all. It acts as a sort of fine-tuner on the radio to give you your best possible signal. I tried to contact Penta Comstat, a land-based communications station located north of Sydney, but the signal that I was getting from them was nonexistent. I had to do something about it."

Carter started to weigh his options.

The northeaster would create an upwind leg from the "invisible" starting line (a line between the start boat on the east side of the harbor and a buoy to the west) to the Heads and beyond. This would in turn mean tighter maneuvering and skilled handling. Collisions were a distinct possibility. A downwind start with the harbor ablaze with bright color spinnakers would have been a visual bonus on such a beautiful summer day. It wasn't to be.

The smallest yachts, those around thirty feet in length, like Jim Dunstan's tiny 1981 race winner, *Zeus II*, had just six crew members aboard. The maxis, measuring some seventy-eight feet long, had around twenty-six aboard—the equivalent of two rugby league teams.

At 12:50 P.M. the *boom!* from a cannon aboard the start boat and the raising of flags signaled the ten-minute countdown. Every thirty seconds the helmsmen would ask the crew how much time there was to the start gun. The helmsmen and tacticians were talking, fine-tuning their start strategy while the man on the bow and others amidships warned of any yachts that might be too close.

Boom! Another cannon shot signaled five minutes to go. Most crews were now beginning to line up their yachts, hustling for a good position. The lookout on the tip of the bow was sending hand signals back to the brain trust in the cockpit. Three fingers up, three boat lengths from the line; two fingers, two lengths; one finger, one length; closed fist, on the line and holding. The calls differed according to position, but one thing was for certain—no one wanted to cross the line early.

On the dot of 1 P.M., Australia's golden girl of swimming, Susie O'Neill, tugged the cord that fired the cannon starting the race. It was a clean start. But there was already drama. On the eastern shore the race's biggest boat, the eighty-three-foot *Nokia*, had collided with *Sword of Orion* and Hugh Treharne's cruiser-racer, *Bright Morning Star*. *Sword of Orion* was damaged, with stanchions supporting the lifelines—the safety fence around the yacht's perimeter—torn out of the deck and a small crease in the aluminum mast. Treharne checked his boat and discovered the damage to *Bright Morning Star* was superficial. *Nokia*'s only wounds were scarred topsides near the bow. Crews heatedly debated who was right and wrong and hoisted protest flags, bright red squares with a dovetailed trailing edge. But there was nothing more to do but get on with the racing and sort out the rest in the protest room in Hobart.

The incident didn't detract from the stunning spectacle of 115 yachts pushing their way toward the Sydney Heads in a strengthening sea breeze. The armada of spectator craft joined the charge, churning the narrow laneways reserved for them along the shore into a blur of whitewater. The race yachts tacked from one side of the harbor to the other, and after only minutes of racing the maxis, *Sayonara*, *Brindabella*, and *Wild Thing* were at the head of the pack.

Less than fifteen minutes after the start, *Sayonara* showed the fleet the way around the first buoy off South Head. It continued in this authoritative manner, rounding the offshore mark ahead of the rest before turning south, setting her spinnaker aloft, and accelerating away in perfect downwind sailing conditions.

"Sayonara, Sydney."

Sailing into a Brick Wall

A southerly buster is a summertime weather phenomenon that spreads its influence over much of the New South Wales coast. It is a bit like Nature turning on the air-conditioning to bring relief from the oppressive heat and humidity. Known originally as a burster, it has its origins in the early days of European settlement. For many decades inner-city Australians called it the "brickfielder" after the clouds of red clay dust it carried in from the St. Peters brickyard.

"It is a particularly viscous form of cool, southerly change— a shallow cold front that becomes trapped on the eastern side of the Great Dividing Range that runs down the Australian east coast," says Roger Badham. "It is locally enhanced by the strong temperature gradient across the front. The most violent southerly busters arrive in the Sydney region in the afternoon or evening, enhanced by the afternoon heating ahead of the change. They move up along the coast with clear or partly cloudy skies, sometimes with scattered thunderstorms.

"Southerly busters are most vigorous on the Illawarra and Central Coasts, particularly between Ulladulla and Newcastle. Immediately ahead of the buster the wind dies, then the southerly winds build very quickly (usually over ten to fifteen minutes) to 30 or 40 knots with occasional gusts up to 50 or 60 knots as it passes. However, the strong winds are generally short lived, easing to less than 30 knots within a few hours."

Sometimes a southerly buster is nothing more than a slight glitch in the Sydney to Hobart, a chilly whisper blowing only 20 or 30 knots and disappearing almost as quickly as it arrives. But occasionally they charge up the coast gusting up to 80 knots. They often follow strong northeasters, and the challenge for all racers is to predict just when they will hit. When the change does arrive, the yacht must quickly be converted from a downwind racing configuration into one that will cope with the approaching blast. The wind rapidly rotates through 180 degrees.

Sometimes the front's arrival can be quite daunting, heralded by a rolling, cigar-shaped, lead-colored cloud that stretches from horizon to horizon. Often there will be no visual warning in a clear sky, the only harbinger a sudden darkening of the ocean surface ahead as the wind whips the water. In just minutes a light breeze from astern can be replaced by more than 40 knots on the bow.

It's like sailing into a brick wall.

There is yet another unpredictable and challenging element for racers when a southerly buster blows—the fast-flowing southerly current that streams down the New South Wales coast, bringing warm tropical water from Queensland's Coral Sea. It can run like a river at three or more knots. Pit that massive current against a 40-knot gale from the opposite direction, and the ocean soon swells into liquid mountains.

The *Sayonara* team had impressed everyone with some slick work after their spinnaker blew apart just south of the Sydney Heads. In less than three minutes a new one was set. But in those conditions the American entry would have stiff competition. *Brindabella*, sporting a powerful new asymmetrical spinnaker, was pushing out to sea in search of the strongest current. She had drawn level with *Sayonara*; close behind, the syndicate-owned *Marchioness* was making its move.

Together with *Wild Thing*, the big trio headed the race at speeds approaching 20 knots. It was exciting, satisfying, but intense racing. Boat speed was paramount. Sails were continually trimmed while the helmsman worked the yacht down lingering blue swells in an effort to promote surfing. Long, white wakes streamed astern like vapor trails. There was constant talk about the weather, especially when the menacing gray-and-white clouds of a thunderstorm forecast for the evening could be seen building to the south. Belowdeck, navigators devoured the latest meteorological information from weather facsimile receivers.

Aboard *Young Endeavour*, radio operator Lew Carter and his assistants, Michael and Audrey Brown, were still hampered by communication problems. Just south of Sydney, Carter decided to contact the technician who'd installed the radio. His advice to Carter was to "continue with it for a while and see how you get on." That didn't sit too comfortably with the trio. Carter realized that the last opportunity to correct any problems would be off Wollongong, forty-five miles south of Sydney. Again he contacted the technician.

"I wanted him to know that I wasn't happy at all," said Carter. "We thought we were going to get a hectic Hobart, and we needed everything to be spot-on with the radios. The guy said that he had another radio at home. My problem was how the hell to get it on board. Fortunately for us, the police launch *Nemesis* was proceeding down the coast with the fleet as far as Eden. The obvious solution was to have the technician drive from Sydney to Wollongong with the new radio. He could be picked up by *Nemesis* there and carried out to us.

"There was quite a swell running—about three meters—and a strong wind blowing, but still the *Nemesis* crew did a marvelous job. The technician was worried about how he would get on and off *Young Endeavour* in those conditions, so I pulled a bit of a con job on him and told him all would be OK. I knew that once I had him on board I had no more worries. It wouldn't worry me if he couldn't get off, because we'd have our new radio and that was all we wanted. He could come all the way to Hobart with us as far as I was concerned. As it was, we did get him off and home. Four minutes after he left we had our first 'sked' with the fleet—loud and clear."

By 3 P.M., two hours after the start, Roger Badham had returned to his home south of Sydney. The moment he arrived he went straight to his office and hurriedly downloaded the latest weather prognosis from the international computer models.

He didn't like what he saw.

That afternoon he told a journalist, "I've just looked at all the latest charts and there's only one thing I can say. If I were on half those yachts out there this afternoon, I'd be taking my spinnaker down right now and turning back to Sydney. They're going to get hammered. There's a bomb about to go off in Bass Strait. A low is going to develop and intensify. They're going to get 50 knots, maybe more, and huge seas. This race is going to be worse than 1993."

The low-pressure system that formed over Bass Strait had its genesis in a sharp, cold, upper air trough that slowed, tilted, and deepened as it engaged warm, humid air pulled in from the northeast. Badham described it as "a textbook frontal low pressure development," quite common across the waters immediately south of Australia. The cold upper air mass showed up clearly on satellite images as it crossed the Great Australian Bight on the days immediately preceding December 26. Cut off from the upper air westerly flow when the system deepened to the surface during the early hours of Sunday, December 27, it was this "cold pool of air" that brought summer snow to the high country of Victoria and New South Wales that day.

The official race forecast issued from Sydney at 1450 hours (2:50 P.M.) on December 26 read as follows:

SYNOPTIC SITUATION: A HIGH NEAR NEW ZEALAND IS RIDGING ONTO THE CENTRAL NSW COAST. A LOW AT 995HPA NEAR LORD HOWE ISLAND IS SLOW MOVING. [Hectopascals, hPa, are equivalent to millibars, mb; thus, 995hPa is the same as 995 mb.] A COLD FRONT IS OVER CENTRAL VICTORIA.

WARNINGS: STORM WARNING IS CURRENT SOUTH FROM MERIMBULA.

GALE WARNING IS CURRENT SOUTH FROM BROKEN BAY.

WIND: NORTH TO NORTHEAST WIND 20/25 KNOTS AHEAD OF A W/SW CHANGE 25/35 KNOTS, WITH STRONGER GUSTS, EXPECTED NEAR JERVIS BAY AROUND MIDNIGHT–2 A.M. AND THEN NEAR SYDNEY AROUND 3 A.M.–5 A.M. SUNDAY. WIND MAY TEND BRIEFLY NORTHWEST 15/20 KNOTS PRIOR TO THE CHANGE.

WAVES: 1 TO 2 METERS, RISING TO 3 METERS OFFSHORE WITH W/SW CHANGE.

SWELL: 1 TO 2 METERS.

WEATHER: SCATTERED SHOWERS AND THUNDERSTORMS DEVELOPING TONIGHT AHEAD OF THE CHANGE, THEN CLEARING TOMORROW.

OUTLOOK FOR NEXT 48 HOURS: WINDS MODERATING NORTH OF JERVIS BAY SUNDAY NIGHT. GALE TO STORM FORCE W WINDS SOUTH OF JERVIS BAY EXPECTED TO MODERATE MONDAY EVENING.

The Bass Strait forecast issued from the Victorian Bureau of Meteorology office at 1646 hours read:

EASTERN BASS STRAIT: NORTHEASTERLY WIND 20/30
KNOTS IN THE FAR EAST AT FIRST. A WEST/SOUTHWEST
CHANGE AT 20/30 KNOTS EXTENDING THROUGHOUT THIS
EVENING AND INCREASING TO 30/40 KNOTS TOMORROW
MORNING AND TO 45/55 KNOTS DURING THE AFTERNOON.
SEAS/SWELL 2 TO 4 METERS INCREASING 3 TO 5 METERS DUR-
ING THE MORNING AND 4 TO 6 METERS DURING THE AFTER-
NOON.

According to that forecast, there was going to be one hell
of a battle in Bass Strait.

The crews hadn't yet heard the latest reports, but already the
experienced sailors suspected something big was brewing.
The northeasterly wind was strengthening all the time and
was now well above the predicted velocity of around 25
knots. The sea breeze and favorable current remained so
strong throughout the afternoon and evening that the entire
fleet was ahead of the race-record pace set by the state-of-
the-art German maxi, *Morning Glory*, two years earlier. Lew
Carter, Michael Brown, and the *Young Endeavour* skipper, Lieutenant Commander Neil Galletly, noted that the fleet was flying. They were twice as far from Sydney as they were most
years.

"We discussed with the skipper what we would do," recalls
Carter. "We always talk tactics throughout the race because
it's important for us to be in a position where we can be of
assistance if needed, even though that's not our primary role.
We try to keep ourselves about mid fleet, maybe with a leaning toward the back. We were up on the bridge and had a bit
of a chat about the weather patterns and the current. We'd
had a look at the chart and were talking about the problems
that we might experience down the bottom, off the southeast
corner of the mainland.

"The depth of the water drops dramatically as soon as you get beyond the 100 fathom line down there. We were thinking about the convergence of three to four knots of very warm current from the north against the waves from a southwesterly change. We decided if we were going to have any problems, it would be there."

They were right.

By midafternoon Gary Ticehurst had reconfigured the ABC helicopter so that it was ready to cover the race, and he and his two passengers, Scott Alle, a producer for the ABC, and cameraman Peter Sinclair, began their chase of the yachts down the coast.

"The plan was, as in most years, to lay over at Merimbula for the night," recalls Ticehurst. "We usually plan to arrive in Merimbula about half an hour before last light—it's 185 nautical miles south of Sydney. With such a strong following wind I was hoping we could cover the lead yachts and then come back in. On the way to them, and while flying over the smaller yachts, we were listening to the weather forecasts. They were predicting 40 to 50 knots. They said the change would come about midnight with local thunderstorms all the way down to the coast.

"Sure enough, they were spot-on with the latter part. You could see the lightning. It was that typical, sultry gray afternoon and you could feel the change coming. One thing that was pretty impressive was the speed at which the entire fleet was traveling south. The forecast for 40 to 50 knots the next day didn't concern us. In fact it excited us. I thought, this is going to be a little bit tougher than just a southerly buster. This is going to last a day or two. We're going to get some action—great vision.

"When we arrived at Merimbula that evening, we literally

had to poke our way around the thunderstorms to get to the airport. There were so many of them. It was pouring with rain, torrential rain. We were certain then that the fleet was going to cop it overnight—there'd be a few things going on. We wanted to be out over them at first light."

Throughout the afternoon and early evening the crews enjoyed exhilarating rides. Then, as darkness closed, there came the added spectacle of the huge thunderstorms Ticehurst had encountered, moving out from the land and across the course.

"What we saw was almost unbelievable," said John Messenger, sailing master of the maxi *Marchioness*. "The lightning was all over the place—horizontal and vertical. It was horrific. It lit up the night. It was incessant. The trouble was, we didn't know if the storm was going to bring the change or not. We were always on full alert. There was a bit of apprehension on board." *Marchioness* was at least level with and possibly ahead of *Sayonara* and *Brindabella*, which were farther out to sea. That situation changed in an instant.

"The wind was coming from around 035 degrees and blowing at around 20 knots. We had the spinnaker on and were really flying. We were surprised that the wind didn't drop when the thunderstorm got to us. Instead it held and began flicking between 035 and 350. We were forever chasing it, changing course all the time to keep the wind at the right angle over the stern. It was as though the wind couldn't make up its mind what to do. Suddenly one big wave got under our quarter and lifted the stern. We lost control and broached wildly. Now this is a big boat, but she stayed down on her side for what I guess was between three and four minutes."

Two burly blokes hung on to the wheel, keeping the rudder hard over in a desperate bid to get *Marchioness*'s bow back toward course and give it a chance to come upright. A brief lull in the wind and the influence of another wave let the rudder bite the water—but all too quickly. With most of its twenty-two crew members clinging to a near-vertical deck, *Marchioness* bolted back upright, then took off downwind out of control at 20 knots. This time it speared off course the opposite way—to leeward. A classic flying gybe ensued.

The wind filled the mainsail from the opposite side, and the boom whistled across the yacht like a giant scythe. At the same time the spinnaker went aback. *Marchioness* was knocked flat once more, and the spinnaker filled with water instead of wind. Sheets and lines were tangled across the deck and under the hull.

John Messenger called for a cessation of racing. All sails were lowered and the spaghetti-like mess of sheets, wires, and lines was tidied up. It was thirty minutes before sails were hoisted and *Marchioness* rejoined the race.

With the northeasterly wind approaching 40 knots, Geoff Ross's *Yendys* (Sydney spelled backwards) was starting to do things a Beneteau 53 cruiser-racer had never done before: vibrating and humming and at times hitting 20 knots. By 10 P.M. the crew knew the time had come to take down the 1.5-ounce spinnaker. If they didn't, the rig might be ripped from the boat, especially if they broached and were knocked down. Just as the drop procedure started, *Yendys* went out of control, and the broach they'd sought to avoid was upon them.

"We were knocked well over," said Ross. "I was up to my thighs in water in the cockpit. The guy at the front of the boat for the drop, Peter Seary, wasn't clipped on and was sucked clean off the bow by the force of water. He was gone. What happened next was almost unbelievable. He shot down the side of the boat in the water and before you could even blink a huge wave picked him up, lifted him over the lifelines, and dumped him on the deck at the back of the cockpit. We were in a hell of a mess by then, and it would have taken a long while to turn back if we'd lost him."

By that time the spinnaker had all but taken itself down; it was blown to bits except for a small piece that fluttered like a flag from the halyard near the top of the mast. Seary went straight to the mast as though nothing had happened, clipped onto a halyard, and was hauled to the masthead to retrieve what was left.

Surprisingly, there had so far been no retirements. But this was soon to change. One of the race favorites, Ray Roberts's bright yellow forty-six-foot sloop *ABN Amro Challenge*, was the first to come to grief. It was spearing through the night when a sudden, sharp jolt hit first the keel and then the deep blade of the spade rudder. They had hit either a large sunfish or floating debris. The yacht careered out of control in an instant. The rudder had been ripped off and their race was run. It was a bitter disappointment for codesigner Iain Murray, who was aboard and hoping for a big win.

Around the same time another of the handicap honors contenders, Ron Jones's near new *Sledgehammer*, started limping back to port. The steering cables had chafed through.

Other crews, like that aboard Charles Curran's sixty-footer, *Sydney*, were reveling in a great run down the coast. But *Sydney*'s race end was nigh. At 11:30 P.M., after averaging 18 knots for the previous ten hours, the crew heard a massive bang from the stern.

"We had the spinnaker up and were absolutely flying," said sailing master Dave Kellett. "While we searched for the cause of the first bang, there was another. We discovered that the lower rudder post bearing had shattered, and the rudder post was wobbling around. It didn't take much to realize that if we pushed on, the rudder post could break free and become a giant can opener. It would have opened up the hull."

They lowered the spinnaker, then the mainsail, then waited patiently for the forecast southwesterly change. When it arrived they set a small headsail, turned the bow northward, and headed home.

Champion offshore yachtsman Roger Hickman, skipper of *Atara*, had completed twenty of the twenty-one Hobart races he had entered.

"The first night we had one of the most wonderful runs downwind you could want," recalls Roger. "There was more lightning in the sky than I'd ever seen. At one stage I asked Peter Gardner, who's an extremely experienced sailor, if he wanted to have a drive. He said, 'No, Hicko. It's your boat, so you play with it.' So play I did. I have to say that at the same time the situation was starting to concern me. I kept recalling what Ken Batt, the meteorologist, said not long before we left: 'You're going to have a lot on, Hicko.' He does a wonderful job representing the Bureau of Meteorology for the race, but unfortunately he's shackled by enormous bureaucracy. He and the other forecasters can't come out and make a punt on weather and give us a good guide. It always has to be so substantiated.

"What he said left me in no doubt that we were going to have plenty on once the change came. So we were already gearing up for 45 or 50 knots. We have a policy on *Atara*, and any other boat I race for that matter, that at 40 knots you get the mainsail down, roll it up on the boom, and then put the cover on it so that it can't catch water or blow away. That way you're as safe as houses. We just run with the headsail because you can get it down quickly if you have to and it doesn't go anywhere, like blow over the side. Our plan in a blow is to go to the storm trysail [a tiny, loose-footed triangular handkerchief of a sail that sets where the mainsail would otherwise have been] with a No. 4 headsail, whereas most boats go to the storm jib and then to the trysail."

Different styles of yachts employed different techniques going into that first night. The strengthening northeaster, which was registering more than 35 knots on some sections of the course, was surprising a growing number of experienced sailors. Even *Winston Churchill* was bowling along with a bone in her teeth—a big white bow wave that was cut and curled away like shavings from a bar of soap before disappearing into the night. John Stanley was enjoying it.

"We set the spinnaker at a gentlemanly pace after turning south at Sydney, then proceeded down the coast, knowing all the time that we were going to be hit somewhere along the line that night. We were out to make the most of the northeaster while it was on and get down the track as fast as we could. The breeze got fresher and fresher to the point where we couldn't overload the old *Winston Churchill* too much. So we took the spinnaker off. It was probably blowing around 30 knots at that stage. We then poled out a No. 2 headsail until that too proved to be too much. We pulled that headsail off and gybed inshore when the wind started to back toward the north and northwest. It was around 35 to 40 knots then."

The *Kingurra* crew was also concerned with the way the weather was developing. "It was just beautiful sailing through the afternoon and early evening," said Peter Meikle. "We were doing 12 knots over the ground with between 2 and 3 knots of current assisting us. At that point we knew we were in for a little bit of a belting, but all the time things were beginning to not add up. We had no idea what we were in for, but we were uneasy: it just didn't seem quite right. It certainly seemed strange that the northeasterly was continuing to strengthen. I remember thinking when we got down to the 2.2-ounce spinnaker that things were a bit odd.

"The one good thing about it all was that on the first night out, as is always the case on *Kingurra* in a Hobart race, there was a roast coming up. We had this enormous hunk of beef in the oven with all the trimmings. The game for Peter was to see if he could get the roast out of the oven and served before the change came through. That was probably foremost in the minds of at least half the crew. The other half didn't plan on eating."

Up front, *Sayonara* and *Brindabella* were surfing down wave after wave and maintaining amazing average speeds. But the conditions were no longer concurring with the forecast. Larry Ellison sensed things were changing, and changing fast.

"We thought things were getting a little bit screwy when we were hitting 42 knots of wind running away from Sydney. We were doing 24 to 26 knots under spinnaker."

The downwind roller-coaster ride continued well into the night. As midnight approached, many yachts had replaced their spinnakers with poled-out headsails, a snugger rig that was easier to control. The grand prix boats hung on to their "kites" until the wind began its abrupt change in direction toward the west, then southwest. Sometime between 1 A.M. and 3 A.M., the southwesterly hit the entire fleet with a vengeance.

"At 0230 hours the wind went to 350 degrees from 020 degrees, and the sea became difficult," recalls Roger Hickman. "We had hit speeds of 19 knots plus and had done eighty-six miles in four hours and ten minutes with between 2 and 3 knots of favorable current. I felt the fun was up. We downed the 0.9-ounce chute [spinnaker], then put up the jib-top and poled it out. We gybed and then settled down. All boats our size were either behind us or retired. *Ragamuffin* was out of sight and *Ausmaid* was a white light to seaward. The breeze swung quickly to the west, around 20 to 25 knots. With the No. 4 and two reefs we were in good shape."

"Mayday, mayday, mayday." The chilling call penetrated the airwaves at around 2:30 A.M., December 27. Crews on race yachts across the course scrambled to their radios. "This is *Challenge Again, Challenge Again, Challenge Again.* We have a man overboard!"

The incident had occurred when the forty-one-foot fiberglass production yacht went into a wild broach—a near capsize. The moment the man overboard shout went out the experienced crew did everything they could. Owner Lou Abrahams, a Sydney–Hobart race veteran out of Melbourne and one of Australia's best offshore sailors, had been hurled across the cabin from his seat at the navigation station during the broach. Though dazed, he clambered back to his seat, and his index finger went straight to activating the MOB (man-overboard) button on the GPS (Global Positioning System) unit. At least that would define the search area and increase the chance of recovering the man. Watch Captain Fraser Johnston, a similarly experienced ocean-racing sailor and professional yacht delivery captain, was jolted from a light sleep.

"I'd just dozed off after finishing my watch," Johnston recalls. "We'd had little sleep that night because we'd been sailing so hard downwind. The next thing I knew the boat was broaching and I was pinned in the aft quarter berth. I heard, 'Man Overboard,' and thought, 'Oh, Christ, here we go.'"

As he struggled to free himself from the bunk and fight his way to the cockpit, his mind flashed back to the 1993 race. He had been aboard *Atara*, the yacht that extricated John Quinn from his five-hour, death-defying battle with the ocean in almost the same spot. Johnston knew that everything needed to go like clockwork if the man was to be recovered. They would probably get only one chance. "I ripped straight up on deck and asked in haste who it was. There was uncertainty. Someone shouted out, 'We think it's young Nick.'" All that mattered, though, was to get back to the person, whoever it was. Johnston could see that the helmsman, Col Anderson, was taking the necessary steps.

"All I saw was a blur go across the boat in front of me," recalls Anderson. "This body was hurled through the air, from the weather side through the gap between the deck and boom. With the yacht heeled over so far, he missed landing on the leeward rail and went straight into the tide. I pulled the boat up onto a reach so we could turn and go back to him on a simple reciprocal course when we were ready. Then I started the motor and called on the guys to make a quick check for lines over the side. We didn't want to foul the prop.

"Fraser was over the back trying to sort out the man-overboard buoy. It was a tangled mess with thin cord going everywhere. I shouted that there was only one thing to do—get all the bloody mess on board before we put the engine in gear, because even a little bit of shit cord is enough to wreck your prop. I remember seeing some of the crew coming on deck still half asleep, wondering what the hell was going on. All I could do was shout to them to get the mainsail and jib down."

Although the crew were trying desperately to get the main and headsail down, somehow the long cords connecting the components of the man-overboard system had tangled around the rudder while the yacht had been lying on its side. As he called for a knife, Johnston heard someone finally identify the man overboard. It was "Skippy"—Victorian policeman Gary Schipper—and he had a flashlight.

Johnston cut the man-overboard buoy free and let it down,

then headed for the next most important thing: the engine control. He called on crew to prepare ropes to throw to Schipper when they got close to him. He checked once more for lines in the water, then engaged the gearshift lever. "It was terrific that Skippy still had the torch. But just as with the Quinn rescue, there was much excitement going on—the adrenaline was running. You must make sure you don't make a silly mistake under those circumstances."

One crewman, Richard Grimes, had kept his eyes glued to Schipper from the moment he hit the water. He pointed to him at all times so Anderson knew where to steer to get back to him. Schipper's life depended on it.

"We'd pulled down a headsail and stuffed it downstairs, so everyone below had been disturbed," recalls Gary Schipper. "They were all awake—which turned out to be a good thing. We'd changed from the reacher to the No. 4—no real drama—and were flogging along with probably 25 to 35 knots coming across the deck from the west. I was coming back to the cockpit from the bow. I had a safety harness on and it was attached to the jackstay. The problem was that there were sheets and stuff across the jackstay, so I couldn't get all the way back. I decided to unclip myself from the jackstay and then reattach on something closer to the cockpit. I wasn't concerned about doing that because the boat was sailing nicely—we hadn't broached at any stage.

"Wouldn't you know it, just as I unclipped we got hit by a rogue wave at the stern, under the boat. It knocked the stern to leeward, caused the boat to go into a broach, and laid her over on her side. I had been on my knees, braced against the cabin side. When we broached I overbalanced and wound up sliding across the cabintop on my stomach, straight over the safety rail and into the piss. I didn't even touch the rail. I was flying. I remember grabbing hold of a winch as I went, but it was slippery and I lost my grip. It's hard to stop my weight in full flight—147 kilos [323 pounds]. What I didn't realize at the time was that I had a waterproof flashlight in my hand and took it with me.

"I was fully rigged in foul-weather gear, thermal underwear, and seaboots, but the water was warm. It was small consolation. One of the crew thought quickly enough to grab another floating torch, turn it on, and hurl it into the water toward me. That would also help locate me when they could turn back.

"When I surfaced the boat was probably ten or fifteen meters from me and moving away, still at a reasonable pace. The first thing I could think of was that the weight of water in my boots and gear would be pulling me under. I knew I wasn't going to be able to swim for the boat. I thought, *Don't panic.* For an instant I remembered what John Quinn said after he'd spent five hours in the water in the 1993 race—he just tried not to panic.

"After about ten or fifteen seconds I realized I had the flashlight in my hand. I turned it on, and it worked. Hallelujah. I was able to shine the torch on the boat. They had stopped probably 250 meters from me. I knew they'd see me with the flashlight—but that wasn't my foremost concern at the time. I wanted to get out of my harness and other gear so I could tread water more easily. But it was bloody impossible to get my harness off, because everytime I stopped using my arms to tread water I started to sink. I just had to continue breast stroking.

"I eventually got one boot and a sock off. That was bloody difficult because, like so many others, I'd taped my boots on to keep the water out. It was a lot of effort for a small result. Every time I tried to do something with the harness or my boots I started going under. The guys seemed to take forever getting back to me. Obviously they'd had their problems getting sails down and trying not to get any lines over the side and around the rudder or propeller. All I can say was that I was feeling very, very lonely. I was already exhausted. I was breathing heavy, probably because of the adrenaline rush. I was tiring, but I just kept treading water.

"When I saw the boat coming toward me I was still worried. I didn't know if they could still see me. I kept trying to shine the flashlight at them from above my head. The rest of the time it was just under the surface. Before long I realized they had me spotted. That was a relief. But when they made their run at me to pick me up I thought I was going to get the bloody bow right through my head. Fortunately it missed."

"It was pretty scary for Skippy," recalls Col Anderson, "but I had to get the boat really close to him. I had to be certain that the guys could grab him. It ended up that getting the yacht there was the easy bit. Getting him back aboard was hard."

Strong, eager hands grabbed whatever they could that was attached to Schipper and clung desperately to it. Their arms were now his lifelines. The crew were lying on their stomachs on the deck, leaning out over the side, and all the while the yacht was bucking and the waves were trying to tear him away. If he were ripped from their grasp he would almost certainly drown.

"A couple of the young guys grabbed me," Schipper recalled, wiping away tears. "Suddenly I saw them as my kids. They were clinging on to me; they didn't want to let me go. They were going to save me. They were terrific. They were all over me, leaning down over the side, hanging on to me, attaching bloody ropes everywhere so they wouldn't lose me."

The rough seas, Schipper's bulk, and problems with a special sling designed to lift crew back onto a yacht's deck made it a perilous and daunting task.

"The biggest problem for everyone was that I was so bloody exhausted I just couldn't help them. Every time I got near to being in the sling I slipped out. Eventually they clipped a halyard on to my safety harness as well as the sling and finally winched me up to deck level. Then, while I was still suspended, they guided me across the cockpit and lowered me into the cabin, where I collapsed." Schipper had been retrieved little more than ten minutes after going over the side. Abrahams checked with him and the rest of the crew on how they felt about the race. Their decision was to continue.

Postscript: That fateful day fifty-seven sailors were rescued, but six died at sea. Five boats were sunk and seven abandoned. Many experienced sailors vowed never to go near the race again.

THE LAST GRAIN RACE

ERIC NEWBY

Storm in the Southern Ocean

On the 20th of March Moshulu was in a position near the Snares, a group of uninhabited islands in latitude 48° southward of New Zealand. At midnight on the 19th we had come on deck at the muster to find the ship under full sail, flying along at 13 knots with a NNW wind, the seas boiling out from under her bows.

I had first wheel and it needed the greatest attention to keep the course. She had to be steady, so I kept my eyes and my whole attention on the card, grimly determined that if *Moshulu* was to be lost by broaching to, it wasn't going to happen while I was at the wheel.

At two bells (1 A.M.) I was relieved. Soaked through and

very cold I was happily going below for a period of "påpass" when the mate told me to summon the watch. One by one I shook them into reluctant wakefulness whilst he roamed about impatiently on the deck above.

"Where you were all bloddy night?" he demanded when they were all finally on deck. "Kom on. Bräck bukgårdingarna på kryss royal."

As we stumbled aft along the slippery deck to the mizzen royal buntlines we cursed the mate audibly and the captain more secretly. By the time Yonny Valker and I had been aloft and furled the main royal, which was heavy and sodden with rain, and cleared up on deck, it was a quarter past two, and I was overdue for look-out. I need not have been anxious to reach it, for Sedelquist failed to relieve me at three and I spent an hour and three-quarters looking at nothing but rain.

At last the end of this interminable "utkik" drew near. At twenty to four I saw the light lit in the starboard fo'c'sle where the påpass was waking the other watch. At two minutes to, I saw the dark figures congregating beneath the break of the midships deck for the muster. There was a short interval while the mate counted; an interval when, finding one man short, he despatched the påpass to find the missing man—in this case "Doonkey," who had either been overlooked or was not shaken hard enough. He was greeted with jeers of disapproval when he shambled out on deck.

"Orlright," said the mate. "Lösa av ror och utkik, in frivakt." The helmsman was relieved and there was a struggle at the steel doors as the free watch went below.

"Klara lanternor," I said to Vytautas as he relieved me. "It's bloody cold and you can see damn all."

"Not so fine, yerss?" said Vytautas, who was a good deal warmer and drier than I was myself. "She is going."

"So am I," I said and went off in a hurry to report "Klara lanternor" to the officer of the watch.

Very cold and very miserable I went below, resolved to do something to elevate my spirits. At utkik I had decided that I would open a 5 lb. can of marmalade which had cost me 3s 6d in Port Lincoln. Now I did so and cutting myself a massive slice of bread, I spread it on thickly. The marmalade looked rather insipid but I was not prepared for it to be absolutely tasteless as well. When we had reached Port "Veek" we found that a 5-lb. tin of jam was only 2s 6d, but I had comforted myself that the extra shilling was well spent in order to obtain a superior article. I thought now of all the splendid jam I might have bought instead. Bäckmann had a big tin of peach jam, one of the most delicious things I had ever tasted. Alvar had fig, Sedelquist quince, Hermansonn loganberry—all good fully flavoured stuff. Only I had managed, in a country with a vast growth of every kind of fruit, to pick on some with neither taste nor smell of any kind.

I soon found that nobody was very keen to offer me their jam in exchange. One day I offered my marmalade to Sedelquist. "Have some jam, Sedelquist," I said, pushing my hateful marmalade towards him.

"Oh you noh," he said, "there's damn all oranges in your jam. It tastes of olt bolls to me."

"Balls?"

"Yes, olt goolf bolls. You should try quince. Veree good."

"I should like to very much—"

"It's a peety," he went on, "that your marmalade isn't bettair."

Thirteen days out from Spencer's Guff we crossed the 180th meridian and suffered two Fridays in succession. Two Fridays were not popular. Sedelquist was angry because he had been deprived of the two Sundays he had hoped for; I was depressed because it meant an extra day of "Backstern"; only Yonny Valker, that rigid medievalist, was happy, secure in the knowledge that here was a problem nobody would have the patience to explain to him.

"Koms to blow," said Tria to me on the afternoon of the first Friday as I came on deck to pour the washing-up water over the side.

"Good."

"No, no. Not good. Koms to blow bad," he replied anxiously.

I asked him how he knew.

"I don' know how I know. There's someting fonny, someting noh good in the vind." There was nobody about on the bridge deck, so I asked him if I could look at the last entry in the logbook in the charthouse.

"Orlright," he said reluctantly. "Don' let kapten see you." The captain did not like finding the crew in the charthouse. I looked hastily at the open book and read the noon position:

"24.3.39. Lat. 51° 4S, Long. 176° 37′ 16W. Course East. Run 282. Barometer 4 A.M. 758 millimetres; Noon 754 millimetres. Wind WSW, force 4."

I glanced at the barometer. It had been falling steadily since 4 o'clock on Wednesday morning, the 22nd. On that day, except for some light northerly airs, we had been becalmed on a sea as grey and unvarying as a featureless plain. The albatross had vanished. At midnight on Wednesday the wind had been a gentle breeze from the NW, and by the afternoon of Thursday, the 23rd, *Moshulu* was logging 12 knots with WNW wind, force 5. At 8 it had shifted to the west, the yards were squared, the spankers and the gaff topsail were taken in and she ran before it. The time was now 4 P.M. on the 24th, the wind WSW. The air was full of masses of white and grey cloud moving rapidly eastward above the ship, which was being driven and lifted forward with a slight see-saw motion on the crest of seas of immense depth and power. These seas did not seem to be raised by wind; instead they seemed the product of some widespread underwater convulsion. All round the ship the sea was surging and hurling itself into the air in plumes of spray, occasionally leaping over the rail by the mizzen braces and filling the main deck with a swirl of white water. The air was bitter; I could see Tria's breath smoking.

"It looks all right to me," I said.

"I don' say right now," said Tria. "But very soon this blody ting gets so much as she can stand. Lissun when you go aloft."

We were joined by the sailmaker, who stood for some time looking up at the main royal with the wind straining in it, then over the rail at the mounting sea. "Going to blow," he said.

Hilbert came racing down the deck from the Vaskrum for'ard, dressed in nothing but wooden clogs and fresh long underwear, his teeth chattering. All he said was: "Vind," and vanished into the starboard fo'c'sle. The first mate looked down at us from deck. "Going to vind a little too mooch," he began conversationally.

"For Christ's sake," I said, rather too audibly.

"What the hell are you doing?" he demanded, noticing me.

"Backstern, sir."

"Backstem doesn't take all bloddy day. Get down in the hold for babord'svakt for knacka rost."

I went below to where the port watch were working suspended on platforms over one of the 'tween-deck hatches. The only vacant space was next to Taanila, even more gnome-like than usual in goggles. I slipped in beside him and he turned as the platform gave a lurch. "I tink . . ." he began. In that moment I wondered exactly what he was going to think.

Was he going to think that I needed a knife inserted in some delicate part? Was he going to remind me yet again of my unfortunate nationality? Or was he going to tell me his opinion of "knacka rost"?

"I tink it is going to . . ."

"Don't tell me, let me guess—to vind."

"Yo, yo. How you know?"

"Because I'm bloody clever."

At 5 the heavy chain sheet to the fore royal parted on the port side. We just managed to get the sail in before it blew itself to pieces. The remaining royals had to come in, and the flying jib, then all hands went aloft for the main and mizzen courses. All through the night there were two helmsmen. The wind increased and the seas rose higher and began to pour into the ship again. In the watch below I lay awake listening to the clang of freeing ports along the length of the main deck as they opened to the pressure of water and closed as the ship rolled away, tipping the sea right across her so that the same process took place on the other side. With more apprehension I listened to the sound of water trickling steadily into the fo'c'sle through a cracked port above Bäckmann's bunk. This seemed to constitute a far greater threat to our comfort than the more spectacular effects outside.

At 5.30 on the morning of the second Friday, *Moshulu*, still carrying her upper topgallants, began to labour under the onslaught of the heavy seas which were flooding on to the deck like a mill race. It was quite dark as six of us clewed-up the mizzen lower topgallant, and although from where I was at the tail of the rope I could see nothing at all except the hunched shoulders of Jansson ahead of me, I could hear Tria at the head of the line exhorting us. The sail was almost up when the wind fell quite suddenly and we all knew that we were in the trough of a wave far bigger than anything we had yet experienced. It was far too dark to see it at a distance, we could only sense its coming as the ship rolled slightly to port to meet it.

"Hoold . . ." someone began to shout as the darkness became darker still and the sea came looming over the rail. I was end man. There was just time to take a turn with the clew-line round my middle and a good hold, the next moment it was on top of us. The rope was not torn from me; instead it was as though a gentle giant had smoothed his hands over my knuckles. They simply opened of their own accord and I unravelled from it like a cotton reel from the end of a thread and was swept away. As I went another body bumped me, and I received a blow in the eye from a seaboot. Then I was alone, rushing onwards and turning over and over. My head was filled with bright lights like a bypass at night, and the air was full of the sounds of a large orchestra playing out of tune. In spite of this there was time to think and I thought: "I'm done for." At the same time the words of a sea poem, "ten men hauling the lee fore brace . . . seven when she rose at last," came back to me with peculiar aptness. But only for an instant because now I was turning full somersaults, hitting myself violently again and again as I met something flat which might have been the coaming of No. 4 hatch, or the top of the charthouse, for all I knew. Then I was over it, full of water and very frightened, thinking "Is this what it's like to drown?" No more obstructions now but still going very fast and still under water, perhaps no longer in the ship, washed overboard, alone in the Southern Ocean. Quite suddenly there was a parting of water, a terrific crash as my head hit something solid, and I felt myself aground.

Finding myself in the lee scuppers with my head forced right through a freeing port so that the last of the great sea behind me spurted about my ears, I was in a panic that a second wave might come aboard and squeeze me through it like a sausage, to finish me off.

Staggering to my feet, my oilskins ballooning with water,

too stupid from the blow on my head to be frightened, I had just enough sense to jump for the starboard lifeline when the next wave came boiling over the port quarter and obliterated everything from view.

Swinging above the deck on the lifeline with the sea sucking greedily at my boots, I began to realize what a fortunate escape I had had from serious injury, for the alacrity with which I had leapt for the lifeline in spite of the great weight of seawater inside my oilskins had convinced me that I had suffered no damage except the bang on the head.

The sea had taken me and swept me from the pin rail of the mizzen rigging, where I had been working, diagonally across the deck for fifty feet past the Jarvis brace winches, on the long handles of which I could so easily have been speared, over the fife rails of the mizzen mast, right over the top of No. 3 hatch and into the scuppers by the main braces outside the captain's quarters.

"Where you bin?" demanded Tria accusingly when I managed to join the little knot of survivors who were forcing their way waist deep across the deck, spluttering, cursing, and spitting seawater as they came.

"Paddling," I said, relieved to find that there were still six of us.

"Orlright, don' be all bloody day," he added unsympathetically.

"Tag I gigtåget. One more now. Ooh—ah, oh, bräck dem."

"What happened?" I asked Jansson.

"That goddam Valker let her come up too mooch," said Jansson. "I bin all over the bloddy deck in that sea."

On the second Friday *Moshulu*'s noon position was 50° 19′ S., 170° 36′ W. In 23 1/2 hours she had sailed 296 miles.* This

---

*When running to the east in southerly latitudes a day, noon to noon, is about 23 1/2 hours.

was the best day's sailing with cargo she ever had with Erikson. It was only bettered by the Germans on very few occasions. Twice in 1909 on a voyage from Newcastle, NSW, to Valparaiso when loaded with nearly 5,000 tons of coal she ran three hundred miles.

At midnight the wind was SW, force 6, and in the early hours of Saturday morning I went aloft with Hermansonn in a storm of sleet to make fast the main upper topgallant. It was now blowing a fresh gale, force 8, and the yard was swinging like a mad thing; we had a terrible time with this sail. Some of the gaskets had been caught in the buntline blocks on the yard and were immovable, others were missing. The sleet numbed our fingers until we almost cried with cold.

Below us, in the fore and mizzen rigging, eight boys were having the time of their lives furling the lower topgallants; on the mizzen two buntlines had carried away to starboard and the sail was being clewed-up to the yard with lines taken to the capstan on the main deck, where from time to time ton upon ton of white water poured over the rail, causing those heaving at the capstan bars to abandon their efforts and leap for the lifelines.

"OOH, what bloddy cold," screamed Hermansonn. "Ut, Kossuri, you strongbody, you rosbif, ut, ut på nock."

As we reached the yardarm there was a great ripping sound that seemed to come from below, and we both hung dizzily over the yard to see whether the upper topsail had blown out. Then, in spite of the wind and our precarious situation, Hermansonn began to laugh. I knew then that I had suffered some dire misfortune as Hermansonn laughed in that way only when a disaster happened to someone else.

"Ho, ho!" he boomed above the gale. "Ho, ho, focking fonny!"

"What?" I screamed in his ear. "Tell me."

"Your trousers, ho, ho. English, no good."

It was true. My oilskin trousers, unable to stand the strain to which they had been subjected, had split from end to end.

This was an accident of the worst kind. To find myself halfway across the Southern Ocean, in the stormiest seas in the world, with defective oilskin trousers, was calamity.

At the moment however there was no time to worry over such things. The wind was awe-inspiring. Not only was it so strong in the gusts that we could do nothing but hang on until it lessened, but it moaned in a way which I had never heard before, rising and falling like the winds heard about old houses in the wintertime. It seemed, in spite of its force, to be the last part of some even more violent disturbance that was taking place at a great distance. This then was what Tria had meant when he told me to listen when I went aloft.

But in this weather there were still worse jobs on deck where the carpenter and two helpers were trying to caulk the closet. As the ship started to run downhill into the valley between two seas, she would bury her bows nearly to the fo'c'sle head, so that the water surged into the pipes and shot into the compartment in a solid icy column like the jet emitted by a whale, leaving them half drowned and spluttering.

At noon the wind was WSW, force 9, and there was a vicious sea running. We were carrying upper and lower top-sails, the foresail, forestaysail and jigger staysail. I spent the morning with a sail-needle, seaming up my ruined oilskins, while overhead the starboard watch struggled to reeve fresh buntlines on the mizzen lower topgallant. The outer steel doors of the fo'c'sle were fast, but not being close-fitting they let the water in. Soon there were more than six inches of water in the compartment reserved for our seaboots and oilskins, and half as much in the fo'c'sle itself. Every few minutes I had to leave my stitching and bail with a cocoa tin to prevent the fo'c'sle being flooded still more. Everyone else was asleep. As old soldiers do before an action, they were absorbing sleep greedily like medicine, and lay snoring happily in the midst of tumult.

For the noise was unbelievable. In the fo'c'sle the shrieking of the wind through the shrouds and about the upper yards now bereft of sail, so awe-inspiring on the open decks, was here only a murmur subordinated to the shuddering and groaning of the hull under stress and to the sounds of water; water thundering over the ship in torrents, water sluicing out through the freeing ports, water trickling into the fo'c'sle in half a dozen different ways, and sloshing about the floor.

By the time I had mended the trousers, the free watch was nearly over. I was "Backstern," and having made sure that Kroner had put on the washing-up water, I waited for a lull to dash forward to the fo'c'sle head from where I could look back along the ship.

Moshulu was running ten knots in the biggest seas I had ever seen. As I watched, the poop began to sink before my eyes and the horizon astern was blotted out by a high polished wall, solid and impenetrable like marble. The poop went on dropping until the whole ship seemed to be toppling backwards into the deep moat below the wall of water that loomed over her, down and down to the bottom of the sea itself. At the moment when it seemed that this impregnable mass must engulf us, a rift appeared in its face and it collapsed beneath the ship, bearing her up so that what a moment before seemed a sluggish, solid hulk destined for the sea bed was now like a bird skimming the water, supported by the wind high above the valley.

This was noon.

In the first part of the afternoon the barometer was low, 742 millimetres. At one moment *Moshulu* would be riding the crests in brilliant sunshine, the next swooping down a great incline of water peppered by rain and hailstones, yawing a little from her course and beginning to roll, taking sea as high as her charthouse. Everyone was soaking wet and none of us had any more dry clothes. Everything in the Vuitton was wet as well. All through the afternoon we were kept busy making new wire buntlines, cold work with no movement in it, but by coffee-time one of my shirts had dried over the galley fire and I put it on rejoicing. But not for long.

As soon as I came out on deck I heard a voice calling me. It was the captain, in leather coat and tweed cap, like a huge backwoods peer I had seen in a *Tatler* that the sailmaker had somehow saved from destruction.

"Here you," he said. "Take up some slack on the crojack sheet."

I plunged down on to the maindeck, where I was immediately knocked flat by a sea coming inboard. After this initial soaking, I no longer cared whether I was wet or not, only leaping for the lifelines when big dangerous seas came aboard.

At six there was a slight easing in the wind. I happened to be coming from the wheel, when once more the captain had something in mind for me.

"We'll see what she can stand," he said in a speculative way, like a gambler about to stake a large sum on an uncertainty.

"Aloft and break out the main lower topgallant. Lively now." As I went I heard Sedelquist, who had been at the wheel with me, say: "Crazy focker." Privately agreeing with him, I swung myself on to the pin rail and into the main rigging. Aloft the wind seemed as strong as ever, and I looked down to a deck as narrow as a ruler on which the tiny figures of the watch were clustered, waiting to perform the ticklish job of sheeting home the sail which I was about to loose from its gaskets.

A distant cry borne on the wind told me that they were ready.

I cast off the gaskets on the weather side, hauled up a good
slack on the buntlines, and, scuttling into the rigging, clung to
the shrouds for my life. The yard began to plunge and whip,
the buntlines plucked at the blocks seized to the shrouds,
making the ratlines tremble underfoot.

"She'll never stand it" was the general verdict when I
regained the deck.

With the sail sheeted home there was too much strain on
the entire sail structure and at eight o'clock the upper topsail
sheet carried away and the sail had to be taken in, together
with the lower topgallant we had recently set.

Thus reduced, we drove on in the darkness with both topsails set on the fore and mizzen, the main lower topsail, the
foresail and one fore-and-aft sail—the jigger staysail.

This was the night of the second Friday, March 24th. We
were fed up and though we cursed *Moshulu* and the captain
too, we were pleased with him for pushing her to the limit.

"This kapten is proper strongbody for vind," said Sandell
after an issue of rum and a good dinner of Lobscouse—a sus-
taining hash made from pounded hard biscuit, potato and
"Buffelo."

"—the kapten," replied Sedelquist, who was absolutely cyn-
ical about all men. "Vonts to get his name in the papers, I
shouldn't vonder."

"We'll be in it too, if he does," I said.

"Yes, in the bloddy paper but on the front with beeg black
lines all round 'missing.' That's what we'll be."

It was too cold to argue. I slipped into my bunk dressed in
my long underwear with two pullovers on top. On my head
was a very hairy balaclava helmet, so that I looked like the
subject of some hitherto unpublished photograph of a military
man in the lines about Sebastopol.

The fo'c'sle no longer seemed a human habitation. There

were several inches of water on the floor, and trousers, seaboots and oilskins that had slipped from their hooks were moving gently backwards and forwards the whole length of it with a sucking sound. Wedging myself as firmly as I could in a steady position, I tried to read the *Times* leader on the dismissal of Dr. Schacht, but the subject seemed so remote and unimportant and the light was so bad that when Alvar said "Light ut" I extinguished it without argument.

Just before midnight the voice of the påpass woke me. My long underwear was steaming like a kettle. Outside it was fearfully cold. Because it was my utkik I put on as many layers as I could: a wet hairy shirt and trousers that I had bought in the East India Dock Road, two more pullovers in addition to the two I was sleeping in and my heavy pilot coat. Everything was dripping with water.

"Remember *Admiral Karpfanger**–keep good utkik, plenty ice around here, maybe," screamed Tria cheerfully in my ear, and left me.

At the lookout I peered ahead of the ship and could see nothing. The air was full of spray which rose like mist about the ship. The wind was strong enough to lean on. High above in the darkness the rest of the watch was bending a fresh chain-sheet for the main upper topsail.

With the new sheet bent we started to wind the yard into position. The gearing on the winch was very low and it was a slow job to raise it. By three in the morning it was in position and we had set the sail, together with the main lower topgallant which the captain was determined she should carry.

But it was no use. The barometer continued to fall, and at five the starboard watch had to furl it again. This was on the morning of March 25th.

---

*German training ship, originally named *L'Avenir*, that was lost with all hands in the Southern Ocean, February 1938.

"Going to blow, I tink," said Tria.

"What do you think it's doing now?" I asked him.

"Notting."

"Golly."

After breakfast I was at Backstern, extremely bad-tempered because I had been washed away when crossing the foredeck to the starboard fo'c'sle and had lost all the hot water.

Suddenly Taanila appeared. "Kom," he said.

"Why? I'm Backstern."

"Styrman, he say 'BRÄCK GÅRDINGARNA PÅ STOR ÖVRE MÄRS.'"

"This is it," said Kroner as I went aft. "Upper topsails. It's going to be really big."

"It's the blasted Backstern that worries me. There's no water."

"I'll put some on for you," he answered. "It'll be there when you come back."

"Maybe I shan't," I said, nearer the mark than usual.

When we were all assembled the mate slacked away the handbrake of the upper topsail halliard winch and set it spinning. The eighty-foot yard began to descend in its greased track on the fore part of the mizzen mast, and as the weather sheet was progressively eased we clewed-up to windward and manned the buntlines. With the weather clew up, the lee side was easier and the sail was furled without incident.

The fore upper topsail was the most difficult. All the buntlines jammed and more than half the robands securing the topsail to the jackstay had gone. The outer buntline block had broken loose and was flailing in the air, so that when we reached the lowered yard eighty feet above the sea, we hesitated a moment before the "Horry ops" of the mates behind us drove us out on to the footropes, hesitated because the bunt of the sail was beating back over the yard. The wind was immense. It no longer blew in the accepted sense of the word at all; instead it seemed to be tearing apart the very substance of the atmosphere. Nor was the sound of it any longer definable in ordinary terms. It no longer roared, screamed, sobbed or sang according to the various levels on which it was encountered. The power and noise of this wind was now more vast and all-comprehending, in its way as big as the sky, bigger than the sea itself, making something that the mind balked at, that it took refuge in blankness.

It was in this negative state of mind that could accept anything without qualm, even the possibility of death, that I fell off the yard backwards. I was the last man out on the weather side and was engaged in casting loose a gasket before we started to work on the sail, when without warning it flicked up, half the foot of a topsail, forty feet of canvas as hard as corrugated iron, and knocked me clean off the footrope.

There was no interval for reflection, no sudden upsurge of remorse for past sins, nor did my life pass in rapid review before my eyes. Instead there was a delightful jerk and I found myself entangled in the weather rigging some five feet below the yard, and as soon as I could I climbed back to the yard and carried on with my job. I felt no fear at all until much later on.

It needed three-quarters of an hour to make fast the weather side. Time and time again we nearly had the sail to the yard when the wind tore it from our fingers.

My companion aloft was Alvar.

"What happened?" he said when we reached the deck.

"I fell."

"I din' see," he said in a disappointed way. "I don' believe."

"I'm damned if I'm going to do it again just because you didn't see it."

"I don' believe."

"Orlright," I said. "The next time I'll tell you when I'm going to fall off."

"Dot's bettair," said Alvar.

At noon on Saturday the 25th, our position was 50° 7′ S, 164° 21′ W. In the 23½ hours from noon on the 24th *Moshulu* had sailed 241 miles and made 228 between observed positions. Her previous day's runs were 296 and 282, but the violence of the sea and the necessary reduction in canvas were slowing her increasingly.

The barometer fell and fell, 746, 742, 737 millimetres. The sun went down astern, shedding a pale watery yellow light on the undersides of the deep black clouds hurrying above the ship. It was extremely cold, colder than it had ever been, blowing a strong gale force 9. Big seas were coming aboard. I felt very lonely. The ship that had seemed huge and powerful was nothing now, a speck in the Great Southern Ocean, two thousand miles eastwards of New Zealand, three thousand from the coast of South America, separated to the North from the nearest inhabited land, the Cook Islands and Tahiti, by two thousand miles of open sea; to the South there was nothing but the Antarctic ice and darkness. She was running before seas that were being generated in the greatest expanse of open ocean, of a power and size unparalleled because there was no impediment to them as they drove eastwards round the world. She was made pigmy too by the wind, the wind that was already indescribable, that Tria said had only now begun to blow.

At this moment, for the first time I felt certain of the existence of an infinitely powerful and at the same time merciful God. Nearly everyone in the ship felt something of this, no one spoke of it. We were all of us awed by what we saw and heard beyond the common experience of men.

I had second wheel in the watch till midnight with Jansson to help me. We relieved Yonny Valker and Bäckmann.

"Törn om," I said, mounting the platform next to Yonny and feeling with my foot for the brake pedal.

"Törn om," repeated Yonny, showing me that he was ready to be relieved.

"Othhnordotht," he lisped, giving me the course (we were running before the storm ENE), and then added as he relinquished the wheel: "No more babords."

It seemed reasonable. The ship was pointing ENE½E, but with the rolling it was difficult to keep her right on course and I supposed that he had already given her as much port helm as she needed.

I was soon disillusioned. Yonny had left me with the wheel hard to starboard and she continued to run off in that direction.

Before Tria awoke to what was happening *Moshulu* was pointing southeast. Unfortunately he lost his head; shrieking wildly he began to turn the binnacle hood towards Jansson so that he could see the card, but only turned the hood sufficiently for the card to be invisible to both of us. At this moment the first mate arrived and, thinking Jansson was at fault, began to give him hell. Not even the fact that I was standing on the weather side convinced him that I was helmsman.

It needed the four of us to return the ship to her course, and she took some terrific seas aboard. Afterwards the mate laid into Jansson until the latter's nose began to glow red.

"It was my fault," I shouted, trying to make my voice heard above the wind.

"Shot op, shot op!" bellowed the mate with such violence that I dared not say another word. "Shot op, or by *helvete* be jus' too bloddy bad."

I shut up.

"I'm sorry," I said to Jansson afterwards.

"Orlright," he said, "not dead, but nearly. We'll make some cocoa in the Doonkey Hus."

As the barometer went on falling, the wind rose. At 4 A.M. it fell to 733 millimetres and the wind blew force 10, Beaufort notation, a whole gale of wind. The starboard watch took in the main upper topsail at three o'clock and the ship ran before the storm under lower topsails and the foresail; the whole of the afterdeck was inundated.

"A liddle more," said Sandell, "She'll take a liddle more than this."

Day broke at last, slowly because clouds, black as night, pressed upon the ship. Hail, driving rain and flurries of snow fell. At five the watch was called. We knew the reason before the mate gave the order.

"Undra märs skot," said Sedelquist. "Got to slack those lower topsail sheets before it's too late."

The main deck was like a reef with occasionally the tops of the winches and the hatches breaking the surface, and it seemed strange to me that a week ago, when we had been securing the hatch covers with heavy timbers, the precautions had seemed superfluous, almost too adequate, and yet now I found myself wondering what would happen if one of those awful cliff-like seas caught up with the ship and pooped her.

On the deck we were caught in a roaring flood and jumped for the lifelines hanging on minutes at a time, but with her topsails eased she ran better and there was less danger of the sail blowing out.

At six o'clock, cold yet exultant, we went below for coffee.

"She's a real ship," said Sandell. "I've never seen a ship like this. Blows like strongbody. Mos' ships you'd have the foresail off her and heave-to. Lovs vind, lovs it. But my God if ve have to take the foresail, be someting."

The clouds cleared and a whole gale of wind blew out of a clear blue sky. At eight the wind reached its greatest velocity, force 11 on the Beaufort scale, a wind in which a wooden ship might well have foundered, and a lesser than *Moshulu* would

have hove to, drifting to leeward, lying on the wind under a
storm trysail.

All through the storm the pigs had been setting up despair-
ing cries, as well they might, cooped in their narrow steel
coffins. At six o'clock we cleaned out their sties, a difficult job
in a ship running before a great gale. It took three of us to do it.

"For Chrissake, don' let them go," grunted Tria as we levered
the iron troughs through the door of the sty with crowbars.

He had no sooner said this than Auguste and Filimon,
believing that the ship was about to founder, charged the barricade of hatch covers with which we had fenced them in,
intent on finding a place in the boats. The barricade collapsed
and Filimon, who was leading, shot between Tria's legs, upset-
ting him in the nasty mess we were shovelling up. Auguste followed him closely, and they both went glissading away on
their behinds into the lee scuppers, from which we had difficulty in rescuing them.

"Better eat them before they go overside," I said as we
struggled with Auguste, who was threshing about under water.

"I don' care how soon we eat that Filimon," Tria said.

Moshulu continued to carry her sail and the storm entered its
last and most impressive phase. We were cold and wet and yet
too excited to sleep. Some stood on the fo'c'sle head but only
for a short time as the force of the wind made it difficult to
remain on two feet. Others stood beneath it and gazed out
along the ship, watching the seas rearing up astern as high as a
three-storeyed house. It was not only their height that was
impressive but their length. Between the greatest of them
there was a distance that could be estimated only in relation to
the ship, as much as four times her entire length, or nearly a
quarter of a mile. The seas approached very deliberately,
black and shiny as jet, with smoking white crests gleaming in

the sunshine, hissing as they came, hurling a fine spume into the air as high as the main yard.

I went aloft in the forerigging, out of the comparative shelter of the foresail, into the top, and higher again to the cross-trees, where I braced myself to the backstays. At this height, 130 feet up, in a wind blowing seventy miles an hour, the noise was an unearthly scream. Above me was the naked topgallant yard and above that again the royal to which I presently climbed. I was now used to heights but the bare yard, gleaming yellow in the sunshine, was groaning and creaking on its tracks. The high whistle of the wind through the halliards sheaf, and above all the pale blue illimitable sky, cold and serene, made me deeply afraid and conscious of my insignificance.

Far below, the ship was an impressive sight. For a time the whole of the afterdeck would disappear, hatches, winches, everything, as the solid water hit it, and then, like an animal pulled down by hounds, she would rise and shake them from her, would come lifting out of the sea with her freeing ports spouting.

Opening my camera, I attached the lens hood, but the wind blew it into the sea. The mist of spray rising all about the ship made it almost impossible to see anything through the viewfinder. There was no need for the range-finder. I simply set the scale to infinity and pressed the button, and even that was difficult enough.

Later, I was standing on deck just aft of the charthouse when a monster wave reared over the main rail and exploded on the house itself. As it came I shut the camera but was too late to shut the case.

In an agony of mind I went down to the fo'c'sle. The camera was very wet. The film was undamaged. I up-ended it and a thin trickle of water ran out of the Compur shutter. The rest of the watch were observing me with interest.

"I'll have to take it to pieces or it'll rust up," I explained.

"Good," said everybody. "Now."

"No, when the storm finishes. The thing's full of springs."

"Put it in the offen," said Sedelquist. "I should ask the kock. Dry heem out."

By noon *Moshulu* had again run 228 miles. Since the storm began we had crossed 18 degrees of longitude. Now the barometer rose steadily. The starboard watch reset the fore and main upper topsails and all through the afternoon we were resetting sail. Big seas were still coming aboard and we frequently deserted the halliard winches for the lifelines. Sent aloft to overhaul the buntlines, I returned in a filthy temper because I had dropped my knife overboard.

By 9 P.M. the gale had passed, the wind had fallen, but there was still a tremendous sea running. The weather was clear and cold with overhead a thin crescent moon. At two in the morning of Monday, the 27th, we reset the main royal and in an hour or two more we were in full sail again.

Postscript: Eric Newby went on to become one of the most prolific travel writers of his generation, and thirty years after the trip on the *Moshulu* he published a companion volume of photographs entitled *Learning the Ropes: An Apprentice on the Last of the Windjammers*.

After Peter Nichols's marriage had failed and a debilitating depression set in, he left England in the wooden twenty-seven-foot *Toad* to cross the Atlantic alone, hoping the voyage would serve as a balm to his broken spirit. His introspective journey is abruptly interrupted when the boat springs an irreparable leak and slowly begins to sink.

SEA CHANGE

Alone Across the Atlantic in a Wooden Boat

PETER NICHOLS

July 24

Twenty-second day out of Horta.

We have been tearing along all night with the main slightly reefed, and at 0200 I go out on deck to roll the reef deeper. It is windier than an hour ago. Maybe because of the large dark rain cloud passing astern of us.

Below, I am unable to go back to sleep, feeling we are still overcanvased and hearing the sloshing in the bilges.

An hour later the cloud is gone and the wind is the same, about a steady twenty knots. I go forward and drop the genoa. I sit astride the bowsprit in the dark, bunching up the genoa and tying it to the whisker stays. I grip the four-inch-wide teak spar with my thighs like a bronco rider. My feet on the bob-stay dip in and out of the warmish water as the bow rises and falls. I'm still not wearing a harness, not yet, it's not at all bad out. Just a lot different from what it had been for so long. And there is so much noise now: waves tumbling over themselves, and *Toad*'s insistent charging through them, and the steady cataract sound of the white water tumbling along both sides of the hull.

The boat is much happier under reefed main and staysail. Me too. I go below and fall asleep.

Still blowing this morning. Amazing difference from a few days ago. At noon we'll clock a good run at last. America is a thousand miles away but seems infinitely closer today. I feel it now just over the horizon. I picture it, New England in August: clams, lobsters, station wagons, sneakers and tattered sweatshirts; and toothsome American girls, strong, corn-fed, happy, impossibly normal. I imagine bringing *Toad* alongside some gray-bleached dock festooned with floats, stacked with lobster pots, and meeting one of these splendid, freckly girls. The ordinariness of it makes it seem so far beyond my reach. Is it real, or is it a J. Crew catalog?

At 0900 I notice a new sky. It is still blue and sunny, but high up there is now a lot of streaky cirrus.

If clouds appear as if scratched by a hen,
Get ready to reef your topsails then.

I get out Alan Watts's book and find this sky in Photograph 2: "Sky which means deterioration. The warm front of a depression is probably on its way . . . the wind will increase . . . rain is likely later."

The sea is up, too, after several days of this wind, confused and lumpy. A southerly swell now dominates over a steady procession of smaller waves from the northwest. *Toad* is being knocked about, slapped on the nose by the northwesterly lumps. But we are still making good progress, moving at five knots, heading northwesterly, straight for Maine.

However, Maine is still about one thousand miles away. I have been thinking of making for Bermuda, now four hundred miles due west. But with the wind up and from the southwest, I can't push *Toad* any closer to Bermuda than we're heading. When and if the wind shifts or drops, we will head that way.

A lot of water below, and more, always more, coming in. I pump now when I'm not doing anything else.

At local noon, 1330, my sights show we have made 112 miles in the last twenty-four hours. The log mileage is 121, so there is some current with the northwesterly swell which has set us back ten or eleven miles.

At 1500 and again at 1600, I roll up more of the main onto the boom. *Toad* is equipped with a roller-reefing gear that pulls the mainsail down and rolls it around the boom. Operated by a ratchet and pawl, it does its job quickly and neatly. I can roll up half the mainsail in about a minute. The remainder sets well on the mast, maintaining a taut, efficient airfoil shape. I can roll it down to stormsail size in two minutes. There is a photograph of this gear in Hiscock's *Cruising Under Sail*. Turner's roller-reefing gear, it's called, manufactured in the 1930s. It works much faster than the modern system, laughably known as "jiffy" reefing, for its supposed speed of operation, which is what I found on all the new boats I've skippered or delivered.

Later in the afternoon I tune in to the shortwave weather forecast given by the U.S. Coast Guard station November Mike November in Portsmouth, Virginia, to see if they mention this weather. Two gales are moving east off the eastern seaboard, but that's way north, around 45° north.

And at 1800 I roll up still more of the main. The wind—I finally admit it—is much, much stronger now. It's blowing about thirty knots, a gale. We are being knocked and slammed about now. It is impossible to think of getting any closer to Bermuda at the moment. If I had thought of it days ago . . .

No matter how much I pump, water is now constantly sloshing over the floorboards. It has become wet and grimly depressing below. Gallons of water pouring without letup into an old boat bouncing around in the middle of the ocean without a proper life raft undermines your confidence, I find. I'm used to seeing an ocean of water outside, but a lot of it inside the boat where by essential principle it's supposed to be dry can get you down.

Just keep pumping. The Coast Guard forecast doesn't mention any weather system around here, so maybe it'll quiet down again soon. We'll go to Bermuda or maybe still poop on to Maine. It's hard to adjust to the fast-changing reality of life aboard: I keep thinking everything will be okay.

July 25

Haven't slept much. That sloshing noise. I worry about drifting off and letting too much water come in. When I do doze I dream we're sinking. Waking is hardly less nightmarish, with water above the floorboards.

The rain predicted by the Watts book comes in the night, with a low dark caving-in of cloud and those spatial hallucinations that make me feel we are turning and hobbyhorsing through great amorphous rooms. The strangest sensation, not unpleasant, but so strong tonight, probably because this is the lumpiest sea and weather of this voyage so far, and because I'm tired and it's easy, even a relief, to get carried away into it.

I have to watch myself. I know from all my book reading of sailors at sea and my own encounters with exhaustion that this is when you make mistakes. You let things go, let yourself and your boat down. I have to be vigilant. I have to eat to keep strong, and somehow I have to sleep. I have to sleep soon too, otherwise I risk getting so tired that when I wake up there will be too much water in the boat and I'll have lost the battle. Later this morning I'll nap.

We are converging with shipping lanes between northern Europe and ports in the Gulf of Mexico. We would never be seen by any lookout aboard a ship in such conditions. Nor would *Toad* be spotted on radar with all the wave clutter. And we've stopped moving now, so if I did see a ship looming up out of the murk, it would take long minutes to attempt evasive maneuvers. I'm relying on the statistical unlikelihood of collision, as John Letcher did for a while. We are hove-to, staysail backed and the reefed main sheeted flat amidships, bobbing quite comfortably, pointing west, probably making a knot of leeway to the northwest, which is where we want to go. I want to see if heaving-to, reducing our motion, slows the water coming in. Can't tell yet. It's four o'clock in the morning.

Under way again at 0800. Tried napping, and maybe dozed a little but not much. Just as much water coming in, so we might as well keep going and we're making good time in the right direction. The wind is still a steady twenty-eight to thirty knots.

A lot of water, in fact, is coming in. More than yesterday. It is unhinging to have this much water coming in and no visible hole in the boat. I pump all the time now when I'm not doing anything else vital. Sleep is vital, but I can't seem to manage it. The floor is continually underwater now. I wade through the interior of the boat. Yet I seem to be able to keep it around that level.

Local noon is 1335, and I'm lucky enough to get a sight of the sun for latitude. Earlier this morning I managed two quick snapshots of a hazy but sufficiently distinct orb through cloud. We're at 35° 18′ north, 52° 45′ west. Eighty-three miles since noon yesterday, which is good for being hove-to and slowed down. This boat sails well.

Marking my penciled X on the chart, I find we are again at one of those spots on the ocean where I've been before. Two years ago, on July 16, J. and I were just three miles away with the cats aboard *Toad*, bound for the Azores. A year ago, on June 28, we were five miles away on *Sea Bear*, a boat we delivered from Florida to England.

Sea Bear was a Moody 33, a modern plastic boat designed by Angus Primrose, the English yacht designer who had the great misfortune to go to sea in one of his own boats— something designers rarely do—a Moody 33 called *Demon Demo*. Primrose sailed it across the Atlantic in the OSTAR (the London *Observer* Single-handed Trans-Atlantic Race), during which, in not particularly severe weather, *Demon Demo* was rolled upside down, losing its rig. Primrose was sailing the boat off the U.S. East Coast several years later, supposedly alone, while Mrs. Primrose remained in England, when again *Demon Demo* capsized during a gale. This was a bad Gulf Stream storm, a northerly gale blowing against the north-setting current creating dangerous seas. J. and I were coming down the Chesapeake from Annapolis in a new bareboat, to deliver offshore to the Virgin Islands, when this same storm brewed up. We were lucky enough to hear about its approach on the radio and sat it out in Little Creek Harbor at the mouth of the Chesapeake. Offshore, a number of boats got into trouble, and when *Demon Demo* capsized, Primrose, who was not in fact alone, but with a young lady, launched the life raft and got his passenger into it. She later said that before he had a chance to follow her, another wave broke over the boat and down it went, taking its creator.

Sea Bear was ugly and uncomfortable, though fast, and we were luckier than its designer with the weather. At one point we spent five days and nights flying a large spinnaker and traveling at its maximum hull speed of between six and seven knots through dense fog south of the Grand Banks, frightened to death of meeting a ship or an errant iceberg, but knowing there was not much difference between slow and fast in such a situation.

This afternoon we're being knocked about too much, and tons of water are filling the boat, so I heave-to again, feeling, for the first time, a little desperate, unsure if I am able to handle what's happening. I want to keep moving, get closer to Bermuda, but moving seems to make the leak worse—although, finally, it's hard to tell. My attitude is changing fast. For a while, around teatime, that English ritual so suggestive of warmth and coziness that I observe most days at sea, I lose my nerve and think of putting out a mayday call. It's not warm and cozy at all aboard the boat now, but wet and loud and fucking terrifying.

Never mind, then, have a nice cup of tea.

" 'Ere, 'ave a nice cuppa tea, luv," I say aloud in my best Eastender charlady accent. " 'At's right, put the kettle on. Lovely! An' a bit of that bread—why don't you toast it, luv? You got this bleedin' oven wiv a grill, use it! Go on! Give yourself a lit'le treat, then. All you bin froo. Yes, lovely! An' a bit of that jam. A proper tea! 'At's it!"

Whoever she is, she's wonderful. She makes me a lovely tea. And keeps cooing, "Love-lee!" as she does it. I'll hang on to her for a bit.

I should sleep. I'm tired—you're exhausted, you've *got to*

sleep—but I'm afraid to let myself go all the way, because I don't know at what point, if I stop to sleep, the water coming in will become too much ever to get ahead of again. If *x* amount is coming in now and I can keep ahead of it, can I pump out enough water after *y* minutes of sleep? I don't know the answer, and I'm too terrified to get it wrong. And behind that is the fear that once asleep I simply won't hear the alarm.

This evening I do a marathon stint at the pump, getting glimpses of solid floorboard for a few minutes. Then I turn on the radio and hear McCoy Tyner on the Jazz Hour. I make spaghetti.

I eat my bowl of spaghetti sitting on the saloon bunk with my feet up out of the water on a towel in front of me. Looking around the cabin, I'm intensely glad J. isn't here tonight to see this water sloshing over the floor, to see *Toad* reduced to this. To fear for it now as I do. We had more good times than bad aboard this boat, I still think. Most of all when we pulled up the anchor and sailed somewhere. We worked in concert, and felt our boat respond. Once we had fixed it up, the vision we shared of a sailing life seemed, for a short while, to come true. Our three-month cruise from the Virgin Islands to Florida by way of Puerto Rico, the Dominican Republic, and the Bahamas was the nearest we came to reaching paradise together.

It takes time to become part of a place, especially in a pit stop for transients, and after nearly three years of floating around St. Thomas and St. John, just as we were about to leave, we seemed finally to have arrived. People knew us and our rugged little boat. Ed Dwyer, who ran Water Island Charters and had given us so much work and become a friend, offered all the charters both of us might want and deliveries of new boats from the east coast down to the Virgins. Dieter, the German blacksmith, asked us to run his sixty-five-footer for its first charter season. We said no, thank you, pleased at the recognition, but we'd had it with the Virgins. It had been mostly heartbreak and effort. We were already gone.

Two days before we sailed away, we got another kitty from the Humane Society, a black skinny thing with huge ears. Ed Dwyer said he looked like a bat. We called him Neptune. He was to be a friend for Minou, who pummeled him and ignored him before he finally fell in love. But it was me Neptune chose to favor. After two days of hiding aboard, he appeared on my chest one morning and began rubbing his nose against my whiskery chin, purring like an outboard. He became "my boy" and I loved him more than Minou.

We sailed first to San Juan, Puerto Rico, where we met an American sailor, Rick, and his Spanish girlfriend, Cruz, whom he had picked up in the Canary Islands while crossing the Atlantic. His boat was a nice, rather run-down old wooden double-ender; but what made it noticeable was the thing that looked like an umbrella without any fabric open and lashed to the top of the mast. It was a lightning protection device, he said. He had already been struck twice (*"¡Aïe!"* said Cruz, remembering) and designed his umbrella, after consulting numerous books, to ward off future attacks. Two years later when we were passing through Horta, in the Azores, Bob Silverman (whose house and lifestyle there I admired) gave us more news of Rick and his wonderful bad luck. Approaching Fayal the year before, Rick had taken a nap, the wind had changed, and his wind-vane-steered, umbrella-protected boat had piled into the foot of a cliff at the west end of the island. Rick and Cruz, wearing only shorts and T-shirts, jumped onto the rocks as the boat sank beneath them and spent the entire night scaling a steep cliff until they were crawling through the hydrangea bushes on level land at dawn. They

were found bloody, shocked, insensible, and brought to the
local hospital. When they recovered, they were given a ride
on to England aboard another yacht. As that yacht entered
the English Channel it was run down and sunk by a French
trawler. Rick and Cruz were both injured, but made it ashore
to England alive. I don't know if they went sailing again, but
I'd bet anything he did. He had too much bad luck going for
him to leave it at that. People like that are persistent, and lucky
too in a funny way, because they always survive, despite any
amount of wreckage and dead or injured people they leave in
their wake. Rick is still out there, sailing toward a fresh disaster, with a really unlucky, unsuspecting companion unaware
of what's about to happen.

From Puerto Rico we sailed on through fabled waters. La
Isla Española, Columbus named the large, lush, high island
he found to the south of his first landfall, in honor of his Spanish patrons. Hispaniola it became, and still is, shared by the
states of Haiti and the Dominican Republic. On the quiet
Christmas night of 1492, the *Santa María* grounded on a coral
reef off the north coast, near what is now Cap Haiten. It stuck
fast and was abandoned, leaving its Spanish timbers to rot
in the New World. On this bloody island sugar plantations
worked by Carib and Arawak Indian slaves were the first
planted endeavor of the colonial aspirations from across the
Atlantic.

We stopped at several ports in the Dominican Republic.
Samaná, described in our guidebook as a picturesque village
on the east coast, had recently been razed and rebuilt by the
government in readiness for a hoped-for onslaught of tourism.
It had rows of project-looking concrete buildings in which
the dispossessed people of Samaná now lived like glum squat-
ters, empty concrete hotels, and wide concrete roads leading
nowhere.

It took us four days to sail the ninety-odd miles from Puerta Plata, on the Dominican Republic's north coast, to Great Inagua, the southernmost island of the Bahamas. We got about halfway there and the wind died and we lay becalmed. We sat under the awning and ate the incredible-tasting avocados and pineapples we had bought in Puerta Plata. ("How much are the avocados?" "Sixty cents a dozen." *"What?" "Bueno,* forty cents.") We read. And we listened to the Voice of America tracking Skylab as, unplanned, the space station fell out of its orbit and began hurtling earthward at so shallow an angle that NASA wasn't really sure where it was going to crash onto the planet's surface. Most of the earth's surface, the VOA announcers pointed out reassuringly, was covered with water, so people on land shouldn't worry. And much of the eighty-ton, eighty-two-foot-long Skylab would burn up in the long oblique plunge through the atmosphere, so what did reach that remote spot of water somewhere would simply be a few tons of white-hot flaming debris. The coverage, as the fiery descent began, made it all sound like a sporting event, the commentators excitedly reporting that now it was over the Bering Sea, dropping fast, then streaking southeast across the Canadian tundra, now over open ocean, hurtling down the Atlantic; it was anybody's guess where it would land; NASA's latest estimates were being revised; it's got to be starting to burn up about now—

I looked up, scanning the sky to the north for what would at first appear as fireworks but then very quickly grow infinitely bigger, imagining that we might actually be unluckier than Rick and Cruz and have a space station drop on us. It seemed worse not having an engine, not having the option of cranking it up and then, once the fiery comet of debris was sighted, being able to steam out of its way at five knots.

However, it wasn't even a close call. Skylab scattered itself over the eastern Indian Ocean and western Australia, hopefully not disturbing even so much as a wallaby, or any Aussie yachties.

The Bahamian islands stretching south and east from Nassau, the capital, on New Providence Island—the Exuma Cays, Cat Island, Long Island, San Salvador (generally agreed to be Columbus's first landfall in the New World), Crooked and Acklins, Mayaguana, and Great and Little Inagua—are known to the Bahamians as the Out Islands. Perhaps because they are really *out there*. They lie north of eastern Cuba. They offer no facilities to the visitor, and the world largely passes them by. To me they felt as remote from the rest of the world as any place I've ever been.

We were sailing in the wake of one of my sailing heroes. In the sixties, Eric and Susan Hiscock sailed *Wanderer III* across the Atlantic to the Caribbean, the Bahamas, and the U.S. East Coast. *Toad* followed *Wanderer*'s path through the Out Islands and we stopped at many of the anchorages mentioned in Eric's book *Atlantic Cruise in Wanderer III*: French Wells, Calabash Bay, Big Major's Spot. In these places I took photographs of *Toad*, riding to anchor just where *Wanderer* had, copying Eric's plates in the book as closely as I could. I even surreptitiously lured J. to spots on the sand where Susan had stood, where the composition was a perfect match, and then pressed the shutter. J. would admonish me, telling me to focus on our trip, not the Hiscocks', but it gave me a little thrill.

The Bahamas lie at the edge of the Great Bahama Bank, a plateau of sand almost five hundred miles long, which separates the islands from Cuba. The average depth is fifteen feet, and often in the atmosphere over the bank miles ahead, you can see "bank blink," a pale green reflection of the shallow water below. On the other side of the islands, in places only several hundred yards from the bank, is the Atlantic Ocean, with depths plunging quickly to fifteen thousand feet. In the cuts between the islands, where these waters meet, tidal currents are strong—far stronger than *Toad*'s sail-powered ability to breast them. We had to play the tides like sailors of old. Navigation was all "eyeball": gauging depths and bottom type by the color of the water and the state of the tide by a glance ashore as we shot through cuts and ran, tacked, jibed, and beat through an endless maze of tiny islands and labyrinthine coral reefs, around great mushroom-shaped coral heads that sprouted from the sandy bottom with only a dark patch to warn of their position. Our passage up through the Out Islands was our final exam in handling a small boat under sail. We had heard the scuttlebutt about the Bahamas: it was a tricky place and many boats were lost there. But we did fine.

The Out Islands seemed deserted that summer. In our first month there, we saw only one other yacht, a singlehander on a tiny boat heading south. The Out Islands even had their own lonely sound, which we always heard when we stepped ashore from the dinghy: a soughing made by the trade wind through the casuarina pines that grew with the sea grape along the shore. It reminded us both of the wind in the pines in Mallorca when we were children.

In three months we spent one hundred dollars on vegetables, limes, and ice cream bought at tiny shack stores in Out Island villages, and on cold beer when we hove in sight of a bar. We carried no beer aboard because we had no refrigeration and didn't like it warm. At the end of every day, anchored in quiet water watching the brief and always beautiful tropical twilight, we drank glasses filled with rum, crushed limes, water, and a little sugar. During the day we drank gallons of water, of which we always had plenty because we caught it from passing squalls in our cockpit awning, which emptied through a small tube straight into our tanks. We dove every day for grouper, crayfish, or conch, for us and "the boys." I used a Hawaiian sling rather than a speargun: a sling-shot made of surgical rubber bound to the side of a hollow wooden handle. The spear goes through the handle and is pulled back and released. You had to get close to your quarry, and then pull and fire. We saw shark and barracuda but we didn't bother them and they didn't bother us. We ate well on whatever I speared four or five nights a week with rice or veg-etables, and spaghetti or rice on nights when we were glutted on fish or crayfish—the southern lobster. We found wild papaya and coconuts. We baked bread. We grew as brown and fit as savages from swimming and diving for our food and hauling up the anchor and raising sails and winching sheets and walking entirely around every island we anchored at.

This was J. and I at our best, working our boat together, feeding ourselves, exploring each passing island and moving on. We felt we could have lived like this indefinitely, we dal-lied and zigzagged, but we were moving inexorably closer to the States and the end of our cruise.

In the Berry Islands, north of Nassau, we sheltered in a landlocked bay as Hurricane David roared up through the Bahamas and passed sixty miles south of our hurricane "hole." The roof of a solitary house ashore behind us blew off, but our anchors—three of them, triangulated for a hold against any change of wind direction—held firmly, and we weathered the blow looking out our portholes at the spume-filled air, and listening to Florida radio stations a hundred miles away that tracked the storm. The local Bahamian sta-tion had switched, near the height of the storm, to a live, end-less, imploring church service as a means of ultimate storm protection for its listeners. When the hurricane had passed, we found crayfish, disoriented by churned-up sand and strange currents, walking drunkenly along open sandy stretches of bottom, out of their usual holes in the coral, and we picked up eight of them in five minutes and ate them all the way to Fort Lauderdale.

We spent six months in Fort Lauderdale, and another year anchored off Dinner Key south of Miami. A dispiriting time when we tried to make enough money to sail away, but there was never enough, or as much as we thought we would need. I hadn't yet read Sterling Hayden's autobiography *Wanderer* (Hayden was a sailing ship master before he became what he called a male starlet), in which he writes: "To be truly challenging, a voyage, like a life, must rest on a firm foundation of financial unrest. Otherwise you are doomed to a routine traverse." We did some delivery work: sailing new boats from Florida and Annapolis to the Virgins for charter companies, a ten- to twelve-day trip, usually an unpleasant beat to windward all the way, in crappy boats not designed or prepared to go to sea but for a doodle around the gentle Virgins. I bought a good sextant in a varnished wooden box from Sy Carkhuff, who had sailed around the world with it, and my sun and star sights improved on these offshore passages. I also worked as a boat carpenter around Dinner Key, and J. did some boat painting and varnishing.

We plunged back into our old malaise. We fought more often and more unkindly. A constant dull unhappiness grew between us by the steady accretion of little episodes. The same way a coral reef is built.

After eighteen months we decided to leave again. Rather the way we'd felt when we left the Virgins: it was time to flee. We knew we didn't have enough money to get as far as New Zealand, a year's voyage with no possibility of making money on the way, so we headed east across the Atlantic.

This voyage was not the happy uninterrupted dream sequence of our Out Islands cruise. We sailed out of No

Name Harbor on Key Biscayne, into the Gulf Stream a couple of miles offshore, where the wind died and we were swept away north in the five-knot current. That first evening we had a terrible fight, shouting at each other. I remember the shouting but not what it was about, but it's never about what sets it off. The weather remained light all the way to Bermuda, and it took us fifteen days to get there.

After two weeks in Bermuda, the bilges filled with water the day we left, frightening us, but we discovered it had been coming in through the unsecured forward hatch—and then it stopped. The Azores, three weeks out. A month on Fayal. Then a week to the European mainland, rounding Cape St. Vincent on a sunny afternoon and Portugal looked so pretty, but we were screaming at each other. *"I'm sick of you! I'm sick to death of you!"* I remember yelling at J. hoarsely, and her yelling it back.

We almost put the boat ashore just north of Tarifa at the entrance to the Straits of Gibraltar. We had tacked in toward the land all night seeking a lee against the tremendous blast of a *levante*, an easterly gale blowing out of the straits. Tack after tack after tack, exhausting ourselves, we became drenched and cold inside our oilskins, and a dulling numbness came over us. In the misty dawn we saw ahead the lights of cars on the coast road shown on our chart, but we didn't see that this was well inland from the beach. Before we were aware of it in our blunted state, we were in the waves off the beach. We had expected the water to flatten out as we approached the shore, with the gale blowing off the land, but so great was the force of the wind that they were still high and breaking only yards from dry sand. We let the sheets fly, the sails flap, and I jumped straight into the water off the bow and stood hip deep and pushed *Toad*'s bow off into deeper water. A day later we ghosted into Gibraltar, the northern Pillar of Hercules, and the remarkable juxtaposition of a hideous English suburban town on the shores of the Mediterranean.

Our final break came not with a bang but a series of whimpers. We left *Toad* in Ibiza, one island short of our destination of Mallorca because we could bear to sail no farther together. I left almost immediately for London. J. followed two months later, after she had found a home for the cats with someone in Germany because there was no bringing them to England with a six-month-long quarantine. That must have destroyed her, giving them away, that and the abandonment of our home for a studio I was renting from my mother. We spent an unhappy winter and spring together in London. I was trying to write again, after years of thinking but doing nothing about it. J. hated sharing me again, particularly with the people we saw in London, whom she found to be superficial. She hated the way she felt about herself around me. That summer we got the job delivering *Sea Bear* from Florida to England. In the early fall we sailed *Toad* from Ibiza to England. Our final passage together. Martin came with us as far as Motril on the Spanish mainland, where we met Whit, who so disapproved of scrimshaw, and J. and I had one more fight. She left Martin and me in a bar there one night and when I got back to the boat I found a note from her: "I know when I'm like this I'm my own worst enemy, making you want to abandon me."

We spent two weeks at sea being quiet and careful with each other. We made love for the last time. We got pummeled by the equinoctial gales off the Western Approaches to the Channel. We left *Toad* at its winter berth off Flushing and listed it with a local yacht broker.

One day, back in London, after food-shopping by myself in Waitrose on the King's Road, I went home and told J. I couldn't live with her anymore. I did this instinctually, appalled at myself, in the face of my love for her and my feeling that she was the best person I knew or might ever know and my vision of what we could have been together. None of that seemed to help. I was exhausted with trying to make her happy, sick of seeing myself at my worst through her eyes, and seeing her at her worst, frightened of the way we fought like two alpha wolves trapped in a cage, wounding each other and going for those same raw wounds the next time.

She had expected it all along—almost from the day of our wedding, I realize now. It came as proof of the inerasable lesson she had learned as a nine-year-old girl on vacation with her parents when one day her mother vanished with the handsome tennis pro: the people you love will leave you.

She didn't fight me; she didn't say, *Let's work this out.* She took what I said as absolute as a papal decree and boarded a train to Nice to stay with her mother. She saw the Bergstroms again, and Leif asked her if she wanted to be part of a crew with him delivering a motor yacht to Florida. She went, about six weeks after we split, and they are still together.

I have thought, since leaving her, that we might have been perfect together if we could have met for the first time as the people we were when we split up—or perhaps quite a bit later. People who had acquired some knowledge of marital relations and could use it to make one work. Or if we had stayed together and rebuilt our relationship as we had rebuilt *Toad*, cutting out the rot back to what was clean and sound, and building on the good stuff. But I didn't see how we could do that anymore than meet each other again for the first time.

I started running. I got up early every morning and ran through the dark around Bishop's Park in Fulham, beside the Thames. I ran longer and longer distances. Across Putney Bridge and down the towpath along the river to Hammersmith. Five miles, then ten miles. It seemed the only thing in the world I could do that did something in return for me. The longer I ran, the better I felt.

I went on the dole (I gave my occupation as boat captain, and, there not being any such jobs at that time in Fulham, I was given £90 a week).

I ran the London marathon in March.

I spent most of my time in my little studio, writing, and reading boating books, magazines, and taking my sextant out of its varnished box and looking at it. I felt marooned. David and Martin were well embarked on their careers, but not in positions from which they could help me get in. I found my old portfolio of ads and thought of trying to get back into advertising. I wrote and drew new spec ads. I wrote one for Seiko watches, about how Peter Nichols used his to navigate across the Atlantic. But it was a bad time to try to get back in, I was told.

I wondered what I was doing, and who I was, alone, in my thirties, now, living at home with my mother, broke and on the dole. Such thoughts flew at me like van Gogh's dark crows between two and four o'clock in the morning, and I had no answers.

Increasingly I thought of *Toad*. Unsold, waiting. I thought of sailing it somewhere by myself. I felt capable of this now; I knew this would make me feel better about myself.

Finally, it was all I could think of.

July 26

Spent most of the day in the cockpit. In my foul-weather gear, my harness on now because I'm getting some sleep, sitting upright over the pump, back against the cabin, nodding off between strokes. Rocked and bounced to sleep. Getting real sleep too, must be, because I'm dreaming vividly. Dreamed

we were approaching the Azores. Woke up once and saw
Maine ahead, for sure, all those granite shores and fir trees.
Straight out of *WoodenBoat* magazine. Eggemoggin Reach, I
guessed. Thought about getting up and going forward to
unlash the anchor and then it wasn't there and I realized we
still had about eight hundred miles to go. A lot of dreams like
that all day.

Hove-to. No sailing. Boat full of water, although I can go
below and wade around pretty easily.

I put the battery (a Die Hard car battery, which powers my
tape deck and VHF radio) into the cooler, which is floating
where the engine would be. I have to keep it dry, keep the
VHF working.

No sun today, so no position. No one makes me tea either.
Not that sort of day. Or else she's on holiday.

Odd, but there's this white stuff in the water today, all
around the boat, particularly as we roll in the swell. Little
white bits, like chunks of barnacle you scrape off the hull
when you haul out, only a little smaller. In the water around
the boat. Waves cleaning the hull? The stuff sinks slowly. I
watch it go down. Bits of something.

I think it's windier today, if anything. A real gale, over
thirty knots. The seas are up from yesterday—but they would
be, after days of this.

Might try the radio later, put out a call, see if anyone's
there.

An endless night, pumping when I'm not dozing. Pump-
pump-pump. Back and forth, back and forth, a rhythm building, like prostration for prayer. It's cloudy, but through the
cloud comes the dim illumination from a new moon somewhere above, giving the night shape and texture: gloomy
rooms with inchoate frescoed ceilings, dark, heaving walls.

July 27

At dawn I see a ship off to the north, four or five miles away. Very hazy, dawn light and misty air, but it stays there and keeps going like a real ship while I stand up and watch it.

I go below and call it up on the VHF.

"Hello ship at about 35° 43′ north, 53° 03′ west, this is the sailing yacht *Toad* several miles off your port beam. Do you read? Over."

An answer, from a Dutch ship. He claims it's not him I see because he doesn't see me anywhere off his port beam, or on radar. He tells me I'm probably seeing another ship. I don't care. I have rehearsed what I want to say.

"I am in a severely leaking condition. I am en route to Bermuda. I may have to abandon ship. Would you please radio the U.S. Coast Guard station November Mike November and let them know my position and situation, and ask them to alert shipping in this area to keep a good lookout in case I have to abandon ship?"

The Dutch ship will have a shortwave transmitter. My VHF will transmit no farther usually than you can see from its aerial at the top of the mast: maybe twenty miles, possibly farther at sea in good conditions.

"You need to get off now?"

I'm not prepared for this question.

"*Jacht*, you want to abandon ship now?"

"No, thanks. I'm hoping to make it to Bermuda. But my boat is leaking, and I may have to abandon ship later."

"*Ja*, okay."

I wait a little while, then call back to see if he got through, but I get no answer. I call several more times without a response. I go back on deck and look to the northwest, but the ship is gone. It's still blowing about thirty knots.

Immediately, I start thinking I should have said, "Yes, I'm sinking. I have to get off now. Please save me."

What constitutes sinking? I wonder. Is *Toad* sinking? Even now, this is almost a new concept. It has a leak, but is it *sinking*? How bad is it? How accustomed to it have I become?

What if I don't see another ship?

When do I let go?

I pump for a long time, but there is still water over the floor below. I go down to find something to eat. No bread left. There is some muesli. I haven't made a proper meal for several days. Spaghetti, when was that? I look in the lockers around the galley, not really seeing what I'm looking at. Didn't I have some peanut butter?

I drift, standing in the galley, holding on while the boat lurches back and forth, my mind blank.

"Hello, *Toad*!" An incredibly cheery voice on the radio, which I've left on. "Little boat *Toad*!" An Indian accent. "Hello! Hello! Hello!"

I pick up the mike. "Yes, hello. This is *Toad*."

"*Toad*, yes! Good morning! How are you?"

How am I? "I am leaking, thank you. How are you?"

"Oh, yes, you are leaking!" A definite chuckle. "That is what we are hearing! But we are fine, thank you! Very good, very good!"

The Indian accent, beloved of comics and mimics in England, is thick, and irrepressibly cheerful. It sounds like Peter Sellers, escaped from *The Party* and running amok on the high sea. If I were anywhere else—hearing this on the phone, say—I would know it was a joke.

And even here I say, "Who is this?"

"We are the ship *Laxmi*. We are calling to see if you need help. How are you, really?"

"Where are you?"

"We are here!"

We are here is not a position a professional seaman would be likely to give. The sense of joke compounds, turns surreal.

"I mean what is your position, please?"

"But we are right here, *Toad*! Look! Look out the door, please!"

Still holding the mike, I step up on the galley counter and look out—

A ship is *right* behind us, on top of us. I could whack a badminton birdie onto its deck. Big, black, rusty, a cargo ship of some sort. LAXMI written on its bow. The bridge towers overhead, and eight or ten grinning Indians are crowding the rail above my head, waving as if I were Prince Charles. I can hear them shouting: "Hello, *Toad*!" I wave back.

"You see!" says the laughing voice on the radio. "We are here!"

"Yes, I see," I answer back into the mike.

We all wave for a while.

"Well, do you want to come with us?"

That question again. Get off or wait? For what? It's still blowing. I'm not doing well. I'm tired and dopey. And I don't think the leak is going to slow down when the wind drops. I've reached a crossroad.

"Where are you going?" I ask.

"We are going to Burma!"

"Burma?"

"Yes, Burma! You know, next door to India!"

What a thought! What might be waiting for me in Burma? Perhaps I could turn into a Somerset Maugham character, become an old Burma "hand." Manage a rubber plantation, wear baggy shorts and a pith helmet, and start drinking a lot of gin. Trim my mustache to an RAF shape and marry the daughter of a missionary, Celia, with whom I would have brittle fights on the veranda after dinner. Go quietly mad. Or perhaps go native—"poor chap, bad business"—and meet a Burmese woman and raise a bunch of beautiful Eurasian children. Or become a Buddhist monk. Or would I find my appointment in Samarra, the death I had unknowingly been headed toward all along? I think of these old clichés and realize I know nothing at all about the modern Burma. All the more reason to go.*

Here at the crossroad, *Laxmi* is unmistakably the less-traveled road, forking toward Burma. And, with some disappointment in myself, I fail to rise to the occasion.

"No, thanks, *Laxmi*. I'm trying to get to the States. Or Bermuda."

"You are sure?"

"Yes, thanks." And now I'll always wonder.

I ask *Laxmi* to radio the Coast Guard at NMN in Portsmouth, Virginia, to tell them about me and my situation. They promise to do this and, with lots of waving and wide white smiles, they steam off to the southeast.

Will this be the last ship I see? I'm sure not. It's the second I've seen in an hour. We must be bang in the middle of the shipping lane.

A little later *Laxmi* calls back. They're in touch with the Coast Guard, who are asking for an ETA in Maine or Bermuda. Eight to ten days, or three or four for Bermuda, I tell my pal aboard *Laxmi*. In our last exchange, he gives me a position check, which puts me considerably farther to the northeast than where I think I am. One of us is about forty miles off.

The sun appears at 1030 and I get two LOP snapshots. I

---

*Since this voyage, I have learned something of Aung San Suu Kyi and the troubles of modern Burma.

work them out and find that I am, in fact, where I thought I was. I believe in my navigation, and wonder whether *Laxmi* will make Burma after all.

With the sun comes a sudden dramatic moderation of wind and weather. By noon it's a nice day, blowing about twelve knots. The sea is still lumpy, but it's time to crack on more sail, which will steady us and get us moving. I'm invigorated. I feel wide awake.

I go up on deck and unroll all of the main. Then I go out on the bowsprit, sit down on it, and start untying the genoa.

My feet and legs and the bobstay chain are plunging in and out of the water as *Toad* rises and falls in the leftover swell. At the lower edge of my vision I suddenly register a large dark shape in the water immediately beneath my feet. I'm back on deck, well inboard, saying out loud "Je-sus *Christ!*" before I know it. It was huge, dark brown, and bobbing at my feet with a curious undulating motion, as if sniffing me.

I lean over the edge of the deck and look down. My God, what is that? The weirdest creature I've ever seen, huge too: flat, ragged, torn, waving in the water—

It's the sheathing. Delaminated from the bow, hanging off the hull in a long wide flap of heavy cloth, brown with dried resorcinol glue, waving up and down in the water with the motion of the waves. I move out onto the bowsprit again to get a better look and see the same waving flap down the other side of the boat too. The Cascover has delaminated at its joint at the bow and peeled back down both sides of the boat, at least halfway back, as far as I can see. Great obscene flaps waving from amidships. How long has it been like this?

I see those white bits in the water again, and now I know exactly what they are: old caulking, dried and brittle, washing out of the seams.

Dizzy, with a cold feeling in my stomach, I rush below and

look at the hull up forward. Plain as day, seawater is pouring in, welling arterially, through most seams, as far back as the saloon, and farther. White bits of old caulking have also been pushed in and are lying on the planking and down the sides of the frames. Everywhere. Haven't I seen this until now? Known, without looking overboard, how bad it was? I don't know. If I saw it, I pushed away its meaning.

I don't know if I've been holding my breath, but now I can't breathe. I rush topside again.

I sit in the cockpit. I'm feeling dizzy. Hard to breathe. I sit, holding on. Minutes pass.

The boat, I realize—I knew it all along—is quite sound. All those sister frames, and the new laminated floor frames I put in just two years ago before we left Florida. The boat is as strong as ever. But the sheathing is off, the caulking gone or going from half the seams in the hull's planking. The boat has turned into a colander.

Nothing I can do about it . . . is there? A hole I could patch: I could saw up the plywood beneath the bunks and nail it over ten holes. But this . . . I think of Robin Knox-Johnston caulking *Suhaili*'s leaking seam underwater with a complicated patch. Eight feet of seam on both sides of the boat. What would he do here with the equivalent of forty fifteen-foot-long kerfs sawn through the hull? And certain to lengthen.

Toad is gone. I know this absolutely as I sit here in the cockpit on what is now becoming rather a nice day. The sun is out, the sea is going down.

Knowing this, I look at the boat around me. The teak vent boxes I built on the cabin roof. The stainless steel guardrail stanchions I installed. The winches, the rigging. The new compass Martin and I hooked up. The slight imperfection beneath the paint on the cabin side that I know is my plug of a hole made by Henry's useless depth gauge. I look up and down the boat and I cannot see an inch of it that I haven't remade according to my idea of what would make *Toad* the best it could be. Now I know that the leak will not get better but worse, that I can't keep ahead of it, that I must get off, save my life, and let *Toad* sink.

I have never thought of *Toad* as "she," the way many think of their boats. My brother David liked to call it "him." To me *Toad* doesn't have a gender, but it is certainly something far more than the sum of its wood and bits and pieces. With every screw and bolt and pass of a paintbrush that J. and I gave it, this boat made these its own, and added something of itself. It has absorbed more love into its fibers than any amount of paint or varnish, until this has become part of its matrix. What *Toad* is to me now is a thing that was made and lives from that love.

And I believe *Toad* loves me back.

So as I sit in the cockpit and look at it with tears pouring down my face, I am careful to keep quiet. I don't say anything. I'm not going to tell it what is going to happen now.

I sheet the main amidships, heaving-to, and wait for local noon. I get a latitude sight. I work out our position with unusual care, thinking about our drift since the morning LOP sights. We're at 36° 08′ north, 53° 12′ west. Three hundred miles northeast of Bermuda; eight hundred miles from Maine.

At 1400 I put out my first mayday call on the VHF. I say into the mike, according to international radio etiquette: "Mayday, mayday, mayday. This is the sailing yacht *Toad* at 36° 08′ north, 53° 12′ west, requesting assistance." "Mayday, mayday, mayday. This is the sailing yacht *Toad* at 36° 08′ north, 53° 12′ west, requesting assistance."

No reply. I repeat it a few more times, then stop. I haven't been heard. Probably no ship within range. I'll wait an hour and try again. I'll do this every hour on the hour, but for no

more than two or three minutes, to conserve battery power. I
know this part of the ocean, I know this is a shipping lane. I've
spoken with two ships already this morning. Another will
come along. I cling positively to this thought so I don't have to
think about getting into the dinghy and sailing for Bermuda.
I think instead of what to take when a ship comes along and
takes me off. I start to pack.

This is a good time to go through my wardrobe and get rid
of a few things. At this singular moment in my life, an article
comes to mind, written by Michael Korda some time ago in
The New York Times Magazine. It was on the subject of a man's
irreducible minimum wardrobe. A man can make do, Korda
wrote, with one suit and two shirts. He can wash the shirts in
a basin at night, hanging them up to dry, and if the suit is
made of a decent wool, he can hang it in the bathroom when
he takes his shower, and the steam will remove any wrinkles. I
wondered, when I read this, how Korda, scion of the family of
cinema titans, who grew up surrounded by wealth and abun-
dance, who has himself become a famous editor in chief of a
publishing house and best-selling author, came by such
knowledge, which would indicate both impoverishment and a
great concern to maintain appearances, and why he would
write about this during the prime of his own adult success.
These tactics and concern might have come from his uncle,
Alexander Korda, a penniless Hungarian refugee who made
himself into a movie tycoon and married Merle Oberon. I
suppose the fear of loss of newly gained wealth, and how to
manage without it, and regain it, is carried subconsciously
down through several generations. It might have been something Michael Korda learned at the knee of his illustrious
uncle, essential information that any man must carry to make
his way in the world, and that, I guessed, is why Korda was
moved to write the article and pass it on.

Anyway, I think of it now as I go through my own clothes. I don't have a suit, but I do have a blazer, wool, and I stuff it into a sailbag. I'll pull it out when I have my next shower. I have a number of shirts, out of which I select two Brooks Brothers button-downs, and several T-shirts. A pair of venerable jeans. Underwear, socks, a hankie Martin gave me. I hope this will do. I have no idea what this next boatless phase in my life will bring, or what I will have to become in it, or how often I will have to shower with my blazer.

I look around at my books. Hundreds of them stuffed into the shelves above the saloon berths, over the chart table, in the back of the galley. Years of selecting and collecting. Mostly they are books about boats and the sea. How to design them, build them, sail them. By the designers, builders, and sailors I most respect. Like William Albert Robinson, whose seventy-foot brigantine *Varua* is my favorite boat in all the world. Robinson circumnavigated in a small ketch called *Svaap* in the 1920s, and then designed *Varua*, his "ultimate" ship, with Starling Burgess, and in it he experienced the "ultimate" storm: "Again and again that night, I asked myself why I was there—and had no better answer than that perhaps this was the very thing that had drawn me into this voyage: an unexpressed urge to experience a real Cape Horn gale." Robinson built *Varua* in his own shipyard in Gloucester, Massachusetts, starting construction in 1939—the same year *Toad* was built— and then sailed it to Tahiti, where he lived for the rest of his life. He wrote about this ship and his life sailing it around the Pacific, and through the Roaring Forties to Chile, in two of my favorite books, *Return to the Sea* and *To the Great Southern Sea*. But if I take them, what do I leave behind? *Skiffs and Schooners*; *Boats, Oars and Rowing*; and *Spray*? All by R. D. "Pete" Culler, who learned marlinspike seamanship from a man "who had learned his seamanship under men who had sailed

with Nelson." Bill Tilman's *Mischief in Patagonia*? My Knox-
Johnston, Moitessier, Crowhurst books? *Sailing Alone Around
the World* by Slocum? Chapelle's *Boatbuilding*, and *Yacht Design-
ing and Planning*? . . . My Hiscocks, for fuck's sake? It doesn't
matter that I've read them all; they are my library, I refer to
them constantly, for reassurance more than anything, to know
that this world I've read about and want to be a part of exists,
and I feel a chill intimation of a coming loneliness at the
thought of leaving them all behind.

I take the Hiscocks, all nine of them; Eric's complete oeu-
vre, hardbacked, blue cloth, Oxford University Press. They
are salt-stained, half-ruined, broken-spined, dust jackets long
disintegrated, the foundation of my library—and of who I am,
for they describe all I want to do and the world in which I
want to do it—and upon them I will build once more from
scratch. The rest I hope I can find again.

At 1500 I make another mayday call. No response—until,
minutes after I've stopped and gone back to my packing for a
new life, a clear static-free voice fills the cabin:

"Ship calling mayday, this is the *Almeria Lykes*. *Almeria Lykes*
responding to mayday, come back."

For all my desperate confidence of being picked up, relief
floods me. I think: *Wow, that was fast.*

"Yes, *Almeria Lykes*, this is the sailing yacht *Toad*. I'm at 36°
08′ north, 53° 12′ west, and I am sinking. Over."

The voice on the radio, a voice of calm, of authority, tells
me that he is about twenty miles from my position. (He talks
in a seigneurial first-person singular: not we, not the ship,
but "I am about twenty miles . . .") He is a container ship, on
his way from Rotterdam to Galveston, Texas. He asks me
how sure I am of the position I have given. Pretty sure, I
reply, within a couple of miles—sure that if they come to that
position I will see them. The voice responds that he is on his

way. He will be there in an hour. He will remain standing by on the air.

I hang up the mike and look around *Toad*'s saloon. After six years, an hour more. After an immeasurable moment I resume packing. I can, of course, take more than these clothes, the Hiscocks, and the grab bag I had ready to take in the dinghy (in fact, I will leave my Neal's yard peanut butter and Gibbon's *Decline and Fall* behind), but already I can see myself afoot in America. I have about $60 and an English Barclaycard Visa with a £100 limit. I will be starting my new life in a Texas bus station. I will have to hump everything, God knows how far, or for how long. I must travel light. I must be ruthless.

I am a sailor. This is how I hope to make my living. So I put my varnished sextant box into the cockpit. Into the sailbag, on top of my irreducible wardrobe, I cram all my charts, my Filofax with my Coast Guard hundred-ton license and my passport, oilskin jacket and pants and seaboots. In go the Hiscocks, camera, exposed film, envelopes of loose photographs, and my logbook of this voyage, the last entry reading:

> 1500: Mayday call replied to by *Almeria Lykes*, a container ship
> bound for Galveston. Gave him my position and he said he'd
> be here in an hour.

My Seiko is on my wrist, and around my neck is my Azorean scrimshaw of *Toad*.

For J., I throw in her five hardback diaries.

On top of them I place the folder containing the novel I've been trying to write. I suspect it's not what I want it to be. I yearn to write something great and wonderful—much better than this novel—but I don't know yet what that might be.

I take my Olivetti up into the cockpit, put it next to the

sextant box, look up and see the ship on the horizon. Black and square. It looks like a building. I go below and call him on the radio, tell him I see him, give him his bearing from me—let him work out the reciprocal, I'm too busy.

I go back up into the cockpit and start pumping, partly because I can't stand the sight of so much water below, also because I don't want *Toad* to sink before the ship gets here. I don't know how long it will take the ship to maneuver alongside or how all that will work.

The ship is now about three or four miles away. He calls over the radio to tell me he's spotted me, made visual contact.

I watch it get bigger and bigger, its shape and details growing more definite. It's ugly, slab-sided, tier upon tier of containers—red, gray, blue, rust—stacked high above the black hull along its entire length. Almost no superstructure visible except the bridge at the very front, right up in the bow where it doesn't belong according to all the laws of ship aesthetics as I know them. The closer it gets, growing huger and uglier, the less it looks like a ship. Finally, it has the size and appearance of a mall nearing the end of construction: rectangular, black, and nine hundred feet long, I will learn later this afternoon. Mr. East would hate it, feel it was an abomination. I don't know how to feel. It looks like Armageddon and it's coming to save me.

The ship—ALMERIA LYKES I see on its bow, and LYKES LINES in enormous white three-story letters along the black hull—approaches from windward, leaving us becalmed in a short chop. His voice comes up out of the cabin, from my radio, to tell me that he's going to stop, drift down to me, throw me a line to fasten at *Toad*'s bow. He will then move ahead at his slowest speed, several knots, and we will be pulled in alongside the hull. He will drop a rope ladder, which I am to climb up.

Soon the ship is all I see. It drifts toward us, sideways, blotting out half the visible world. The black hull stretches from horizon to horizon along *Toad*'s starboard side and goes all the way up to the sky.

My hackles rise—no metaphor: the back of my scalp is contracting tightly. This is against all my small-boat sailor's instincts. I should clap on sail and get away from this monster that can mean only one thing to *Toad*: damage. The last time I was on a small boat this close to a larger one was with Bill on *Mary Nell* as the Russian lassoed us and pulled us in and *Mary Nell*'s masts both snapped like dry twigs.

Toad is half turned toward this black wall, now about fifteen feet away. Instinctively, with no thought at all, I dance across the cabin top, over the foredeck, out onto the bowsprit. I stand on the very tip, holding onto the forestay. The black steel plate—pitted, dull, and uneven up close—is closing fast. *Toad*'s angle is all wrong.

I look up for a moment: high above me, peering over the top of the hull, I see a man with long blond hair and a mustache. He's waving. Waving me back.

The ship is a foot away. I stick out my foot now, bracing the other on the bowsprit, to push it off, or push us off. Suddenly this is a collision, that's all I know.

And we collide: the tip of *Toad*'s bowsprit, four inches from my foot, meets the black wall. There's a *crack*—I'm flying through the air, still holding on to the forestay—and then I land back on the cabin top by the mast. The bowsprit is broken, snapped immediately on contact. The forestay, attached to the end of the bowsprit, under tension from the mast and rig, has whipped backward, carrying me with it like Tarzan on a jungle creeper. I land at the mast (which remains upright, held by the inner forestay, which was not set up when the mast fell backward in St. Thomas harbor five years ago). I look at the jagged broken stump of sprit in the bow, and the other piece lying by my foot, and think about how to fix it . . . and then I pull myself away from this thought and push myself toward what must be done.

A shout from above: I look up again and the blond man swings a coil of line right above me, which as I watch turns into a helix as it falls through space and drops onto *Toad*'s foredeck. I fasten the end to the oversize bronze cleat on the foredeck that I took off the Chris Craft lying on the hard in the Lagoon one night years ago.

The small chop, the collision, perhaps even my attempt to push us off have caused us to drift away from the ship's hull. But now the ship begins to move slowly ahead. Tension straightens the line at *Toad*'s bow, and we are pulled forward and in against the black hull. *Toad*'s three-quarter-inch larch planking smacks and bumps against the black steel and I just try not to think about it.

A bright orange rope ladder drops down over the side of the ship astern of us. Someone starts letting out the line holding *Toad* alongside and we are eased back along the hull until we are bobbing and thumping against the ladder. Small, thin lines are dropped down into the cockpit where my bags are packed and ready.

The blond man is now about thirty feet directly above me. I can hear him clearly. He tells me to tie my bags to the small lines. I do this and crewmen haul them up over the side. They are careful with the sextant, keeping it from banging into the steel on the way up. Four items altogether: a sailbag, the sextant, the typewriter, and a Bellingham overnight bag.

"Is that it?" the blond man asks me when they're up and out of sight.

"Yes, I'll be right up." And I go below.

I look around. Apart from the water now at my knees, all

looks normal aboard *Toad*. Very neat, just as I like it aboard a small boat crammed with years of collected belongings. The kettle on the stove. It's past teatime.

There remains an hour or two of daylight. I know what I must do. I take the bread knife, bend and crawl into the space behind the galley, where the engine would have been, and cut the one-and-a-half-inch-diameter plastic hose between the cockpit drain and its gate valve through the hull. Water begins to gush in, spouting. *Toad* must sink before dark. So no other yacht will smash into it, waterlogged but still floating, and sink with it. Full of love and memories, *Toad* is now an obstruction to safe navigation.

I climb back up into the cockpit, grab the orange polypropylene, and start up the rope ladder. An unreal, dislocating sense of what I am doing, deserting and abandoning the thing I love—a suddenly familiar and reverberating sensation—weighing me down. About a thirty-foot climb.

I'm standing on the ship's high deck. The blond man—he's about six-foot-four, looks like a Viking, or like a young Hulk Hogan—grabs my hand and shakes it, grinning.

"Hey, I'm Dan. How you doing?"

The other crewmen around me are also grinning. They introduce themselves. They are all American. This is an exciting episode in the middle of a monotonous trip for them. They're all thrilled.

I'm not sure what I say, but farther along the deck I see someone casting off the line to *Toad*'s bow. He drops it into the sea.

Dan speaks into a portable VHF he's holding in his hand. A moment later the ship shudders. It begins a long arcing turn around *Toad*, which I find I can't take my eyes off.

I'm walking along the deck behind Dan, who's talking to me, though I have no idea what he's saying. This is just like a dream: I observe, but I am completely detached, disembodied from the scene. We go forward, up steps, into the superstructure below the bridge. Inside we continue up steel stairs.

I'm shown into a stateroom, so vast as to confirm that this is a dream. A double bed, a bathroom en suite. It looks like a motel room, but bigger than most. Windows look out at the sea—I crane my head, but I can't see *Toad.* Dan tells me to make myself comfortable, have a shower, and come up and meet the captain, who's on the bridge, one deck up, whenever I'm ready. The other guys bring in my four items of luggage, all I own in the world. Then they all leave.

Again, I look out the window, but I can't see it. *Toad* is behind us somewhere, to port. I leave my stateroom and run—so, so dreamlike with the uphill roll of the ship against me, holding me back—down a long hallway to a door. Through it, I'm outside, on a wing far above the ocean.

Toad is astern, a quarter of a mile away, maybe, looking not quite itself with its stump bowsprit, and conspicuously low in the water. But it still looks good, the paint and varnish glinting in the low sunlight.

Its bow is pointing straight at Maine.

Postscript: Peter Nichols went on to write a bestselling book about the 1969 Golden Globe race around the world, entitled *A Voyage for Madmen.*

In August of 1979, over three hundred yachts participated in the six-hundred-mile-long Fastnet Race from the Isle of Wight near the coast of England to Fastnet Rock near the Irish coast and back. The calm skies suddenly erupted into a force 10 gale with sixty-knot winds. The 2,500 sailors involved were tossed about by forty-foot breaker waves as a massive rescue effort was made to try and save them.

"FASTNET, FORCE 10"

JOHN ROUSMANIERE

Toscana: To the Western Approaches

Longer *foreknowledge of the* approach of Low Y probably would not have decreased the havoc caused by the storm in the Western Approaches. We in *Toscana*, an American forty-eight-foot sloop whose home port was Westport, Connecticut, had come too far to drop out of this Fastnet race simply because of a few warnings about bad weather, and I don't believe that David Sheahan would have stopped racing before the conditions actually deteriorated to the point where survival was the overriding consideration. Of the two dozen or so other boats in the Fastnet fleet that lost men overboard, suffered incapacitating damage, or were

abandoned by their crews, perhaps one or two—but no more—
might have run for shelter if the "Fastnet, force 10" warning
had been made during the BBC Radio 4 shipping bulletin
early on Monday morning. The challenge of sailing through
rough weather is indisputably one of the attractions of ocean
racing. Whether or not the challenge has been compromised
by the death and destruction that occurred in the Fastnet race
gale, it was pure and golden to the men and women who
started the race at Cowes on August 11, 1979.

This summer gale, packing all the violence of a midwinter
North Atlantic storm, could not have appeared at a more
unlucky moment. If it had arrived a day earlier, most of the
boats would have been within sight of the safe harbors indent-
ing the English Channel, where they might have found shelter
before the wind abated sufficiently for them to continue racing. And twelve or fifteen hours later, the smaller, more vulnerable boats would have been within easy reach of the safe
ports along the southeast coast of Ireland.

Attacked by surprise, at night, halfway between England
and Ireland, most of the fleet had to rely only on seamanship
and luck. For many crews, neither was sufficient. At its worst,
the gale was fiercer than any storm ever experienced by the
overwhelming majority of the sailors caught in it.

Since it was first sailed in 1925, the Fastnet race has been
one of the major goals of racing yachtsmen throughout the
world. Other ocean races are longer (transatlantic and Honolulu races run more than two thousand miles) or, if the same
length, cover more blue water (unlike the Fastnet, which runs
along a coast for almost half its length, the Bermuda race is
across part of an open ocean), but the Fastnet race is the international standard of ocean yacht racing. Alfred F. Loomis, historian of the sport, called the Fastnet "the Grand National of
ocean racing." That Loomis, an American, referred to an

English and not an American horse race is no coincidence. Until quite recently in the United States, yachting has been the preserve of white Anglo-Saxon Protestants who, like Loomis, tend to evaluate their institutions by English standards.

I myself am almost purely WASP, despite my French name (and it is probably Huguenot, anyway). A French commissary worker helping out during the American Revolution left the name in Newport, Rhode Island, when he sailed home in 1783. His only American son, Lewis, was a successful Newport publisher until he invested in merchant ships. They were soon unlucky in meeting their schedules, and Lewis, finding himself bankrupt at age thirty-seven, slit his throat with a shoemaker's knife. One of Lewis's sons, William, "followed sea," according to a nephew. Nothing else is known of sailor William. Another son, John, became the foreman of the printing department of the *Boston Daily Advertiser*. Much is known of John. The family avoided the sea for three generations until my father became interested in sailboat racing and won junior and intercollegiate championships in the thirties. He passed that interest and some of his skill on to me. Though he never sailed in a Fastnet race, he had raced in Scotland and our library was full of British sailing books—in brief, although I challenged most WASP principles, I never questioned the dogma that yachting was best conducted in waters off the British Isles, and that ocean racing achieved its greatest fulfillment near Fastnet Rock.

Races across the Atlantic and to Bermuda, Nassau, Spain, and Baja California, races around the Florida Keys and the length of two Great Lakes, races up the East Coast and down the West Coast all passed, but the Fastnet remained the gleam in my eye. When I was thirty-five, Eric Swenson (another WASP) asked me to sail with him in 1979 on a transatlantic race to Ireland, a short Irish cruise, and then the Cowes Week series of five races off the Isle of Wight, followed by the Fastnet race. I hadn't the time for both parts of the schedule. Despite my affection for long offshore passages, in which the simple man-in-nature pleasures of living aboard are stretched out for weeks on end, I told Eric that I would be there for Cowes Week and, of course, the Fastnet.

"Impressive Cowes Week Had Its Dramas" ran a headline in the *Isle of Wight County Press* on the eve of the start of the Fastnet race. It was an understatement. Over eight hundred boats raced daily off a single starting line, dodging press boats, the Royal Yacht *Britannia*, ferries, and sometimes each other. One sailor broke his arm when a Brazilian boat rammed an Australian boat. Another Brazilian boat was holed and almost sunk by an Argentinian boat. A Belgian skipper died of a heart attack during one race, and on another day, a Belgian crew member was dragged across a deck by a runaway sheet and knocked unconscious. Former prime minister Edward Heath's *Morning Cloud* lost her rudder during the overnight Channel race and was later badly gouged by vandals while she sat at her mooring. In one race in heavy winds, two sailors on different boats were badly injured in the head by flying booms. One, a Japanese sailor, was carried off his boat at the end of the race, but the wound to an Englishman was so severe that he was immediately taken from his boat in a photographer's rubber dinghy, from which he was hoisted by an air-sea rescue helicopter and taken to a hospital. And during the last race of Cowes Week, sailed in a force 8 to force 9 gale, we in *Toscana* picked up a man in mid-Solent from his capsized powerboat.

Whether random accidents or incidents in a pattern of omens, these events did not affect the start of the Fastnet race. A fleet of 303 yachts, the largest ever to enter the race, was sent off by the Royal Yacht Squadron's cannon at ten-minute intervals between 1:30 and 2:30 P.M. Saturday, August 11. There were six divisions, based on size of boat. The largest entrant was *Kialoa*, John Kilroy's seventy-nine-foot sloop from Los Angeles, California. The smallest were two twenty-eight-footers, *Billy Bones*, owned by two French sailors named Boudet and Seuly, and *Arkadina*, owned by an Englishman named A. J. Boutle. The average boat was thirty-eight feet, two inches long and probably weighed about fifteen thousand pounds. Twenty-two countries were represented, among them most of the major European, North and South American, and Australasian nations. Nineteen of those countries had entered teams in the competition for the Admiral's Cup, considered by ocean-racing sailors to be their sport's unofficial world championship. Almost every one of the fifty-seven Admiral's Cuppers had been built within the previous eight months and was a highly refined, relatively lightweight, single-purpose racing boat. Going into the Fastnet race, Ireland was leading the Cup series with the United States, Australia, and Hong Kong (many of whose sailors were Englishmen with dual citizenship) trailing in that order. According to the fleet roster circulated before the start by the Royal Ocean Racing Club, 165 entrants were British, 55 were French, 16 were Irish, and 12 were American. The only entry requirements were that the boats have an International Offshore Rule rating, used for comparing boats of different sizes and characteristics against each other, of at least 20.1 feet and that they carry certain required safety equipment, including flares, life jackets, man-overboard floats, lights, a radio receiver, and a life raft. Virtually any cruising sailboat larger than twenty-eight feet might have qualified to sail in the race.

Weather forecasts issued at Cowes on the eve and day of the start anticipated moderate to fresh winds over the succeeding three days, with a likelihood of strong winds by Tuesday.

No boat or crew should have had any difficulty with those conditions, and, given the forecasters' reputation for occasional exaggeration, this forecast should not have deterred anybody from starting the race. However, it was (and still is) fair to assume that any crew that enters a six-hundred-mile race off the English coast is prepared for bad weather. Although recent Fastnet races had been sailed in light winds, the race has been considered a rough one from its genesis, in 1925.

Ocean racing—competition between sailing yachts over distances greater than two hundred miles—has been a popular sport only since the mid-1920s. Developing first in the United States, with long races across the Atlantic, to Hawaii, and on the Great Lakes, the sport as we know it today began with the 1923 race from New London, Connecticut, to Bermuda. Intrigued by the novel idea of racing long distances in small boats, English yachtsmen set about to found their own contest. The first Fastnet race was sailed in 1925, though not to unanimous approval. Many Englishmen thought their waters too dangerous for the requirements of racing, one of which is that the crew carries on in rough weather even to the point of risking damage to the boat. An influential critic was a yacht designer, Claud Worth, who counseled caution. A privately arranged race between two owners would be one thing, he wrote in the sporting magazine *The Field*, "but a public race might very well include some owners whose keenness is greater than their experience. If the weather should be bad, so long as there is a head wind they would probably come to no harm, for a good boat and sound gear will generally stand as much driving as the crew can put up with. But when running before anything approaching a gale of wind and a big sea in open water, conditions are very deceptive. It requires much judgment to know whether a following sea has reached the dangerous stage. I have more than once been compelled very reluctantly to heave-to and watch a fair wind running to waste, and have soon after had reason to be very thankful that I was safely hove-to in good time.

"But if one had been racing one would probably have been tempted to carry on, knowing that some other competitor might take the risk. These conditions might not occur once in a dozen races, but the magnitude of possible disaster should be taken into account."

Worth knew his English weather. During the gale-torn 1931 race Colonel C. H. Hudson was swept overboard and lost from the fifty-one-foot cutter *Maitenes II*, of which he was a part owner. Yet Worth's worries did not apply in this case. *Maitenes II* was hove-to, her crew deciding not to risk running before a force 9 westerly gale, and Hudson apparently did not observe the old rule of keeping one hand for oneself and one hand for the ship. (This incident apparently was overlooked in 1979 when the press and the Royal Ocean Racing Club reported that the only prior fatality in the fifty-four years and twenty-eight runnings of the Fastnet race was a man who died of a heart attack in 1977.)

The 1957 race was the roughest Fastnet race before 1979. That gale was anticipated, however. In his book *Yacht and Sea*, the Swedish yacht designer Gustav Plym described an abrupt conversation he had with the Royal Ocean Racing Club's commodore before the start. "Any last-minute orders?" Plym asked. "None whatever," answered the commodore. "There is a gale warning, but there is no real vice in it. Good luck."

The 1957 race started in a Channel gale that eventually built to force 9, and twenty-nine of the forty-one starters dropped out before reaching Land's End. The remainder of the race was relatively easy. On board Plym's *Elseli IV*, "our experience gave us strength. . . . There was no thought of giving up—at least not in the skipper's mind, and whatever the crew may have thought they were too well disciplined to whisper a word about it." Plym described "high-breaking mountains of water" and "the screaming sound in the rigging" that was like "the shriek of a woman in despair." The motion of the boat was so wild, he wrote, that sleep was impossible and "it was a relief to be called on deck after a couple of hours." Another of the twelve finishers was a badly leaking American yawl, *Carina*, whose owner, Richard S. Nye, said to his crew as she crossed the finish line at Plymouth, "All right, boys, we're over now. Let her sink." (Uttered within two miles of one of Britain's largest commercial ports, this jest has since been assigned the aura of gospel instruction by the few true masochists who sail.) *Carina* had fallen off a wave, much the way a man might lose his footing on a log that rolls out from under him, and the impact of the nineteen-ton yacht dropping several feet had cracked some of her frames. *Carina* won the race, as she had in 1955. American yachts have won eight of the twenty-eight Fastnet races.

"The seas were positively tumultuous," K. Adlard Coles wrote of the 1957 gale in his book *Heavy Weather Sailing*, a study of bad storms that he and other racing sailors had survived. When I first read this book, I had nightmares about huge breakers, and survivors of the 1979 Fastnet were describing the waves they had encountered as being "just like those frightening pictures in Coles."

We were an experienced crew in *Toscana*, which had just sailed a three-thousand-mile transatlantic race. Eric Swenson, her skipper and one watch captain, had raced her and his other boats in four Bermuda races, and I, the other watch captain, had covered over thirty thousand miles offshore in several boats. The navigator, Captain John Coote, Royal Navy (Retired), had raced in twelve Fastnets and several Bermuda

and Australian races. We may have been one of the few boats
in the race to have women standing watches. If she is quick
and knowledgeable, a woman can be as helpful on deck as any
man, although she may not be as strong. Susan Noyes had
sailed all her life, and Sherry Jagerson had raced to Bermuda
and to Ireland in *Toscana*. The least experienced racing sailor
on board was Stuart Woods, an American writer, but even he
had offshore experience, having sailed in a single-handed
transatlantic race. The boat herself was well designed and
stoutly built for offshore sailing. One of a type called the Swan
47, *Toscana* was designed by the New York firm of Sparkman
and Stephens and strongly built of fiberglass by a Finnish yard
called Nautor. Her oversized rigging made the masts on the
Admiral's Cup boats seem like fishing rods.

In many ways, *Toscana* represented the old traditions of
ocean racing, once a gentleman's sport in which a few hundred friends and acquaintances cruised in company with and
raced against one another, year in and year out, in boats
designed to go to sea. Over the previous half-dozen years, a
group of young yacht designers, sailmakers, and builders had
developed and crewed in a new breed of sophisticated and
extremely fast boats for a generation of highly competitive
owners. At the very top level of racing, the Admiral's Cup
fleet, these owners bought and sold boats annually in order to
keep up with developments in design and construction. In this
nautical equivalent of Grand Prix automobile racing, the
boats were shipped from country to country for a handful of
important regattas. While there was no professionalism in the
sport in the sense that winners receive cash prizes, there was a
kind of semiprofessionalism in which boat and equipment
manufacturers stood to gain in the long run when they and
their products helped Grand Prix yachts win important races
and regattas. The boats usually were financed by wealthy

men whose fortunes derived from real estate, manufacturing, and other entrepreneurial enterprises. Most of them sailed in their boats, sometimes in command and sometimes as a privileged crew member; a few, like owners of race horses, were content to stay ashore. Built in some cases with experimental materials, rigged with the most sophisticated equipment, and nurtured with hundreds of thousands of dollars, these yachts were the Ferraris of the sport.

By comparison, *Toscana* was a Mercedes-Benz. Her owner, who had raced production sports cars, had no desire to own one of those exotic boats. Although fast, many of the new racing machines were difficult to steer and often very uncomfortable. Excess weight was eliminated with passion: their galleys were skimpy, their toilets were separated from the living areas by a curtain (if at all), and their interiors had all the charm of the inside of an airplane's wing, with strengthening struts and structural members jutting into the bunks and living areas. Eric Swenson liked his comfort, and his *Toscana* had a freezer in the galley, hot and cold running water, two enclosed toilets with showers, six built-in bunks (one a double berth), several lockers for hanging clothes, and enough teak and other hardwoods laid over the fiberglass to build a small, elegant house. Hanging on her stern was a swimming ladder, which Swenson justified by claiming that it was an excellent means for recovering men who had gone overboard, but which many Grand Prix skippers would have thrown right off the boat as excess weight. (Swenson might not have had a Grand Prix skipper of such seriousness on board to begin with; while he respected their talents and dedication, he felt that theirs was a different type of sport from his.)

After the start, we cleared the Needles, at the western entrance to the Solent, and sailed out into the English Channel in a wind that died to force 3. It was from the southwest, dead ahead, and we beat to windward at six to seven knots, choosing the tack that would take us closest to our objective, a point 180 miles away called the Lizard. We alternated watches four hours on, four hours off between 7:00 P.M. and 7:00 A.M. and at six-hour intervals during the day. Francie McBride, the pretty, chatty Irish cook, served up meals at the watch changes, and once expressed chagrin when she realized that she had not brought the correct type of cream for a complicated dessert pudding. My watch was four—John Ruch, Susan Noyes, Nick Noyes, and myself (the Noyeses are unrelated)—and John Coote volunteered to come on deck to steer while we made sail changes, which was often.

People who say that ocean racing is boring have never worked hard at it. Racing rules, modern technology, and the boat owner's money have provided large numbers of sails, each of which has a specialized purpose and can be readily substituted for another sail as the wind lightens, strengthens, or shifts in direction. *Toscana* carried eighteen sails in bins in the forwardmost of her three cabins, on the sole (the floor) of the main cabin, and in a bin in the after cabin. Nine of these sails were jibs that we set off the headstay, which leads from the top of the mast to the bow. Each jib was designed to be used in a particular wind strength or direction, and if either changed by as little as a couple of knots or five degrees, the crew would change to another jib. The sails were known by numbers or by names: the number 1 (of which we had two) was the largest, number 2 the next largest, and so on down to the number 4; the drifter was used in very light winds, the reaching jib was used only when sailing across the wind (whereas the numbered sails might be used either when reaching or when beating into the wind), the blooper, or big boy, was set when running, and the tiny storm jib, smaller even than the number 4, was reserved for the very rare force 9 or stronger gale. We could change jibs quickly since *Toscana* was equipped with a twin-slotted plastic foil that was secured over the headstay. The boltropes on the luff, or forward edge, of the jibs were fed into the slots as the halyard was hoisted. To change sails, we hoisted the new sail in the free slot on another halyard and then pulled the old sail down. In theory this worked well; in practice it jammed regularly.

Besides the nine jibs, we also could choose from among three staysails, which were set either free or on the forestay, which ran from two-thirds of the way up the mast to a point on the deck six feet behind the bow. These relatively small sails generally improved the boat's speed when reaching.

In addition, *Toscana* carried four spinnakers of various weights and sizes. These huge multicolored nylon sails were set when we reached across the wind or ran before it. The smallest spinnaker was used in strong winds when we thought we might be overpowered with the largest one set. Finally, we had aboard a spare mainsail and a storm trysail, a very small mainsail set, as the name implies, in bad gales. Neither the spare mainsail nor the trysail was required by the rules that applied in the Fastnet race, but like all the other boats, we were obligated to carry the storm jib.

The permanently set mainsail was equipped with three reefs, which we could use to change the sail's shape or to decrease the square footage of sail exposed to the wind as the breeze strengthened. With the third reef tied in, the sail was approximately 60 percent its maximum, unreefed size. With three reefs in the mainsail and the storm jib or forestaysail set, we would carry about one-third the square footage of Dacron that would be up with the full mainsail and number-1 jib hoisted.

Each sail was trimmed with at least one sheet (spinnakers have two sheets) with which we could establish the optimum shape for a given wind strength and direction. We could also alter sail shape by adjusting halyard tension with powerful stainless-steel winches and by changing the bend of the mast and the altitude of the boom with hydraulic pumps on the backstay and the boom vang. At any moment, we could make as many as eight adjustments, most of them synergetic— changing one control often required alterations in two or three others. I enjoyed fooling around with all this gear and could sail an entire four-hour watch at night or a six-hour watch during the day without once sitting still. Sometimes I should have sat still and left things alone. Not only did all this nervous energy drive my watchmates crazy, but impatient sail trimming was as likely to slow a boat down as it was to speed her up.

We measured *Toscana*'s ability to use the wind best in a variety of ways. If a boat of about her size were alongside, we could compare speeds by sight. If competitors were out of sight, we evaluated our performance by "feel"—the tug of the steering wheel and the boat's motion through the waves—and with the help of a veritable dashboard of instruments directly in front of the helmsman. From left to right, there were an anemometer for wind speed, zero to sixty knots; an apparent wind indicator that showed the direction of the wind relative to our heading; a speedometer, which flashed out digital displays of our speed through the water to a one-hundredth of a knot; and a depth sounder, which indicated the amount of water beneath the hull. Steering by these dials and by the compass, mounted in the binnacle squarely in front of the wheel, was a bit like driving a car at high speed in heavy traffic. The helmsman's eyes constantly flickered from one indicator to the other as he tried to sail the course at the highest speed, and with the corner of his eye he kept a watch for waves, which, if they were from astern, might increase our

speed, or, if from ahead, could slow us. At night the helmsman could not see much beyond the dials, which were lit with
faint white or red lights, and had to anticipate waves through
the motion of the boat.

As we beat toward the Lizard, we changed sails with
almost every alteration in wind strength. The crew carefully
folded the jib that had been doused, bagged it in a blue sack,
and dropped it below through the forward hatch. Sometimes
as soon as we had changed sails, the wind died or increased to
the point where we had to change right back. Somebody
would have to go below and push the heavy, bulky sail up
through the hatch, where another person lugged it on deck.

Most if not all of our competitors had at least the same
number of sails and instruments and were racing as aggres-
sively as we were in *Toscana*. From time to time, another boat
would sail across our bow or wake. Sometimes she was
smaller than *Toscana*—in light winds, little boats can sail as fast
as big boats—sometimes she was a bit larger. The second day,
Sunday the twelfth, a freighter steamed out of the fog at ten
knots only a couple of hundred yards ahead. We sailed to
within a quarter mile of the Eddystone Light with no evidence of the lighthouse's existence other than its mournful
horn and its bright rotating light two hundred feet up. Fog is
caused by a mixing of cool water and warm, damp air. In some
areas, fog comes before wind; in other areas, it may come
before bad weather. I did not know enough about the English
Channel to be certain just what this fog meant, but I was not
happy to be in it in a shipping lane.

Late that night, we bore off around the Lizard, set the
reaching jib, and headed toward the Runnelstone buoy, just
off Land's End. When our watch was relieved by Eric's at
11:00 P.M., *Toscana* was reaching at nine knots. When we
returned to deck at 3:00 A.M., for the dawn watch, we were

still sailing fast. The dawn watch is my favorite time of day offshore. The crew on deck has a ringside seat for the sun's early pyrotechnics, which, in the unpolluted air over the sea, are quick and orange, unlike the slow red dawns over land. The sun quickly warms fingers that have been chilled during the darkest, coldest hour of night that comes just before dawn. What appeals to me most about watching the sun rise at sea is the chiaroscuro effect of the new light softening the hard edges of objects and people in those last minutes of blackness.

Dawn often brings a drop in the wind. That morning, the breeze quickly died from a solid fifteen knots to a calm, and when members of Eric's watch poked their heads up through the hatch at 7:00 A.M. to relieve us, we were struggling to inch the boat's speedometer up over one knot. *Toscana* and the dozen or so boats around her were inscribing slow circles over the groundswell rolling in from the southwest. For the first time since the race started forty-two hours earlier, we were out of wind. We were at sea, in the Western Approaches.

I dozed over breakfast—we had worked hard on deck for eight of the ten hours of darkness. When I finished that huge English breakfast, I thanked the cook and went aft to the owner's cabin. Susan, Nick, and John slept in bunks in the main cabin, but following tradition, the watch captains and the navigator slept aft, in the owner's cabin that was almost under the cockpit and, therefore, most directly accessible to any deck crew who needed advice. By sheerest coincidence, bunks toward the stern of a yacht are more stable (hence easier to sleep in) than those farther forward. Eric and I traded off in one bunk. John Coote did not stand watch, so he had the starboard bunk in perpetuity, although he rarely used it and spent most of his time in the seat at the navigator's table, on the starboard side of the main cabin across from the galley. There, he operated the radio direction finder, the only electronic navigation tool we were allowed to use, and plotted our positions and courses. He also chatted with Francie, patiently answered the barrage of questions that came from the nine men and women standing watches ("Where are we? How many miles to the Rock? What's the weather forecast?"), and leaned his considerable bulk against the cabin side for catnaps. When the BBC shipping bulletins were about due, he took his portable radio aft and into his bunk, where he curled up and, in quiet privacy, dozed through the farm news until the weather forecasts came on.

I slept soundly for five hours that morning. When awakened for lunch, I dressed and went into the main cabin. A wet, badly torn spinnaker lay at the foot of the companionway and we were heeled well over to starboard. Coote filled me in on the details: the wind had finally filled in from the northeast ("A strange direction, don't you think?") and Eric's watch had set the spinnaker. Later, the wind strengthened and veered through east to south. While they were dousing the spinnaker, the other watch witnessed the unhappy spectacle of the cloth being blown by a hard puff right out of the tapes that defined its edges. They retrieved the fragments and threw them below.

After lunch, I briefly went on deck to sniff the weather. It was chilly and spray was in the air. Back below into the warm, dry cabin, I alerted my watchmates to the cold and went aft to dress in four layers—long underwear, heavy shirt, sweater, and foul-weather gear.

An hour into our watch, at 2:00 P.M., Coote slid open the cover over the after companionway, poked his head up, and said, "Southwest force 4 to 5, veering to west force 6 to 7. Fastnet Rock reports force 6 southwest." He looked absently at the steering wheel for a moment, then pulled his head below under the closing cover. That summary of the BBC's 1:55 shipping bulletin came as no surprise. We were reaching at eight and a half knots in about twenty-five knots of wind on the anemometer. Since about four knots of the wind's force was apparent wind created by *Toscana*'s motion, we already had the force 5. The sky to the west was bifurcated. To the southwest, off our port bow, there were high white cirrus clouds. To the northwest, off our starboard bow, there were darker altocumulus "mackerel scales." I remembered the old seamen's warning: "Mackerel scales, furl your sails." Which was more correct, the forecast or the clouds with their suggestion of harsher weather?

We reached all afternoon, always on the verge of reefing. The wind stayed between twenty and twenty-five knots and the boat was handling well. At six o'clock, I went below to warm my hands and hear Coote's summary of the 5:50 BBC shipping bulletin. The prediction continued to be for no worse than force 6, but the wind was expected to veer to northwest. There was a chance of a force 8 gale at Fastnet Rock, now ninety miles to the northwest. I tapped the barometer. Since the start, it had fallen from 1020 millibars (30.1 inches) to 1010 millibars (29.8 inches), still comparatively high. The BBC reported that it was at 1005 millibars (29.7 inches) and dropping slowly at Valentia Island, forty-six miles northwest of Fastnet Rock. Despite the various omens of accidents, injuries, fog, calm, and clouds, the forecast and the barometer gave us little reason to worry about storms—although we could expect a force 8 near the Rock when we arrived there in ten hours, at 4:00 A.M. Tuesday morning.

An hour later, the watch changed in the middle of a rain squall, and, grateful for the timing, we went below to a beef curry dinner and a bottle of red wine. We were down to our last few bottles, which were fine sleeping aids for the off-going watches. The great mystery on board concerned the whereabouts of a case of white wine, which somebody claimed to have brought aboard at Cowes and which had somehow disappeared. Losing a case of wine in a forty-eight-foot boat would appear to be impossible, but apparently it had happened, and Coote, whose wine it was, spent his spare minutes ransacking lockers. If this story had not been true, it might have been invented by somebody trying to inject levity into the otherwise serious business of taking a boat offshore. (The wine was never found.) After dinner, I went aft into the owner's cabin, shed my four layers of clothes, and climbed into the cocoonlike bunk to snuggle under a blanket against the blue canvas lee cloth. This restrained me from rolling out of the bunk and down to the cabin sole.

I slept well for over two hours. When I first sailed offshore, in my late teens, I never had a problem with sleep, but I never had any responsibility either. Captaining a watch may have put me in closer tune with the boat: when she rests, I rest; when she works, I work. *Toscana* must have sailed along restfully for those two hours ("snoring along on an easy reach" is how Alfred Loomis aptly described such a sail), for I slept comfortably until awakened by a new motion. She was pitching and rolling wildly. Overhead, voices shouted, "Ten knots! Ten-point-*two*! *Ten-point-two-five knots!!*"

I reached into the bin beside my head for my glasses and put them on and crawled out of the cocoon. My left shoulder against the lockers on the port side of the cabin—the boat was heeling at least thirty degrees—I walked in my underwear through the door to the main cabin, grabbing the support bar in front of the stove. Downhill, John Coote dozed in the navigator's seat. In a moment, his eyes opened and he said, as though continuing a conversation, "They are doing over ten knots with the number 3 and one reef in the main. They should have the second reef in."

I swung downhill using the wooden companionway ladder

as a support, coming to a stop against the end of the navigator's table. The built-in clock read 10:20. Forty minutes to the
change of watch. Coote pointed with a pencil to an encircled
X on the chart. About fifty miles to the Rock.

"How do we rig the third reef?" he asked gloomily.

"We get the bravest, tallest man on the boat to stand on the
boom and pass the free reefing line through the leech cringle."
I did not relish this chore. The week before, during Cowes
Week, booms had laid open two heads; six months earlier, a
boom had crushed the skull of a man during a race off
Florida; a year ago, my closest friend had twice been knocked
into hospital emergency rooms by flying booms. Booms are
not to be messed with in rough weather.

I looked around the cabin. My three watchmates and the
cook were asleep in the bunks. The lee cloths secured to the
two uphill bunks bulged around heads, buttocks, and shoulders. The two in the downhill bunks were sleeping more on
lockers and the side of the hull than they were on their mattresses. I climbed up to the galley, turned on the propane gas
valves, lit a burner, and put the pot over the flame. I slid back
aft to dress: damp long underwear, damp wool socks, damp
green turtleneck jersey, damp gray wool sweater, my last dry
corduroy trousers, fingerless leather gloves (my hands would
soften in the spray). I pulled my foul-weather gear out of a
locker and tugged on the suspendered yellow pants, which
covered me from insteps to armpits. With a clownish balancing act, hopping on one foot, I shoved my feet into the damp
yellow boots.

I inched forward again to the galley, with new security on
the nonskid soles of the boots, and spooned instant coffee and
condiments into four mugs: black for Nick, powdered milk
and sugar for Susan and John, powdered milk for me. Leaving the other three mugs lying against a low rail around a

shelf, I put my mug in one of the two stainless-steel sinks, turned off the gas, picked up the pot, and very carefully poured boiling water into the mug. As I picked it up and sipped at the coffee, I reflected on how calm I felt, how cautiously and purposefully I seemed to be moving. At any other time, I would have held the mug with one hand while trying to pour the water with the other. Inevitably, in the bouncing and heaving of the boat, my arm would have lurched and a drop or two would have spilled and scalded my hand. Had I slept that well? Was I anticipating something?

I had felt and moved this way once before, while preparing to parachute out of a U.S. Army troop plane. Then I had carefully put on my field gear and parachute, had moved cautiously through the inspections and into the plane, had sat quietly as the plane took off and circled over the drop zone, and had, with a keen sensitivity to my hands, stood up, hooked my harness to the static line, and shuffled to the door to jump, slow motion it seemed, into the air eighteen hundred feet above red Georgia soil.

Toscana: Battle Scene

Water dripping from her frizzy hair, Sherry Jagerson came below at 10:40 to awaken the new watch. The blackness and the roar of waves and wind burst through the open hatch into the sanctuary of the dimly lit cabin. As my watchmates rolled out of their bunks, I poured water and handed them their coffee. "You're already up?" John Ruch asked sleepily.

I drank my coffee carefully, put the mug in the sink, and went aft once again and pulled on my blue parka, insulated with foam to keep me afloat if I went overboard, and a brown wool hat. Leaning against a locker, I untangled the nylon straps of the safety harness and put it on. At the end of the six-foot-long tether was a heavy stainless-steel mountain climber's hook, which I snapped into the buckle to keep the tether from tangling in my legs. Moving stiffly in the six layers of clothing and the harness, I walked forward, climbed up the companionway ladder, pulled back the heavy Plexiglas hatch cover, and stuck my head up into the gale.

Sliding out of the hatch on my belly, I grabbed the safety line rigged between the companionway and the cockpit with one hand and reached behind me with the other to pull the hatch cover securely shut. I duck-walked aft, looking downwind to keep spray off my face, and, when I reached the cockpit, found a spot of bench to sit on among the four dark figures that braced themselves against the wind and the mad jerking of the boat. I hooked my safety harness to the line and concentrated on the rows of whitecapped waves that marched downwind from us. When my eyes were adjusted to the dark and my internal rhythms were more or less in synchrony with *Toscana*'s lurches, I turned and studied the glowing instrument dials: wind speed—thirty-five, forty, thirty-seven knots; relative wind angle—ninety, one hundred, ninety degrees; boat speed—(dropping as we went up a wave) 9.95, 9.82, 9.50, 9.3, (increasing down a wave) 9.46, 9.70, 10.01, 10.25.

I turned the other way and wiped the spray off my glasses with my fingers. At the helm was Dale Cheek, an Oklahoman and former skipper of a Greek charter yacht who had turned up at the dock in Cowes one day looking for a crew berth. Fortunately for us, we took him, and Eric asked him along for the Fastnet race. Dale was struggling with the wheel. The king spoke, marked with a bit of line, stands vertical when the rudder is centered. Now it was horizontal, so the rudder below us was pushing thousands of pounds of water to one side, risking damage (perhaps), slowing us down (probably), and hindering Dale from steering the course (certainly).

"Eric, we should shorten down," I said.

"I agree," he said. "This blow just came up. We put up the number 3 only an hour ago."

"Another reef and the number-4 jib?" I asked.

"I think the forestaysail."

"Will it be enough sail to get us around the Rock? We'll have to tack, and the waves must be breaking there."

"That's five hours away," Swenson said. "Look how fast this is building."

We stared at the anemometer. The pointer now was between forty and forty-five knots. I looked around. Each of my watchmates was on deck, so we had nine pairs of hands. Eric took the helm.

"Okay," I said loudly. "First let's get the second reef in, next let's set the staysail, then let's douse the number 3."

Nobody budged. A large wave broke on deck and spray flew over us and halfway up the mainsail. Blobs of phosphorus, nature's light show, glowed for a few seconds on the sail and our foul-weather gear before sliding off and running out the cockpit drains.

I unhooked my harness, slid to leeward under the safety line, and grabbed an end of a spare jib sheet that lay on the leeward seat. I walked forward with the end along the starboard deck, leaning thirty degrees to port to stay upright and bracing myself against the boom with my left hand. Halfway forward, I leaned down and snapped the harness hook onto the jackwire that ran along the deck, glancing aft to see John Ruch and Doug Parfet, from Eric's watch, dragging the forestaysail out of the main hatch and forward along the port deck. Down to leeward, up to my shins in water gushing up from the starboard rail, I passed the sheet through a block on the deck and tied the end to a rail near the mast.

We turned to the reef. I lowered the main halyard six feet,

and Doug and John pulled the sail down against the force of the wind and secured a ring sewn in its luff under a stainless-steel hook on the boom. Then Doug helped me crank the halyard up taut on the winch. The three of us took turns at winching in the reefing line that ran from the leech into the boom and forward. It was arm-wearying work. With the reef tied in and her mainsail's area decreased by about 15 percent, *Toscana* seemed to straighten up slightly.

Next, the change of headsails. Doug and John pulled the forestaysail out of its bag and, their wet hands slipping on the snaphooks, slowly hanked the sail onto the forestay and then hoisted the sail. Nick trimmed the sail in, on an after winch, cleated the sheet, and came forward to help us douse the number 3 hoisted on the headstay. Doug, John, Nick, and I sat down shoulder to shoulder on the foredeck, facing to leeward with our safety harnesses hooked onto the jackwires. We grabbed at the foot of the sail, but the wind stretched it like sheet metal and we could not grip the cloth.

"Eric," I yelled aft, "bear off, bear off!"

A wave broke over the bow and our heads and shoved the four of us to leeward into the lifelines, our safety harness tethers stretched to their limits. With water trickling under our clothes and sea boots, we untangled ourselves from the lifelines and climbed back uphill. The boat leveled as Eric steered her off the wind. When we grabbed the jib again, its cloth softened as it was blanketed by the mainsail. Aft, Susan cast off the halyard. The wind and friction in the slot into which the luff was fed at first kept the sail from coming down. John and Doug slid forward and pulled together on the luff, and the sail gradually dropped in six-foot folds into Nick's lap and mine, and we smothered the heavy Dacron cloth with our bodies. Eric headed back up to the course to the Rock.

"Damn," Doug shouted, "the sail's stuck in the groove!" A

few inches of the luff had jammed. If we were unable to free it, we would have to lash the sail on deck, where it would catch wind and water and eventually blow overboard, taking the lifelines and possibly even the stanchions with it.

"We'll cut it away," Doug said. I tossed him my knife and he slit the sail just above the jam-up and pulled the luff out of the slot. He opened the halyard shackle, shook the sail's head out, and secured the shackle to the bow pulpit, the stainless-steel thigh-high cage that all this time had restrained him from being washed or heaved overboard as the bow lifted and plunged through a ten-foot arc.

While we held the jib on deck, Doug crawled aft and opened the forward hatch. We slowly stuffed the sail below, first with our arms and then with our legs. Waves broke on deck and water poured into the forward cabin down the creases and folds. When the sail was entirely below, John dropped through the hatch and, from inside, closed and locked the cover.

Susan, in the cockpit, yelled something.

"What?" I shouted back.

"How's the trim on the staysail?" She was still racing.

"I can't see. Where's a light?" Somebody shined a large torch on the sail.

"On course, a little high, a little low, on course," Eric chanted as the waves threw *Toscana* either side of our course.

"Ease it out a little," I yelled aft. When the shape looked right at a moment when Eric said, "On course," I shouted to Susan, "That's fine. Hold that."

We unhooked ourselves and walked aft, sliding our hands along the lifelines and crouching like boxers to absorb the motion of the deck, which tried to propel us into the nearest wave. We were soaked after our half hour's work on the fore-deck. Stumbling into the cockpit as a wave smashed the boat amidships, I slid under the safety line to the low side and around the steering wheel.

"Keep your harnesses hooked on, damnit!" Eric said in as near a roar as his gentle voice could command.

When I touched the wheel with my right hand, the palm of the wet leather glove slid across the elk hide cover that insulated the helmsman's fingers from the cold stainless steel of the wheel's outer rim. I squeezed the rim tighter and said, "I've got her, Eric."

He sidestepped uphill to windward and I followed, grabbing the wheel with my left hand where he released it with his right. The wheel turned through twenty degrees as we rocked and pitched. When Eric released his grip entirely, I slid my left hand to where his had been, at the ten o'clock position. With my right hand at three o'clock, I could turn the wheel clockwise to keep the boat from rounding up when waves struck her amidships and she heeled. When the waves slid under her transom and we surfed off course, I pulled the wheel counterclockwise to bring her up. I had never worked harder at steering a boat. The instrument dials now read: wind speed—forty-five, forty-three, forty-six knots; relative wind angle—ninety, one hundred, eighty-five degrees; boat speed—8.61, 9.20, 8.83, 9.45 knots. We had traded some speed for improved control.

Eric's watch went below. After half an hour, we were again overpowered: too great of an angle of heel, and excessive strain on the rudder.

"Get the navigator on deck to take the wheel," I told Susan. "We have to tie the third reef in."

She opened the hatch and stuck her head below. Almost before she had finished passing along the message, John Coote was on deck in his bright blue foul-weather gear.

"The zero-zero-fifteen shipping bulletin predicts force 9 to force 10 from the southwest, veering to northwest," he said as he crawled into the cockpit. "It looks as though we have force 9 already."

"What's the barometer?" I asked.

"Down to 986 at Valentia, rapidly falling." The barometer had dropped nineteen millibars, or half an inch, in only seven hours. The clouds had been right.

"Could you steer while we try to tie in the third reef?" I asked Coote.

"Gladly."

"We'll have to lower the main," I told him.

"Good luck," Coote said as he took the wheel.

Nick and John went forward to the base of the mast to lower the mainsail. We had only two reefing lines at the outer end of the boom. One, which was red, was holding down the second reef that we had just tied. The other, which was green, held down the first reef and was now redundant, since the second reef had superseded it (reefs in mainsails are like slats in venetian blinds; as each reef is tied in, several more feet of sail are removed from the flow of the wind). We had to pull the green reefing line out of the first reef and lead it through the third reef, but to get at the line, we would have to be able to get at the end of the boom, which was now ten feet to leeward, tripping through waves.

As Nick and John pulled the mainsail down, Susan and I trimmed the mainsheet until the boom was waving over our heads. Most of the sail flogged to leeward. I stood on the cabin top, hooked my harness into the safety line, and leaned over the boom to steady it. I pulled at the green line, but, wedged under the red line in the second reef, it would not budge.

"Ease the red line," I yelled forward. Only twenty feet away, they did not hear a word I said. "*Ease the red line!*" I screamed. Nick looked at me, trying to read my lips. "God-dammit, the *RED* line, *ease the RED LINE!*"

Nick knelt down on deck and reached for a winch. The green line went slack.

"No, the red one, the *OTHER* one!"

He nodded and reached for another winch. The red line eased out.

"That's enough!" I showed Nick the palm of my left hand and he cleated the line. I freed the green line and reached far over the boom for the third reef cringle, a heavy steel ring. The cringle flapped wildly and banged my fingers. I thought, even in twenty knots of wind this would not be easy. I finally grabbed the cringle with the middle finger of my left hand, held it long enough to pass the green line through it, and then pulled the line back to the boom and, using a bowline knot, secured the end through a metal plate.

"It's made!" I shouted, and I crawled off the boom and into the cockpit. Coote, behind me, whistled a loud sigh of relief. Nick and John tied down the cringle in the luff and winched the mainsail up. The head seemed barely halfway up the mast. Susan eased the mainsheet, and the men forward pulled down the leech cringle with the green line, led around a winch.

I relieved Coote at the helm. "You know," he said, "we were going along quite nicely with only the forestaysail up." Nick and John came aft and, panting, threw themselves down on the windward cockpit seat.

Continuing to increase, the wind was now in the mid to high fifties. We were going no slower yet the steering was slightly easier even though the waves came in confusing pat-terns and at times tossed the boat around wildly. After a while I said, "I hope you don't mind, but I think I should do most of the steering. Let's keep two people on deck. The other two can go below to warm up." I was chilled.

"Go ahead," Nick said. "If you get tired, let me know." Nobody went below.

As the wind built over the next two hours, the seas continued to grow larger. They broke with surprising frequency. For a while, I watched for the big ones over my left, windward, shoulder and tried to steer down their faces so they would not break over us. *Toscana* was not too large to be rolled over by a wave. A sixty-one-footer, *Sorcery*, was rolled in the North Pacific in 1976 and her mast, rigging, and lifelines were swept overboard as though a huge knife had sliced along her deck. In a confused sea like this one, churned up by a rapidly building and shifting wind blowing over relatively shallow water, there was always the chance of a giant wave rearing over and capsizing us.

But the night was too dark, the bad waves were too frequent, and I was too awed to continue the lookout. Their great size and speed distracted me from steering. Yet with my eyes straining ahead, I could still sense from the motion of the boat and increasing volume of the roar when the bad ones were coming, like moving walls, and would shout warnings to my watchmates, who sat huddled in the cockpit. They could only pull their heads into their foul-weather jackets and parkas and hold on tight. One wave broke over us, knocking my glasses off until they dangled by the safety strap, collapsing my wool hat over my face, and filling the cockpit. Another big one slid out from under us and *Toscana* fell into the next trough with a crash that dislodged the lock on the forward hatch and opened the cover halfway, letting in a flood of water. John went below to close the cover and to pump.

For the first two hours, the only steady lights were those in the instrument dials, which I could barely make out through my soaked glasses, and the port running light on the bow, which turned the forward waves red. After a bad breaker smashed into the man-overboard light that hung on the life-lines behind my back, the light turned on as it flipped into the cockpit. Its flashing strobe had us helplessly blinded until John muffled it and turned it off.

For a frightening moment, we saw a green running light ahead, which indicated that we were on a collision course with a boat heading back from the Rock. The light disappeared for a couple of minutes and then showed up again down to leeward. A collision between two boats each going over nine knots would have been fatal to both. The sky briefly cleared at about 1:30, revealing a half-moon with its crescent, oddly, facing down. I thought, that's the center of the depression.

Coote had told us to begin looking for Fastnet Rock light at 2:00 A.M., when we should have been within its eighteen-mile range, but it did not appear until almost an hour later. Instead of dead ahead, it was fifteen degrees on the port bow—we had been pushed to leeward farther than anticipated. As we trimmed the sails and headed up, the wind continued on the gradual veer that had started just after midnight. Instead of reaching at 9.5 knots in a southwesterly, we were now beating at six knots into a northwesterly, still not making the course to the Rock. *Toscana*'s bow started to pound into waves from the new direction. I thought, I've never seen worse, but God save the little boats. *Toscana* was stable enough to carry sail to keep her speed up in this sea and wind, but a thirty-five-footer could carry little or no sail area upwind in force 9 or more. With little speed, she could not be steered around the worst waves and could be badly battered.

Eric and his watch relieved us at 3:00 A.M. Cold and stiff, we went below. As I slowly peeled off the layers of sodden clothes, I heard the normally imperturbable Coote shout, "That's Clear Island and it's only a mile and a half to leeward.

Tack! Tack *now!*" The bow swung through the eye of the wind with a roar of waves and wildly flogging sails. The staysail continued to flap after we were around. "The sheet's untied," I heard Sherry shout. Running feet pounded forward. I crawled into the sleeping bag. My shoulders ached and I shivered with cold. I pulled my knees up under my chin in the fetal position and instantly went to sleep.

Sometime later, I was awakened by a light shining through a porthole. Coote was shouting, "We're clear now, Eric. You can bear off to course."

I sat up and looked out the port. To leeward was Fastnet Rock, its baroque lighthouse almost hidden by spray. Between *Toscana* and it sailed a small cruising boat plugging along through the waves with only a storm jib up. I heard Eric, in the cockpit, say with amazement, "What could that little boat be doing out here on such a night?"

Postscript: By the time the race was over, 15 sailors had died, 5 yachts had sunk, 24 crew had abandoned ship, and 136 sailors had been rescued. Only a fourth of the boats finished the race.

Saint Brendan was a sixth-century Irish monastic saint who was often called "The Navigator," and whose legend included a quest for blessed islands and sea monsters. In 1976 the Irish explorer Tim Severin built an ox-leather curragh and over several summers sailed from Ireland to Newfoundland via the Hebrides, Faroe Islands, and Iceland to demonstrate that the saint's fantastic voyage was at least physically possible.

THE BRENDAN VOYAGE

TIM SEVERIN

Emergency

The weather treated us almost too kindly. For the first week we had no more than light airs and calms, and *Brendan* drifted slowly westward away from Iceland. It was a convenient time to settle down and readjust oneself to the medieval way of life, remember the lessons of the year past, and pick up once again the special rhythm of an open boat in northern waters. At Trondur's suggestion, we adopted the watch-keeping system favored by Faroes fishermen. We divided into two watches—Trondur with Arthur; George and myself—and the two watches worked four hours on and four hours off around the clock. It was a system that allowed each watch to decide its own arrangements. When the weather was fine, one man steered the boat while his partner could rest, or read, or cook a light snack. When the weather grew worse, the two watch-keepers would take the helm turn and turn about, just as they saw fit. When it was very rough, as we were to learn, twenty minutes at the helm was as much as a man could endure before he became completely numb. Only at noon did we break the four-hourly pattern. Then we worked two dog watches of two hours each and prepared the main hot meal of the day, which all four of us would eat together. And this season we shared the chore of cooking, which was a far better arrangement.

In some ways it felt as if we had never interrupted the voyage for the winter. Our old companions the whales promptly paid us a visit. When we were still well inside the circle of Faxafloi Bay off Reykjavik a school of minke whale surfaced and blew around us, and a young minke about thirty feet long and consumed with curiosity spent fifteen minutes cruising along up and down each side of the boat, some twenty yards away, puffing and snorting, and rolling under us. Two mornings later, again in a flat calm, a large colony of seals popped up to inspect her, their heads bobbing like sleek footballs all around *Brendan* as the seals gazed curiously at the leather boat. Then, all at once, they sank beneath the water and vanished from view.

We had human visitors, too—a passing fisherman who presented us with lumpfish from his catch, which Trondur skinned and cooked up into fish stew; and a party of hunters in a speedboat. They had been shooting guillemot for the pot, and they also gave us part of their catch, much to Trondur's delight. He plucked, boiled, then fried, and finally sauced the guillemot with sour cream to produce as fine a meal as any

French chef. "One guillemot," he announced judiciously as he ladled out our helpings, "is same as two fulmar, or three puffin, all good food."

Trondur was obviously back in his element. He fashioned a new fulmar-catching device, a deadly flower of wicked-looking hooks sprouting from a corked float which bobbed along in our gentle wake. Below the surface, at the end of our safety line, he also towed a massive hook-and-feather on a heavy wire trace. It looked big enough to catch a shark. Everywhere one turned, there was evidence of Trondur's activities: coils of fishing line, lead weights, boxes of fish-hooks, chunks of whale blubber ready for fulmar bait, a stone for sharpening fish-hooks, and the occasional loose feather where he had plucked his latest gull prey. Trondur lavished the most care on his harpoon. During the winter he had made a beautiful new one. Its brass shank fitted into a long wooden shaft, and the attack end carried an exquisitely made spear point of steel, shaped like a leaf. This spear point was also set in brass, with an off-set attachment for the harpoon line so that as soon as the harpoon struck, the head broke free and the pull of the line twisted and buried the head in the flesh. For hour after hour Trondur would sit hunched over the harpoon head, lovingly honing it to a bright, razor edge. On the thwart beside him lay the harpoon shaft, its handle wrapped with leather thong for a grip. With the leaf-shaped point in his hands, identical in size and shape to the Stone Age spearheads of flint recovered from archaeological excavations, it occurred to me that the whole picture symbolized nothing so much as age-old Man the Hunter.

Seven miles above our heads we could sometimes see the silver dots of airliners flying between Europe and America, drawing their vapor trails across the sky. In just six or seven hours these aircraft were making a journey that it would take

Brendan many weeks to complete, if we succeeded in our passage at all. How, I wondered, would those airline passengers comfortably seated in their chairs, with their film headsets and plastic meal trays, react if they knew that far below them four men in a leather boat were crawling at less than two miles an hour across that innocent-looking ocean, only a couple of feet above its surface, and dependent largely for their survival upon skills and materials that had not changed in a thousand years?

In the first four days *Brendan* had progressed so sluggishly that we could still see the snowcapped peak of Snaefellsjokull on the horizon behind us. In the clear northern air it was difficult to gauge just how far from land we had come. This clarity of the air was another factor, along with twenty-four hours of useable daylight in high summer, which must have helped the early voyagers in these northern waters. The Norsemen had used the peak of Snaefellsjokull as their departure point for Greenland. Norse shipmasters would sail west from Snaefellsjokull until the mountain sank below the horizon, and soon afterward, by looking ahead in clear weather, they would have been able to distinguish the first peaks of Greenland. From land to land along this track the distance between Iceland and Greenland is about 250 miles, and the mountains at each end make perfect landmarks, thus reducing a major gap in the Stepping Stone Route westward. On a fast passage the navigator might not be out of sight of land for more than one or two days. Also the phenomenon known as the Arctic Mirage may have helped them still further.

The Arctic Mirage, known in Iceland as the Hillingar effect, is a northern equivalent of the well-known desert mirage. The Arctic Mirage occurs when a stable mass of clear air rests on a much colder surface. The result is to change the optical properties of the air so that it bends the light like a giant lens. Objects far beyond the normal horizon now appear within view, floating above the horizon, and sometimes turned upside down and stacked, one image above the other. Sextant readings become unreliable, and the theoretical horizon may extend for a distance limited only by the resolution of the human eye. Highly favorable conditions for the Arctic Mirage occur over Greenland, where a mass of high-pressure heavy air rests on the great ice cap, while the high-altitude Greenland glaciers supply a bright source of reflected light for the mirage. So it is possible that Irish and Norse mariners, venturing out from Iceland's coastal waters or gale-driven westward, saw this distant light of Greenland well beyond the normal limits of the visual horizon and suspected that land lay in that direction.

Brendan's slow advance made her an easy mark for the patrols of the Icelandic Coast Guard service, whom Petur Sigurdsson had instructed to keep an eye on us for as long as possible. First the Coast Guard spotter plane circled us, then the guard ship *Tyr* came to investigate. As usual Trondur had a fishing line into the water. "We're only fishing for fulmars, not cod," I radioed to *Tyr* as she steamed inquisitively around us. "Jolly good, and good luck, *Brendan*," came back *Tyr*'s reply as she churned off on her duty to protect Iceland's two-hundred-mile fishing limit from poachers. I turned to Trondur. "By the way, did you tell your fishermen friends in Faroes that last year we ate grey fulmars, which they say are poisonous?"

"Ya," he replied.

"What did they say?"

He grinned. "They say we are crazy."

Coming from Faroes fishermen, I thought to myself, that was the best compliment we had received so far.

Our next visitor was the patrol boat *Aegir*, which sent across a rubber dinghy. Standing bolt upright in the dinghy was a junior Coast Guard officer, clutching a brown box as if it would explode at the slightest tremor. "The captain sends this with his compliments. I hope it's all right," he said, gingerly handing over the box. I opened it. Inside was an enormous cream cake; on the cream sailed an outline of *Brendan* piped in red icing. Beside it was an envelope addressed:

HIGH COMMAND OF THE GREENLAND SEA

CAPT. TIM SEVERIN

BRENDAN

ADDRESS POSITION 63°56′ N; 23°17′ V

The letter inside read:

Hello Tim, old boy.

You better start whistling for a wind. For added assurance we will make a powerful woodo [*sic*] dance in your behalf, at the Dance halls in Reykjavik tonight.

Seriously we all here wish you all smooth crossing and may God be with you all your remarkable journey. The steward sends you a small token of his admiration and wishes you all the best.

Good speed.

Capt. Gunnar H. Olafsson.

As I finished reading the note, *Aegir*'s boat crew was already scrambling back aboard their vessel. The rubber dinghy was whisked aboard; a burst of smoke from her twin exhausts, and *Aegir* went throbbing past us at full speed, her crew waving and three long blasts on her siren to wish us farewell.

The weather continued to be very mild. It was difficult to believe we were in such ill-reputed northern waters. With only a gentle swell on the sea, Trondur could trail astern in the rubber dinghy, sketching *Brendan*, and George was able to clamber around the gunwale, adjusting ropes and leeboards to his precise satisfaction. The sun shone brilliantly through the clean air, and sank down in magnificent sunsets. Only the cutting edge of the wind reminded us that we were less than one hundred miles from the polar pack ice. When the wind blew from the north, from the ice, it sliced through one's defenses. Before emerging on watch, it was wise to struggle first into cotton underwear, then a suit of woollen underclothes, then the heavy Faroes underwear, two pairs of socks, trousers and shirt, and two sweaters, before leaving the protection of the living shelter and tugging on oilskins. The technique was to wear as many layers of warm clothing as possible and to dress up before going outside. Otherwise even a gentle breeze stripped away all body heat in a few minutes, and it was difficult to get warm again. As the temperature dropped each of us produced his own choice of clothing. Arthur sported a selection of shapeless woollen hats and a vast pair of padded Navy watch-keeping trousers. George had stocked up with soft Icelandic woollen socks and gloves. I preferred home-knitted mittens reaching halfway up my forearms. But Trondur outshone us all when he appeared in a magnificent furry Chinese beaver hat, its earflaps waving so that it was difficult to tell where the beaver fur left off and Trondur's luxuriant tangle of hair and beard began.

We were finding that life aboard *Brendan* was much more comfortable with four persons instead of five. The extra space was invaluable. We could stow our spare clothes and equipment properly, keeping out only our personal belongings, safely packed in watertight kit bags. Also our daily rations, originally packed for five men, now gave us ample food. What with the fulmar that Trondur was catching, and our store of smoked and dried meats, we were eating far better than the previous season, and our morale lifted accordingly, even when we had to chip half-frozen honey from the jar. A

constant supply of hot drinks—coffee, beef extract, and tea—
kept the watch warm; and our fresh supplies survived well. In
temperatures that seldom rose above forty degrees Fahren-
heit, nature was providing us with a free cold larder, a fact that
would have been doubly important to the medieval seamen
who sailed that way before us and had to rely on fresh provisions more than we did.

On May 12, an exhausted bird arrived on board to remind
us that migrating birds also took the same route between the
continents. Scarcely larger than a sparrow, we identified it as a
wagtail when it fluttered down, totally worn out, and landed
on the steersman's head. It refused crumbs and water, but
later hopped forward along the gunwale and took up resi-
dence in a sheltered hole in the forward bulkhead of Trondur's berth. By next afternoon it had gone, flown on its way,
though we jokingly accused Trondur of having eaten it for a
midnight snack. The little wagtail's journey lay along age-old
migration paths that could have been another clue for the
medieval sailors that land lay west of Iceland. But such clues
would have had to be treated carefully. Flocks of migrating
birds moving high overhead in spring and autumn indicated
the direction of distant lands to watchers. But it required special knowledge to interpret these signs correctly. The watchers
needed to know something of the habits of the particular birds
to know just how far or how directly they flew on their migra-
tions. On *Brendan* we ourselves were witnessing an example of
this lore. The previous July whenever we saw puffins flying
over the sea, we knew that we were close to land. But now in
May we saw flights of puffin one hundred and more miles
from the nearest shore. In May the birds were foraging far
and wide for food, whereas in June and July, depending on
where they laid their eggs, they restricted their hunting to
areas close to the nests. On such knowledge could depend the

difference between a successful and a futile voyage of exploration.

For our safety, I tried to report *Brendan*'s daily position to the shore radio stations, who passed the information on to the Coast Guard. So whenever the sky was clear, I took sextant readings and calculated our position. To set our course, there was only one golden rule: keep sailing west, always west. With each wind change, we simply altered course to make whatever westing we could manage. If the wind headed us, then we turned north or south, and moved at our best angle of ninety degrees to the wind, until the wind changed again. Calculations of leeway and the effect of ocean current were hit and miss. We judged *Brendan*'s leeway simply by looking at the angle of the safety line to the boat, which could be as much as thirty degrees; and our speed and distance were broadly a matter of guesswork. In light air, *Brendan*, especially when heavily laden, was moving too slowly for the trailing log to be effective, and the log reading was often 40 percent wrong. By a simple test we found it equally accurate to throw a chip of wood into the water by the bow, time how long it took to pass the steering paddle, and then calculate our speed.

Friday the thirteenth proved to be our best day's progress to date. A breeze of force 3 or 4 pushed *Brendan* along for sixty miles, and because the wind moved out of the north and into the east, we immediately noticed the rise in temperature. For lunch we ate an enormous cassoulet of beans and smoked sausage, after Boots had scraped the sausages clean of their green fur of mould.

"Let's test some of our dye," I suggested to George as we lounged replete from the meal and wondering what to do to enliven the afternoon. Some bottles of dye powder had been given to us in case of emergency. The theory was to drop the dye into the water where it would be visible to a searching aircraft. "It will color the water an iridescent orange," George read aloud from the label on the bottle. He unscrewed the cap and tipped the phial of powder overboard. The powder promptly turned green—not much use in a green ocean. "Perhaps the maker was color blind," commented Arthur. "Or his stuff doesn't quite work right in near-freezing water," I added. Five minutes later, however, George himself turned a spectacular blotchy yellow. Some of the powder had blown back and landed on him, and he spent the rest of the day looking like a strange species of leopard.

Next morning brought the first real snag of the second stage of the voyage—the kerosene cooker mutinied and refused to work on either burner. This was totally unexpected. All last season the cooker had functioned perfectly. Now I pulled out a box of spare parts and went to work to strip down the cooker, only to find that most of the spares did not fit. Someone at the factory must have made a slip-up when packing the spares. Superficially, this was merely irritating; but in the long run I knew that it could turn into a major setback. The kerosene was our only source of heat. If the stove failed, we would be left without hot food or drink at a time when a hot meal might make the difference between an efficient crew and an exhausted one. Of course we could sail forward, eating only cold provisions, but it was not a cheerful prospect. Even the Eskimos rely on hot food during long journeys; and we still had at least 1,500 miles to go in an open boat. After four hours of work crouching over the cooker, I finally coaxed one burner to work on makeshift replacement parts. But the other burner was never to function again, and for the rest of the voyage I was acutely aware of just how much depended upon that single blue flame.

Now the weather, after a spectacular display of the northern lights, began to flex its muscles and behave more as if we were in the far North. The wind swung to the southwest and built up ominous black thunder clouds ahead of us. *Brendan* stopped in her tracks and began to shy sideways, northward, under an overcast sky and steady drizzle. An unfriendly swell heaved up the sea and occasionally splattered aboard as wave crests. Trondur commented on the bilge water which was now surging and lapping under his sleeping bag near the bows. "I hear water," he said, "but it is not wet . . . yet." He was amusing himself by fishing for the cloud of Little Gulls which hovered in our wake. They swooped and pecked at his line, even carrying it with them into the air, but their beaks were too small to be easily caught; and only rarely did Trondur reel in a victim which he could add to the larder of seabirds hanging off *Brendan's* stern. "Is there any gull you would not eat?" I asked him. He thought for a moment. "The Eskimo, they catch two, three hundred auk. This they put inside dead walrus and bury for many weeks, then they dig up and eat. This I have not tried, but maybe it is not so good." Even so, Trondur looked mildly hungry at the prospect.

Saint Brendan's day, May 16, was the last day of "normal" weather—thick overcast with occasional rain showers that were just short of turning into sleet. It was in stark contrast to our Saint's day the previous year when, nearly thirty degrees warmer, we had waited in Brandon Creek preceding our departure from Kerry. Now in 1977, in the middle of the Greenland Sea but more relaxed and experienced, we toasted the Saint in Irish whiskey twice—once before lunch, and once in the afternoon when the wind turned briefly into the north-east and gave us a short push in the right direction. "Ouch!" grunted Boots when he leaned over the gunwale to dip his pannikin into the water for the washing up. "If that's any sign, I'd say we'll see ice at any time."

"Cold, is it?" I asked.

"Bloody freezing," he declared. "I wouldn't fancy my chances of falling into that. It rains just as much here as it does in Ireland, but there's a difference: if you touch metal in this cold, it hurts."

All day long the rain continued to come down, and despite the improvement to the living shelter, the water seeped in. A fine fat puddle formed on the thwart near Boots's berth; every lurch of the boat sent a trickle down on his head. Just before midnight, out of the darkling mist behind us, loomed the patrol ship *Thor*. On Petur Sigurdsson's instructions she had come all the way to check our aircraft VHF radio, which was not giving a proper signal, and how *Thor* managed to locate us in that gloom and swell we never knew. It was near miraculous. She had to come within six miles of us before her radar could pick up an echo from *Brendan*. It was like discovering the traditional needle in a haystack. After an hour in which we tested the VHF set between the two vessels, *Thor* slid away into the darkness. She had come well off her normal patrol route, and I knew that henceforth *Brendan* had passed out from under the umbrella of the Icelandic Coast Guard unless there was a dire emergency. Ahead of us lay only the bleak coast of Greenland, whose only permanent inhabitants in those latitudes were a tiny band of meteorologists at the small weather station of Tingmiarmuit. During the last few years the sea ice had been growing worse and worse, and even the East Greenland Eskimos who had once hunted along the coast had abandoned that region as too inhospitable.

As if to underline my sense of foreboding the weather continued to deteriorate. The next day began with fog, mist, and drizzle, and the barometer began to fall rapidly past 980 millibars. A sullen swell from the southeast warned us that heavy weather was on the way. George and I made ready. We dug out a tarpaulin, and stretched it as tightly as possible over the waist of the boat. Two oars acted as a ridge pole, and left a tunnel underneath the tarpaulin just big enough for a man to crawl into if he had to work the bilge pumps. The Irish monks carried leather tents and sheets of spare leather aboard their curraghs and presumably rigged themselves a similar shelter to throw off the breaking seas, otherwise a severe gale would have filled and sunk their boats.

By noon our lack of freeboard was growing dangerously apparent. *Brendan* was so heavily laden for the long passage direct to North America that, as the wind and waves increased, she promptly heeled over and began to scoop water aboard. Bilge pumping became a regular chore; and when the watches changed, Arthur and George climbed forward to reduce sail, rolling up the foot of the mainsail and tying in the reefs. Then we ate a hot stew of sausage, and waited for whatever the gale would bring.

By now I had abandoned any attempt at a westward course. The wind was too strong for *Brendan* to do anything but run away from it. On the charts I could see we were being driven farther north than I had planned. In a sense we were being embayed, just as we had been embayed on Tiree in the Hebrides. Only now it was on a giant scale. Ninety miles ahead of *Brendan* lay the pack ice off the east coast of Greenland. From there the ice edge ran north and then curved east, sweeping back toward Iceland, so that we were being pushed into a great embayment of ice. For the moment, we had plenty of sea room, but a day or two of gales would put *Brendan* into the pack icc. It was not a prospect I relished, but there was nothing we could do about it while the heavy weather lasted.

We were not the only victim of the strong winds. Another migrating bird landed on *Brendan*. This time it was a small brown-and-white water pipit traveling its long migration route to a summer home in Greenland. The high winds must have sapped its strength, because the exhausted creature dropped into the sail, slid down, and lay quivering on the cabin top. It was too tired to protest when George picked it up, and put it out of the wind until it regained its strength. When the bird felt active enough, it hopped curiously about the steering area, perched briefly on George's hat, and then, still wary of humans, decided to spend the night on a coil of rope lying on top of the cabin shelter. There it stayed all night, where the helmsman could see it, balancing and bobbing to the swing of the boat, and unperturbed by the slap and rattle of the main-sail above its head. The little fluffy shape made a companion-able fellow creature in the dark loneliness of the night watch; but the bleak conditions were too much for it. By dawn it was stiff and cold, dead of exposure.

Our next radio contact was encouraging. My radio call to Reykjavik was picked up and answered by the coast station at Prins Christianssund on the southern tip of Greenland. Prins Christianssund is a lonely outpost lying only a few miles from Cape Farewell and it handles the radio traffic for vessels rounding the Cape, so *Brendan* was now, in radio terms, at the halfway point between Iceland and Greenland. The weather also gave us a brief respite. The wind eased, though it left a heavy swell behind it, and we could prepare another hot meal. As I reached for the pressure cooker, Boots called out from the cabin, "Careful of the camera!" I thought he was talking in his sleep because as usual he was snug in his sleeping bag.

"Watch out for the camera," he called again.

I stopped, puzzled. "What do you mean?" I asked.

"It's in the pressure cooker."

"What!" I couldn't believe he was properly awake. "What did you say?"

"In the pressure cooker," he repeated as if it were the most natural place in the world to keep his camera. And in a sense it was. I removed the lid of the cooker, and there nestling in the vegetable cage was his precious camera, dry and safe, if smelling of onions. Thenceforth no one filled the kettle or put a saucepan on the stove without first checking that it did not contain our photographer's equipment.

Soon, for the third time in as many days, the wind turned against us and picked up strength. Our spirits fell with the barometer. For three days now we'd been struggling in circles, covering the same patch of ocean with no progress. It was very disheartening. Enhanced by the almost constant rain, the sea took on a permanently hostile look. From one point of view the huge swells were impressive. They came as great marching hills of water, heaped up by the wind blowing counter to the main ocean current. They were grand monuments to the power of Nature. But seen from a small open boat, they depressed the spirit. It was difficult to judge their height, but whenever *Brendan* sank into the troughs, the swells were far higher than her mainmast. The entire mass of the wave loomed over us, and became as much of our surroundings as the sky itself. If I was talking to George at the helm, it was disconcerting to see a great slab of water loom up behind and above his head not more than twenty yards away as if to topple on him. Ripples wriggling down its face, the water wall rushed toward the boat; then George's head would suddenly begin to lift against the backdrop as *Brendan* rose to the swell. Abruptly the skyline would appear, and all at once there was the broad unfriendly vista of Atlantic rollers stretching all the way to Greenland, before *Brendan* sank once again into the next trough and the grey-blue water closed in about us.

At 6:20 A.M. on May 20, we picked up a faint signal from Prins Christianssund which gave the weather forecast I had been dreading: we were due for a southwest gale, force 8 rising to force 9 of about forty-five miles an hour, precisely from the direction in which we were headed. We scarcely needed the warning. The ugly look of the cloudy wrack ahead of us was enough to advise us that we were in for heavy weather. Sure enough, within an hour, we were struggling first to reef the mainsail, then to lower it altogether and lash it down. Only the tiny headsail was left up to draw us away downwind and give the helmsman a chance to jockey the boat among the ever-larger seas which now began to tumble and break around us. Even as we worked to belay the mainsail, it was clear that we had left one precaution too late; the heavy lee-board should have been taken in earlier. Now the weight of water had jammed it solidly against the hull. Each time the boat heeled to the pressure of the wind, the leading edge of the leeboard dipped into the sea and, like a ploughshare, carved a great slice of water from the ocean, over the gunwale, to pour solidly into the bilges. In ten minutes the water inside the boat was swirling above the level of the floorboards, and the watch—George and I—could feel *Brendan* growing more and more sluggish. This was dangerous, because she was no longer rising properly to the seas, and the loose water was heaving back and forth, unbalancing her.

Clearing the leeboard was typical of the workaday chores aboard. George and I scrambled forward. The holding thongs of the leeboard were taut from the tremendous strain of the water, and the knots defied our efforts to clear them with mar-linspikes. Water continued to pour in with every roll of the hull. George pulled out his knife and slashed through the thongs, while I hung on to the leeboard to stop it being swept away. Lurching and clumsy in our heavy clothing, we man-handled the unwieldy leeboard into the boat. The work was slippery and dangerous. We knew a single misstep could send either of us sliding overboard with no chance of survival in those chill waters. Next we tugged the tarpaulin into place to

shoot off the breaking seas that leaped the gunwale. Ten minutes pumping and the water level in the bilge was down to a
safer margin.

Then it was time to pay out the main warps in loops from
the stern to slow *Brendan* down. I was fearful that she would
somersault or slew sideways and roll clean over if she went
too fast down the face of a wave. Finally we poured whale oil
into our oil bag, pricked holes in the canvas, and dangled the
bag from a short stern line. The oil bag left a streak of oil in
our wake which partly quenched the worst of the wave crests
directly behind us, but it was all the helmsman could do to
keep *Brendan* running directly downwind of the slick where it
would do any good. Each wave swung the little boat out of
control; she threatened to broach and spill, until the trailing
rope loops took hold with a thump that shook the steering
frame, and literally hauled her straight. Looking back one
could see the tremendous strain on the ropes, literally tearing
across the surface of the sea under pressure, the spray rising
from them like smoke. In this fashion we fought the gale, and
in the next five hours of flight we squandered every mile of
hard-earned progress from the previous day. And there was
no end in sight for the gale.

Arthur was off-watch, asleep in the main shelter, when the
first drenching took place. George was at the helm; I was
crouched under the forward tarpaulin steadily pumping out
the bilge water. As if in slow motion, I felt *Brendan* begin to tip
forward, bows down. The boat seemed to hang there at a
weird angle. Curious, I thought to myself, she usually levels
off more quickly than this. Then George bellowed, "Pump!
Pump as fast as you can!," and I heard the heavy onrush of
water down the length of the boat. *Brendan* squirmed like a
gaffed salmon and began to level off. Water bubbled and
gushed out of the floorboards beneath me. Frantically, I

redoubled the speed of pumping, and heard the thump, thump, thump of George briskly operating the bilge pump near the helmsman. Trondur emerged from his shelter, crawled to the starboard midship's pump, and aided in emptying the boat. When the water level was under control I climbed back and peered into the shelter.

There I saw Arthur sitting, disconsolate. On all sides he was surrounded by sodden clothing. His sleeping bag was sopping wet and his hair plastered to his scalp. "I'm afraid half the shelter is soaked, and my cameras have been drenched," he said.

"A big wave broke over the stern and traveled up the boat. It pushed in the rear flap of the shelter and poured on top of him," George explained. "Did it drown the radios?" I asked anxiously. "I don't think so," Arthur replied, "though there's spray all over them." I removed my wet oilskins, crawled into the shelter and dabbed carefully at the sets with a strip of dry cloth. Then I tentatively flicked on the power. To my relief the radios came to life. "Better sponge up the puddles as best you can," I advised Arthur. "There's a spare dry sleeping bag which Edan was using. Meanwhile, I think I'd better put extra plastic bags around the radios in case we get pooped by another wave."

It was lucky I did so. When the watches changed, George and I peeled off our oilskins, crawled inside, and lay down in our sleeping bags. Trondur and Arthur took it in twenty-minute spells to nurse *Brendan* through the seas.

George and I were half asleep, when out of nowhere there came a thunderous roar, an almighty crash, and a solid sheet of water cascaded into the cabin. It brushed aside the rear flap, slammed over the thwart, and hit with such force that water sprayed onto the shelter roof lining. The water was icy, straight from the East Greenland current. Underneath us in our sleeping bags, the sheepskin mattresses literally floated off the cabin floor. A moment later, there was the frigid shock as the water soaked through the sleeping bags. "Pump her! Quick, pump her! She's heavy!" somebody shouted. Frantically, George clawed out of his sleeping bag and raced out of the shelter, wearing only his underwear. In the same movement he had scooped up his immersion suit, which was hanging on the steering frame, zipped himself into it, and was swarming forward to get to the bilge pumps. At the helm Arthur was desperately wrestling with the steering paddle, trying to keep *Brendan* straight to the waves. Trondur, his oilskins glistening, was peeling back the small awning over the cooker and getting ready to bail. For want of a bucket, he had grabbed up the largest saucepan.

Ankle-deep in water in the cabin, I took a quick look around to see if anything could be saved from the water. Virtually all our gear was saturated. A book floated forlornly across the floor; the sleeping bags lay like half-submerged corpses. Water was sloshing everywhere. Quickly I jotted our last estimated position, tore the leaf from the message pad, and stuffed it in my pocket. If *Brendan* filled and sank, our only chance was to broadcast a MAYDAY with an accurate position advice. I thrust the small VHF transmitter, spare batteries, and a microphone into a satchel which I placed, ready to be grabbed, on top of the radio board. Then I, too, clambered into my immersion suit and went forward to help George, who was ratcheting away, flat out, at the port midship's pump. As I passed Trondur, I could see what a shambles the steering area had become. He was standing up to his knees in water, steadily scooping away, while around his legs bobbed pots and pans, jars of food, empty sea-boots, and wet rags. This was a full emergency.

Pump, pump, pump. The two of us heaved back and forth

at the pump handles, sending two feeble little squirts of water back into the ocean. Curled up in the wet darkness beneath the tarpaulin, one had a heightened sense of the crippled motion of the boat. *Brendan* lay almost stopped in the water, dead and sluggish, while the water inside her swirled ominously back and forth. She was so low in the sea that even the smaller waves lapped over the gunwale and added more water to the bilges. It was a race against the distinctive rhythm of the sea. As I heaved frantically at the pump handle, I wondered if there was another wave waiting to break and fill her. Would she stay afloat? And what a godforsaken place for this emergency to happen—halfway between Iceland and Greenland. What had the experts said? Survival time in this near-freezing water was five minutes or less.

Pump, pump, pump. A glance through a chink of the tarpaulin revealed the cause of our distress. The full strength of the Atlantic was showing itself. Whipped up by the gale racing clear from Greenland, the waters were thrashing in wild frenzy. The main motion was the steady pounding of huge waves from the southwest, overtoppling their crests in a welter of foam. Flickering across the surface as far as the eye could see were spume streaks drawn out by the gale across the skin of the water. Here and there cross waves slid athwart the main wave direction and collided. When they met, they burst upward as though cannon shells were landing. It was an awesome sight.

Pump, pump, pump. It took forty-five minutes of nonstop work with pumps and Trondur's saucepan to reduce the water in the boat to a safer level and lighten *Brendan*. Then we could assess the damage. Structurally *Brendan* seemed as tight as ever. The steering frame was still in place, and the seams of stitching had held. It was easy to see where the wave had struck. It had come aboard at the unprotected flank of the boat, through the open gap beside the steering paddle. Right in the wave's path stood the metal cooker box. It had taken the full brunt of the wave. One side of the box was stove in and completely twisted. The retaining clip had been smashed open, and its rivets sheared off cleanly by the force of the blow.

The scene inside the cabin was heartbreaking. Everything on floor level, which was most of our equipment, was awash in water trapped on top of the plastic sheet we used as a base for our living quarters. We opened the flap that led forward beneath the central tarpaulin, and one by one I handed through to George the dripping floor mats, sodden sleeping bags, sheepskins oozing water, soaked clothing. Everything was saturated in icy, salt water. Only the radios and equipment perched above floor level had been saved, together with the contents of our personal kit bags, which, thank heavens, had remained waterproof. Our spare clothes, at least, were dry.

George was shivering with cold and pulled on proper clothing at last. "Christ," he muttered as he struggled into a sweater, "I hope your theory is right that body heat will dry out our sleeping bags. I don't fancy being this wet for the rest of the voyage." As soon as the shelter was clear of gear, I concentrated on trying to get rid of the water on the floor, mopping up puddles and stabbing drain holes in the plastic floor with a knife. After half an hour's work it was obvious we would have to be content with the glistening wet interior. The shelter would never become any drier. Back from the tarpaulin tunnel, George passed everything we had evacuated, except the three sheepskins and one sleeping bag. These were so saturated that even after we had tried to squeeze them dry, the water poured out in rivulets.

Exhausted, George and I crawled back into the remaining

two sleeping bags, trying to ignore the fact that we were drenched to the skin and the sleeping bags lay clammy upon us. For nearly thirty-six hours we'd been working with scarcely any sleep.

Boom! Again a heavy wave came toppling over the stern, smashed aside the shelter door, and poured in, slopping over my face as I lay head-to-stern. We sprang up and tried to save the sleeping bags from the flood. But it was too late. In a split second the situation had returned to exactly where it had been before. Water was everywhere. The bilges were full, and the cabin was awash. *Brendan* was near-stationary before the breaking seas, and George and I were wading around the cabin floor with icy water soaking through our stockinged feet.

Once again it was back to the pumps for an hour, rocking back and forth at the pump handles, hoping silently that another wave would not add to the damage while *Brendan* was handicapped. Then back to the same chore of stripping out the cabin contents, squeezing out the sodden items, mopping up and returning everything to its place. I flicked on the radio. There was a heart-stopping moment of silence before I realized that the radio had been knocked off-tune in the hectic scramble. As soon as I had corrected the fault, I put out a call to try to report our position in case of disaster. But no one was listening. We were many miles off any shipping lanes, and with the radio's tuning unit drenched with water and the waves overtopping the aerial more than half the time, I thought it was very doubtful that we were putting out a readable signal. The little VHF set had fared even worse. Water had got into it, and it would only squeak and click in frustration. I switched the set off before it did itself an electrical injury.

"We've got to do something about those big waves," I said.

"We're exhausting ourselves pumping and working the boat. This can't go on. The cabin will soon be unlivable."

The crew looked at me with eyes raw-rimmed from exhaustion and the constant salt spray. The wind buffeted the mast and plucked at the tarpaulin; the waves kept up their ceaseless rumble and roar; and for a moment I seriously wondered what on earth the four of us were doing here in this lonely, half-frozen part of the Atlantic; cold, drenched, and very tired, and out of touch with the outside world.

"I propose we put up an oar as a mizzen-mast," I went on. "Rig a mizzen staysail and put out the sea anchor so that she rides nose up to the waves. It means taking a risk when we peel back the tarpaulin to dig out the oar—a wave might catch and fill her—and it will be a dangerous maneuver trying to turn the boat around. She could be caught broadside. But the curragh men of Aran ride out heavy weather, head to wind, hanging on to their salmon nets as sea anchors."

I saw Trondur was looking very doubtful. "What do you think, Trondur?" Of all of us, Trondur had by far the most experience in these heavy northern seas.

"What we are doing now is right," he said. "It is better that *Brendan* is this way to the waves. Now she can move with them." He twisted his hands to imitate *Brendan* zigzagging down the combers. "If we have sea anchor," Trondur continued, "*Brendan* cannot move. When big wave hits the bow, I think tarpaulin will break and we have very much water in the boat. Water in stern of *Brendan* is not so much problem. Watcr in bow, I think, is big problem. Now we must stop water in stern and in cabin."

But how? What we needed was some way of closing the large gap between the cabin and the helmsman's position. But even if we cut up a sail as an awning, or used some of the forward tarpaulin, which we could ill afford to do, I doubted if they would withstand the pressure if we rigged them over the gap. We needed something extremely strong, yet something which we could erect at once in the teeth of the gale.

Then I had it. Leather! Under the cabin floor lay a spare oxhide and several slightly smaller sheets of spare leather. They were intended as patches if *Brendan* sprang a leak or was gashed. Now they could be used to plug a far more dangerous hole in our defenses. At the same moment I remembered, absolutely vividly, an encyclopedia illustration of the Roman army *Testudo*, the "tortoise" under which the Roman legionnaires advanced against a town rampart, holding leather shields overlapping above their heads to ward off missiles thrown by the defenders. Why hadn't I thought of it before?

For the third time, I began emptying out the contents of the cabin, peeled back the floor sheet with a sticky ripping sound, and prized up the leather sheets where they had lain on the deck boards. "Get a fistful of thongs," I told George. "I want to lace the hides together." He crawled forward.

I shoved the leather sheets out of the cabin door. They were stiff and unwieldy in the cold. So much the better, I thought, they will be like armor plate.

Quickly I pointed out to Trondur what needed to be done. Immediately he grasped the principle, nodded his understanding, and gave a quick grin of approval.

Then he was off, knife in hand, scrambling up onto *Brendan*'s unprotected stern where the waves washed over the camber of the stern deck. It was a very treacherous spot, but it was the only place where the job could be done properly. With one hand Trondur held on to his perch, and with the other he worked on the leather sheets we passed up to him. Every now and then, the roar of an oncoming breaker warned him to drop his work, and hold on with both hands while *Brendan* bucked and shuddered and the wave crest swirled over the stern. Meanwhile, Arthur at the helm kept *Brendan* as steady as he could, and George, balancing on the port gunwale, pinned down each sheet of leather to prevent it being swept away by the gale. Trondur's job was to cut a line of holes along the edge of the oxhide in the right place for the leather thongs to lash down and join together the tortoise. With the full power of his trained sculptor's hand, Trondur drove his knife point again and again through the quarter-inch-thick leather, twisted and sawed, and carved out neat hole after neat hole like a machine. It was an impressive display of strength. Then George fed the leather thongs through the holes, tied down the corner of the main hide, and laced on the overlapping plates.

In less than fifteen minutes the job was done. A leather apron covered the larger part of *Brendan*'s open stern, leaving just enough room for the helmsman to stand upright, his torso projecting up through the tortoise. Leather cheek plates guarded the flanks.

Boom! Another breaker crashed over the stern, but this time caromed safely off the tortoise and poured harmlessly back into the Atlantic; only in one spot did it penetrate in quantity, where I had plugged a gap beneath the leather apron with my spare oilskin trousers. So great was the force of the water that the trousers shot out from the gap, flying across the cockpit on the head of a spout of water.

The tortoise won the battle for us that night. Several more potentially destructive waves curled over *Brendan*, broke, and shattered themselves harmlessly against our leather defenses. Only a fraction of that water entered the bilges and was easily pumped back into the sea. Poking up through his hole in the leather plating, the helmsman had a hard and bitter time of it. Facing aft and steering to ride the waves, he was battered achingly in the ribs by the sharp edge of the tortoise while the wind scoured his face. From time to time a breaker would flail his chest, and it was so uncomfortable that each man stayed only fifteen minutes at the helm before he had to be replaced, his hands and face numb in the biting cold.

But it was worth it. Even if we were losing the distance we had made and were being blown back in our tracks, we had survived the encounter with our first major Greenland gale. We had made *Brendan* seaworthy to face the unusual conditions of those hostile seas, and we had done so with our own ingenuity and skills. Above all, we had succeeded by using the same basic materials which had been available to Saint Brendan and the Irish seagoing monks. It was cause for genuine satisfaction.

Greenland Sea

By eight o'clock next morning the gale had eased enough for us to begin sorting out the jumbled mess in the cockpit created by the waves that had washed aboard. Shelves were knocked askew; canisters of food had leaked. The lids had sprung off plastic boxes, and their contents now swam in murky puddles. When the salt container was tipped, its contents ran out as a liquid. All the matches we had been using, and the lighters, were ruined; to light the stove we had to resort again to special lifeboat matches which ignited even when damp. Sea water had burst into the kerosene lamps so that even the mantle had been broken behind the glass of the pressure lamp. Gloves, socks, scarves, hats, all were soaked, and there was no way to dry them except by body heat. The pages of my daily journal, which were written on waterproof paper, had been so badly soaked that most of the allegedly indelible ink had run. Each page had to be mopped off with a rag. Nor could I raise contact on the main radio with any shore station until that evening our signal was picked up by one of the Icelandic Airlines regular flights between Reykjavik and Chicago, and the pilot promptly relayed our position report to his air traffic control center, who in turn passed on the message to the Coast Guard that we were safe. That at least was one worry out of the way: the last thing I wanted was for our friends in the Icelandic Coast Guard to start searching for us on a false alarm. They had been magnificently generous in offering to keep track of *Brendan*, and I had the reciprocal responsibility not to put them to unnecessary trouble.

The wind dropped, but the weather did not really relent. It produced rain, fog, a brief calm, then more rain, and more fog. For half a day the wind obliged us by going into the northeast, and we bowled along sometimes at six or seven knots, rapidly picking up valuable mileage in the right direction. But then it turned again into the south and we were forced to slant even closer to the ice edge. All this time we kept up our efforts to dry out—mopping up again and again, sponging and bilge pumping, trying to beat back the water.

Whether the medieval Irish seafarers had to endure such bleak conditions is doubtful. Most historians who have studied climate agree that the climate of the North Atlantic between the fifth and eight centuries was often warmer than it is today. But they are cautious about the precise details. Quite simply, too little is known about the reasons for climatic change, and the experts are still gathering evidence of exactly what happened. The leading English historian of climate, Professor H. H. Lamb, had studied the early chronicles for references to floods, harvests, and other records of climatic change. "Briefly, there is good reason to believe," he had written to me, "that there were periods, particularly between A.D. 300 and 500 or perhaps as late as 550, and again between 900 and 1200, as well as a briefer period coinciding approximately with the eighth century A.D. in which there was an anomalously high frequency of anticyclones about the 50 latitudes and sometimes higher latitudes which must have reduced the frequency of storms and made the possibility of safe voyages to Iceland and Greenland higher in those times than in most others. However, it is quite clear that the variation of climate was not sufficient to rule out the possibility of a disastrous storm at any time."

Professor Lamb's conclusions were supported in part, though not in every instance, by the recent analysis of ice-core samples drilled out of the Greenland ice cap by Danish and American scientists. The horizontal layers in these ice cores represent annual snowfalls in Greenland extending back for more than a thousand years. A technique has been devised to calculate the temperatures in those years by measuring the amount of the heavy oxygen isotope trapped in each layer. Again, the evidence shows various warmer periods in Greenland's history, including one between A.D. 650 and A.D. 850.

Several scholars had already pointed out that the weather was much more suitable for trans-Atlantic voyages when the Norsemen were reaching Iceland and then went on to colonize Greenland. But there were at least two other favorable intervals, sometimes overlooked by the historians: a period in the eighth century just before the time Dicuil had been writing of the Irish voyages to Iceland, and an earlier opportunity in the sixth century closer to the time of Saint Brendan himself. Dicuil's information also throws a revealing sidelight on the more general climatic picture provided by the scientists. Dicuil declared that in about A.D. 800 the Irish monks had been setting out on regular voyages to Iceland *in February*, a time of year which modern sailors would certainly not recommend as the best season for the passage. But wind and weather in February, in Dicuil's day, were suitable for the voyage, more evidence that the early medieval climate was not the same as it is in the mid-twentieth century.

Of course the air temperature over the North Atlantic in early medieval times was only one factor in the problem of climatic history and the Irish voyages. Nothing is known of such vital matters as the prevailing wind direction, or the frequency and seasonal distribution of storms in those earlier centuries. However, it does seem likely that there was less sea ice on the Greenland coast for most of this time. The Norse sailors who voyaged from Iceland to the Greenland settlements in the early years were not unduly hindered by the Greenland ice. And it is reasonable to suppose that with higher temperatures at the time of the Irish Christian voyages, the sea ice would not have presented the problem it does today. Appropriately enough Páll Bergthorsson, a meteorologist at Iceland's Weather Center, had checked back through the Icelandic records and shown how the variations in winter temperatures could be directly related to the amount of sea ice appearing off Iceland. Now Páll and his colleagues were watching the Greenland weather maps on behalf of *Brendan* and, whenever possible, sending us weather forecasts by radio.

An improvement in the climate of the North Atlantic in the Middle Ages may explain why the *Navigatio* had so little to say about bad weather during Saint Brendan's epic voyage. In general, his curragh seems to have been troubled as much by calms as by gale-force winds. But this was due in part to the Saint's good sense in restricting the main stages of his voyage to the summer, though there was one occasion when he was taken by surprise by the weather: after their narrow escape from the hostile sea monster who attacked them, only to be defeated and killed by another sea creature, the travelers beached their curragh on an island. Here they found the carcass of the dead monster where it had been washed ashore, and Saint Brendan told his men to cut it up for food. This gave them extra supplies for three months. But the travelers had to spend all three months stranded on the island because foul weather at sea, with heavy rain and hailstorms, kept them from putting out in the curragh. Some commentators had suggested that this unseasonal bad weather indicates that the monks had landed in South Greenland, where the weather can be notoriously foul even in summer. A bad Greenland summer, it is claimed, would have caught the Irish monks unawares because they were accustomed to better summer sailing at home.

A more intriguing clue to the possibility that the Irish navigators landed in Greenland is to be found, once more, in the writings of the Norsemen themselves. When the Norse first discovered Greenland they reported coming across "human habitations, both in the eastern and western parts of the country, and fragments of skin boats and stone implements." The eminent American geographer, Carl Sauer, argued that these skin boats and stone dwellings were much more likely to have been left behind by Irishmen than by the Eskimo, because at that time—as far as all research can show—there were no Eskimos living in South Greenland. The Norse settlers in South Greenland did not encounter any living Eskimo, nor have archaeologists found Eskimo relics of that time in that area. What the archaeologists have found is evidence that the only Eskimos in Greenland when the Norse arrived belonged to the Dorset culture, whose early traces are confined to the north of the country. Just as important, the only habitations, other than tents, known to have been used by the Dorset people were very characteristic subterranean burrows, sometimes roofed with skins. These burrows would certainly not be described as "habitations of stone."

This being so, Carl Sauer asked, then whose skin boats

and stone habitations did the Norsemen find in South Green-land? Surely the Irish, because cells are typical structures built by Irish monks all over the west coast of Ireland and in the Hebrides.

Had the Norsemen stumbled across the traces of the Irish monks who fled there as refugees from Iceland when the Norsemen drove them on? Or were these relics left by Irish hermits who had voyaged direct to Greenland from the Faroes or from the Hebrides? The Norse sagas do not give any more information about the size or shape of these "habita-tions of stone," but with *Brendan*'s experience to help, another point now arose: the "skin boats" the Norsemen found were not likely to have been Eskimo kayaks, because the skin cover of a kayak will perish if it is not regreased and looked after very carefully. The skin has not been tanned in the true sense, as *Brendan* was, and will disintegrate when abandoned any length of time on the shore. By contrast, the oak-bark-tanned leather of the Irish curraghs was extremely stable and durable, and could last for a very long time indeed. Perhaps, then, the skin boats of pre-Norse Greenland were Irish ocean-going curraghs.

As we now struggled toward Greenland's coast, *Brendan*'s modern weather-luck was causing me real anxiety. The gales had not only forced her around in a futile circle in the Green-land Sea, but the boat was being pushed much farther north than I had anticipated or wanted. To clear Cape Farewell and its eighty-mile-wide shelf of pack ice striking out from South Greenland, *Brendan* needed to head southwest. But she was being frustrated by the constant foul winds. So I decided to take a gamble: we would steer close to the ice. There the local wind often blows parallel to the ice edge, and *Brendan* might find the wind she wanted so desperately. But the danger was obvious; if we were caught by an easterly gale, *Brendan* would be driven headlong into the pack ice with very little chance of anyone reaching us in time if we got into trouble. Petur Sigurdsson of the Coast Guard had told me not to be worried by the ice. "We call it the Friendly Ice," he had said with a twinkle in his eye. "Coast Guard patrol ships have found shelter many times from the storms by entering the ice. The sea is always calm there." But he was speaking of steel-built ships, and I was not so sure that *Brendan*'s leather hull would withstand an ice collision.

I did not have to explain the risk to *Brendan*'s crew. They watched the pencil line on the chart, which showed our daily progress, inching nearer the Greenland coast. Each man kept his own counsel but it was clear that they appreciated the importance of every slight variation in the wind direction. The foul weather continued to afflict us all the next week and began to take its toll. There can be few places where the daily fluctuations of weather have a greater and more immediate effect than on the crew of an open boat in such waters. Whenever it rained—which was several times a day—we spent our time off-watch huddled in the shelter or under the tarpaulin, patiently trying to stem the trickles of water. When the air temperature hovered within a few degrees of freezing and the wind got up, the wind chill was harsh enough to restrict us to our damp sleeping bags as much as possible, despite the fact that the sleeping bags were still clammy. The trick, we found, was to keep rotating the bags so that the bottom side of the bag, which oozed a film of water, was periodically turned uppermost and had a chance to dry out. Grudgingly, we hoarded our last remaining dry clothes. The near-swamping had taught us to keep some dry clothes in reserve in case they were needed in a real emergency, and so we continued to wear our damp garments, even though it was a penance to pull on wet socks and trousers, push one's feet into wet sea-boots, and squelch to the helm on a rainy cold night.

Yet under these conditions, we remained remarkably cheerful, provided only that *Brendan* was making progress in the right direction. Sails were carefully adjusted; arms plunged into the icy water to haul up the leeboards; the helm painstakingly set to just the right angle. It was when *Brendan* was stopped or being driven back by headwinds that life became wearisome. All of us knew that the only answer was to be stoically patient, to watch and wait and bide our time until the winds turned in our favor. There was nothing else we could do.

Each man reacted in his own way. As sailing master, George must have felt the most frustration. With the wind against him—or no wind at all—there was little he could do to help us reach North America. Yet he never lost his meticulous sense of care for *Brendan*. He checked and rechecked ropes for wear, readjusted lashings, stripped down and reassembled the steering frame when it became slack, moved the leather chafing pads to fresh positions. Inside the shelter, he was equally careful about details. With his army training he always left his sleeping bag neatly rolled, his gear carefully wrapped and stacked and out of harm's way, and one could set a clock by his well-regulated watch-keeping routine.

Arthur was the complete reverse—a rumpled, chaotic, easygoing shambles. Arthur's sleeping bag, if Arthur was not in it, was usually serving as a squashed-up cushion. His stock of sweaters and scarves ran loose and turned up in strange places, until we finally banished his sodden naval trousers from the cabin, when they threatened to take over the entire living space. It was a standing joke that Arthur never remembered a hat. Invariably he lurched out of the shelter to begin his watch, and a minute later his head would pop back with a plaintive "I say, could you pass my cap, please. I'm not sure where it is, but it should be somewhere."

Arthur always had the bad luck. If a sneak wave broke

unexpectedly over the gunwale at mealtime, it was Arthur who was sitting in the wrong place so that he received the cold sea water down his neck or in his pannikin. When it began to rain heavily, it always seemed to be as Arthur was about to start his watch. "Arthur!" George would sing out cheerfully. "There's a thundercloud ahead. It must be time for you to take the helm!" With unwavering good nature, Arthur remained unruffled by his mishaps. Only his suit of green oil-skins suffered. They seemed to wilt under Arthur's tribula-tions, and adopt their own personality. The rest of our oilskins hung neatly over the steering frame ready for use; but Arthur's green jacket and trousers were always to be seen, crumpled, battered, and inside out in a corner of the cockpit. "It hardly seems worth putting them on," Arthur would say as he poured a cupful of sea water from his jacket hood and shrugged his way into the soggy garments. And likely as not, he would discover that the inside of his boots were full of water, too. And there was no mistaking which were Arthur's sea-boots; his feet were so large that he was obliged to wear agricultural rubber boots, specially ordered from the makers, and their ribbed soles had treads like tractor tyres.

Trondur had spent so much time at sea in boats that he had developed his own brand of patience. "When do you think the wind will change?" I would ask him. Trondur would look at the sky, at the sea, and pause. "I say nothing," he would announce calmly, "sometime north wind." And when the weather was really atrocious, with driving rain, poor visi-bility, and an unpleasant lumpy sea that had *Brendan* stagger-ing to the waves, he would say "Is not so bad. It can be worse than this in winter," and go about his work with such calm assurance that he raised all our morale. Trondur always found something to keep himself busy. If he was not fishing for fulmar, he was sketching shipboard scenes or working

over his drawings, sometimes using the frayed end of a match-
stick to spread the ink wash. The inside of his berth under the
bow tarpaulin was a veritable artist's atelier. He had rigged up
a hammock of fishnet which contained his paper and pens, his
ink bottles and pencils, and the inevitable box of fish-hooks.
Drawings and half-finished studies were hung up to dry, and
one could sometimes see a needle and thread scrapings of
leather where he had commandeered a spare bit of oxhide
and was stiching up some knick-knack, perhaps a little box for
his ink bottles, or a leather pendant carved with a Celtic cross.

On the whole, there was little idle conversation among the
crew. Like dry clothing, we tended to dole out our thoughts
and our comments little by little, knowing that there was much
empty time ahead. One side effect, George noticed, was how
our conversation actually slowed down. George was using a
tape recorder to make a sound track for a film about the voyage, and when he played back the day's recording he found it
was very frustrating. One person would ask a question. There
would be a long pause; and then the reply would come back.
Nor did George's tapes reveal much of our thoughts. By and
large, each member of *Brendan*'s crew kept his opinions to himself, and in an old-fashioned way concentrated on running the
boat and minding his own affairs. By unspoken agreement it
seemed the best way of enduring our ordeal.

Sailing aboard *Brendan*, we were finding, was becoming a
very personal experience despite our shared adventure. Each
man reacted in his own way to events, and his experiences
did not necessarily mix with the ideas of his companions.
Nowhere was this more true than on watch. Then the
helmsman was often the only man to see the distant single
spout of a whale, the sudden jump of a dolphin, or a changing
pattern in the sky. Some incidents passed in a flash before there
was time to rouse the other crew members—others happened

so slowly and gently that they were perceptible only to a man obliged to wait by the helm for two hours at a stretch.

Watch-keeping in a gale was perhaps the most personal experience of all, because then the helmsman was acutely aware that the lives of the other three depended on his skill. Every big wave during his watch brought a challenge which only the helmsman could judge and meet. Each wave success-fully surmounted, and rolling safely past under the hull, was not noticed by the rest of the crew. But to the helmsman it was a minor victory, only to be forgotten in the face of the next on-rushing wave behind it.

Some moments, by contrast, were seared in the memory of the man concerned. One such incident occurred on May 23, when *Brendan* was yet again running north. It was the dusk watch, and although the wind was only about twenty-five knots, it was blowing counter to the East Greenland current and kicking up a short, breaking sea, with an occasional rogue wave which raked the boat. We were all very tired. The day-long moan of the wind and the roar of the combers sapped one's concentration. Watch by watch we had been climbing into our immersion suits, strapping ourselves to the steering frame with our safety lines, and holding on to the tiller. George happened to be forward under the tarpaulin, pump-ing out the bilge; Arthur and Trondur were in the shelters in their sleeping bags; I was alone at the tiller, steering through yet another maelstrom of sea, cliff after cliff of water rising up behind the boat. Each wave demanded a heave on the tiller bar to bring *Brendan* to the correct angle to her adversary.

Almost casually I happened to glance over my shoulder, not toward the stern to where the waves were coming from, but to port and away from the wind. There, unannounced by the usual crashing white mane of foam, was a single maverick wave. It was not particularly high, a mere ten feet or so, but it was moving purposefully across the other waves, and now reared nearly vertical along *Brendan*'s length, while *Brendan* was already locked solid in the crest of a regular breaker. "Hang on," I yelled at the top of my voice, and grabbed at the H-frame.

Brendan began to tip away from the face of the new wave. She leaned over and over until, on the lee side, I found myself looking almost straight down at the water and still hanging on to the upright of the H-frame. "My God, she's going to capsize!" I thought. "She can't possibly hold this angle without tipping over. What's going to happen to the men in the shelter and under the tarpaulin? Will they be able to get out?" It was a long, very unpleasant moment. Then instead of capsizing, *Brendan* began to slide sideways down the face of the wave.

The next instant, the wave covered *Brendan*. It did not break in a spectacular roar of white water or tumble over her in impressive foam. It did not even jar the boat. It simply enfolded her in a great mass of solid water which poured steadily across *Brendan* like a deep steady river. Sea water swept across the tortoise and plucked at my chest. Looking forward, *Brendan* was totally submerged. Not two yards away, the cabin top was completely covered. The life raft, which was strapped on top of it and stood twenty-one inches higher, was under water. Only the masts could be seen, projecting up from the water. *Brendan* seemed to have been absorbed into the body of the wave. In a curious distraction, I thought how her long, low profile and the two stubby masts looked exactly like a submarine with its periscopes hidden in the wave. And like a submarine emerging, *Brendan* struggled up from the sea. The air trapped under the tarpaulin and in the shelter simply pulled her up out of the wave. The water swirled off quietly, and *Brendan* sailed on as if nothing had happened. I was amazed. At the very least I expected the whole cabin to have been twisted and all the tarpaulins split. But when I clambered up on a thwart to survey the damage, everything was still intact.

The only casualty was my peace of mind. From my vantage point at the helm I knew exactly how close we had been to capsizing. And when my watch ended and I crawled into my sleeping bag, I found that I could not sleep although I was bone-weary. The rumble of every big wave sweeping down on the boat made me tense up to await a certain disaster. I did not get a moment's rest, and when the watches changed again, I mentioned the rogue wave to Arthur. "Yes," he said. "Everything inside the cabin went an underwater green." And that was where, by tacit agreement, we left the subject; and did the same a couple of days later when George had a similar bad experience thinking that *Brendan* was about to roll over during his watch. Such episodes in our lives seemed best left without discussion.

Only seventy or eighty miles from the edge of the Greenland pack ice we were at last rewarded with a break in the weather. On the morning of May 25 a much-needed calm succeeded the high winds, and we could enjoy the revival of sea life around us. On the horizon great flocks of gulls were circling and diving. As they flew closer, we made out the bursts of white spray beneath the birds where a school of dolphin was hunting the same shoal of fish from below. Then a separate, excited group of dolphin approached. They were escorting one single, very large, very fat fin whale. As usual the whale changed course to visit us, and brought his dolphin escort with him. When he was close, the whale gave a deep puff, sank down, and swam under *Brendan*'s hull. But his dolphin escort stayed at the surface, leaping and jumping, twisting and turning all around us like gamboling dogs. Glancing astern of *Brendan* we could see the turbulence thrown up by the whale's broad flukes, coming to the surface and flattening the small waves, so that for a moment it looked exactly as if *Brendan* had her own propellers churning up a wake. Then the big whale surfaced, blew twice, and circled round us for one last look before he puffed off to the east, his spout visible for four or five miles.

It was, in fact, a typical "whale day." George was leaning over the gunwale to scoop up a pot of salt water to boil the lunchtime potatoes when he glanced up and said in a matter-of-fact voice, "There are five big whales watching us, just astern." "What sort are they?" I asked. "I'm not sure; they seem different," George replied. Trondur stood up and looked over the stern. "These are sperm whale," he said, and we watched as yet another of the whale species cruised quietly up to *Brendan* to take a look at her, their strange blunt heads shoving steadily through the water. One member of the pod swam to our bow to have a closer inspection and then all five moved majestically on their way, not bothering to dive but wallowing on the surface.

The calculated risk of running close to the ice edge paid off. On the afternoon of May 25, the wind began to blow steadily from the northeast, and *Brendan* started to move parallel to the ice edge, heading toward Cape Farewell. Prins Christiansund Radio broadcast a gale warning, which proved to be correct. All that night the wind stayed near gale force, and the night watch awoke to the chilling sound of hailstones crackling off the tarpaulins like the sound of crumpling cellophane. There was another gale warning the following morning, and the morning after that, too, and also on the third and fourth days. But now the wind always came out of the north or northeast, and *Brendan* fairly scampered along, helped by the East Greenland current which pushed her even faster, giving us an extra twenty or twenty-five miles a day. On May 26

Brendan put up her best performance, 115 miles on the log in twenty-four hours. This equaled her best day's run the previous season, and would have been a respectable achievement for a modern cruising yacht.

The scrawled comments on the daily log sheets summed up the conditions of those Greenland days; "fog," "drizzle," "thick mist," "gale warning" were repeated monotonously. Under such adverse conditions, Arthur's cameras began to give trouble. The salt atmosphere was penetrating their delicate mechanisms and the shutters seized up. Painstakingly Arthur disemboweled the cameras into dozens of little pieces on the shelter floor, cleaned and oiled the bits, and from two camera bodies salvaged one camera which worked if he gave it a hearty cuff between shots. We had now been more than three weeks at sea and our fresh food supplies were running out. We ate the last of the apples, and regretfully finished off the cheddar cheese. There was still plenty of smoked and dried meats, but our German black bread was a disappointment. It had turned sour, and there was green mould on every slice when we opened the packets. But the reduction in our stores and the amount of water we had consumed now meant that *Brendan* was nearly a third of a ton lighter, and she was beginning to ride a little more easily.

Living conditions daily grew more basic. The contents of the cabin had been stripped down to essentials—there remained only our sleeping bags, a kit bag of clothes for each person, a radio, a sextant, a bag of books, and the cameras— nothing else. Also the shelter was beginning to smell strongly with the permanent smell of wool drying out, of leather, and of damp, unwashed bodies. We were growing accustomed to living with permanently wet hair, wet shirt sleeves where the water oozed past the cuffs of the oilskins, wet socks, and wet sweaters. Fortunately no one suffered any illness, not even cuts or sprains. The only problem was Trondur's hands, which puffed up with fat red swellings on knuckles and fingers with a pitted sore in the center of each swelling. But Trondur only shrugged and said it was a normal affliction for fishermen who handled nets and lines in cold water. The rest of us merely came off watch with fingers like dead white cucumbers, grained with cracks of grime, and it took a couple of hours for the normal color to return.

We began to treat the daily gale warnings from Prins Christianssund with a certain downbeat humor. We joked among ourselves that the wind never seemed to reach the ferocious speeds that were forecast, though our little barometer agreed with the pressure readings that were being broadcast. A series of low pressure centers, sometimes as low as 970 millibars, were rubbing shoulders with the Greenland high pressure gradient where the gale winds blew. We wondered whether we were avoiding the worst of the winds because *Brendan* was so low in the water and sheltered by the troughs of the waves. Certainly we did not feel the full blast of the gales, and we were surprised when we received a worried message from Páll Bergthorsson to say that a ship, not sixty miles from *Brendan*, was reporting a wind speed of force 10, full storm. The message was relayed by an Icelandic fishery research boat, *Arni Fridriksson*, which was operating to the north of us, and when *Arni Fridriksson* finished her tour and left for home, our radio link with Reykjavik was broken and we felt even more isolated. The high winds and poor visibility grounded the aircraft in South Greenland, and even the Ice Patrol plane, which was supposed to look for us, was unable to fly due to bad weather.

On May 29 *Brendan* at last cleared the tip of the ice ledge extending south from Cape Farewell and we breathed more easily. We were now crossing the wide approaches to the

Davis Strait which divides Greenland from North Labrador. Here, to our frustration, we came into an area of calms, light airs, and pea-soup fogs. Almost every wind, when it did come, arrived from the south and west, and *Brendan*'s advance slowed to a crawl. Once again, the pencil line of our course again began to zig and zag and make erratic circles on the chart.

"May 31st" read a typical day's entry in the journal. "Began calm, but a northwest wind by noon, and we altered the course more directly for Newfoundland. Then the winds turned southwest, and we are virtually hove-to, lolling through the water. Nothing of interest."

Tedium became our new enemy. Once or twice we glimpsed enough sun to make it worthwhile to hang the sleeping bags in the rigging and to try to dry out our clothes. But usually the weather was too foggy or too damp for any success. And it was so cold that the next migrant to land on *Brendan*, another water pipit, also failed to survive the night and perished. To pass the time, there was a shipboard craze for fancy rope work, and *Brendan*'s rigging sprouted complicated knots and splices, intricate lashings, and every item that could possibly be embellished with a Turk's head was duly decorated. To add to the boredom, there was an increasing sense of remoteness brought about by our limited horizon, which seldom exceeded three or four miles because of constant fog. Often the fog banks closed in so thickly that we could see no more than fifty yards in front of the vessel, and it was impossible to distinguish the line between air and sea, so that *Brendan* seemed to be suspended in a muzzy grey bowl. The only consolation was that there was very little chance of being run down by a ship. These were desolate waters, crossed only by an occasional fishing boat on its way between North American and the Greenland fishing grounds. Nor were there many coast stations either, and so *Brendan* gradually fell into a gap in the communications network. The radio voice of Prins Christianssund grew fainter and fainter until finally it could only just be heard. Then came the day when their signal vanished entirely and we still could not make contact with the Canadian stations ahead of us. Above, we heard the airliners reporting their positions to air traffic control, but they did not reply to *Brendan*'s calls and we seemed very alone.

On June 11, we picked up a Canadian Coast Guard radio station broadcasting an advisory message to all ships, giving *Brendan*'s description and announcing that as nothing had been heard from *Brendan* for sixty hours, any vessel sighting her or hearing her signals was to report to the Coast Guard. Frustratingly, we could not reply ourselves to the message because of heavy atmospheric interference. But on the following day a sudden improvement in conditions allowed both the Canadian and Greenland radio stations to pick up our position report and the Canadians advised us of the position of the main pack-ice edge off Labrador. According to their observations, the main pack ice was retreating steadily northward, and from the chart it looked as if *Brendan* would be clear of the Labrador ice. Only a week earlier the Canadian news bulletins had been describing the fate of the ferryboat *Carson* about two hundred miles east of us. The 8,273-ton *Carson* was built as an icebreaker, but on her first run of the season up to Goose Bay, she had hit ice and sunk. Fortunately the weather was ideal and she was close to shore. Military helicopters had rescued her passengers from the ice floes without loss of life, but her sinking was a grim warning.

Thirteen seemed to be our lucky number, because on June 13 we finally got a favorable wind, and *Brendan* ran up the miles all that afternoon and the following night. During the evening watch George mentioned that he was disappointed. "It seems a pity to have come all this way, and never to have seen any ice. I don't expect I'll ever be up here again," he said. Next morning at dawn, George was making himself a cup of coffee. "Hey!" he called in delight. "Ice. I do believe it's ice." There, floating by like some strange Chinese carnival dragon, was a queerly contorted chunk of ice, bobbing gently like a child's toy. "There's another chunk, just ahead," George said. We all lined up to watch. *Brendan* was beginning to slide past humps and bits of loose ice. They were extraordinarily beautiful, lurching and dipping and occasionally pieces splitting away and breaking free. And then the whole chunk of ice would revolve as its balance changed, spinning over to reveal some entirely new profile. All the while the constant surge and wash of the swell on the ice came to our ears as a low, muted roar.

Trondur beamed with pleasure. "Good," he said. "Now we see more birds and more whales. Near ice is good fishing."

I pointed away to the east. "Trondur, what is that white line over on the horizon? It looks like ice blink, according to the description in the pilot book. Do you think there is pack ice in that direction?"

"Yes," he said, peering in the direction I was pointing. "Yes, there is much ice."

I was puzzled. According to the latest information, there should not be any ice in that direction. "I expect it's a big isolated raft of ice broken from the main part," I said confidently. "According to the most recent ice report we should be clear of the main ice, and there shouldn't be any pack ice in this area. I expect we've come between the land and some stray drifting ice."

I was wrong. Unwittingly, I altered course to starboard to pass inside the ice "raft" and sailed down toward the ice blink. As we came closer, the ice edge became more definite. It was an awesome sight. The solid edge of the ice was made of brilliant white floes, which shimmered in the strong sunshine. Every hundred yards or so, the carcasses of larger and thicker floes had been driven in the lighter floes and jammed there. These larger floes were made of multi-year ice, ice from several years of freezing, and broken chunks of icebergs. These larger pieces stood above the general level in strange sculptured shapes, some soft and round like melted butter, others grotesque and jagged, all sharp edges and spines. A fringe of smaller ice debris drifted along the main edge, and into *Brendan*'s path. We wove our course between them, innocently admiring their shapes. They looked like little boats, pieces from a jigsaw or sea serpents. One small floe was banana-shaped and was promptly dubbed the "ice curragh."

Treacherously the wind began to shift into the northwest, and try as we might, we could not prevent *Brendan* from sidling closer to the ice edge. The sun clouded over from time to time, and the pretty shapes looked less enticing. "The swell is really grinding the ice," commented George. "Look at that big, dark-colored floe over there. Look how it's lifting and falling." He was pointing out a sizeable block of ice, perhaps the size of a two-storey house, which had a distinctive, ugly grey band along its lower edge. Each time the swell moved it, this chunk of ice rose up ponderously, tilted, and then came smashing down with its dark underbelly so that the water gushed from the undercut edge. "It wouldn't be very pleasant if *Brendan* got driven under the edge of that one," I commented. "We'd be pulverized as if by a steam hammer."

Steadily we glided past the ice edge, keeping it to port. Arthur was taking photographs, George steering, and Trondur sat on the shelter roof, gazing at the marvelous vista. In the distance, across the hummocks and rifts of the lesser ice, we could distinguish the massive shapes of true icebergs locked in the depths of the ice field. "I don't think we're going to clear the tail of the ice raft," said George in a worried tone, "it seems to stretch a long way ahead, and we're drifting down toward it rather fast." A nagging fear took shape in the back of my mind. We were about 160 miles from land, and a long distance from where the main pack ice was reputed to be. But this ice looked remarkably solid. George spoke again. "What if we're just running ourselves into an ice bay? I can't see how we would get out without being crushed."

I glanced inquiringly at Trondur. "*Brendan* must find a hole in the ice. There is safe," he said and, pulling out his pencil, sketched what he meant—*Brendan* should try to find an open patch within the body of the pack ice and lie there as if in a lagoon. But the ice edge was unbroken. There was no gap and no haven, least of all for a skin boat. Just at that moment George exclaimed, "A ship!"

It was the first vessel we had seen since the patrol ships of the Icelandic Coast Guard. Low on the horizon she looked like a fishing boat skirting the edge of the ice raft. "I'm afraid she won't see us against the ice," I said. "White sails against white ice, and even our radar reflector will just look like a small blob of loose ice."

Suddenly George had a brain wave.

"The signal mirror!" he exclaimed, and quickly dug out the little metal mirror from its storage place.

Blink! Blink! Blink! We took it in turns to focus the sunlight on the distant ship. When first sighted, she had been heading almost straight at us, but then she had turned aside to steam parallel with the ice edge. Blink! Blink! Blink! "Let's hope we can get some fresh food," Arthur muttered longingly. "I rather fancy some fresh milk and bread." Blink! Blink! "She's turning, she's seen us!"

Quarter of an hour later the boat was almost within hailing distance. George peered through the binoculars. "Her name is *Svanur*, and hey! Trondur, I do believe she's a Faroese boat."

Trondur beamed with anticipation. He cupped his hands and bellowed a string of Faroese across the water. His shout was greeted with a mass of waving arms from the boat's crew, who were lining the rail. "I wonder what they're thinking on *Svanur*," George said, "meeting up with a leather boat off of the ice."

"One thing is sure," I replied, "when they hear Faroese coming from *Brendan*, they'll know it can only be Trondur Patursson."

In fact the Faroese fishing boat knew all about *Brendan*, not only from our visit the previous year to the Faroes, but also via the mysterious network of sea gossip which links the fishing boats and small freighters plying the far North Atlantic. The voyage of the leather boat was a topic of conversation in the Icelandic and Greenland ports; and *Svanur* had just come down from Greenland, loaded with a cargo of shrimp to be landed at Gloucester, Massachusetts. All northern ships, her skipper later told Trondur, had been asked to keep a special watch for us, and Greenland radio had been broadcasting our last known position. Nevertheless, had it not been for the bright flash of the signal mirror, *Svanur* would never have spotted *Brendan*. Her captain had already changed course away from the ice when the mirror had caught the attention of the watch and *Svanur* closed to investigate.

Trondur pumped up the little rubber dinghy and paddled across to *Svanur*. After ten minutes he came back. "The captain says there is very heavy ice all ahead of *Brendan*. *Svanur* has been steaming six hours and could not find a way through the ice. Also he has heard on the radio from another ship which cannot get through. He says the ice is very thick." I saw that *Svanur*'s steel bows had ice dents in it. If *Svanur*, a well-built fishing boat designed for those waters, was backing off the ice, then it was wise for *Brendan* to do the same. It seemed that the ice had moved since the last reports and was a good deal farther south. Trondur continued: "*Svanur*'s captain said if you want, he will pull *Brendan* around the corner of the ice where we can pick up the wind again. *Svanur* is going this way."

"Please tell him that I accept his offer."

Trondur paddled back with a tow line and soon *Svanur* was plucking us out of danger. More Brendan Luck, I reflected, that the first boat in three weeks should show up just when *Brendan* was blundering into an ice trap. Doubtless we would have been able to work ourselves clear of the ice once the wind had changed, but in future I would be more wary of the ice reports. The pack could move and change its boundaries faster than the Ice Patrol could keep track of it, and next time, I promised myself, I would keep *Brendan* to seaward of it. I did not know what a broken promise that would soon turn out to be.

It took only three hours for *Svanur* to pull *Brendan* out of her predicament, and then she cast us off. Trondur, who had stayed aboard *Svanur* for the tow, came back with a bag of frozen bread, a sack of potatoes, the supply of milk which Arthur had wanted, and a great box of frozen shrimp.

"That's a splendid haul," I grunted, taking the box from Trondur's hands. "Yes," he replied, "*Svanur*'s captain lives not so far from us, on the island of Hestor." Only the wandering Faroese fisherman, I thought, could make so light of a chance meeting off the pack ice.

We were still busily stowing this welcome supplement to our rations when George exclaimed, "Good Lord—it's another ship." Sure enough, rolling down from the north was a grey-painted vessel. She had a strange profile, with a cut-back ice-breaker bow and a crow's nest fixed to her foremast. "This place is like Piccadilly Circus," I said. "Two ships in a day. Everyone has to come round this corner en route to or from the Arctic."

"Let's hope that ship has seen us," muttered George. "She's bearing straight at us."

The look-out aboard the newcomer had spotted *Brendan*. The vessel slowed down and then stopped about two hundred yards from *Brendan*. She was the U.S. Navy ship *Mirfak*, and we could see her deck officers leaning over the wing-bridge to gaze curiously down at us.

"What ship are you?" *Mirfak* asked by radio.

"*Brendan* out of Reykjavik and bound for North America," I replied.

There was a long pause.

"Can I have that again?" came a puzzled voice.

"*Brendan*, out of Reykjavik and bound for North America. Our boat is an archaeological experiment. She's made of leather and testing whether Irish monks could have reached America before the Vikings."

Long pause.

"Say that again."

I repeated the information. Another pause as the khaki-clad officers peered at us.

"I had better take this down in writing," said *Mirfak*'s radio operator. "Where did you sail from?"

"Reykjavik, this season."

Another incredulous pause. "Where?"

"Reykjavik in Iceland. We've had pretty good weather this side of Greenland, but we took a battering between Iceland and Greenland."

"I should say so. Things can be pretty bad in this steel tub. I can't imagine what it's like in your little boat."

Mirfak, as it turned out, was a U.S. Navy supply vessel returning from Sondrestrom Fjord in Greenland and a regular visitor to Arctic waters. Meeting *Brendan* was a complete surprise.

"Can we give you any help?"

"Some fresh vegetables and meat would be very welcome if you can spare any. We ran out of fresh food a little while back."

"That's easy. But how will we transfer the stuff to you?"

I smiled to myself at the thought of a leather boat advising a navy ship. "That's easy. We'll send you a boat." I turned to George. "Your turn in the dinghy."

So *Brendan*'s little rubber dinghy paddled off again, a tiny dot against *Mirfak*'s tall flank. We saw crewmen lowering sacks on the end of the line to George, who was heaving up and down on the swell. Then George gesticulated upward.

Ten minutes later he pulled back to *Brendan*, the dinghy low in the water. "I had to stop them," he puffed. "They gave me so much food it would have swamped the dinghy." Piled around his legs were sacks of oranges, apples, yet more milk, tins of coffee, slabs of meat. It was an incredibly generous haul.

"Look at that lot," said Arthur. "Marvelous! We ought to set up a corner shop at the ice here and trade with passing vessels. We'd never starve."

"And I left behind three more sacks of food they had ready on deck for us," George added.

As *Mirfak* picked up speed to continue on her way to Bayonne in New Jersey, I made one more request. "Could you give us a position check, please?"

"Yes," came the reply. "We're getting a read-out from the satellite now."

That was a nice touch, I thought to myself—a medieval leather boat receiving her position from a twentieth-century navigation satellite. Then *Mirfak* was gone, and *Brendan* was left rocking on the swell. The wind had died completely, and the sun went down in a spectacular mauve-and-orange sunset, the sky streaked with radiating patterns of high clouds that complemented the brilliant white of the ice field stretching away on our starboard side. We ate a delicious supper of Greenland shrimp and turned in that night, listening to the ceaseless mutter and grumble of the ice floes rubbing against one another on the Atlantic swell.

Postscript: Severin's crew successfully landed on the island of Newfoundland on June 26, 1977.

NOTES ON THE CONTRIBUTORS

STEVEN CALLAHAN is a naval architect and an editor-at-large for *Cruising World* magazine.

GORDON CHAPLIN is a journalist, a screenwriter, and the author of *The Fever Coast Log*.

SIR FRANCIS CHICHESTER (1901–1972) became a sailing legend in England and later wrote *Alone Across the Atlantic*.

PETE GOSS served in the Royal Marines for nine years and now lives in Cornwall.

THOR HEYERDAHL (1914–2002) was a Norwegian ethnographer of international renown, having penned *Aku Aku* and *The Ra Expeditions*.

DEREK LUNDY is the author of *The Way of a Ship* and *The Bloody Red Hand*.

BERNARD MOITESSIER (1925–1994) wrote numerous books about the sea, such as *A Sea Vagabond's World*, *Sailing to the Reefs*, and *Cape Horn*.

ROB MUNDLE, an Australian journalist and former television weatherman, is the author of *Ocean Warriors* and *Life at the Extreme*.

ERIC NEWBY (1919–2006) wrote *A Short Walk in the Hindu Kush* and *Slowly Down the Ganges*, among many others.

PETER NICHOLS penned *A Voyage for Madmen* and has worked as a professional yacht captain. Born in Britain, he now lives in Northern California.

JOHN ROUSMANIERE is the author of eighteen books, including *A Berth to Bermuda* and *After the Storm*.

TIM SEVERIN lives in Ireland and is the author of *The Sindbad Voyage* and *In Search of Genghis Khan*.

PERMISSIONS

ALSO EDITED BY CECIL KUHNE

NEAR DEATH IN THE MOUNTAINS

True Stories of Disaster and Survival

In these thrillingly true tales of narrow brushes with death, Cecil Kuhne has amassed a wide range of stories that show the awesome power of the mountains: from the haunting story of the famed mountaineer's daughter who succumbs to high-altitude sickness while scaling the peak for which she was named, to a daring escape of three Italian soldiers from a British POW camp during World War II and their subsequent climb of Mount Kenya, and many others. Spanning five continents, from the frosty tip of Mount McKinley in the dead of the winter to the unexplored vastness of the Himalayas and beyond, this is a pulse-pounding collection of disaster and survival at the top of the world.

Travel/Adventure/978-0-307-27935-4

Forthcoming from Vintage Departures in summer 2008 . . .